CHOOSING THE GOOD

CHOOSING THE GOOD

CHRISTIAN ETHICS IN A COMPLEX WORLD

DENNIS P. HOLLINGER

Baker Academic

A Division of Baker Book House Co
Grand Rapids, Michigan 49516

© 2002 by Dennis P. Hollinger

Published by Baker Academic
a division of Baker Book House Company
P.O. Box 6287, Grand Rapids, MI 49516-6287

Printed in the United States of America

Library of Congress Cataloging-in-Publication Data

Hollinger, Dennis P., 1948–
    Choosing the good : Christian ethics in a complex world / Dennis P. Hollinger
        p.   cm.
    Includes bibliographical references and index.
    ISBN 0-8010-2563-X (pbk.)
    1. Christian ethics. I. Title.
BJ1251.H585 2002
241—dc21   2002018590

Chapter 11 is adapted from Dennis Hollinger, "Pluralism and Christian Ethics," *Christian Scholar's Review*
30, no. 2 (winter 2000). Copyright © 2000 by *Christian Scholar's Review*. Reprinted by permission.

Unless otherwise indicated, Scripture quotations are from the New Revised Standard Version of the Bible,
copyright 1989 by the Division of Christian Education of the National Council of the Churches of Christ
in the USA. Used by permission.

Scripture quotations identified KJV are from the King James Version of the Bible.

Scripture quotations identified NIV are from the HOLY BIBLE, NEW INTERNATIONAL VERSION®.
NIV®. Copyright © 1973, 1978, 1984 by International Bible Society. Used by permission of Zondervan
Publishing House. All rights reserved.

For information about Baker Academic, visit our web site:
www.bakeracademic.com

CONTENTS

PREFACE

The complexities of our world often generate cynicism or despair over the possibility of choosing the good in moral decision making. Many assume that the competing moral voices, the multifaceted nature of dilemmas, and the limited human perspective make it impossible to have a clear sense of the good, right, and just in our complex world.

Despite such challenges —and they are real—this book attempts to set forth a broad framework for doing ethics with humility yet confidence. *Choosing the Good* has two primary objectives: first, to provide a textbook that surveys the essential issues pertinent to understanding the discipline of Christian ethics and reflecting on the moral life; and second, to suggest a particular approach to doing Christian ethics in a complex world. As to the first goal, I have attempted to cover the crucial concepts and issues essential for developing a foundation for ethics, making ethical decisions, and applying moral commitments to a secular, pluralistic world. As to the second goal, I argue in this work that Christian ethics emerges out of a distinctly Christian worldview, and thus we face some significant but not unsurmountable challenges in living and applying such an ethic in a society that typically does not share those worldview assumptions.

The book is structured around four main parts. After an introduction that discusses the nature of the moral life and the discipline of Christian ethics, part 1 examines competing foundational theories in ethics. Every ethical judgment ultimately rests on a larger foundation that essentially guides our thinking as to the nature of the good, the right, the virtuous, and the just. Hence, in this section I set forth and critique the various foundational theories, concluding with my own framework.

Part 2 explores the contexts of Christian ethics, for all ethical commitments and judgments emerge out of particular contexts that give rise to the issues we face, influence the nature of moral reflections, and shape the application of ethical commitments. In particular, this section explores two macro contexts: modernity and postmodernity. Understanding these contexts is important when doing ethics but also for ensuring that we are not co-opted by our context and hence lose a distinctively Christian dimension.

Part 3 then moves to issues inherent in making ethical decisions. First, it explores ways that Christians have historically made decisions and looks at some of the central thinkers throughout Christian history. Second, it examines the use of the Bible in decision making, giving attention to biblical authority in ethics, hermeneutical issues, and the kinds of ethical resources found in Scripture. Finally, this part looks at the role that empirical or factual judgments play in making ethical judgments.

Part 4 turns to applying Christian ethics in culture and society. It looks at the relationship of faith and culture, a crucial issue that influences what we expect of our Christian ethic in society and how we seek to apply this ethic to the sociocultural realities around us. Next it looks at the issue of justice in society, examining the ways in which conceptions of justice influence social ethic outcomes. This section also takes up the challenge of pluralism, asking how an ethic rooted in a particularistic worldview can possibly hope to influence culture and society. Finally, it explores some possible concrete models for carrying out Christian convictions within a complex world.

I am indebted to many people for sharpening and deepening my thinking in ethics and for the writing of this book. First, my thanks to the hundreds of seminary and college students who over the years grappled with me in attempting to think about choosing and applying the good in a complex world. Among these are students in other parts of the world where I taught for short periods: India, Ukraine, and Russia. Second, my thanks to fellow scholars who read and offered feedback on selected chapters: ethicist Stephen Mott, philosopher Caleb Miller, and biblical scholar Boaz Johnson. Third, thanks to my work study assistants at Messiah College who logged hours tracking down footnotes, proofreading chapters, and offering their perspectives and suggestions: Chris Beers, Ryan Rich, and Pat McCullough. Above all, thanks to my daughter Daphne, who meticulously read most of the manuscript, corrected mistakes, and offered thoughtful wisdom through the eyes of a college student. The support and encouragement of my wife, Mary Ann, and our other daughter Naphtali were essential ingredients in bringing this book to fruition. To all of you, "I thank my God upon every remembrance of you."

INTRODUCTION

THE MORAL LIFE
AND CHRISTIAN ETHICS

Tom and Sarah have been married for eight years and during the past four have experienced the anguish of unsuccessfully trying to start a family. They are both thirty-two years old and are feeling the pinch of time regarding their child-bearing efforts. After numerous consultations and attempts at various approaches, they have learned that Tom has a low sperm count. They are now faced with several possibilities. Their doctor at the fertility clinic has laid out the most viable medical option: artificial insemination by a donor. The sperm would come from an anonymous donor, though Tom and Sarah would have a choice concerning the background and characteristics of the donor. The child would be Sarah's biologically but would have no biological link to Tom.

For several years this couple has been praying for a child, believing that children are a gift from God and part of the divine order of things. Should Tom and Sarah opt for artificial insemination, knowing that the procreation would occur outside their own sexual bond with an anonymous biological father? What is morally right and good in this situation? What is the will of God regarding this technology and their married life together?

The Acme Advertising Agency has just signed a contract with the Jordan Company, a new clothes and cosmetics manufacturer. Jordan wants to capitalize on a lucrative market for new clothes and hair styles: young women in their late teens and early twenties. Their plan for doing so relies on developing a full media advertising campaign, one that will depict "The Awesome Jordan Look." The campaign will consist primarily of TV ads showing young women with the "Jordan Look" in sexy situations, surrounded by adoring guys.

One of the company's new "Jordan Look" product lines is a wave-setting lotion called Natural Wave. After several weeks of brainstorming and tests with the product, the Acme team hits upon an idea for a new TV commercial for advertising Natural Wave: While the voice-over (narration) introduces the viewer to Natural Wave, the camera will show a drinking straw being soaked in a bowl of the lotion. Drinking straws curl up when soaked in Natural Wave, and the camera will show this. The commercial will *not*, however, *actually say* "Natural Wave will curl your hair just like this straw." (Afterward, the camera will depict a wavy-haired "Jordan Look" girl with a handsome man at her side.)[1]

Michelle is a vice president for personnel at the Jordan Company and has just gotten wind of the proposed advertising strategy and content. Marketing and advertising lie outside her responsibilities within the company, but as a Christian she has attempted to carry out her profession with integrity and high moral standards. She has a sense that the Natural Wave advertisement has gone beyond what the product can actually yield, and she is offended by the sexual overtones of both the clothing and Natural Wave advertisements. What should she do? Should she risk her job or at least alienation within top-level management (who likes the ads) by objecting? Since she is not in advertising or marketing, should she ignore the situation? And what about responsibilities to her family, who depend on her income? Should she leave the company?

In 1999, the United States joined with NATO forces in a massive air war against Yugoslavia. Slobodan Milosevic and his armed forces had for years been practicing ethnic cleansing, most recently against Albanians, the majority group in the province of Kosovo. In response to Milosevic's actions against the Albanians, NATO bombing targeted military resources, government buildings, key transportation routes, and industrial complexes that supported the Yugoslavian armed forces. In the process, numerous civilians were killed, including personnel at the Chinese embassy (bombed by mistake) and Albanian refugees forced by the Serb military to flee from their homes. The entire infrastructure of population centers in Yugoslavia was virtually destroyed.

During the war, Stephen is serving as a high-level official in the State Department of the United States with access to detailed classified information regarding the Kosovo situation. He has direct access to military leaders and even the president. He knows the horrors committed by the Yugoslavian regime, but he is not at all convinced that the NATO response can be effective. Moreover, while he believes that some wars are just, he is not sure that this one meets the just war criteria. What should he do? What kind of person is he if he goes contrary to his convictions? And what bearing should his faith have on this international situation?

These three scenarios engender the kinds of questions human beings have raised for centuries. What should we do in situations in which we have a sense that right and wrong is involved? What kind of people should we be in the midst of the push and pull of responsibilities we feel toward others, institutions, and even nations? How should we live in the midst of a complex world or in those situations that are not so complex? And what is the basis for our judgments on these issues? These are the questions of the moral life, and these are the kinds of issues dealt with in the discipline of ethics.

The Moral Life and Christian Experience

This is a book about Christian morality and Christian ethics, so invariably we will grapple with such scenarios from a particular perspective, one shaped by Christian beliefs, values, virtues, and moral ideals. But how does the moral life and Christian ethics relate to the whole of Christian experience? Where do moral decisions and personal character fit within the Christian life?

It might be helpful to think of two broad dimensions of Christian experience: the internal and the external. The internal dimension is our personal relationship with God. It is the realm of spirituality in which we experience a vital relationship with our maker through faith in Christ, nurtured by prayer, worship, Bible reading, meditation, and other spiritual disciplines. The internal dimension of Christian experience incorporates certain affective responses that almost immediately emerge in life situations, because of God's presence and empowerment. Those of us in the Western world tend to think of this internal dimension in highly individualistic terms, but the biblical model also incorporates a strong communal spirituality in which piety and disciplines are expressed in the context of a community of believers.

The external dimension of Christian experience is the outward expression of the inward spirituality. It is Christian reality being manifest in everyday life. This dimension can be divided into two parts: word and deed, or as some have put it, proclamation and presence. The word or proclamation part is the verbal expression of faith. It involves carrying out Jesus' Great Commission to "make disciples of all nations, baptizing them in the name of the Father and of the Son and of the Holy Spirit, and teaching them to obey everything that I have commanded you" (Matt. 28:19–20). Christians believe that divine realities and the gospel can be communicated, defended, and cognitively applied to various situations. The preaching/teaching of God's Word and evangelism are among the main aspects of this part of the external dimension.

But this dimension also involves deed or presence. As Christians we are called to live out the spiritual realities in the midst of the situations in which God places us. The gospel is not only spoken but also lived and evidenced in the actions of those who follow Christ. A full-orbed Christian mission will always involve both word and deed, and they should never be pitted against each other as Christians have sometimes done.

Ethics and the moral life seem to fit into the external dimension and the deed or presence segment. Morality is about the good and right actions we display in the midst of our vocations, families, churches, communities, cultures, societies, and personal interactions. It involves the kind of presence we exhibit

11

in the various responsibilities we are given in life. But, of course, all of this is an oversimplification. Life is never quite as neat and tidy as these categories. While it is true that ethics and morality are primarily about deeds and the kind of presence we exude in the external world, they are never far removed from the internal dimension, for ethics and morality, as we will see, are not only about *what we do* but *who we are*. What we do is a reflection of who we are, and who we are is sometimes shaped by what we do. Jesus put it this way: "For it is from within, from the human heart, that evil intentions come: fornication, theft, murder, adultery, avarice, wickedness, deceit, licentiousness, envy, slander, pride, folly. All these evil things come from within, and they defile a person" (Mark 7:21–23).

The moral life then must always be tied to the internal dimension of Christian experience, and the internal dimension must always demonstrate itself in the external dimension, including both word and deed. To emphasize the external without the internal is ultimately to fall back on a works righteousness, which assumes that the moral life can emerge from human nature on its own accord. Some Christians have argued that morality is fundamentally about a natural law that all human beings can exhibit by nature apart from direct divine initiative or guidance. While people clearly have some sense of the good God desires and can exhibit some actions that reflect that good, Christian ethics is far more than a natural enterprise. It is not only rooted in a particular Christian understanding of reality but is also nourished and sustained by spiritual and divine resources beyond our natural proclivities.

But just as the external without the internal is imbalanced faith, so too is an internal emphasis without the external. Such an emphasis falls prey to unhealthy mysticism and piety that will make little impact on the way we live and act. It is faith without works, which the New Testament so directly condemns as non-faith:

> What good is it, my brothers and sisters, if you say you have faith but do not have works? Can faith save you? If a brother or sister is naked and lacks daily food, and one of you says to them, "Go in peace; keep warm and eat your fill," and yet you do not supply their bodily needs, what is the good of that? So faith by itself, if it has no works, is dead.
>
> James 2:14–17

The apostle Paul argues for the importance of both the internal and the external dimensions in Ephesians 2:8–10: "For by grace you have been saved through faith, and this is not your own doing; it is the gift of God—not the result of works, so that no one may boast. For we are what he has made us, created in Christ Jesus for good works, which God prepared beforehand to be our way of life." While ethics and the moral life cannot earn God's grace, God's internal working of grace will always be manifest in the ethical life. Paul then immediately goes on to deal with the first great social ethic issue faced by the early church, the racial-cultural divide between Jews and Gentiles. The divisions and hostility could be overcome in Christ because the internal working of God's grace could make a difference in how social groups lived together. Ethics and spirituality are never far apart.

The Nature of Ethics and the Moral Life

But what exactly are ethics and the moral life? Generally speaking, the moral life is behavior in which we have a sense of oughtness and obligation. It involves those decisions in which we are aware that one choice may be better or worse than another, not from a functional or economic standpoint but from the sense that we feel obligation, right and wrong. Not all choices in life are moral. For example, when we go to the grocery store and choose a box of cereal from the numerous varieties available, we generally assume that such a decision is not a moral one. The kind of toothpaste we use is generally not a moral or ethical issue. But suppose we discover some interesting facts about these products, namely, that our favorite cereal is produced in a foreign country that employs young children who are forced to work ten hours a day and six days a week, and that the toothpaste we use is produced by a company known to be a major polluter of a river near its plant. At this point our shopping may turn from the routine to questions about whether we ought to support a company through buying its product, not from the standpoint of price, quality, or personal taste but from the standpoint that there may be right and wrong implications in the purchase. Our conscience now raises questions about our shopping practices, and we have entered the realm of morality.

Or take the case of John, a salesperson at a pharmaceutical company. John has just received an offer from a competing company that would provide better pay than his current job. One might be prone to think this is not a moral decision, since there seem to be no pressing right or wrong questions involved in the decision. But as John begins to probe further into this offer, he discovers that he will be traveling 50 percent more than he does with his current job and thus away from home. He has two children, ages thirteen and eleven, and his wife is employed outside the home as well. As John asks additional questions about the company's products, he discovers that he will be required to sell RU-486, the abortion pill. Clearly, at this point John is faced not only with a job decision but one that has moral ramifications. The decision he makes carries with it questions that have to do with right, wrong, conscience, obligation, and commitments that touch the core of who he is as a person.

There is a tendency today to turn moral issues into amoral ones, to argue that many of the decisions and choices we make are merely personal choices that lie outside the ethical purview. For example, in the current debate about euthanasia or physician-assisted suicide, some argue that this is not a moral issue but simply a matter of controlling one's life. Ethical questions need not be raised. In the same manner, abortion is described as a matter of personal choice, lying outside the pale of morality and particularly outside the realm of society's ethical concern. Several years ago I had a conversation with a man who worked for a military industry making armaments for war. As we talked it became evident that he saw his work as an amoral enterprise, for he said, "Until today I had never let myself think about the uses of my work. I simply saw it as an application of engineering technology. The moral aspect never entered my mind."

Despite this amoral tendency today, the moral life emerges in those personal, institutional, and societal decisions that carry with them a sense of right and wrong. Moreover, morality is not only about the big decisions; it bears on the daily lives we live in relation to God, self, others, our culture, and the entire world. It involves the core of who we are as human beings living daily in the pursuit of God's will, the morally good. As Jeremiah the prophet put it, "Stand at the crossroads, and look, and ask for the ancient paths, where the good way lies; and walk in it, and find rest for your souls" (Jer. 6:16).

Ethics is the discipline that studies the moral life. If morality refers primarily to behavior and character, ethics is the discipline that tries to provide guidance and perspective in making decisions and forming character. Ethics can perhaps most easily be understood as the systematic study of standards of right and wrong, justice and injustice, virtue and vice, with a view toward applying those standards in the realities of our lives. Or as Arthur Holmes put it:

> Ethics is about the good (that is, what values and virtues we should cultivate) and about the right (that is, what our moral duties may be). It examines alternative views of what is good and right; it explores ways of gaining the moral knowledge we need; it asks why we ought to do right; and it brings this to bear on the practical moral problems that arouse such thinking in the first place.[2]

Ethics is a normative discipline as opposed to a descriptive discipline. The descriptive fields of study are those that attempt to recount human and institutional behavior in various spheres such as psychology, sociology, anthropology, economics, history, and political science. Ethics, however, is normative or prescriptive in that it attempts to establish norms, standards, and perspectives that guide human and institutional behavior and character. "Confusion about ethics as a discipline is very understandable, because it is a unique area of study. Most disciplines deal with 'is' questions. Who was Sigmund Freud? What is a dangling participle? . . . Moral dilemmas belong to a different category. . . . In ethics, right means something different than correct."[3]

As a discipline ethics begins to emerge when we move beyond being directed merely by tradition or cultural rules and expectations to reflect on what we ought to do and be. It involves a conscious attempt to analyze the moral situation and options before us and to designate the moral good in the midst of the options. As such, ethics often raises questions about the status quo or the conventional ways of acting and being. We normally think of ethics as a subject studied in colleges, seminaries, or church education programs, but any time we analyze our moral choices and ask what we ought to do and be, we are engaged in ethics.

The Disciplines of Ethics

The study of the moral life actually involves several disciplines. While this book is a work in Christian ethics, there are other contexts and commitments for the study of ethics.

One of the disciplines is philosophical ethics, which studies the moral life from within a framework of philosophy and utilizes a rational approach apart from any religious or professional commitments. Classical Greek philosophers such as Plato and Aristotle engaged in this discipline of ethics. While they differed in moral foundations and perspectives, they pursued ethical analysis from the standpoint of natural reasoning or observations about the world. In the twentieth century, many philosophers have utilized analytical philosophy[4] as a framework for exploring the nature of moral situations and the meaning and validity of moral terms such as *justice, goodness, virtue,* and *right.* In fact, earlier in the twentieth century, one school of analytical philosophy, logical positivism, argued that ethical judgments are not really propositions or meaningful statements; they are purely emotive, arousing feeling, and hence belong to psychology or sociology. Only empirical statements (such as those of science) or analytical statements (such as those of math and logic) can be verified and are thus meaningful. A. J. Ayer, for example, argued that "the exhortations to moral virtue are not propositions at all, but ejaculations or commands which are designed to provoke the reader to action of a certain sort. Accordingly, they do not belong to any branch of philosophy or science. . . . A strictly philosophical treatise on ethics should therefore make no ethical pronouncements."[5] In recent years, philosophical ethics has tended to return to more traditional approaches, emphasizing various normative frameworks that can be applied to given moral issues, while continuing to clarify and define the meaning of ethical concepts.

A second discipline is professional ethics. Over the years, numerous professions have attempted to develop normative principles to guide professionals in carrying out their work and conducting their relationships with clients or constituents. Medicine, for example, has for hundreds of years been guided by a professional ethic rooted in codes such as the Hippocratic oath, the oath of Maimonides, or more recently, the Declaration of Geneva (1948). These statements of medical professional ethics set forth the guiding vision for carrying out one's vocation and set parameters around the behavior toward patients and fellow physicians. Business, education, social work, psychology, and other fields have established ethical codes to guide professionals so as to minimize the misuse of one's position or power and to ensure fair treatment toward the recipients of their professional work. This discipline of ethics has tended to lean toward professional etiquette rather than ethics, but in recent years various professions have begun to draw on other ethics disciplines to develop more in-depth guidance for their statements. Indeed, medical ethics (now called bioethics) and business ethics have evolved into penetrating analyses that are in some senses ethical disciplines in their own right.

The third discipline in ethics is religious or, in the case of this work, Christian ethics. In this approach, ethics emerges from within the larger framework of religious beliefs, commitments, and values. Christian ethics as a discipline has often looked significantly different from philosophical ethics, not so much in its conclusions about issues as in how it arrives at those conclusions. Christian ethics is done within the confines of a specific worldview that gives account of who we are as human beings, what is fundamentally wrong with the human condition, and what remedy exists for that malady. Christians are a people of the Book, and thus they look to the Bible as divine revelation to guide their understanding of both reality and the moral good. Christian ethics may at times utilize reason, as in philosophical ethics, or human experience, as is often evidenced in professional ethics, but fundamentally it draws from a specific Christian understanding of reality to guide the moral life. As a result, Christian ethics is never far removed from theology or biblical studies, for these provide foundational assumptions for discerning the moral vision and norms for ethical decision making. Moreover, the Christian ethic will always embody a concern not only for cognitive understanding but also for inward motivations and empowerment in carrying out those visions and norms amid the realities of a complex world.

Christian Ethics

Christian ethics, like the other moral disciplines, incorporates two main parts: theoretical ethics and applied ethics. Theoretical ethics seeks to identify, clarify, and define ethical norms, standards, principles, and virtues. It attempts to articulate which ethical guidelines are most salient for choosing the good and why. In Christian ethics, this is often called theological ethics. Theologians and ethicists have articulated numerous norms that serve Christians in making judgments: love, justice, integrity, holiness, human dignity, freedom, peace, and so on. They have also explicated various assumptions that influence moral understanding and perspective: the nature of God, humanity, salvation, the kingdom, life, and death. Theological ethics attempts to define these notions and to weigh them against each other as competing claims in the moral arena.

For example, love has often been understood as the *summa bonum* (highest good) of Christian action. But Christian thinkers have given differing renditions of the exact nature of love as a moral virtue (related more to character) or a principle (related primarily to behavior). Some have argued that the *eros* conception of love from the Greek tradition, with its emphasis on natural desires of the human self, has been replaced by the *agape* love of the New Testament, a totally unselfish love that seems to negate self and natural desires.[6] Other theologians and ethicists (such as Augustine and Thomas Aquinas) have contended that while *eros* is not used in the New Testament, there is a place for natural loves of passion if directed toward a proper good, and at times even the human self can be a proper good. These kinds of discussions and clarifications are part of theological ethics and provide a significant foundation for the second part of moral reflection: applied ethics.

Applied ethics involves the application of moral norms, principles, virtues, and theological assumptions to the particular issues faced by individuals, the church, institutions, and society. It attempts to understand the exact nature of these issues, the competing claims within each issue, and the various moral responses. It then seeks to connect moral norms and ideals to the issue to provide guidance for action and character. In today's complex world, ethicists deal with a wide spectrum of problems including war and violence, bioethics, sexual ethics, family ethics, economic ethics, business ethics, environmental ethics, media ethics, political ethics, and racial/ethnic ethics.

Sometimes a distinction is made between personal applied ethics and social ethics, but the pressing issues of our day invariably involve personal and social dimensions. Business ethics, for example, involves institutional policies and procedures, but sooner or later the person in the corporation has to decide whether to acquiesce or challenge those policies and procedures. Euthanasia and physician-assisted suicide are often described as intensely personal issues, but there are always social dimensions ranging from law to the traditions of medicine to the multiple individuals who may somehow be affected by such a decision. It is best to understand that applied ethics will, or at least should, generally include both personal and social dimensions.

Complexity in Ethics

When we begin to apply moral virtues or principles and theological (or worldview) assumptions to issues, we often discover that it is not a simple process. Seeking the good is frequently complex. To be sure, not every issue is complex. For example, if a woman is contemplating having an affair with a colleague at work in order to meet certain emotional needs, we can respond with certainty that this is not a morally complex issue. She may feel emotional complexity within, but from a Christian ethics standpoint (and even from the standpoint of most other ethical frameworks), her contemplations need go no further: Adultery is immoral and contrary to her marital vows and the nature of marriage as established by God and clearly taught in Scripture. Likewise, if a man is contemplating holding up a local gas station in order to help pay for his son's college education, this is not a complex issue. The contemplations are clearly contrary to biblical norms, theological understandings about the nature of property and human stewardship, and what most human beings throughout history have understood through conscience to be the right thing to do.

However, not all issues are quite so simple. Tom and Sarah (in the opening scenario) could not find direct teaching about artificial insemination in the Bible, though they did find much there about children being a heritage from the Lord. Michelle, the vice president at Jordan, was not sure where her spheres of moral responsibility began and ended, and she wondered how her personal Christian commitments related to a company that had no similar commitments. And Stephen at the State Department felt numerous competing moral claims concerning the bombing of Yugoslavia: Jesus' teaching on non-retaliating love, Paul's teaching on the state not bearing the sword in vain, the notion of justice, and the responsibility to carry out his work in accordance with the decisions of the government and those over him. All of these individuals encountered moral complexity.

What makes an issue complex? One factor is that sometimes the specific course of action is not immediately clear based on the Bible, theological reflection, or even reason. Many of the issues we face today are not directly discussed in the Bible, and even the great thinkers of the church down through the centuries never faced them. In the Bible, for example, there are no *direct* discussions about war, genetic engineering, environmental pollution, organ transplant issues, or the responsibility of a corporation to its shareholders. Issues such as these are then complex because the moral response is not immediately evident, and thus we are often faced with more than just two possible responses. As Richard Higginson notes, "Most moral dilemmas are really more like multilemmas—we need to invent a new word!—because there is a variety of choices involved."[7]

A second factor in making an issue complex is that we sometimes encounter competing ethical claims. Stephen, for example, needed to decide which moral or biblical injunction took precedence in his dilemma: love, justice, obedience to the state, the example and teachings of Jesus, or vocational agreements and commitments. In regard to many of the ethical issues of a complex world, humans come to different judgments because they differ on which ethical principles or virtues carry the greatest moral weight in the decision or which biblical text is most relevant to the situation at hand.

A third and related factor that makes an issue complex is the competing players involved. To which individuals (or institutions) affected by our choice do we grant the greatest moral significance? For the pharmaceutical salesman contemplating a job change, is it his family or the company? For Michelle, is it her management colleagues, the consumers who will buy the product, the shareholders investing in Jordan Company, or her family? Ethical issues are often complex because we sense moral obligation in various, often conflicting, directions.

A fourth factor that renders an issue complex is the factual or empirical judgments that inevitably surround it. Sometimes it is difficult to get hold of the facts, particularly within a large corporation or nation, and at other times we simply find differing interpretations of what is happening. From Stephen's vantage point at the State Department, the bombing of Yugoslavia was a dead-end street, but others, also with insider information, sided with President Clinton, believing that the air strikes would eventually bring Milosevic to his knees.

Because issues can be complex, some of our decisions may involve choosing the wise course of action rather than the absolute moral good. This is certainly not always the case, for even in the midst of complexity, we are often able to discern clear directions. However, we must be open to the fact that in regard to some ethical judgments, our focus will be more on the wise, judicious course of action than on the absolute right course of action. Such seems to be the case in the New Testament discussions about buying and eating meat offered to idols. The Bible clearly indicates that buying and eating the meat are not in themselves morally wrong, for "nothing is unclean in itself." However, "If your brother or sister is being injured by what you eat, you are no longer walking in love. Do not let what you eat cause the ruin of one for whom Christ died" (Rom. 14:15). Here and in other texts Paul encourages believers to choose the wisest course of action in light of the needs of others, but such action is not of the same nature as taking the life of another human being or committing fraud within one's company. It is the most judicious response rather than an absolute moral good or evil.[8]

It is important to understand that complexity in ethics is not the same as moral relativism, the belief that "what is right and wrong, good and bad, true and false varies from time to time, place to place, and person to person. There are no absolute standards of truth or morality, but these depend on where, when, and who you are."[9] Moral relativism is different from a descriptive cultural relativism that notes that in fact there are sometimes differing moral standards and practices in various cultures. For example, some cultures give moral sanction to polygamy while others do not. Moral relativism, however, would go one step further and argue that from an ethical perspective, polygamy can be morally wrong in one culture and morally right in another. "In this view, there is nothing behind the demands of morality except social convention."[10] In the modern and now postmodern world, many people espouse relativism with the claim that there are no absolutes. Relativism is not only contrary to a biblical worldview but also rests on a self-contradiction, for the statement that everything is relative is itself an absolute statement.

In the midst of complex issues, we may have to choose between competing moral claims, but we are nonetheless entering into the dilemma with moral and theological givens or absolutes to guide us. It is the very nature of the issue that compels us to choose which moral claims and theological or worldview perspectives are most relevant to this particular issue. Moreover, as Lewis Smedes once pointed out, "We have no ideal world in which to find out what God expects us to do; we have only this changing and broken one. . . . And obedience to unchanging commands must adjust to changing conditions."[11] But that in no way implies that the moral and theological guides are themselves relativistic, sometimes binding and at other times not. In the midst of complexity, we are still armed with moral and theological certainties and constants, and we will need to find the most significant and relevant of these guides and norms for the issue at hand.

Christian Ethics, Pastoral Care, and Public Policy

Several years ago I was delivering a lecture on bioethics at a theological seminary. As part of my address on reproductive technologies, I gave the students the case study of Tom and Sarah and their dilemma regarding artificial insemination with a donor. I then asked the students to respond ethically to this case from within a Christian ethics framework. The students' responses went something like this: "We need to empathize with Tom and Sarah in their childlessness"; "We ought to assure them of our love whatever course they choose"; "There should not be any laws or societal restrictions on their right to artificial insemination." It became evident that very few students were thinking ethically. Instead, most of them were responding from either the perspective of pastoral care or public policy; few were actually doing Christian ethical analysis.

Christian Ethics

Christian ethics is rooted in the very nature and actions of God and in our worldview as Christians. From these foundations it sets forth the ideal actions and character to which God calls us. While all men and women may have some insight into the moral designs of God via reason and human experience, Christian ethics always goes further in both its content and its motivation. This is so because Christian ethics is not only rooted in God's character and actions and a biblical worldview but also emerges out of a personal relationship with God through Christ and is nurtured and sustained in the context of a body of believers, the church. Christian ethics then is the moral ideal to which God calls us precisely because of a covenant relationship we have with him.

Though we live in a broken and fallen world and often fail to live up to God's designs, the brokenness and fallenness are not normative for Christians. We will certainly take account of the world and the human situation in our moral analyses, but ultimately we will look to God's character and actions and the specific moral implications that flow from the Christian worldview. Therefore, as Tom and Sarah explore their dilemma, they will certainly want to be guided by far more than a vague notion of love, feelings of hurt, or human freedom. They hopefully will look at God's design of marriage from creation, God's own covenant relationship with his people as a model, and the nature and meaning of God's gift of sexual intimacy.

When we do Christian ethics, we are indeed working with a particular understanding of God, life, humanity, and the world, and we are responding out of a specific relationship with God. Both the content of our ethics and the motivations for our responses should reflect the Christian worldview and the covenant relationship with God through Jesus Christ. The moral ideal will indeed be very high.

Pastoral Care

Pastoral care should not be divorced from Christian ethics, but it is not identical to it. Pastoral care is the attempt to express grace, love, forgiveness, empathy, compassion, holistic healing, and accountability in the context of the Christian church. Historically, it has included such things as counseling, rites of penance and forgiveness, prayers for healing, and general care for hurting people. We certainly have a moral responsibility to administer these graces to people in need, but the care and mercy we show is not the same as Christian ethics per se.

Pastoral care is often needed in situations in which God's moral designs have been broken or in which moral failure confronts our ethical norms. Generally speaking, Christian ethics tends to focus on the law of God (though depending on what we mean by law, ethics is certainly broader than this), while care tends to focus on mediating divine grace. The problem comes when we reduce one down to the other. Pastoral care cannot be reduced to ethics, and ethics cannot be reduced to pastoral care. If we reduce our care to ethics, we will lack empathy, love, and understanding in applying ethical norms to people's lives; if we reduce ethics to pastoral care, we will end up with a minimalistic ethic of shallow love or humanistic care.

A clear illustration of this can be seen with regard to divorce. The Christian moral assumption is clearly on the side of permanence in marriage, as established at creation, as evidenced in the biblical notion of covenant, and as directly taught in various biblical texts. From a biblical standpoint, there may be legitimate divorces, but even in legitimate divorces,[12] and certainly in non-legitimate ones, the ethical ideal of permanence should always be held central. However, in the midst of pastoral care, if one enunciates the moral ideal (or law of God) without sensitivity to issues threatening the marriage, the care will likely be ineffective, and the couple may not be led to a place where they are open to hearing God's moral designs. And if a divorce does occur, which is always less than God's ideal in even the most legitimate cases, and one practices ethics without pastoral care, it will be difficult for the divorcees to experience redemptive grace.

At the same time, however, ethics cannot be reduced to pastoral care. We do not decide what is morally right or wrong on the basis of compassion and empathy, though we always have a moral responsibility to express them in a caring relationship. If we stop with compassion and empathy on the issue of divorce, we will never reach God's designs, and more than likely we will let our emotional involvements determine our ethics. This is particularly a temptation in our postmodern culture, in which we have experienced what Philip Rieff has called the "triumph of the therapeutic."[13] There is a tendency to reduce ethics to caring when we make compassion or self-actualization the primary framework or the highest good for ethical deliberation. Oliver O'Donovan rightly reminds us that compassion can never stand alone. "Compassion is the virtue of being moved to action by the sight of suffering. . . . It is a virtue that circumvents thought, since it prompts us immediately to action. It is a virtue that presupposes that an answer has already been found to the question, 'What needs to be done?'"[14]

Tom and Sarah will certainly need pastoral care in the midst of their anguish and personal journeys with regard to childlessness. Friends, family, and pastors should express empathy, compassion, a listening ear, and understanding as they struggle with their plight. But the ethical task before them will not be determined by pastoral care; ethics and pastoral care are different modes of discourse and thinking.

Public Policy

Public policy is the art of the possible within the *civitas*. When a political order is defined and dominated by one worldview system, such as Christendom in the Middle Ages or Islam in some countries today, the relationship between public policy and religious ethics is fairly clear. But in the midst of pluralistic societies with many competing ideologies and religious frameworks, the relationship between Christian ethics and public policy is much more complicated and ambiguous.

Public policy and the law are usually the ethical minimum of a society. In most pluralistic societies, and sometimes even in Islamic societies in which religion and law are closely merged, the religious ethic goes much further than the civil law and policy formulations of the government. There is a tendency today to eliminate religiously based ethics from public square debates and allow only secular versions to influence the shape and motivations of public life. Such forms of secularization not only cut off the culture from rich resources needed in a complex, pluralistic world but also severely limit the rights of those who live their lives in the light of religious commitments. At the same time, some religious believers in pluralistic societies err in attempting to force their religiously rooted ethic on an unbelieving society. This raises conflicts within society and in the case of Christianity is also contrary to biblical understandings of Christian morality.

Law and public policy can never do what Christian ethics can do. Clearly, the law can and must eliminate racial and ethnic discrimination that fails to grant civil rights and opportunity to all citizens. But the law cannot produce love, reconciliation, and the dethronement of prejudices within an individual. American history reveals that the legal and public policy changes regarding civil rights emanated primarily from a Christian-based ethic that pushed society to establish laws and structures that could procure justice. Thus, public policy and the law have an important role to play in society and certainly need to be open to the positive influences that can come from a transcendent ethic, but those laws and formulations will never be the same as Christian ethics. The last section of this book deals further with the relationship between Christian ethics and society and grapples specifically with how the Christian ethic can interface with the larger pluralistic society that increasingly does not share the worldview and commitments from which that ethic emerges.

Conclusion

The moral life is an important dimension of Christian faith and an integral part of any culture and society. The rest of this work explores ethics and the moral life from within the framework of a Christian worldview and commitment. While there will be some overlap with philosophical and professional ethics, the book will reveal clear differences between Christian ethics and the other two disciplines. It will also show the complexity of ethics, especially given the kind of world in which we find ourselves today. Finally, it will reveal that Christian ethics is a distinct way of thinking; it is different from not only other disciplines of ethics but also pastoral care and public policy.

PART 1

THE FOUNDATIONS
OF CHRISTIAN ETHICS

Mrs. Williams was a thirty-five-year-old single mother of two. After almost a decade on the welfare rolls, she had begun to free herself from dependency by taking a job as a cashier at a local grocery store. She had just received her first check, and on the way home from cashing it at the bank with pride, she was held up at gunpoint by a drug addict who needed quick cash for another fix. He grabbed her wallet with over two hundred dollars in cash and fled into the twilight of the evening. Virtually every person would agree that this was a morally reprehensible act. But why was this an unethical action?

To answer that question, we are driven to foundations. Every attempt at devising an ethic assumes some kind of foundation, which is essentially the root framework for deciding what ultimately makes actions or character good or bad. Humans have bedrock assumptions, either implicit or explicit, that serve as the basis for their moral actions and their ethical reflections. The foundation then serves as the primary factor in determining what it means to choose the good and usually carries a glimpse of how that good will be attained in the rough and tumble of real life.

This section examines the key foundations that have been articulated throughout history and in the present. Chapter 1 explores the theories that vied for ascendency throughout much of the modern world: consequentialism versus principle ethics. Chapter 2 examines a recent reaction to those foundations but one that goes far back in history: character or virtue ethics. Each of these theories is, I believe, inadequate as a foundation for discerning the good in a complex world, especially from a Christian perspective. Chapter 3, therefore, sets forth a theological foundation for ethics, rooted in the specifics of a Christian worldview.

1

Consequences versus Principles

When Karla Faye Tucker was executed in 1998 as the first female victim of capital punishment in the United States in over fourteen years, the event set off a new round of ethical debates concerning an old issue. Shortly after her death, a conversation on the issue took place on a radio talk show. The proponent of capital punishment argued that it was a necessity to deter crime. Capital punishment is a moral good because it is a constant reminder to people that we cannot live together as a society if individuals take life into their own hands. The state's execution of one who commits such a crime is necessary to prevent further deterioration in our culture. It is needed for the general welfare and happiness of all people.

The opponent of capital punishment indicated that all life is precious and to be valued, and we have no right to take the life of an individual even when that person has committed a heinous crime. He contended that we all know intuitively that human life must be respected and valued, and when we engage in capital punishment, we are only devaluing life in our culture. It is inherently wrong to take a human life, except in cases of self-defense (including war), and we have an obligation to preserve it.

The two debaters represented two traditional approaches to thinking about ethics and the moral life, though each side of this issue could have employed the other's foundation. The proponent of capital punishment in this case was employing an ethic of consequences, believing that what makes actions right or wrong is the results, which all humans can clearly calculate and assess. The opponent employed a principle ethic, believing that some things are inherently right or wrong, and humans know which is which through moral principles or rules. For some these rules or principles are derived from reason, for others from religion, and for still others they are self-evident from the processes of human history. The consequentialist approach is sometimes called teleological ethics,[1] and the principle approach is also known as deontological ethics. Both are under-

27

stood as foundations for moral judgments and embody particular approaches in the decision-making process: Consequentialists utilize an evaluation of results, and adherents of principle ethics utilize rules and principles.

Consequentialist Ethics

Consequentialists believe that the ultimate criterion or standard of right and wrong is ends or results. Committing adultery, for example, is not inherently wrong in and of itself, but through our life together as human beings the consequences that arise from adultery may render it morally suspect. One tells the truth as a consequentialist, not because truth telling is itself a moral obligation but because in most situations truth telling produces the best results. Consequences are the foundation of ethics.

Of course, appealing to consequences as a grounding for ethics immediately raises the question, Which consequences? or What type of results? Generally, consequentialists have contended that the results calculated are not moral principles or virtues but nonmoral results. Since all human beings by nature seem to pursue happiness (or pleasure) in life, happiness is the prime candidate for the nonmoral consequences utilized in the evaluation process. But, of course, this raises another question: Happiness for whom? And it is here that we can divide the consequentialist approach into several schools of thought, most notably ethical egoism and utilitarianism.

Ethical Egoism

Ethical egoists argue that ethics is rooted in consequences but specifically those that relate to the individual moral actor. That is, one ought to do whatever will produce one's own highest good, determined by the amount of pleasure or happiness that the person will receive from the action.

At first glance this might appear to be an ethic of pure selfishness—do what satisfies me. And indeed at a popular level many people engage life in that manner. When Robert Bellah and his cohorts wrote *Habits of the Heart*, they interviewed hundreds of Americans to discover how they understood and justified their moral foundations. They found that many people operate from a kind of individualism in which personal happiness is the overriding criterion. Brian, for example, was a man who attempted to give more attention to his family and children than to his career and material success, yet in his discussion with the researchers, he continually reverted back to his own personal preferences and happiness: "I just find that I get more personal satisfaction from choosing course B over course A. It makes me feel better about myself." And as the writers described it, "Morally, his life appears much more coherent than when he was dominated by careerism, but to hear him talk, even his deepest impulses of attachment to others are without any more solid foundation than his momentary desires."[2]

But ethical egoism is far more than selfish impulses. It has been set forth as a moderate, rational ethic intended to be the best possible way to achieve the good. As Alexander Pope, the eighteenth-century British poet, put it, "Thus God and nature formed the general frame/And bade self-love and social be the same."[3]

One of the first to articulate this foundation was Epicurus (341–270 B.C.), the Greek philosopher who garnered a significant following in the city of Athens. People from all over Greece and Asia Minor came to sit at his feet in the garden where he taught, attracted perhaps as much by his charm as by his mind. Epicurus was a materialist who believed that all knowledge comes from the senses, which portray the world as it really is. He did not deny the existence of the gods, but he believed they had nothing to do with the realities of everyday life. From this framework he concluded that in regard to morals we naturally pursue personal pleasure and therein is goodness. Personal pleasure is the highest good and the main goal of life, but it is never to be an unbridled pleasure. Rather, for Epicurus, hedonism (the pleasure principle) must always be pursued through self-restraint, moderation, and detachment.

Epicurus believed that the body is ultimately the source of our pleasure, but he also believed that there are different types of pleasure. For example, bodily experiences of pleasure are momentary and secondary to the pleasures of the mind (which as a materialist he believed was an extension of the body), and passive pleasures are more valued than active pleasures. True pleasure, which the individual ought to pursue in life, is, in the words of Lucretius, one of his primary students, "Produced by the reason which is sober, which examines the motive for every choice and rejection, and which drives away all those opinions through which the greatest tumult lays hold of the mind."[4] The ethical egoism of Epicurus was thus "an austere hedonism"[5] and clearly different from the kind of hedonism often associated with the name Epicurean, usually referring to a sensual pursuit of pleasure.

Many years later another defense of ethical egoism was rendered by Adam Smith, the eighteenth-century Scottish philosopher and economist. Smith began his career as a moral philosopher and reflected this perspective in his first major work, *Theory of Moral Sentiments.* A few years later he began to apply his thinking to economics and in 1776 wrote his famous treatise *An Inquiry into the Nature and Causes of the Wealth of Nations,* the work that has often given him the title "the father of modern capitalism." In *The Wealth of Nations,* Smith argued that in economic life each person should seek his or her own good, unfettered by governmental interference. He believed that self-interest (not selfishness) was the highest good in economics because the world was structured in such a way that from it everyone would benefit. In economics "we are led by an invisible hand to promote an end which has no part of his [a human being's] interest. . . . By pursuing his own interest, he frequently promotes that of society more effectively than when he really intends to promote it. I have never known much good done by those who affected to trade for the public good."[6]

The ethical egoism of Smith was not unbridled selfishness. Smith "did not trust the morality of the market as a morality for society at large. . . . He envisioned a capitalist economy within a society held together by noncapitalist moral sentiments."[7] Nonetheless, Smith did see self-interest as the foundation and guiding principle for economic life, assuming a kind of providential "invisible hand" that ensured its positive outcome. Certainly, not all subsequent theories of capitalism or market economies have assumed self-interest as the highest good, but it was the foundation of Smith's economic thinking.

In the twentieth century, the clearest rendition of ethical egoism was given by Ayn Rand, a novelist and philosopher who championed an ethic of "rational self-interest." Born in Russia, Rand immigrated to the United States in 1926 at the age of twenty-one. She soon began her writing career and in 1943 produced her best-known novel, *The Fountainhead.* In this and other works, Rand set forth her philosophy of objectivism, which contended that society functions best when people pursue their own self-interests. She advocated individualism over collectivism, egoism over altruism, and believed that these were self-evident through reason. As an atheist she rejected any transcendent source for ethics and knowledge.

Rand strongly rejected altruism as a basis for the moral life because rationally it is an impossible concept. "The man who attempts to live for others is a dependent. He is a parasite in motive and makes parasites of those he serves. The relationship produces nothing but mutual corruption." In place of such altruism, she contended, "The first right on earth is the right of the ego. Man's first duty is to himself. His moral law is never to place his prime goal with the persons of others. His moral obligation is to do what he wishes, provided his wish does not depend primarily upon other men."[8] For Rand, this rational egoism was a reflection of the order of things. Nature and reason simply teach us, she said, that when each person seeks to preserve his or her own self, the world is a more orderly place.[9] Freedom, justice, and self-esteem can come to fruition only when we follow the path of rational self-interest.

An Evaluation of Ethical Egoism

How do we assess ethical egoism as a foundation for ethics? We must first note that, contrary to the way some Christians have operated or critics have supposed, the Christian perspective does not negate or obliterate the self. In the Christian worldview, the individual certainly counts in the moral maze precisely because humans have been created in the image of God and thus have inherent worth, value, and dignity. A proper kind of self-love is affirmed, for

Jesus himself said, "You shall love your neighbor as yourself" (Matt. 22:39). It is also significant to note that self-interest seems to be a major factor in why people become Christians; few embrace Christ because of altruism but rather because salvation offers them something they need.

But despite this affirmation of a proper self-love and interest, ethical egoism must be found wanting for a number of reasons. From a purely rational standpoint, many argue that it is self-contradictory, since it would not be to one's advantage for all others to pursue their own interests. For this to work, there would need to be some kind of preestablished harmony within the world that would ensure that self-interest results in the best for all. And this, of course, was the assumption of both Adam Smith (from a theistic perspective) and Ayn Rand (from an atheistic perspective). But when we look at human nature and the history of the world, there is scant evidence for this assumption. Both history and our experiences in everyday life reveal clear evidence that self-interest is often at the heart of personal, societal, and international evils. Thus, ethical egoism is a self-defeating enterprise.

From a specifically Christian standpoint, ethical egoism faces a number of problems. For one, it runs contrary to *agape* love, which from both biblical teaching and the example of Jesus is a self-giving and self-sacrificing love. In the biblical framework, authentic selfhood is not found in seeking one's own interests but in being other-oriented, yet without negating one's own self. In contrast to the autonomy implicit in the ethical-egoist claims, Christians understand the human self as a dependent being, as evidenced even in the creation story. From the beginning we learn that humans can best fulfill what God intended through a dependence on their maker and through interdependence with other human beings. Genesis 2:18 states, "It is not good that the man should be alone; I will make him a helper as his partner," which is not only an affirmation of marriage but also an indication of our need for other people in life. Contrary to Rand's thought, this is not a parasitic condition but one in which the self chooses to give up autonomy in a life of community with God and others to be truly human and authentic.

Ethical egoism as a foundation for ethics is a dead-end street. Not only is it self-contradictory and contrary to the Christian understanding of things, but it would also appear to allow self-centeredness to hold sway. That is at the heart of most moral failures.

Utilitarianism

Like ethical egoists, utilitarians believe that the moral good is rooted in consequences, but they look to a different set of consequences—namely, those that relate to the greatest number of people. The greatest good for the greatest number is the utilitarian mantra, and that good is calculated not on the basis of a moral virtue but on the nonmoral good of happiness or pleasure. Utilitarianism emerged in the eighteenth and nineteenth centuries when science was becoming queen of the academic disciplines. Many scholars desired to make their field a science, as did a number of moral philosophers. They believed that rather than starting with an a priori rational notion of moral good, one could make ethical decisions through a scientific calculation of the results of human action. They turned to consequences in terms of happiness or pleasure for the greatest number of people in society or the greatest number affected by a given course of action. The principle of utility or usefulness was the only principle for ethics, for goodness essentially resided in what was useful to the people affected by specific actions, and that usefulness was defined by the maximizing of pleasure and the minimizing of pain.

Thus, in the case of capital punishment, if executing a criminal resulted in the greatest amount of pleasure for the greatest number of people, then it was a moral good. Conversely, if capital punishment resulted in pain for the greatest number of people, it was a moral evil. The utilitarians did not believe that all people would be affected equally by this approach, but they did believe it would produce an impartiality in ethics that could be calculated with a fair amount of precision. One could limit or diminish the good of an individual only when it was necessary to secure the good of the greater number.

The first to set forth utilitarianism in a systematic fashion was the British philosopher and jurist Jeremy Bentham (1748–1832). In reaction to what he believed to be the failure of natural rights and social-contract theories (rooted more in principle ethics), Bentham initially formulated utilitarianism as a foundation for progressive social policy and reform. He believed that "nature has placed mankind under the governance of two sovereign masters, pain and pleasure. It is for them alone to point out what we ought to do."[10] The principle of utility meant that one should always seek to determine morals on the basis of maximizing pleasure and minimizing pain. Bentham believed that it was possible to measure these governing masters of human life, and he developed a calculus to determine the amount of pleasure over pain for given situations. He contended that humans could differentiate between different types of pleasures, such as those of the mind and those of the body, but his major emphasis was on the quantity of pleasure over pain. Bentham's "hedonistic calculus" incorporated seven circumstances or factors of pleasure that could be measured: intensity, duration, certainty, propinquity (nearness), fecundity, purity, and extent. He then advised, "Sum up all the values of all the pleasures on the one side, and all the pains on the other. The balance, if it be on the side of pleasure, will give the good tendency of the act upon the whole, with respect to the interests of that individual person. . . . Take an account of the number of persons whose interests appear to be concerned; and repeat the above process."[11] For Bentham, ethics had become mathematics.

John Stuart Mill, nineteenth-century British philosopher, embraced Bentham's utilitarian approach but commended some changes in the way it was formulated. For Mill, the primary calculation was not the quantity of happiness but the quality of happiness or pleasure. Some pleasures, he believed, were worth pursing more than others. The higher pleasures were mental, and the lower pleasures were sensual or physical. One of Mill's most famous statements is, "It is better to be a human being dissatisfied than a pig satisfied; better to be Socrates dissatisfied than a fool satisfied. And if the fool or the pig are of a different opinion, it is because they only know their side of the question."[12] Mill was an empiricist who believed that humans know things through their senses, but his utilitarianism clearly embraced some distinctions based on reason or intuition—namely, that some pleasures were higher than others. For example, he argued that freedom is a pleasure that must receive higher status than physical satisfaction, and hence, the free choices of humans can be limited only to prevent harm (i.e., pain) to others.

Like Bentham, Mill believed that the moral life could be grounded in a nonmoral framework, one in which God or religion was not necessary. Mill did not necessarily reject theism, but he believed it added nothing substantial to moral foundations or decision making. He did, however, believe this approach was compatible with religious ethics, for he wrote, "If it be a true belief that God desires, above all things, the happiness of his creatures, and that this was his purpose in their creation, utility is not only not a godless doctrine, but more profoundly religious than any other."[13]

Since Bentham and Mill, there have been various formulations of utilitarianism, but most of them have fallen into one of two approaches: act utilitarianism or rule utilitarianism. Act utilitarianism focuses on the results accruing from a given act in a given situation. Here the question is, What effect will this act in this situation have on the general balance of good over evil? This tends to be a situational ethic, for the variables of each context determine the outcome and thus the morally right thing to do. An act utilitarian, for example, might argue that one ought to tell the truth in circumstance A because it will produce the greatest good for the greatest number, but in circumstance B, one ought not to tell the truth because the truth in this setting would bring about the greatest amount of pain.

For rule utilitarians, the foundation of ethics is still the greatest good (i.e., pleasure or happiness) for the greatest number, but they develop rules or principles from that foundation. For example, one generally ought to tell the truth, not because truth telling is inherently right but because generally it produces the best result. Rule utilitarians believe that humans need rules and principles to guide them through the moral maze of life, but the foundation for those rules resides in the same location: consequences.

Some utilitarian thinkers in recent times have questioned the premise that pleasure or happiness is the best measure of the good and have argued for other ends as the criteria. A rather interesting variation of this approach was expressed in Joseph Fletcher's *Situation Ethics: The New Morality* in the 1960s, a controversial book that was widely read and utilized for ethics courses during that era. Fletcher was an Episcopalian clergy and professor of ethics who argued that love was the only intrinsic good and thus qualified as the standard by which to judge the consequences of actions. He argued for a situational ethic in contrast to two other approaches to ethics—legalism (an ethic of laws) and antinomianism (an ethic without norms)—and worked from assumptions such as pragmatism, relativism, and positivism (faith and ethics are not proven but posited).

At first glance, it appears that Fletcher was a principle ethicist, in that love was the ultimate principle. He believed that other principles may play an illuminating role, but one should be "prepared in any situation to compromise them or set them aside in the situation if love seems better served by doing so."[14] Love was the only intrinsic good, the only universal in ethics, for "the situationist holds that whatever is the most loving thing in the situation is the right and good thing."[15] But Fletcher added something else to this principle: "Only the end justifies the means; nothing else." He contended that "not only means but ends too are relative, only extrinsically justifiable. They are good only if they happen to contribute to some good other than themselves. Nothing is intrinsically good but the highest good . . . the end or purpose of all ends—love."[16] From these statements, it is clear that Fletcher moved beyond a strict principle ethic to a form of utilitarianism, albeit one in which love rather than happiness was the consequential criterion. Moreover, his arguments regarding particular cases revealed a strong commitment to consequentialist foundations, for he inevitably looked at the results of particular actions and asked how love was best served in that act.

Fletcher went on to write a number of other works, especially in the area of bioethics. Christian elements were significantly missing from his later writings, as he moved toward an almost secular utilitarianism. A vague notion of love still played a role but always in relation to the end results of human action.

An Evaluation of Utilitarianism

How do we assess the utilitarian foundation of ethics? Certainly, utilitarians are to be lauded for their attempts to show that ethics ought to make a significant difference in outcomes and specifically in the way people are affected. The early utilitarians also contributed to understandings of justice, which treated all people from the standpoint of fairness and impartiality. But as a foundation for ethics, utilitarianism faces some significant problems—practically, rationally, and biblically.

From a practical standpoint, utilitarianism assumes that we can objectively weigh the consequences of a given course of action. But this is highly debatable, for often our biggest differences in ethics are over the empirical or factual judgments surrounding an issue (see chapter 8), and those differences only increase when we attempt to assess consequences. The difficulty utilitarianism faces is well portrayed by philosopher J. Budziszewski, who asserts that for this ethic to work, one would have to be able to accomplish the following:

- Identify all possible courses of action
- For each course of action, identify all people affected
- For each person, identify every pain or pleasure likely to result from the action
- Assign each of these pains and pleasures a numerical value
- Calculate the net gain or loss for each person
- Sum up these gains and losses to get a grand total for each course of action
- Carry out the course of action[17]

Beyond the practical difficulty, there are also some rational problems with utilitarianism—namely, its attempts to decide the moral good of consequences that are deemed nonmoral. But is this possible? When utilitarians set forth pleasure or happiness as the consequential criterion, they establish an intrinsic moral ideal, for it is not at all evident how pleasure and happiness can be a nonmoral base of judgment. To put it another way, utilitarianism is always forced to designate a basis for judging consequences, and in doing so, it actually becomes a kind of principle ethic. And even if it were possible to establish a nonmoral criterion, why happiness or pleasure? The utilitarians accepted Aristotle's contention that everything we choose, we choose for the sake of something—except happiness, which is an end, "for happiness does not lack anything, but is self-sufficient."[18] Thus, they asserted that happiness was the logical choice. But that is not self-evident and therefore is a major flaw in utilitarian thinking.

From a Christian perspective, several issues need to be raised in regard to utilitarian ethics. First, it easily leads to an "end justifies the means" perspective, and some means leading toward a good end may not be morally justified. This seems to be inevitable in utilitarianism, because no criteria other than consequences can limit actions. A classic example of this was the proposal set forth by Thomas Malthus in 1798 to deal with overpopulation. Malthus's study of population trends led him to believe that human population growth would far outstrip food production. To curb human growth, Malthus not only commended sexual restraint or contraception but also advocated allowing people to die off through famine, war, and disease. For Malthus, the end result of population balance justified a stance of negligence to human need, for as he put it, "It seems highly probable, that moral evil is absolutely necessary to the production of moral excellence."[19]

A similar approach was heralded in the late twentieth century with the theory of lifeboat ethics. Advocates argued that the carrying capacity of the earth was being outreached by increased population, and the best solution was simply to let some people die.[20] This is, of course, unacceptable to Christians, who believe that all human beings bear the mark of God's image, and thus the weak among us deserve justice as much as the powerful. The means of willfully permitting some to die runs counter to cherished Christian beliefs and commitments. This issue of the end justifying the means gets played out today in a host of issues: war, poverty, human rights, abortion, euthanasia, and the use of embryonic tissue for stem-cell research. For Christians, it ought to raise the moral red flag.

A final concern with utilitarianism from a Christian perspective is that it does not recognize that some things in and of themselves are good or bad, worthy of pursuit or of rejection. In the utilitarian schema, something is valued only to the degree that it produces good consequences. But in the Christian worldview, there are givens that are good, right, and true regardless of their outcome in a particular time and place. The sanctity of human life, honesty, justice, basic human rights, the sanctity and permanence of marriage, and compassion are not goods to pursue because they make humans happier or bring more pleasure—though in the long run they will usually do so. These and a host of other virtues are to be pursued because they are worthy pursuits in and of themselves and because they are ultimately rooted in the nature and actions of God and the worldview that flows from that transcendent reality. Only when we pursue these givens are we able to guard against the kinds of limitations or excesses that utilitarianism can easily produce. This is well illustrated by Steve Wilkens when he notes that utilitarianism has no way of limiting excessive punishment for a minor infraction such as jaywalking. "Most will say that jaywalking is a minor infraction that does not deserve execution—the punishment does not fit the seriousness of the crime. In other words, the sentence violates a sense of justice. However, what is to keep us from exemplary punishment (hanging jaywalkers) under a utilitarian approach if justice is not an intrinsic value?"[21] And we should note that many of the greatest atrocities and violations of human rights in history have been rationalized on utilitarian grounds—that the end results justified the means.

Principle Ethics

Principle or deontological ethics is significantly different from consequentialism in its understanding of ethics and the moral life. According to this approach, moral actions are inherently right or inherently wrong, not dependent on outcomes or other extrinsic factors. This is an ethic of rights, duties, and obligations that we know by virtue of moral principles or rules, which can come from various sources including reason, religion, or the accumulated wisdom of life experience. The foundation for the moral life is that the world is constructed in such a way (often by God, but not necessarily so) that we as humans are obligated to carry out certain moral duties or responsibilities in life. We are to put principles, rules, and laws into effect in the various spheres of living so that we do what we *ought* to do.

In deontological ethics, one tells the truth because truth telling is in itself the right thing to do and hence a moral obligation. It can be negated or put on hold only when another principle or rule supercedes it. Principle ethicists do not always agree on moral judgments about given issues because they often look to different sources for moral guidelines. Even if they draw on the same source, they may value one principle (or rule) over another. Further, even if they agree on the moral principles (i.e., love, justice, non-maleficence), they may render varying definitions and hence a differing moral decision. But principle ethicists do agree on the heart of ethics: Some moral actions are in and of themselves right or wrong, and there are guidelines to help us discern the moral good.

Socrates

Though he left no writings or specific school of philosophy, Socrates (470–399 B.C.) was one of the most influential thinkers of Western history. We know his thought only through the writings of his student Plato. With a passion to serve Athenian society through philosophy and teaching, Socrates was best known for prodding students toward self-examination of their thought, an approach often called the Socratic method. Ethics was at the heart of Socrates' philosophy, and he believed that knowledge was the key to the moral life. People are not willingly immoral; rather, vice results primarily from ignorance. If we know the right we will do the right, said Socrates.

The philosopher personally faced his greatest test in ethics at his death. He was accused of corrupting the morals of Athenian youth by challenging established religion and current practices of democracy. As a result, he was condemned to die. His friends planned a means of escape from prison, but Socrates rejected the scheme. In one of Plato's dialogues, *Crito,* we get some sense of what Socrates thought about the moral life through the response to his friends' plot. He argued that ethical issues must be settled by reason, not emotional appeal. Moreover, ethics must be decided according to the standards and principles of the moral actor, not according to popular thought, for what people generally think may be wrong. And, said Socrates, ethics cannot be built on results from actions, including good ones; rather, ethics must be rooted in the belief that things are intrinsically right or wrong. We have a duty (the Greek *deon,* from which we get *deontological*) to do what is right and avoid what is morally wrong. From these assumptions, Socrates argued against his friends' plan on the basis of principles derived from reason. First, said Socrates, we ought never to harm anyone, and his escape would in effect harm the state by

37

disregarding its laws. Second, we ought to keep our promises, and by continuing to live within the state when he could have left it, he essentially promised to obey its laws. To break the laws would be to break his promise to the state. Third, he argued, we ought to obey our teachers and our parents, and the state is essentially one's teacher or parent.[22]

Socrates gave the classic rendition of principle ethics. Some things are intrinsically right or wrong, we articulate them by moral principles, we have a duty to do the right and avoid the evil, and (in his case) the source of those principles is reason. Ethics, thus, centers in obligations that we have as human beings, and the results carry no weight in moral foundations. Socrates in the end stood by his ethical principles, for he rejected his friends' escape, drank the hemlock, and died.

Immanuel Kant

The name most frequently associated with deontological ethics is Immanuel Kant, the eighteenth-century German philosopher whom some consider the most influential thinker of modern times. Kant never traveled more than a few miles from his home of Königsberg, and when he eventually became a professor at the University of Königsberg, his life was so predictable that the housewives of the town set their clocks by his regular afternoon walk. He grew up in a Pietistic home, a tradition somewhat skeptical of institutional and dogmatic (highly theological) religion but extremely devout in personal faith and morals. Despite his Pietistic upbringing, Kant embraced Enlightenment views of religion, eventually creating conflict with the political powers. Kant acclaimed reason over divine revelation and believed that the existence of God could not be philosophically demonstrated, though God and religious beliefs were a practical necessity to ensure moral living. In his later years, he was appointed rector at the University of Königsberg and in that role was to lead the faculty procession to chapel. Kant would carry out his responsibilities of leading the procession, but he would not enter the chapel and participate. Because of his religious sentiments and published views, he was forbidden by the king of Prussia to teach or write on religious subjects for five years.

Kant believed that reason was the final arbiter of ethics. Morality was not rooted in consequences, metaphysical beliefs, or any other system of thought; it was autonomous in that moral truth stands on its own rational foundations. From this rational basis and the assumption of a good will that can make good choices, Kant set forth an ethic of duty. "The first proposition of morality is that to have moral worth an action must be done from duty. The second proposition is: An action performed from duty does not have its moral worth in the purpose which is to be achieved through it but in the maxim by which it is determined."[23] That is, there must be a rational, universal principle to which one can ultimately appeal, and the moral duties from that maxim are inherently obligatory simply because they are duties.

Kant asserted that there were essentially two kinds of moral statements: hypothetical imperatives and categorical imperatives. We obey the hypothetical imperative as a "practical necessity of a possible action as a means to achieving something else which one desires. . . . The categorical imperative would be one which presented an action as of itself objectively necessary, without regard to another end."[24] In other words, in regard to the hypothetical imperative, we take a course of action because we might regret the consequences if we do not pursue it or because the reward for the action is worthy of pursuit. A business person might, for example, treat a customer with fairness to keep that person's business. Kant saw this as a kind of prudential consideration that always embodied a sense of selfishness; thus, it was always less pure in motive and not really the essence of true, rational morality.

The categorical imperative, on the other hand, is an action or principle we choose without recourse to its benefit or results; it is in and of itself good. For something to be a categorical imperative, it must be universal, and thus Kant set forth the major principle of the categorical imperative: "Act only according to that maxim by which you can at the same time will that it should become a universal law."[25] Kant believed this was rationally self-evident and that all other imperatives (duties) and moral principles derived from this one imperative. He argued, however, that there was another formulation of this dictum, set forth as a "practical imperative": "Act so that you treat humanity, whether in your own person or in that of another, always as an end and never as a means only."[26] Interestingly, this sounds much like the Golden Rule, and it may well be that Kant never entirely shed his pietistic Christian background.

In this second version of the categorical imperative, he fleshed out the broader abstract rendition of the first formulation. When people are used as means rather than as ends, they no longer are free to make rational choices, which was a bedrock assumption of Kant's ethics. And this is precisely the kind of maxim that humans can will (or desire) to be universalized. Kant saw ethics as rooted in rationality and in rationally derived maxims that all human beings can know without appeal to any other authority. Duties and moral actions are in and of themselves right, and we know these ultimately by the categorical imperative, from which arises all other moral directives. For Kant, ethical principles are absolute, precisely because they are universal. Obligations cannot be negated by appeal to particular circumstances in given situations. In real life, humans might have to deal with such circumstances and make prudential choices, but those choices are hypothetical imperatives. They are not the stuff of real morality.

Examples from Christian Ethics

Many people assume that Christian ethics is at heart a deontological ethic. Responsibilities and actions are in and of themselves right by virtue of God's will, revealed through either divine revelation or the general revelation of reason (i.e., natural law). Ethics is essentially applying and living out moral rules and principles. In this perspective, the foundation of ethics is the divine will known in basic laws and principles that God intends us to follow. Christian morality is then understood as following the Ten Commandments, the Sermon on the Mount, prophetic injunctions, or moral directives from the epistles. Thus, for some Christian ethicists and certainly for many practitioners, ethics is deontological in nature.

Some Christian ethicists postulate one overarching principle as the primary foundation of ethics. For example, the social gospel movement in the late nineteenth and early twentieth centuries posited the kingdom of God as the summary principle of Christian ethics. Moral actions were seen to be inherently right insofar as they reflected God's kingdom, revealed in the person and teachings of Jesus. The kingdom of God was a popular notion in the modernist theology of the time, and many ethicists and theologians employed the concept as a principle from which all other principles derived. As Newman Smyth put it in 1893, "The kingdom of God is a human good as well as an individual attainment. It is . . . a reign of God in the personal life, and a good to be acquired through individual character; yet it is likewise a kingdom or society of men, and its good is to be secured in the larger life of humanity."[27]

Others have argued that love is the overarching principle and foundation of Christian ethics. The late Paul Ramsey, well-known twentieth-century ethicist at Princeton University, contended that *agape* love, rooted in the righteousess of God and the kingdom of God, is the primary framework of Christian ethics. Ramsey, unlike some principle ethicists, insisted that "Christian ethics . . . cannot be separated from its religious foundations."[28] Nonetheless, from those foundations comes one principle that controls the substance of all ethical decisions: love. While this love is similar to and can be expressed in philosophical notions outside Christianity, it is ultimately rooted in the Christian framework and is best understood as a "radical disinterested love of neighbor." Ramsey argued that "neighbor-love defines what is 'right' or obligatory. Love for neighbor comprises 'the meaning of obligation,' which some philosophers suppose was disclosed only by Rousseau and Kant. . . . Certainly Christian ethics is a deontological ethic, not an ethic of the 'good.'"[29] Ramsey attempted to work out this framework in varying issues such as war, sexual ethics, and bioethics, with an appeal to covenant love as a major norm for life in today's world.

Other Christians working in the deontological framework have argued for multiple principles. Norman Geisler, an evangelical philosopher/theologian, seeks to build his ethic on universal norms that are binding for all times and all places. While love of God and love of neighbor sum up the divine moral requirements, there are varying absolute norms that lay claim to our lives.[30] He believes, however, that there are times when these universal, absolute norms may conflict with each other, such as in the case of lying in order to save a human life. Geisler contends that in such situations we must appeal to a hierarchy of values or moral principles, which he believes to be both rationally evident and biblically based. For example, preserving human life is a higher norm than telling the truth, and thus in a conflict "one is morally right in breaking the lower norm in order to keep the higher one."[31] Such actions do not abolish the lower norms, and one is not guilty in breaking the lower for the sake of the higher.[32] The heart and essence of ethics for Geisler and others who follow this framework are principles or norms; they are known by reason and clearly established in divine revelation.

An Evaluation of Principle Ethics

What are we to make of the deontological approach as a foundation for ethics? For those working from a rational framework, such as Socrates and Kant, the absence of God in the moral process is an immediate problem. Though Christians have sometimes found Kant's ethic to be fairly compatible with their own, given his emphasis on universal, moral absolutes, the Christian ethic can never be a purely rational ethic, even if we were able to deduce our moral obligations by reason. From a biblical perspective, doing the good is never divorced from the ultimate good, God, in both motivation and content. Ethics cannot be separated from grace, for Christian moral obligation is not a demand but a gift.

This separation of ethics from God and divine grace is a problem not only for nontheistic deontological ethics but also for Christian formulations. Certainly, the Bible contains moral principles and norms that believers are to follow. These norms reveal the will of God. But if we make principles the foundation of ethics, God is functionally not necessary to the process as long as we know the norms. From a biblical standpoint, principles are not the foundation of ethics. They are certainly means by which we know the good and the right, but ethics at its heart is not about obeying principles and rules, and we are not necessarily moral people simply because we obey them. There is something far deeper and richer that is often missing in the deontological foundations—namely, a larger context that forms the heart and essence of ethics. The foundation of ethics is the nature and actions of God and the worldview that flows from that divine reality. Principles or moral norms are set forth in that context.

A clear example involves the Ten Commandments. Christians have sometimes argued that the Decalogue forms the foundation of Christian morality. Clearly, the moral law reveals the broad structure of God's designs, and believers have a responsibility to embody these designs, but they are not the moral foundation. If we start with the commandments themselves, we miss the grounding: God's redemptive act of freeing his people and forming a covenant relationship with them. The preamble to the Decalogue is just as important as

41

the commands themselves: "I am the LORD your God, who brought you out of the land of Egypt" (Exod. 20:2). On the basis of God's actions and his covenant relationship with the people, he then calls them to obedience, and the Ten Commandments give explicit content for following their redeemer.

This framework is evidenced again and again throughout divine revelation. Moral injunctions are set in a wider context. Thus, they are not mere universals that we are obliged to perform; they are not the heart and essence of the moral life. Indeed, when we divorce them from their ultimate grounding in God and God's acts of grace, and when we separate them from the larger Christian story, they become hollow principles with little motivating and sustaining power. This in no way minimizes the role that biblical principles and laws play, but we must understand them for what they are—the epistemological guidance for carrying out the good but not the heart and essence of the good itself. The basic problem then with a deontological approach is its tendency to make principles the end of the moral life rather than God and divine glory. The principles and norms from God's Word are the authoritative means toward that end.

Principle ethics faces some other issues that must be addressed. First, it tends to focus primarily on actions and minimally on moral character. The history of deontological ethics reveals that it grapples almost exclusively with moral dilemmas and how to resolve them. In a complex world, we of course cannot avoid such dilemmas, and we need an ethic that can help us find our way; principles are a necessity in the midst of such complexity. But an ethic that focuses exclusively on what we do, especially what we do in the tough cases, misses large segments of the moral life—such as our daily routines and our character, or who we really are as human beings before God and others.

Another issue that principle ethics faces is resolving conflicts of moral principles or duties. These hard cases may not come every day, but clearly they are part of a complex world in which we must make moral choices. Perhaps the classic example of such a conflict is seen in those who heroically hid Jews in their homes during the Nazi regime and occupation of World War II. When the gestapo came to the door and asked if they were hiding Jews, what should they have done? Here is a real moral dilemma. On the one hand, we have a responsibility to uphold the sanctity of human life, but on the other hand, we have a responsibility to be truthful in our statements. Or take the case of a Jehovah's Witness who, following an automobile accident, is brought to the ER bleeding profusely. The doctor discerns that he will die unless he immediately receives a blood transfusion, but the spouse objects on the grounds of the family's religious beliefs. The doctor is faced with a conflict of moral principles—the preservation of human life and the freedom of religious conscience. What should he do?

Today, many of our ethical quandaries revolve around multiple principles, norms, obligations, or ideals that conflict with one another. Principle ethics can find ways to deal with these conflicts, but when principles themselves are the foundation of ethics, the job becomes more difficult. For example, because Kant wanted a universal principle to guide ethics (the categorical imperative), he could not allow for a lie even to save a human life. Since we cannot universalize the maxim to lie, telling the truth even if it causes a death is our moral duty. This, however, goes against both our intuitive Christian moral sense and several biblical examples in which lying occurs and seems to be legitimate (i.e., Rahab to save the life of the spies, Josh. 2:5; the Hebrew midwives to save the children, Exod. 1:15–21; and Elisha with the Aramcans, 2 Kings 6:19). Because Kant lacks a larger frame of reference for moral judgments and makes universal principles the end and foundation of ethics, he is not able to deal with these kinds of moral conflicts.

Another deontological way of dealing with conflicts of principles is evidenced by Norman Geisler. As we have seen, his hierarchy of values allows for a way to resolve ethical conflicts, for some norms take precedence over others. Geisler's approach contains much that is commendable and is certainly to be preferred to Kant's or those that do not allow for genuine moral conflicts. However, his perspective is lacking in two ways. First, his contention that we can easily discern through Scripture which norms are higher than others is questionable. One can make this case with human life over telling the truth, but when dealing with the complexities of bioethics, business, and environmental ethics, such discernment is not nearly as simple as Geisler makes it out to be.

Second, his perspective would be aided by a larger context, theology, or narrative in which the principles are set. The principles in his schema seem to be ends in themselves and need a frame of reference through which to understand the principles and the nature of conflicts between them. For example, there is much more we can discern about the conflict between human life and truth telling than the mere conflict of two norms, with one higher than the other. We may indeed need to set aside truth for the sake of human life, but we do so recognizing that the truth is, as Allen Verhey puts it, "not for its own sake, but for God's sake and for the neighbor's sake." Moreover, "God is Truth, but when Scripture uses this image it does not refer simply to some correspondence between word and thought. It refers, rather, to something like troth, as in the trustworthiness and faithfulness that come with betrothal."[33] In other words, if our ethics is purely principle-oriented, we miss both the intention of the principle and the character dimension of the moral life. Ethics is always far more than merely following principles.

Conclusion

Consequentialism and principle ethics have been the two primary ways of thinking about the moral life over the past several centuries. But as foundations for ethics both are lacking. While we at times may appeal to consequences in the midst of complexity, and while we will be guided by moral principles, Christian ethics at its heart involves far more. Neither consequentialism nor principle ethics can provide the grounding needed to sustain moral life in a complex, secular, pluralistic world. And neither does justice to the richness of biblical teaching and theological understanding. Both approaches, moreover, seem fixated on moral quandaries and cannot lead to a fuller understanding of the moral life as both action and character, principle and virtue, doing and being.

Thus, in recent years there has been a significant reaction to both the consequentialist and the principle paradigms. One reaction is often called character or virtue ethics, and to that we now turn.

2

CHARACTER OR VIRTUE ETHICS

Stephen was a fifty-three-year-old man who had been faithful to his wife throughout the thirty years of their marriage. Fidelity had been a central commitment of his life in marriage, work, and friendships. He had raised a solid family, been a loving husband, and though tempted, had never committed adultery. His wife had been experiencing emotional trauma, mostly related to menopausal changes of life. As a result, the physical dimension of their marriage had significantly waned. One night, while away from home on an extended business trip, Stephen met a woman at the hotel where he was staying. His loneliness, personal frustration over his wife's situation, and this woman's own emotional needs led them into a deep, extended conversation and before the night was over into a sexual encounter in his hotel suite. Never in his life, until this night, had Stephen committed adultery and broken his marriage vows. How do we judge this man morally? Is Stephen an adulterer?[1]

Consequentialist and principle ethics would make the judgment by focusing on the action per se based, as shown in the last chapter, on either consequences or moral principles. Stephen would be judged morally for what he *did*. But in recent years another perspective has emerged, or better, reemerged: character ethics. According to character ethics, Stephen would be judged not primarily on what he *did* but on who he *is*—his character, the configuration of dispositions encompassing his total life.

Character or virtue ethics argues that the traditional approaches of consequentialism and principle ethics are not only wrongheaded in their foundations and methodologies, but they also ask the wrong question about ethics and the moral life. The key issue is not What ought we to do? but rather What ought we to be? The kind of people we are as evidenced by our virtues, firmly implanted within, is the heart and essence of ethics. And how do we build virtue and moral character? Not by analyzing the results of our actions or by exploring moral duties, principles, and laws. Rather, we develop moral virtue in a concrete community through the stories or narratives the community tells. Morality is thus not about autonomous individuals attempting to discern the right thing to do. It is essentially a particular way of seeing the world, informed by narratives that have long sustained and inspired a community's citizens. And being so formed and shaped in inward disposition, one will then live life in accordance with virtues that flow almost naturally from the moral actor. The foundation of ethics in this approach resides within the community and its narratives; the essence of ethics is character and the virtues that form it.

Character can best be understood as "the inner and distinctive core of a person from which moral discernment, decisions, and actions spring. It is an enduring configuration of the intentions, feelings, dispositions, and perceptions of any particular self."[2] In the medieval period and again in recent years, the proponents of the virtue or character approach have often spoken of habits or dispositions, the patterns of behavior that one does almost without conscious initiation or deliberation. Habits that are deemed desirable are called virtues, and those deemed undesirable are vices. Most virtue/character ethicists emphasize not merely a list of virtues but virtue itself as a configuration of various habits clustered within a given person.

The focus on character is akin to the biblical language of the heart with a strong emphasis on actions springing naturally from the inner core of a person. Character ethics, therefore, would approach love differently than principle ethics. According to the principle or deontological approach, love is a norm or standard that one seeks to apply to a given, concrete situation or moral problem, with the focus on a behavioral response. A character approach to love focuses on the inner disposition of the heart, believing that in real-life situations a loving disposition will automatically demonstrate itself in "doing the right thing." Iris Murdoch gets to the essence of this approach when she writes, "At crucial moments of choice, most of the business of choosing is already over."[3]

To understand this movement in greater detail, we will examine four key figures who have helped to shape this perspective: Aristotle, the Greek philosopher and progenitor of virtue ethics; Carol Gilligan, an educational psychologist who focuses on moral development; Alasdair MacIntyre, the foremost contemporary philosopher of virtue ethics; and Stanley Hauerwas, the major proponent within theological ethics.

Aristotle

While character/virtue ethics is often a reaction to approaches of the modern world (i.e., consequentialism and principles ethics), its proponents emphasize that it is not a new approach. Nearly all contemporary virtue ethicists urge a return to an old tradition, namely, the thinking of Aristotle (384–322 B.C.).

Aristotle was the son of a physician in the court of Macedonia, and initially he followed his father's footsteps in studying medicine. But after his father died, the seventeen-year-old son made his way to Athens and the academy of Plato. For a period of time he then served as the tutor for Alexander the Great and later returned to Athens, where he set up a rival academy to the Platonic tradition. While he was Plato's most celebrated student, Aristotle diverged from his teacher in significant ways, including his view on ethics.

Aristotle differed most fundamentally from Plato in metaphysics, or "first philosophy." Whereas Plato believed that the ideal forms (the unchanging essence of things) exist independent of the specific material objects, Aristotle emphasized that material objects are a unity of matter and form. He did not completely reject the notion of forms, but he believed that humans should focus on what they can experience with their senses. Thus, in contrast to Plato's idealism, Aristotle and his followers were in one sense materialists who looked to the world itself as the starting point for knowledge and even morals.

When Aristotle looked at the natural world, he saw that all things have natural inclinations for which they exist. Human beings, moreover, have certain natural desires and natural capacities, and from these observations he built his moral framework, most clearly articulated in *The Nichomachean Ethics,* named after his son. He asserted that every inquiry and art aims at some good or end. The ends of various actions and arts are not the same: For medicine it is health, for architecture it is a house. But the end of humans is happiness, for humans always choose it for itself and never for the sake of something else. This pursuit of happiness is not a self-centered, emotive, or frivolous pursuit, as we sometimes think of happiness today, but rather well-being, which for Aristotle meant both living well and faring well. This is the natural end of human life and hence the best and noblest quest.

Happiness as the natural end or *telos* of life is closely tied to virtue or excellence, for "he is happy who is active in accordance with complete virtue."[4] Virtue is an activity of the soul showing forth excellence within its particular sphere of activity. Aristotle believed there are two kinds of virtue or excellence: intellectual virtue and moral virtue. We may praise the wise person with respect to his or her mind, but "in speaking about a man's character we do not say that he is wise or has understanding, but that he is good tempered or temperate."[5] The moral virtues are not attained by nature (though they are rooted in nature) but like the arts are attained by repetition, and thus they eventually become habits. "By doing the acts that we do in our transactions with other men we become just or unjust, and by doing the acts that we do in the presence of danger, and by being habituated to feel fear or confidence, we become brave or cowardly."[6] The virtues, said Aristotle, are not passions (like anger, fear, envy, or joy) but states of character. By states of character he did not mean good or bad in general but rather a particular state of excellence understood as a mean between two extremes.

Aristotle's "golden mean" is one of his best-known doctrines. Virtue is always a mean of equidistance between an excess and a defect. This is a reflection of the natural world itself, for "in everything that is continuous and divisible it is possible to take more, less, or an equal amount . . . and the equal is an intermediate between excess and defect."[7] Courage, one of the cardinal virtues, is the mean between the extremes of cowardice and foolhardiness. "It is cowardly to run away from all danger; yet it is foolhardy to risk too much."[8] In similar fashion, generosity is the mean between stinginess and extravagance, gentleness the mean between irascibility and impassivity, and truthfulness the mean between boastfulness and self-deprecation. Virtue is always the golden mean, and any deficiency or excess is always a vice. There is one virtue that by its very nature stands apart from this framework: justice. Justice is not the mean between two extremes, for it "is not part of virtue but virtue entire." "It is complete because he who possesses it can exercise his virtue not only in himself but towards his neighbor also."[9]

For Aristotle, these virtues are natural in that they are inclinations within us. For that reason, his ethic is frequently called teleological, not in the sense of consequentialist theories, which ground ethics in end results, but in the sense that we have natural ends through which we experience the moral life. Whenever we perform actions as human beings, it is in a particular role or sphere with a natural intention in mind. We achieve excellence when we perform according to that end or natural intention of the act. The ultimate end is happiness, and the means by which we achieve happiness are the virtues.

Aristotle assumed that moral actions must be freely chosen and are governed by the intellect in conjunction with the will. Ultimately, however, "Action must proceed from a firm and unchangeable character."[10] Yet he simultaneously contended that character is shaped by our actions and particularly those that are habitual patterns of life. "This is confirmed by what happens in states; for legislators make the citizens good by forming habits in them . . . and those who do not effect it miss their mark, and it is in this that a good constitution differs from a bad one."[11] For Aristotle, the state, community, and parents all have a role in forming moral habits, for they develop not in the abstract but in the concrete realities of life and in accordance with an embodied tradition.

Aristotle believed that we are essentially communal beings, and the most fundamental of our natural communities is the state. "Every state is a community of some kind, and every community is established with a view to some good; for mankind always acts in order to obtain that which they think good. . . . The state or political community, which is the highest of all, and which embraces all the rest, aims . . . at the highest good."[12] The state thus plays a pivotal role in the development of virtue, though its agenda must always be a reflection of and never in conflict with other communities such as family and village. States establish laws, but those laws are not the core of ethics for Aristotle. The core is found in character, and character is fundamentally the harmony of the various virtues that become habitual patterns of life. For Aristotle, this is the heart and essence of ethics, and it is from this basic framework that the contemporary interest in character/virtue ethics has emerged.

Carol Gilligan

Carol Gilligan is not an ethicist but a Harvard professor of education, focusing primarily on the field of moral development. Moral development theorists attempt to show that just as humans go through developmental stages physically, emotionally, and cognitively, so they grow in their moral understanding and reasoning. Throughout much of the twentieth century, moral development theories were rooted in the thinking of Sigmund Freud, Jean Piaget, and Lawrence Kohlberg. But in the 1980s, Gilligan began to challenge the conventional wisdom of that tradition. While moral development theorists attempt to describe behavior rather than commend forms of moral thought and life, it is clear that they cannot avoid the prescriptive dimension. As Craig Dykstra points out, "The study of moral development requires answers to questions that are philosophical and theological as well as psychological, sociological, and anthropological."[13] It is precisely over the ideal of the moral life that Gilligan took issue with the received tradition, and her commendations are similar to character ethics.[14]

For a number of years, moral development theory was dominated by the work of Lawrence Kohlberg, who advanced six stages of development, ranging from a simplistic conformity to other's expectations to a morality of universal, general ethical principles. He described these stages "as sociomoral perspectives on norms in general and upon the justice operations of equality, equity, reciprocity, prescriptive role-taking, and universalizability."[15] As Gilligan began to work within this framework, she noted that females tended to score lower than males in Kohlberg's studies. She came to believe that the problem was not developmental inferiority but the way that morality itself was conceived. Kohlberg and his followers were working from Kant's understanding of ethics with its strong emphasis on universal principles, with a special focus on justice. The justice orientation to moral development, Gilligan contended, basically conceives of morality as a conflict of rights that are adjudicated by rational principles. Kohlberg, therefore, was essentially testing to find out who could achieve a particular form of ethical reflection, one that was biased in a rational, autonomous, justice direction.

In contrast to this paradigm, Gilligan noticed a different voice in women's narratives, a different mode of thinking about morality. The different voice was not found exclusively in females over against males, but it was evidenced more frequently in females than in males and was discovered primarily in their stories and narrative accounts. This new mode she called the "care orientation" in contrast to the old "justice orientation." "The very traits that traditionally have defined the 'goodness' of women, their care for and sensitivity to the needs of others, are those that mark them as deficient in moral development."[16] The traditional justice orientation honored the individuated, autonomous, detached moral observer and debased an ethic that focused on relationships, care, and the narratives that sustain such an ethic.

Gilligan asserted then that the justice ethic approach (the Kantian tradition) was not the only way to do ethics and certainly not the only basis for moral development theory. In care ethics, "the moral problem arises from conflicting responsibilities rather than from competing rights and requires for its resolution a mode of thinking that is contextual and narrative rather than formal and abstract."[17] Whereas the justice approach emphasizes truth, rights, and fairness, the care approach emphasizes context, relationship, and compassion. While the justice approach is discerned rationally by an autonomous thinker, the care approach is discerned through narratives in relational networks of real people. These two approaches need not be mutually exclusive, but they clearly are based on different conceptions of the world, the self, and the nature of moral problems.

The distinctions between justice and care orientations are not just different approaches to moral development but entail different conceptions of morality. "A justice perspective draws attention to problems of inequality and oppression and holds up an ideal of reciprocity and equal respect. A care perspective draws attention to problems of detachment or abandonment and holds up an ideal of attention and response to need. Two moral injunctions—not to treat others unfairly and not to turn away from someone in need—capture these different concerns."[18]

While Gilligan is not an ethicist and does not call her analysis character or virtue ethics, it seems clear that her work has affinities with this approach. Her reaction to the Kantian tradition, her commendation of narrative over rationality, her emphasis on concrete historical situations as opposed to abstractions, and her focus on "a preferred way of seeing" all bear similarities to the historic and contemporary character/virtue paradigm. Gilligan believes that both justice and care ethics have a place in moral development and ethical reflection, but any approach that neglects the care emphasis is clearly deficient. "From the perspective of someone seeking or valuing care, relationship connotes responsiveness or engagement, a resiliency of connection that is symbolized by a network or web. . . . The moral ideal is one of attention and response."[19]

Alasdair MacIntyre

In 1981, the philosopher Alasdair MacIntyre, then at Notre Dame, wrote what was to become the prime shaper of contemporary virtue ethics, *After*

Virtue. Earlier in his career he had written a history of philosophical ethics, but in this work he provides in more explicit fashion an account of what has gone wrong in the modern moral world and a way to amend it. MacIntyre bemoans the aftermath of the liberal Enlightenment ideals and calls for a return to Aristotle and his virtue ethic. He provides a narrative to understand what has happened to ethics in the past several centuries even as he commends narratives of living communities as primary frameworks for grounding moral reflections and behavior. As Max Stackhouse describes it, his writings "are basically about the wisdom of the classical views of virtue, *telos,* and social coherence in close-knit communities in contrast to the foolishness of modernity with its accent on individualism, pluralism, cosmopolitanism, and abstract science."[20] MacIntyre's critique and proposal are especially fascinating in light of his own personal narrative, the pilgrimage of a questioner of theism to a conversion to Roman Catholic Christianity.

MacIntyre believes that "in the actual world which we inhabit the language of morality is in . . . grave disorder."[21] In the modern world, we have no way of carrying on moral debate, for we have no commonly accepted criteria to make such judgments. In a work written several years subsequent to *After Virtue,* he wrote, "We thus inhabit a culture in which an inability to arrive at agreed rationally justifiable conclusions on the nature of justice and practical rationality coexists with appeals by contending social groups to sets of rival and conflicting convictions unsupported by rational justification."[22] Essentially, says MacIntyre, we have ended up with an ethic of emotivism that asserts, "All moral judgments are *nothing but* expressions of preference, expressions of attitude or feeling."[23]

How did we end up in such a state? MacIntyre believes that the main culprit is modern liberalism with its appeals to the autonomous, rational self, abstracted from living histories, as evidenced in the Enlightenment, Protestantism, Kant, liberal democracies, modernist theologies, and a host of other movements and ideologies. The modern world tended to assume that universal moral laws could be established on the basis of reason without being firmly entrenched in a context of people who lived out the moral tradition being espoused. Whether deonotological theories or consequentialist theories (such as utilitarianism), MacIntyre believes they were all doomed to self-destruction, because they focused on finding universal ways of resolving moral conflicts without recourse to a *telos* and an embodied history that could make sense of, guide, and sustain moral assertions.

Even Protestant Christianity cannot escape the scathing critique of MacIntyre. He believes that the Reformation's emphasis on justification by faith left the moral agent alone before God without the stability of a community and without "the conception of human-nature-as-it-could-be-if-it-realized-its *telos.*"[24] Protestantism rejected the notion of *telos,* or the person's natural end, by focusing on moral laws and principles and thus essentially paved the way for secular deontological ethics. It lost the sense of moral character, says MacIntyre, with its emphasis on moral actions, but the actions themselves counted for little in the Christian life. He believes, moreover, that Protestant teachings had the effect of sanctioning "the autonomy of secular activity" and thus handed the secular world over "to its own devices."[25]

The modern moral agenda, whether religious or nonreligious, is a failed agenda in MacIntyre's version of the story. "It was Nietzsche's historic achievement to understand more clearly than any other philosopher . . . that what purported to be appeals to objectivity were in fact expressions of subjective will."[26] The emotivism of our time is the direct result of the liberal, Enlightenment agenda, and Nietzsche's nihilism is the understandable final effect.

What then does MacIntyre see as the solution for ethics? He believes that we need to return to a tradition that was largely abandoned after the medieval period, the ethics of Aristotle. MacIntyre understands ethics as focused primarily on character, not actions, the primary question being, What ought I to be? rather than What ought I to do? With Aristotle he contends that this entails an ethic of virtue that seeks not a discernment of universal moral rules but a discernment of natural ends that embody the good. "Human beings, like the members of all other species, have a specific nature; and that nature is such that they have certain aims and goals, such that they move by nature towards a specific *telos*."[27] What is the end? It is *eudaimonia,* which is best translated blessedness, happiness, prosperity, which according to Aristotle is the state of being well and doing well. The virtues then are those qualities that enable one to achieve that end; they are internalized qualities and habits that shape the core of one's character. MacIntyre, with Aristotle, believes that "to act virtuously is not, as Kant was later to think, to act against inclination; it is to act from inclination formed by the cultivation of the virtues."[28] This is what he means by a teleological ethic. MacIntyre does not completely disregard moral rules or laws, but he argues that applying them is possible only for one who is virtuous and has a proper sense of the end toward which we are intended and the specific ends of particular activities and roles in life.

Unlike the Enlightenment and modernity, which stressed autonomous reason as the path to morality, MacIntyre insists that stories told by particular communities are the primary means to the moral life. He writes, "In all those cultures, Greek, medieval or Renaissance, where moral thinking and action is structured according to some version of the scheme that I have called classical, the chief means of moral education is the telling of stories."[29] The Homeric epics, for example, provide a clear example of the way in which the virtues were taught by stories, the way they were embodied within the community, and the way in which specific forms of action then arose from the status or role of the one carrying out the story in life. The stories not only taught specific virtues but embodied a sense that the virtues must fit together in a web of wholeness. MacIntyre writes:

> It is through hearing stories about wicked stepmothers, lost children, good but misguided kings, wolves that suckle twin boys, youngest sons who receive no inheritance but must make their own way in the world and eldest sons who waste their inheritance on riotous living and go into exile to live with the swine, that children learn or mis-learn both what a child and what a parent is, what the cast of characters may be in the drama into which they have been born and what the ways of the world are.[30]

Ethics, therefore, can never be autonomous and can never be done outside a real-life history of a community that carries on the moral tradition.

MacIntyre never gives a clear indication of what the good or *telos* ultimately looks like. We look in vain in his writings to comprehend the exact nature of the virtuous life or what virtuous people living in the twenty-first century might actually do amid the complexities of our time. He believes, rather, that what is needed is a framework for doing ethics, a social tradition that teaches a morality in its stories and is embodied in a community's life together. MacIntyre seems then to envision ethics as primarily connected to smaller social units in which clear socialization (or moral education) and moral accountability can transpire. The foundation of ethics is communities and their narratives, for they define the community's existence, meaning, and identity and provide the roles and expectations for its members.

Stanley Hauerwas

Stanley Hauerwas is the prophet for a Christian version of character or virtue ethics.[31] A prolific writer and a colorful personality, Hauerwas brings together three unlikely strands in his thinking: a Roman Catholic love of liturgy and sacrament (he taught for a number of years at the University of Notre Dame), an Anabaptist theology of the church, and a Methodist or Wesleyan concern for sanctification (he is a lifelong Methodist). He is currently professor of theological ethics at Duke University Divinity School.

While MacIntyre leaves us without a clear sense of the moral *telos* or good, Hauerwas brings to the table a specific conception of the good and explicit concepts of character and virtue. He brings Christian content and resources to virtue ethics and is bold in asserting the specific community in which it is nurtured, the church. Hauerwas continually emphasizes that there is no such thing as ethics. It always needs a qualifier, so that we can only speak of things such as humanist ethics, existentialist ethics, Hindu ethics, or Christian ethics, never just ethics per se. There is no universal ethic, and there are no universal moral principles, for the moral life is always rooted in, nurtured, and sustained by a particular community with a vision of what it means to be good and human and with communal stories that carry the vision. The notion of a universal ethic is a modern myth, and "the birth of modernity is coincident with the beginnings of 'ethics' understood as a distinguishable sphere or realm of human life."[32]

Ethics in the modern world, he contends, has become autonomous in its attempts to be universal and in so doing has failed to see its captivity to a tradition or a narrative—modernity's story of self-sufficient builder and controller of the world. This is true not only of philosophical ethics but also of Christian ethics with its attempts to develop ethics independent of religion. Hauerwas believes that modern religion essentially followed Kant in his rational universal ethic, and "in many ways Kant became the greatest representative of Protestant liberalism; that is Protestant liberal theology after Kant is but a series of footnotes to his work."[33]

For Hauerwas, Christian ethics "is not first of all concerned with 'thou shalt' or 'thou shalt not.' Its first task is to help us rightly envision the world. Christian ethics is specifically formed by a very definite story with determinative content."[34] The moral life is not about decisions but rather involves a kind of imaginative ordering of our metaphors and narratives about God, ourselves, and the world. "What is at stake in most of our decisions is not the act itself, but the kind of person we will be."[35] And this character formation comes, for Hauerwas, not by normative analysis but by narratives that captivate our hearts as much as our minds. Edward Long once described Hauerwas's method and perspective this way: "We do morals more as an artist encounters his work than as the critic who subsequently makes an analytical or evaluative judgment about the work of the artist."[36]

Early in his career, Hauerwas set forth his thinking about the heart and agenda of ethics in ten theses. His subsequent work has deviated little from them:

1. The social significance of the gospel requires the recognition of the narrative structure of Christian convictions for the life of the church.
2. Every social ethic involves a narrative, whether it is concerned with the formulation of basic principles of social organization and/or concrete policy alternatives.
3. The ability to provide an adequate account of our existence is the primary test of the truthfulness of a social ethic.
4. Communities formed by a truthful narrative must provide the skills to transform fate into destiny so that the unexpected, especially as it comes in the forms of strangers, can be welcomed as gift.
5. The primary social task of the church is to be itself—that is, a people who have been formed by a story that provides them with the skills for negotiating the danger of this existence, trusting in God's promise of redemption.
6. Christian social ethics can be done only from the perspective of those who do not seek to control national or world history but who are content to live "out of control."

7. Christian social ethics depends on the development of leadership in the church that can trust and depend on the diversity of gifts in the community.
8. For the church to be, rather than to have, a social ethic means we must recapture the social significance of common behavior, such as acts of kindness, friendship, and the formation of families.
9. In our attempt to control our society, Christians in America have too readily accepted liberalism as a social strategy appropriate to the Christian story.
10. The church does not exist to provide an ethos for democracy or any other form of social organization but stands as a political alternative to every nation, witnessing to the kind of social life possible for those that have been formed by the story of Christ.[37]

For Hauerwas, Christian ethics must never be divorced from theology, "For theology is a practical activity concerned to display how Christian convictions construe the self and the world."[38] Such a vision is best recognized and sustained through narratives. These narratives are not incidental to the faith but are the forms our Christian convictions take. He believes that once we abstract ethical norms or theological statements from their narrative context, they take on a life of their own that bears little resemblance to their origins. Moreover, he resists the notion that Christian ethics has a methodological starting point. "The dilemma of whether we must do Christian ethics out of a doctrine of God or of man is a false one. For Christian ethics begins in a community that carries the story of the God who wills us to participate in a kingdom established in and through Jesus of Nazareth. . . . Theology has no essence, but rather is the imaginative endeavor to explicate the stories of God by showing how one claim illuminates another."[39]

The heart of the Christian story that guides our moral life is the story of Jesus. Drawing substantially on the thinking of Mennonite theologian John Howard Yoder, Hauerwas asserts that the life and teachings of Jesus, as a manifestation of the kingdom of God, make up the core of what we are called to be in our own character and virtues. "To be like Jesus is to join him in the journey through which we are trained to be a people capable of claiming citizenship in God's kingdom of nonviolent love."[40] And it is in the church that this story is learned, enacted, and proclaimed. Frequently in his writings, Hauerwas declares that the church, rather than attempting to build an ethic that can engage the world, is itself a social ethic. The church is a people of virtue by remembering and living the story of the crucified Savior, which entails not an attempt to control the world by power but a challenge to the powers of the world by the very life of Christ embodied in the church.

According to Hauerwas, the church and its Christocentric narrative stand in stark contrast to the Enlightenment narrative that has dominated modern ethics. The autonomous, productive self, seeking to control life and death, has been the heart of the Enlightenment story. As a result, we struggle with the theodicy question, Why does a good and all-powerful God allow suffering and evil? and in medicine we seek to cure, not to care. "In such a context, medicine becomes the mirror image of theoretical theodicies sponsored by the Enlightenment because it attempts to save our profoundest hopes that sickness should and can be eliminated."[41] As a result, says Hauerwas, modern society lacks a narrative in which to engage the bioethical world.

What then is the foundation of ethics for Hauerwas? That is a difficult question to answer, because he does not like the question; he refuses to do ethics by establishing foundations from which to build. He insists that seeking foundations for ethics has led to its loss of Christian particularism and the centrality of Jesus. "Despite enthusiasm of many religious thinkers for this search for a foundation for morality, such a foundation ironically cannot but make religious convictions morally secondary."[42] But based on his writings, it is safe to say that his grounding of ethics is the story of Jesus, embedded in his community, the church, through the virtues and character of its people. For Hauerwas, ethics does not flow from beliefs about God, Jesus, or the church. Rather, "our convictions embody our morality; our beliefs are our actions."[43]

Assessment of Character or Virtue Ethics

Positive Aspects

An assessment of the character/virtue alternative to consequentialism and deontological foundations certainly reveals some immediate benefits and right-headed perspectives. First, Christians must strongly affirm its focus— that ethics involves more than doing the right thing. The character emphasis draws strongly on the biblical emphasis on the heart and its role in both moral virtue and moral vice, or sin. The word *heart* occurs hundreds of times in English translations of the Bible, and it is clearly the closest concept to character, the innate moral dispositions of the moral actor. The Old Testament *shema* clearly affirms character in the classic text of Deuteronomy 6:4–9:

> Hear, O Israel: The LORD is our God, the LORD alone. You shall love the LORD your God with all your heart, and with all your soul, and with all your might. Keep these words that I am commanding you today in your heart. Recite them to your children and talk about them when you are at home and when you are away, when you lie down and when you rise. Bind them as a sign on your hand, fix them as an emblem on your forehead, and write them on the doorposts of your house and on your gates.

The Hebrew prophets continually proclaimed that the heart was the medium of both moral evil and moral good, as seen in Ezekiel's prophecy:

> I will give them one heart, and put a new spirit within them; I will remove the heart of stone from their flesh and give them a heart of flesh, so that they may follow my statutes and keep my ordinances and obey them. Then they shall be my people, and I will be their God. But as for those whose heart goes after their detestable things and their abominations, I will bring their deeds upon their own heads, says the Lord GOD.
>
> 11:19–21

And Jesus spoke of the heart in relation to the moral life when he taught that an external keeping of the law was insufficient in regard to matters such as adultery (Matt. 5:27–30) and murder (5:21–26). Moreover, he affirmed that the heart is the immediate source of sinful vices (Mark 7:21–22) and of moral renewal, for "the good person out of the good treasure of the heart produces good, and the evil person out of evil treasure produces evil; for it is out of the abundance of the heart that the mouth speaks" (Luke 6:45). When Jesus summarized the requirements of the law, heart and character were paramount: "You shall love the Lord your God with all your heart, and with all your soul, and with all your mind" (Matt. 22:37). All of the New Testament writers echo the same theme and affirm that Christians are called to do "the will of God from the heart" (Eph. 6:6).

The recent emphasis on character and virtue rightly reminds us that the moral life is not only what we do but who we are. Intentions, visions, and dispositions play a significant role in pursuing the morally good, as illustrated by Arthur Holmes:

> If I drive within the speed limit only because a police car is following me, I may be doing what is right, but I do it for prudential rather than ethical reasons. I may perhaps drive within the speed limit merely to annoy my companion and make him late for an important engagement. Then I would be doing what is right from a morally wrong motive. Again, I might keep the speed limit just because my car won't go any faster. Then I would be doing what is right unintentionally.[44]

If we focus only on actions without attention to character, we lose sight of this dimension of ethics—that we can do the right thing but in the wrong way.

Character ethics is right to recapture this internal dimension, and it is certainly correct and biblical in its focus on virtues. When we look at biblical ethics, we find not only the Decalogue with its "thou shalt nots" (which as we will see in a later chapter embody far more than negative prohibitions) but also many listings of virtues. The Book of Proverbs is significantly focused on the virtues of wisdom in everyday life, though clearly the proverbs also stress particular actions. Jesus' Beatitudes in Matthew 5 largely reflect moral virtues or habits that are reflective of who a person is: poor in spirit, meek, merciful, pure in heart, peacemaking, etc. And Paul's list of the fruits of the Spirit are primarily moral and spiritual virtues: "love, joy, peace, patience, kindness, generosity, faithfulness, gentleness, and self-control" (Gal. 5:22–23).

Character or virtue ethics is also to be affirmed for its insistence that ethics is always reflective of a larger vision, or as its adherents put it, a narrative. As will be noted shortly, this approach narrows the focus too much with its insistence on narrative as the only vehicle of this larger vision, but the character/virtue ethicists have rendered a great service by demonstrating that ethics cannot be severed from theology or from a larger vision of reality. Our conception of the good or of the virtuous life is always intimately tied to a larger picture of God, the world, sin, and the patterns of human history.

Negative Aspects

But while character/virtue ethics has much to commend it, there are some shortcomings in this approach as a foundation for ethics. In this evaluation, we need to keep in mind that its proponents almost always set this paradigm over against the traditional foundations of consequences, principles, or theological affirmations. The issues to explore here then are not just matters of focus but rather conceptions of the essence and grounding of ethics, even if many virtue ethicists want to avoid the language of grounding and foundation.

First, there is within the movement an overemphasis on character. If other approaches have almost totally ignored the *being* dimension with a singular focus on *doing*, the character/virtue strand downplays the importance of *doing* with its singular emphasis on *being*. There is no reason that these two dimensions cannot live together as mutual foci of ethical analysis, but the character ethicists too often imply otherwise. Hauerwas, for example, does not deny the need to make decisions but wants to give decision making a different status. When we look to the past, he notes, we often find "that in matters of significance even involving the 'hardest choices' there was no 'decision' to be made. Rather, the decision makes itself if we know who we are and what is required of us."[45] But if we return to the narrative of Stephen from the beginning of the chapter, it is not clear that the problem is merely one of character. Stephen's inner dispositions seem pointed in the right direction, but clearly his act of adultery was immoral and sin. Character ethics too easily glosses over Stephen's actions.

Rather than pitting decisions and character or doing and being against each other, it would be much preferable to see them as complementary. To be sure, character informs our decisions, but the decisions we make also inform our character. There are times when character alone is insufficient for the complex decisions we must make, and we will need to engage in good, hard analysis. This in no way minimizes the role of intentions, dispositions, and habits of the heart, but it does mean that we need a mutual approach that accentuates both being and doing. Our own sinful proclivities mean that while we may give distinct attention to character and even Christian character, it is still possible to act immorally, as Stephen did. To focus almost exclusively on character is to lose sight of this reality.

A second weakness in the character/virtue paradigm is its narrowing of ethical resources by an overemphasis on narrative. Both Hauerwas and MacIntyre emphasize narrative or story as the primary carrier of ethical traditions. Certainly, they are to be lauded for their insistence, contrary to normative statements, that ethics is always set in a large context and arises out of a broad vision of reality. There is no question that narrative has played a significant role in portraying a larger vision or context, but this need not preclude other modes of understanding and communication. Story is particularly set over against more propositional understandings of reality. But why must the two be set against each other? The next chapter contends that worldview forms a basis for ethics, but we understand that worldview not only through story but also through rituals and discursive forms. Some critics have rightly contended that this narrow emphasis allows only for broad strokes in ethical direction and precludes the possibility of more direct moral guidance. The Bible contains multiple forms of ethical resources ranging from narrative, to proverb, to command.

The narrative focus in character/virtue ethics is usually set over against principle ethics. Certainly, principle ethics is inadequate as a foundation (as noted in chapter 1), but it does not follow that narrative ethics must then preclude the use of principle as a form of moral guidance. The nurturing of virtue by means of story in the context of community (the church) is an indispensable part of ethics, but the community also nurtures the moral life through commands, principles, and theological paradigms. These forms of moral guidance need not be portrayed as autonomous and void of a context and vision, as the critics sometimes suppose or as has indeed sometimes occurred. Rather, it is quite possible to see narrative guidance and context as compatible with the use of specific commands and principles. These commands and principles are not the foundation of ethics, and neither are the narratives. But both can work together in providing guidance and context for Christian ethics. We need both the broad strokes of narrative and the more specific pointers of command and principle.

There is a third problem with character/virtue ethics: its overemphasis on community. The proponents of this paradigm emphasize that ethics emerges out of specific communities and is nurtured within those communities. One is sometimes left with the impression that ethics is nothing more than a community's moral vision shaped by its own narratives. This then presents a major problem as we think about ethical foundations from a Christian perspective. Is there no transcendent reality beyond the community itself? And if there is transcendent reality, can one not gain any glimpse of it beyond the particular community in which one finds himself or herself?

It is these questions that have sometimes led to the charge that ultimately character/virtue ethics is relativistic.[46] By reducing ethics to the community and its story, we seem to be left with a kind of postmodern assumption that all truth claims are bunk or merely parochial. Hauerwas wants to direct the truth questions away from a foundationalist perspective that begins with understandings about God, Christ, or the church and toward a perspective in which our "convictions form our character to be truthful." The first task of ethics is to help us rightly see the world, but "if we somehow discover the world is not as that story suggests, then we have good grounds for not believing in, or more accurately, not worshiping the God revealed in the life, cross, and resurrection of Jesus."[47]

But can this perspective really help us discern which narratives are worthy of our commitments? And what happens if we find ourselves in a community that is blatantly racist or flagrantly violates human dignity, supported by its own narratives? On what basis do we reject the operational narratives, practices, and dispositions of a given community? These are the kinds of questions we must face if we opt for a fideistic approach that does not allow the central questions of truth to emerge, except as they are tied to narrative formulations. In rejecting a Kantian, universal, rational ethic, this paradigm goes too far in the other direction by insisting that truth can be tested only within the confines of a community's narrative, to which it is then to be truthful. As Christians we must assert that there is transcendent reality beyond the community's self-understanding and that reality can be known and experienced through God's self-disclosure in the written and incarnate Word. That divine revelation is itself a reflection of the ultimate foundation for ethics—the Triune God. Certainly, we most adequately discern that foundation and its moral directives within the community that commits to live in accordance with transcendent reality. But the reality always transcends the community that names the name of Christ; otherwise Christ and divine revelation are nothing more than the community itself. A community and its narratives alone can never be the foundation of a Christian ethic.

Conclusion

Character or virtue ethics comes much closer as an adequate approach and foundation than does consequentialism or deontological ethics. Its focus on character and virtue, its insistence on a larger vision beyond the moral directives, and its recovery of the role of narrative in moral nurture are to be lauded. But ultimately it is too one-sided in its formulations, and it fails to deal adequately with the following questions: Why be moral at all? What is the basis for saying that one virtue or disposition or action is more laudable than another? How do we respond, as a people shaped in Christian character, to the tough, complex, moral issues that call for a decision? We must move beyond character ethics as we seek a foundation for the moral life.

3

A Christian Worldview Foundation for Ethics

Several years ago, Princeton University created quite a stir when it appointed the Australian philosopher Peter Singer to a tenured professorship in bioethics. Singer had become infamous for his view that killing a live baby may not be as serious as killing a happy cat. He believes that the human treatment of animals is nothing short of tyranny and that animals deserve every bit as much, if not more, protection as a *Homo sapiens,* since animals are self-aware while infants are not. For Singer, infanticide (the killing of an infant) is justified when the child faces a life of suffering and pain. Down's syndrome and spina bifida children are among the candidates for such treatment as is a handicapped baby, if his or her death would both relieve the burden of the child and bring greater happiness to the rest of the family. In similar fashion, Singer believes that euthanasia is morally justified on the grounds that it relieves a person of suffering and misery.

Given the views of Singer, it is not surprising that a large number of protestors showed up at the doors of Princeton, including people with disabilities who by Singer's calculations might never have lived. Many critics have focused on his ethical commitment to utilitarianism as the primary factor in his controversial positions; Singer does indeed approach ethics with a commitment to the maximizing of personal happiness and the minimization of personal pain. But while utilitarianism is one component of Singer's ethical foundation and method, something else is going on in his thinking.

Singer deviates from many traditional norms and sentiments primarily because of his worldview. A worldview is the way we put our world together. It embodies our sense of God or transcendence, our understandings of human nature, our beliefs about what is wrong within the world and how to fix that wrong, and our perceptions about where history is headed. When Singer argues that the sufferings and pleasures of human beings are not necessarily of greater moral significance than the sufferings and pleasures of other species, he is reflecting a worldview different from those who argue that all human life has an inherent dignity. Singer rejects the notion of a moral order "which supposes that human beings are extraordinarily precious because God made them so. He also rejects secular philosophies that depict human beings as possessing a unique and exalted dignity that sharply distinguishes them from, and justifies their 'tyranny' over, other species of animals."[1]

At the foundation of Singer's ethic is a worldview that believes humans are no different from animals and thus of no greater moral significance. Human life has no intrinsic dignity and worth because there is nothing in the universe beyond humans to grant them that worth. As Singer sees it, "We have no need to postulate gods who hand down commandments to us, because we can understand ethics as a natural phenomenon that arises in the course of the evolution of social, intelligent, long-lived mammals who possess the capacity to recognize each other and to remember the past behavior of others."[2] While he employs a utilitarian calculus to justify his moral positions, his own brand of utilitarianism arises from a particular narrative about reality—a worldview about life, death, and human/animal existence on earth.

Worldviews play a significant role in ethics. This is well demonstrated in the following portrayals of two distinct worldviews:

> One, we are a people by blood relationship, who dwell in a sacred universe inhabited by other creatures, including plants, animals, and seldom-seen spiritual beings. The created harmony between us all is constantly jeopardized by human failure to observe the Creator's law. Dangerous and sometimes devastating results follow. Harmony must be restored by appropriate ceremonies and a return to the Creator's law.
>
> Two, we are individuals who have formed societies. We live in a universe that consists of other beings (plants and animals) who are somewhat like us, but inferior. The rest of the universe consists of arrangements of energy and matter devoid of any purpose except for that which we decide to invent. We are in jeopardy as individuals, as a society, and as a species from internal conflicts and wars and the natural environment, unless we can further develop and use our superior intelligence more rationally and effectively.[3]

The first of these portrayals broadly represents the worldview of Native American peoples in North America, while the second represents a secular, scientific, modern worldview of many people in dominant Western cultures. These two ways of conceiving the world engender different directions in environmental ethics and the moral life in general. Both stand in contrast to a Christian perception of reality.

To assert that worldviews are always at the heart of ethical reflections and moral actions is not a peculiarly Christian understanding. Many social scientists believe a profound relationship exists between worldview and ethics. The anthropologist Clifford Geertz argues that there is always an interplay between metaphysics and morals, or worldview and ethos. The worldview of a religious group is the "picture of the way things in sheer actuality are, their concepts of nature, of self, of society."[4] The ethos is the group's tone, character, or moral style, and it is never divorced from the larger perceptions of reality. Geertz writes: "The source of its [a religion's] moral vitality is conceived to lie in the fidelity with which it expresses the fundamental nature of reality. The powerful coercive 'ought' is felt to grow out of a comprehensive factual 'is.'"[5]

All moral reflection, character, and actions are part of a larger drama. As Alister McGrath notes, "Every movement that has ever competed for the loyalty of human beings has done so on the basis of a set of beliefs. Whether the movement is religious or political, philosophical or artistic, the same pattern emerges: a group of ideas, of beliefs, is affirmed to be in the first place true and in the second place important." Thus, for McGrath, "A recovery of Christian doctrine is fundamental to a recovery of Christian ethics."[6]

The foundation of Christian ethics is the Christian worldview, ultimately rooted in the nature and actions of the Triune God. If worldview is the foundation of ethics, then obviously a Christian worldview, our theology, leads to a distinctive approach to ethics, though at points its moral positions may overlap with those of other worldviews. Some Christians throughout history have tried to downplay the role of theology and unite primarily around ethics. But Dorothy Sayers, the great British writer, was on target when she asserted, "It is worse than useless for Christians to talk about the importance of Christian morality, unless they are prepared to take their stand upon the fundamentals of Christian theology. It is a lie to say that dogma does not matter; it matters enormously."[7]

The Christian worldview or theology is manifested in three ways: through a narrative component, a rational component, and a ritual component. All worldviews tend to manifest themselves in these forms. The narrative component, as seen in the last chapter, embodies the stories we tell to make sense of reality. In the Christian faith, this involves the particular biblical stories as well as the overarching biblical story of creation, fall, redemption, and consummation—a paradigm that will be explored in depth shortly.

The second component is the rational or discursive one in which we attempt to give more analytic formulations to our beliefs and commitments. Here we seek to understand systematically the nature of God, humanity, salvation, the work of Christ, the nature of the church, the kingdom, and so on. Traditionally, this is what is known as systematic theology. It is of major significance for ethics because it seeks to show the interrelationship of ideas and the relationship of those ideas to the moral life.

The third component involves rituals. The symbols we use and the rituals we perform both embody and reinforce our worldview. For example, every Sunday in worship we are reenacting our view of reality and thus considering the implications for everyday life. When a marriage is celebrated, we ritualize our beliefs and moral commitments about marriage, family, sexual intimacy, and children. And when we gather as a church community at a funeral, we reenact and reinforce our beliefs and moral commitments regarding the meaning of life, death, and divine providence.

All three components of the Christian worldview play a role in Christian ethics, and all three are needed for the richness of theological commitments. It will not suffice to build theology and hence ethics on only the stories we tell (narrative ethics), for as humans we need all dimensions of the self and all forms of communication to articulate our worldview and then live it out in the moral life. Likewise, to isolate only the ritual component or the rational component is to miss much of the content, motivation, and means for moral enablement.

God, the Foundation of Ethics

Though a worldview provides the immediate foundation for any ethics, Christians will insist that there is something more. The ultimate foundation is the Triune God. Our worldview as believers is not rooted in or derived from human experience or natural sentiments; rather, it is rooted in ultimate reality and made known through the self-disclosure of God in the written Word, the Bible, and the incarnate Word, Christ. From divine revelation it is clear that what ultimately determines the good in human life is God. Geoffrey Bromiley has suggested that Christians should think of God as the ground of ethics, the norm of ethics, and the power for ethical living.[8]

God, the Ground of Christian Ethics

God as the ground of Christian ethics means that our understandings of the moral good, right, wise, and just emanate from the nature and actions of God. As the creator of the universe and the sovereign over all life, God's own goodness becomes the ground or foundation of all human goodness. Goodness is not self-derived but emanates from the fountainhead of all reality. Thus, the good does not exist "independent of the will of God. The source of the good lies not in an idea in the mind of God but in the living God himself who embodies and personifies the good."[9]

This means that Christian ethics is not rooted in principles such as love or justice, nor in virtues embodied in the narratives of communities, nor in the existence of social structures deemed to be part of the created order. All of these may be important elements in Christian ethics, but they do not form the foundation of moral thought, character, and actions. This becomes clear in the biblical patterns of moral teaching, for many parts of Scripture reveal that moral injunctions have a larger grounding that forms the basis for their acceptance. Thus, ethics in the Bible is not blind obedience to laws, principles, or virtues but rather a response to the living, all-powerful God of the universe, who is himself the foundation of those moral guidelines. The content of our moral responses are certainly known and shaped by the biblical norms in their various forms, but ultimately they are reflections of God's character, purposes, and actions in the world.

A good example of this biblical pattern can be seen in the Decalogue, the Ten Commandments. Many Christians jump immediately to the commandments themselves with a view that these form the heart and basis of the moral life. But the Decalogue, as noted in chapter 1, begins with a statement that forms the grounding for these commands: "I am the LORD your God, who brought you out of the land of Egypt, out of the house of slavery" (Exod. 20:2). This preamble gives the foundation: The Hebrew people were to follow these moral laws because God had acted in grace and formed a covenant relationship with them. The heart of the ethic is not following the commands or keeping universal laws but responding to God's covenant and grace. The commandments then spell out what it means to respond to God and neighbor.

This pattern is seen frequently in the Bible. In Deuteronomy 15, generosity and justice for the poor are commanded on this basis: "Remember that you were a slave in the land of Egypt, and the LORD your God redeemed you; for this reason I lay this command upon you today" (v. 15). The pattern is also abundantly clear in the New Testament. For example, Romans 1–11 is essentially Paul's theology describing the fallen human condition, God's response in grace, our justification by faith, and the sanctifying work of the Holy Spirit. After the delineation of all that God has done for us in Christ, chapters 12–16 move to the "therefore" and lay out the ethical responses to God's character and actions. In those chapters, Paul deals with life in community, relationships to the state, and matters of conscience on which believers are sometimes divided. Many of the New Testament epistles follow a similar pattern of the imperative flowing from the indicative.[10]

Love has long been heralded as one of the primary principles or virtues of the moral life. Choosing the good means choosing a life of love—toward God and neighbor. But love in the biblical framework is not an abstract principle isolated from a larger context. It is a reflection of the very nature and actions of God. First John 4:7 admonishes, "Beloved, let us love one another, because love is from God; everyone who loves is born of God and knows God." And later John writes, "Since God loved us so much, we also ought to love one another" (v. 11) and, "We love because he first loved us" (v. 19). Love, therefore, is not a nebulous notion that we determine by our own passions or personal sense of how love is best served in a given situation. Love is grounded in God, and "the content of love must be defined by Divine revelation."[11]

In 2 Corinthians 8:7, Paul writes, "Now as you excel in everything—in faith, in speech, in knowledge, in utmost eagerness, and in our love for you—so we want you to excel also in this generous undertaking." He then provides the foundation for a virtue of giving or mercy: "For you know the generous act of our Lord Jesus Christ, that though he was rich, yet for your sakes he became poor, so that by his poverty you might become rich" (v. 9). And in Ephesians 4:32, "Be kind to one another, tenderhearted, forgiving one another, as God in Christ has forgiven you." Mercy, love, forgiveness, and justice are not normative because they are universal laws that produce the best results, though they indeed may do so. They are not normative because they are part of an abstract moral order known by reason, though by reason we may know something of their moral worth. For Christians, they are normative because they are rooted in the very nature and actions of the Triune God.

If indeed God is the foundation of Christian ethics, how we perceive God (our theology) will make a difference. For example, our understanding of God's work in human creation has a bearing on how we might respond to certain ethical issues, such as cloning. Jonathan Cohen writes:

> The possibility of cloning human beings challenges Western beliefs about creation and our relationship to God. If we understand God as the Creator and creation as a completed act, cloning will be a transgression. If, however, we understand God as the Power of Creation and creation as a transformative process, we may find a role for human participation, sharing that power as beings created in the image of God.[12]

Cohen, in his defense of the latter view, seems to have caricatured the traditional view of God as creator, but his point is well-taken: Our perceptions of God make a difference.

Christian theology has long emphasized that God is both transcendent (beyond us) and immanent (near us). In practice, however, many strands of Christian thought have tended to accentuate one side over the other, as is sometimes particularly evident in church rituals such as music, prayers, and liturgy. To emphasize only or primarily the transcendence of God often turns ethics into an abstract moral law of the universe in which God is essentially not needed. Deism in the eighteenth century was a prime example of transcendence without immanence, and while its moral content was in some ways similar to Christian ethics, it lacked the personal foundation of a God who cared deeply for people, forgave them of their sins, and empowered them to moral living. Conversely, if our conceptions of God are primarily immanent, we will tend to turn our own human purposes into divine purposes, and "God becomes virtually a label for . . . [our] highest values, ideals, and aspirations."[13]

God, the Norm of Christian Ethics

God is not only the ground of Christian ethics. The norms for ethical reflection and moral action and character are reflections of God's own actions and nature. Leviticus 20:26 summarized the broad normative content of the Old Testament this way: "You shall be holy to me; for I the LORD am holy, and I have separated you from the other peoples to be mine." God's own set-apartness or holiness formed the normative framework for the people's journey in the world. Similarly, in the Sermon on the Mount, Jesus taught his disciples to love their enemies, for if they loved only those who loved them, they would not be different from the pagans or the scandalous tax collectors. Then Jesus gave this norm: "Be perfect, therefore, as your heavenly Father is perfect" (Matt. 5:48). The perfection of which Jesus speaks is essentially wholeness or completeness, and thus he was indicating that just as the Father in heaven "makes his sun rise on the evil and on the good, and sends rain on the righteous and on the unrighteous" (v. 45), so they are to show love to all humans, even their enemies. In essence, "Don't discriminate concerning whom you love, because God does not discriminate in his love."

In a sense, we can say that God's character and actions are the standard before us as we live our lives. There is to be an infusion of the very nature of God's patterns in us, as we are in Christ and he in us, to use the Pauline language. When we think about faithfulness to the covenants we make in life, such as marriage, God's own covenant of faithfulness is the norm. God's truthfulness becomes the norm for our integrity in relationships and responsibilities. God's action of justice on behalf of the oppressed and disenfranchised is the norm for our justice. God's purity is the norm for our purity of heart, mind, and behavior. God's action of forgiveness through Christ is the norm for our forgiveness of those who sin against us. And God's grace is the norm for our mercy toward those in need.

When we think about God as the norm of ethics, it is important to recall that he is the Triune God. Certainly, the incarnation of Jesus Christ, the Son, is the most visible expression of God in human history and plays a significant role in Christian ethics. Followers of Jesus are called to reflect his likeness (Rom. 8:29, 1 Cor. 15:49). It is quite telling that for much of the twentieth century Christian ethics as a discipline carried on much of its discourse as if Jesus had never existed. As John Howard Yoder in *The Politics of Jesus*, one of the most significant ethical works of the twentieth century, put it, mainstream ethics operated on the assumption that "Jesus is simply not relevant in any immediate sense to the questions of social ethics."[14] Yoder played a significant role in reminding Christians of the normativity of Christ for life within the world. Some critics have felt that Yoder may have fallen prey to a functional unitarianism of the Second Person of the Trinity, and to the degree that this charge may be true, it is a reminder that Christian ethics must embody Father, Son, and Holy Spirit. The givenness of created realities, the divine commands of Yahweh at Sinai, the life and teachings of Jesus, the discernment of the Holy Spirit in the life of the church must all be operative if we are to embody a trinitarian ethic in which God is the norm.[15] But clearly Jesus, as the very "image of the invisible God, the firstborn of all creation" (Col. 1:15), is a concrete and vital norm for Christian action and character. He is the clearest expression in human history of what it means to be good and the most explicit revelation of God's glory (Heb. 1:2–3) and fullness (Col. 1:19).

God, the Power for Christian Ethics

Christians should never be content only to speak about justice, holiness, righteousness, goodness, and wisdom. We must be committed to *being* and *doing,* and therein lies a major hurdle: "For I do not do what I want, but I do the very thing I hate" (Rom. 7:15). Many people give cognitive assent to doing the good but find both internal and external restraints in actually accomplishing it. Thus, empowerment is clearly an issue to consider in Christian ethics, though it has not been a mainstay in much of the discipline. While humans have certain native capacities for achieving virtue and moral actions, our fallen nature turns us away from the good in both our understanding and behavior. Paul's struggle with his own natural inadequacies (Romans 7) is a universal reality in all human beings. Self-deception and failure of the will are constant threats to the moral life. Biblically speaking there are two main sources of power for ethical living: God's grace and God's presence in our lives, most notably through the Holy Spirit.

The inability of human nature to choose righteousness and goodness leads us to the only solution for both salvation and the moral life: the grace of God manifest in Jesus Christ. After Paul expresses his great struggle in Romans 7, he turns to the remedy of grace: "There is therefore now no condemnation for those who are in Christ Jesus. For the law of the Spirit of life in Christ Jesus has set you free from the law of sin and of death. For God has done what the law, weakened by the flesh, could not do: by sending his own Son" (Rom. 8:1–3). God's grace is not only the mechanism whereby human sin and moral failure are dealt with through forgiveness but also a motivating factor in life for the recipient of grace. As Martin Luther so powerfully reminded the church, God's grace justifies sinners who accept it, and in doing so, Christ's righteousness becomes our own righteousness, a righteousness that overflows into a transformed will and good works. Luther, like St. Augustine, placed "the fundamental ethical problem in the will rather than in the intellect. Hence, the greatest need of man is not to know the good, but to experience a forgiveness to which he can respond so as to draw him beyond his self-concern into a life of joyful service."[16]

Certainly all humans, being made in the image of God, have a general capacity to love, seek justice, maintain orderliness, show mercy, and act with regard to conscience. But as Jonathan Edwards, the great eighteenth-century theologian, philosopher, and preacher, argued, those are a secondary kind of virtue or beauty that are distinct from true virtue, which comes from divine grace. The secondary virtues arise from self-love, and "though self-love is far from being useless in the world, yea, it is exceeding necessary to society; yet every body sees that if it be not subordinate to, and regulated by another more extensive principle, it may make a man a common enemy to the general system. . . . a system that contains millions of individuals."[17] For Edwards, "A truly virtuous mind, being as it were under the sovereign dominion of love to God, above all things, seeks the glory of God, and makes this his supreme, governing, and ultimate end." This is "true grace and real holiness. And no other disposition or affection but this is of the nature of virtue."[18]

Along with grace as an empowerment to the moral life there is the presence of the Holy Spirit. Throughout the Bible the Father and the Son certainly play a role in empowerment, but it is particularly the Holy Spirit who is emphasized in this task. After Paul describes his inner moral dilemma in Romans 7, he turns not only to grace but also to the gift of the Spirit. He asserts that God condemned sin in humans:

> so that the just requirement of the law might be fulfilled in us, who walk not according to the flesh but according to the Spirit. . . . Those who live according to the Spirit set their minds on the things of the Spirit. . . . To set the mind on the Spirit is life and peace. . . . You are not in the flesh; you are in the Spirit, since the Spirit of God dwells in you. Anyone who does not have the Spirit of Christ does not belong to him.
>
> Romans 8.4–6, 9

And, of course, before Christ left this earth he gave this promise to the disciples: "You will receive power when the Holy Spirit has come upon you; and you will be my witnesses . . . to the ends of the earth" (Acts 1:8).

The Holy Spirit receives scant attention in most ethics texts. One exception is Carl F. H. Henry's *Christian Personal Ethics,* in which he devotes an entire chapter to the Holy Spirit and concludes the work with a chapter on prayer. For Henry, "The Spirit is the dynamic principle of Christian ethics, the personal agency whereby God powerfully enters human life and delivers . . . from enslavement to Satan, sin, death, and law."[19] Henry seems to neglect the role of the Spirit in the moral discernment process, but he is certainly right to remind us that "it was the Holy Spirit alone who had transformed the inescapable and distressing 'I ought' which philosophical ethics was compelled to acknowledge and the tormenting 'thou shalt' which Hebrew religion adduced as its complement into the 'I will' of New Testament ethical dedication and zeal."[20]

Thus, Christian ethics is not a natural enterprise. The moral good is defined by God. The Triune God is the ground, the norm, and the power for Christian ethics, and therein is its ultimate foundation. But there is a secondary foundation that is derived from God and provides perspective, normative guidance, and basic orientation to the moral life. This is the Christian worldview, our theological understandings.

The Christian Worldview: The Biblical Story

As soon as we turn to the specifics of a Christian worldview, we are immediately aware of the theological differences that have existed throughout the centuries in the various strands of the Christian church. People are prone to raise the question, Which Christian worldview? Yet there have long been essential core points of agreement in classic Christian understanding. Obviously, the details may get nuanced in different ways, but there is a "big story" undergirding the many particulars of the Old and New Testaments. Most Christians throughout the centuries have accepted this grand narrative, though they may not have spelled it out in quite the same manner. Essentially, it is the story of creation, fall, redemption, and consummation. These aspects form the core of a Christian worldview and the second level of the foundation for Christian ethics.

Creation

Too often when Christians reflect on creation they become embroiled in how it happened, when it happened, and to what degree God may have utilized natural processes. In the midst of the debates, its theological significance is often lost. The Christian worldview, based on divine revelation, embodies several themes regarding creation that are pivotal foundations for ethical reflection and moral thought.

THE GOODNESS OF CREATION

In the creation account of Genesis 1, God pronounces his work good after each day of creative activity. At the end of the chapter comes the grand summary, "God saw everything that he had made, and indeed, it was very good" (v. 31). The goodness of the material created world stands in stark contrast to many competing worldviews of the ancient world and other periods. As Vinoth Ramachandra from Sri Lanka puts it:

> Contemporary world-views would have understood "salvation" as an escape from the sensory, empirical world of human existence. There was no value or purpose attached to the physical realm of space-time events. Meaning has to be sought in detachment from the external world which . . . was less real than the "spiritual" realm. This view is contradicted by the doctrine of creation which sees the world as possessing an intrinsic worth and meaningfulness.[21]

Many competing views of creation see the material world as illusory or the unfortunate result of a cosmic battle between the forces of good and evil. But the biblical story begins with a strong affirmation that the material world, including the materiality of human beings, is intrinsically good. While the fall into human sin marred that goodness and perverted the mind and the will of humans, there remains as St. Augustine argued a metaphysical goodness to the created world. God created humans as whole beings in which the material and immaterial (soul or spirit) dimensions are crowned with goodness.

Unfortunately, the Christian church has often lost this affirmation. Gnosticism and neo-Platonism, with their denigration of the material and lauding of the "spiritual" and esoteric, introduced into the early church an unhealthy asceticism that undermined an important foundation for the moral life. Over the years asceticism has denigrated a positive holistic view of sex, heralded the monastic life over physical or mental work, and debased the calling to live in the midst of culture and society. The disparagement of the physical was already evident in New Testament times, for John had to go out of his way to affirm a real, material incarnation of Jesus: "What we have heard, what we have seen with our eyes, what we have looked at and touched with our hands, concerning the word of life" (1 John 1:1). And Paul combated the forces of ascetic ethics in relation to false teachers peddling their theological wares to churches: "They forbid marriage and demand abstinence from foods, which God created to be received with thanksgiving by those who believe and know the truth. For everything created by God is good, and nothing is to be rejected, provided it is received with thanksgiving" (1 Tim. 4:3–4).

Asceticism, in contrast to the goodness of creation, has had a profound impact on sexual ethics. Many of the Gnostics argued that the sexual act was a sin, and even some mainstream leaders of the church, such as Jerome in the fourth century, so exalted virginity that they believed "the only good of marriage is that it produces virgins."[22] Much of the church came to believe that the only purpose for sexual intercourse in marriage is to produce children, and in so doing it lost the other divine purposes that accompany procreation: the consummation of marriage ("one flesh"), the expression of love, and the experience of pleasure as a good gift of God (Prov. 5:18–19; Song of Solomon). Obviously, sin has twisted sexual desires and caused humans to turn away from God's designs for physical intimacy, but the first and most important thing to be said in a Christian perspective is that sex is good. However, like all of God's good gifts, sex is made for certain purposes and intended for a particular context. In other words, its goodness is fully experienced only in a marriage between a man and a woman.

CREATION IN THE IMAGE OF GOD

At the apex of the creation account, God said, "'Let us make humankind in our image, according to our likeness; and let them have dominion over the fish of the sea, and over the birds of the air, and over the cattle, and over all the wild animals of the earth, and over every creeping thing that creeps upon the earth.' So God created humankind in his image, in the image of God he created them; male and female he created them" (Gen. 1:26–27). Theologians have long debated the exact nature of the *imago Dei* in humanity, but it should be clear from a casual reading that this part of the story stands in direct contrast to the worldview of Peter Singer, with whom we introduced this chapter. All creation is not the same; humanity stands apart in a distinct manner. At least three major themes for Christian ethics can be found in this dimension of creation.

First, the text is clear that part of the image involves a stewardship over the created order. Only God creates *ex nihilo,* out of nothing, but God grants to humans a kind of cocreating and co-caring role for the rest of creation. Because all of creation is good, this "dominion" is not a coercive pillaging for one's own selfishness but rather a tender care so that the needs of all humans might be met and that we might experience joy, aesthetic pleasure, and creativity in our stewardship of the good resources of the earth. Herein is the heart of an environmental ethic for Christians. In the Christian worldview, there is a demarcation between the creator, those created in God's image, and the rest of creation. The distinction between humans and animals, for example, is clearly taught by Jesus when in affirming the value of a sheep who needs our care, he states, "How much more valuable is a human being than a sheep!" (Matt. 12:12). Nonetheless, the rest of creation is a good gift of God, and those who bear a likeness to God should oversee it with justice and care.

Second, the image of God seems to reflect a relational dimension to life that is to be guarded and nurtured. In his image God "creates them male and female." Many theologians have argued that just as there is relationality within the Godhead (Father, Son, and Holy Spirit), so part of the image in us is our relational capacity. As Genesis 2:18 states, "It is not good that the man should be alone; I will make him a helper as his partner." This is not only an establishment of marriage but also an affirmation of human relationships for making us the kind of people God has designed. Our true nature is found not in individualism or autonomy but in mutual relationality whereby we reflect our interdependence with others.

Third, the image of God clearly implies an inherent dignity and worth in all men and women. Even after the fall, humans are said to bear God's image, and this is the basis for treating others with respect and dignity. Genesis 9:6 states, "Whoever sheds the blood of a human, by a human shall that person's blood be shed; for in his own image God made humankind." And James appeals to the *imago Dei* in his discussion of the misuse of the tongue to hurt another person: "With it we bless the Lord and Father, and with it we curse those who are made in the likeness of God" (James 3:9). All humans have a dignity and a worth that are not to be defaced. This forms a major foundation for a Christian ethic of race relations, economic life, human rights, gender relations, and bioethics.

The inherent dignity of all humans stands in contrast to the kind of functional dignity that is part of the ethic and worldview of many thinkers such as

Peter Singer. In a functional dignity, one's value is postulated on the basis of performance, whether that be a particular level of rationality and self-awareness or a certain capacity for relationships. In the classical Christian understanding, our dignity is alien in the sense that it comes from God, but it is then inherent within our very being, simply because we are human. This has profound implications for contemporary bioethics issues such as organ transplants, death and dying issues, abortion, and genetic engineering. While the issues are often complex and by no means solved by monolithic norms, human dignity must always be guarded. Thus, one does not receive a kidney transplant over another person on the grounds that he or she plays an important role in society or the community. Rather, in matters of life and death, all persons should come to a triage situation (e.g., who gets the goods when there are not enough for all) on equal footing. And when it comes to a handicapped child, such as one with Down's syndrome, that child is the bearer of God's image and possesses a dignity that must be protected and nurtured.

A Givenness in Creation

The creation of the world and humanity by God implies that reality is not a mere chance happening in which we then create our own meanings, values, and ultimate commitments. In our fallen state, we do, of course, create our own meanings and commitments, and therein is the problem of humanity and society. But creation implies that God has spoken, given, designed; we as his special creatures are then called to mesh our lives with the ultimate purposes and designs of the creator. Our very capacity to act within the world comes because God has acted with form and order. As the literary scholar George Steiner puts it, "There is aesthetic creation because there is *creation*. There is formal construction because we have been made form. . . . The core of our human identity is nothing more or less than the fitful apprehension of the radically inexpressible presence, facticity and perceptible substantiality of the created. It is; we are. This is the rudimentary grammar of the unfathomable."[23] There is a givenness to creation in which we properly find the meaning of true moral and spiritual goodness.

Of course, the difficulty comes in declaring exactly what is given within the world to which we ought to be congruent in our lives. The idea of a givenness in creation has sometimes been used to legitimize tyrannical governments, unjust economic structures, and the oppression of particular groups of people. "Creation mandates," as they are sometimes called, have often been described in rather static terms that reflect the social and cultural status quo of a given time and place. But just because there has been misuse of a concept does not automatically render it null and void. Oliver O'Donovan reminds us that creation is "not merely the raw material out of which the world as we know it is composed, but as the order and coherence *in* which it is composed." He contends that "by virtue of the fact that there is a Creator, there is also a creation that is ordered to its Creator, a world that exists as his creation and in no other way, so that by its very existence it points to God. But then, just because it is ordered vertically in this way, it must also have an internal horizontal ordering among its parts."[24] For O'Donovan, this ordering is not a static rendering of creation realities, for the resurrection of Christ, which vindicates creation, moves us toward an end in which all things are being made new. Though there are varying interpretations of the exact nature of creation's givens, it makes a huge difference in ethics to affirm them. Without a foundation of creation givenness in some form, we are left with a subjectivistic ethic in which humans, history, or culture become the foundations and norms.

An attempt to delineate the givens of creation would necessitate another book. But two realities that are clearly affirmed in the Genesis account of creation can serve as examples: work and marriage/family. Many Christians seem to view work as a curse and a result of the fall. But work is clearly ordained by God from creation, for God grants to Adam and Eve "in the garden of Eden to till it and keep it" (Gen. 2:15; also 1:26–28). The fall into sin clearly affected the working of the "garden," but from the beginning God gave to humankind the responsibility and privilege of work, through which they would meet their own needs, the needs of others, and experience the creativity inherent in God's creation. The givenness of work means that humans then have both a right and a responsibility with regard to work. If we are by creation *homo faber* (the person as doer or maker), then we are less than human when we refuse to work, are not granted the opportunity to work, or seek to find in work more than what God intended it to be. No wonder the Protestant Reformers so strongly emphasized the doctrine of vocation, which sees God's calling for human life set in the context of work. Any Christian ethic for society must give a priority to the importance and meaning of work, both for the good of the individual and the good of society itself.

A second given of creation is family, understood biblically as the relationships stemming from the marriage of a man and a woman (Gen. 2:23–25). Marriage and family are the means through which human life comes into the world and the means by which humans are socialized and hopefully nurtured in the faith. At the heart of marriage is a one-flesh relationship between a man and a woman, symbolizing a unique and profound relationship that is consummated through sexual intimacy and thus set apart from all other relationships. The givenness of marriage and family has produced a fairly universal reality throughout history and around the world, though the particular forms of family (i.e., extended versus nuclear) and the particular roles within the family have often varied. One of the primary givens is that procreation, socialization, love, commitment, and a one-flesh relationship are to be held together in unity.[25] Today, this givenness is being pulled apart in myriad ways: procreation apart from a marriage commitment, sex without any sense of responsibility for the potential fruit from the act, some of the new reproductive technologies, and the large number of serial marriages through divorce in which children are socialized outside the context of the one-flesh bond. As is evident in societies today, we bear the consequences for living contrary to the givenness of creation.

The Fall

Though God created a good world, and humans were made in his image, things are "not the way [they're] supposed to be."[26] The givens of creation are ignored, the goodness of creation has been distorted, and human actions and character defy God's likeness. The fall, or human sin, is sometimes said to be the one biblical doctrine that is empirically verifiable, for everywhere we see and experience its menacing effects. This is the second part of the biblical story that shapes the Christian worldview and hence Christian ethics.

It is quite clear in any system of ethics that the account of human nature has a profound impact on one's sense of moral thinking and action. Adherence to an Enlightenment, humanistic view of human nature will invariably have consequences concerning expectations for human behavior and political, economic, and cultural outlooks. Essentially, according to this view, moral goodness is an inherent trait in humans that merely needs a bit of prodding through education and positive-reinforcement carrots. Conversely, adherence to a negative, bestial view of human nature will likely result in stringent controls over both society and human life, often without regard for human dignity, value, freedom, and justice. The worldview of the Christian faith is that humans are wonderfully made in God's image, but because of the fall their will is bent, their thinking is deluded, and their character is by nature self-seeking. Such a view rejects both humanistic and bestial (i.e., Machiavellian/Hobbesian) views of humanity. As Blaise Pascal, the seventeenth-century philosopher and mathematician, observed, the philosophers talk about the dignity of humanity, and they tempt us to pride, or they talk about the misery of humanity, and they tempt us to despair. "The Christian religion alone has been able to cure these two vices, not by expelling the one through means of the other according to the wisdom of the world, but by expelling both according to the simplicity of the Gospel."[27] Only here, says Pascal, do we find both our dignity and our misery.

The fall into human sin and our subsequent actions and character do not negate either the goodness or the givenness of creation. As Albert Wolters reminds us, "Sin and evil always have the character of caricature . . . a distorted image that nevertheless embodies certain recognizable features." For example, "A human being after the fall, though a travesty of humanity, is still a human being, not an animal. A humanistic school is still a school. A broken relationship is still a relationship. Muddled thinking is still thinking. In each case, what something in fallen creation 'still is' points to the enduring goodness of creation."[28] Thus, human sin means there is a distortion of creation but not negation or obliteration of its essential qualities. The Bible speaks of sin in many ways: missing the mark, transgression (the breach of a relationship), ungodliness, rebellion, blindness, wandering from the path, unrighteousness, and perversion. At the heart of human sin is a rebellion against God and his grace, but the effects of sin are cosmically felt. One of the best ways to understand the nature of sin and its implications for ethics is to examine the story of the fall in Genesis 3.

THE NATURE OF THE FALL AND HUMAN SIN

The essence of human sin in Genesis 3 is "a grasping for spiritual and moral autonomy rooted in unbelief and rebellion."[29] Though it is primarily a revolt against God, the historic fall, which is affirmed in the experience of all human beings, is widely felt throughout all the world and all relationships. No dimension of humanity, culture, society, or the physical world is unaffected by the pangs of sin. Thus, a major presupposition of Christian ethics is that a wide gap exists between God's designs and human and institutional realities. One of the best ways to understand the story in Genesis 3 and the subsequent human experience is in terms of alienation. In the text, alienation is experienced in four ways.

First, there is an alienation from God, the ground and norm of human goodness. In the Genesis account of the fall, as soon as Adam and Eve turn from God's givens to seek their own autonomy ("when you eat of it your eyes will be opened, and you will be like God, knowing good and evil" [Gen. 3:5]), the sense of alienation from their maker is felt. Indeed, alienation from God becomes the primary reality of human experience.

> They heard the sound of the LORD God walking in the garden at the time of the evening breeze, and the man and his wife hid themselves from the presence of the LORD God among the trees of the garden. But the LORD God called to the man, and said to him, "Where are you?" He said, "I heard the sound of you in the garden, and I was afraid, because I was naked; and I hid myself." He said, "Who told you that you were naked? Have you eaten from the tree of which I commanded you not to eat?"
>
> Genesis 3:8–11

No longer do humans by nature seek and enjoy the presence of God. "As the film maker Woody Allen said in 1993, trying to explain his controversial affair with the young daughter of Mia Farrow, 'The heart wants what it wants.'"[30] Humanity defines goodness over against God and his good givens. God comes to be experienced and seen as enemy, not friend. Humans, of course, have an innate drive for transcendence, but their fallen nature tends to create false gods in their own image, often elevating good divine gifts (i.e., money, sex, power) to gods that are neither transcendent nor personal and were never intended to be the source of life, meaning, salvation, and hope.

The second alienation concerns fellow persons. "The man said, 'The woman whom you gave to be with me, she gave me fruit from the tree, and I ate'" (3:12). Rather than harmony between the man and the woman there is now blame of another for one's own actions. Other people are used as a means of extracting oneself from sinful proclivities and self-created circumstances. The givenness of distinctions between male and female in creation no longer beckons partnership but now turns to domination, inverted desires, power plays, and manipulation, for "Your desire shall be for your husband, and he shall rule over you" (3:16b).

In the alienation that occurs between fallen human beings there is, as Cornelius Plantinga Jr. puts it, a masquerading that distorts the givenness of creation. "Vices have to masquerade as virtues—lust as love, thinly veiled sadism as military discipline, envy as righteous indignation, domestic tyranny as parental concern. . . . Deceivers learn how to present something falsely, and they exert themselves to make the presentation credible."[31] Fallen creatures see in another not a fellow creature bearing God's image but an obstacle to one's own self-defined version of goodness and one's own self-centered passion for autonomy. In the midst of this alienation, we never lose sight of our created need for the other nor lose a native capacity to in some measure love those with whom we have natural bonds. But the relationships are always divided and filled with selfish ambition. We seek to manipulate the other to fulfill our own psychological needs and personal wants.

That, of course, leads to a third dimension of alienation: alienation from oneself. "They [sinful creatures] do not really know themselves, flee no less from self than from God, and try to make this unknown self the center of life in place of God."[32] This alienation was evidenced in the Garden and continues to be evidenced in the form of shame and guilt: "Then the eyes of both were opened, and they knew that they were naked; and they sewed fig leaves together and made loincloths for themselves" (3:7). Humanity not only feels ill at ease with God but ill at ease with one's own self, the self that has become the central point of reference in rebellious autonomy.

The alienation from self is further seen in self-deception: "Then the LORD God said to the woman, 'What is this that you have done?' The woman said, 'The serpent tricked me, and I ate'" (3:13). Eve, and subsequently all people in their fallenness, have a propensity to distort reality and so deceive themselves into believing things that are not the way they really are. Our self-deception attempts to foil truthful accounts of reality about the world, self, and others. Personal narrative triumphs over a metanarrative that is grounded in God, the truth and truthful one. It is through self-deception that fallen humanity with all its education and sophistication is able to do evil and not wince. George Steiner reminds us that a person can be intellectually brilliant and artistically sensible and at the same time morally bankrupt through self-deception. We know, writes Steiner, "That a human being can play Bach in the evening, and play him well, or read Pushkin, and read him with insight, and proceed in the morning to do his job at Auschwitz."[33] After all, Paul Joseph Goebbels, the chief architect of Nazi propaganda, had a Ph.D. in literature from one of Germany's distinguished universities.

The fourth alienation as a result of the fall is alienation from nature. At creation there was a clear distinction between creator and the created. As noted earlier, there were also distinctions within the created world: humans made in God's image, the animal world, and the inanimate world of nature. The world of nature was not the same as either God or the human world, but clearly it was a good gift of God to be cared for and used with temperance. At creation, nature and humanity were not identical but were clearly in harmony. Because of the fall, even nature itself experiences the reverberations of sin and alienation: "Cursed is the ground because of you; in toil you shall eat of it all the days of your life; thorns and thistles it shall bring forth for you. . . . By the sweat of your face you shall eat bread until you return to the ground, for out of it you were taken; you are dust, and to dust you shall return" (3:17–19). What was meant for human enjoyment and stewardly care now stands over against humanity as a threat, and in turn men and women rape God's good creation. Indeed, many troubling ethical issues in the modern world stem from the alienation between people and nature.

The story of the fall, therefore, provides the most basic understanding of what ails the world. Not all ethical dilemmas are a direct result of specific sinful actions (John 9:1–3), but the moral context must always come to terms with global fallenness. Christians must always be suspicious of utopian social schemes, for they do not take account of the fundamental problem within the world. Human sin is understood first with reference to God, but it manifests itself in all relationships within the cosmos. Thus, God's solution, redemption, involves all relationships as well.

STRUCTURAL OR CORPORATE SIN

When we think about sin, we tend to think of individual actions or personal dispositions. Scripture clearly states, however, that individuals are not the only ones to experience sin; structures and corporate realities also bear the scars of sin and manifest the fall. Christians may not always feel at ease with this understanding for a number of reasons. As Greg Foster points out, "We instinctively and rightly value individual freedom and responsibility, and it seems that talk of 'structural sins' in society reduces the responsibility and value of individuals."[34] We feel that such a conception will negate personal responsibility and put the blame on society. As they sang in the musical *West Side Story*, "We're depraved because we're deprived." Moreover, says Foster, "We may disregard structural sin because of a feeling of helplessness. Something may be done for individuals; brands may be plucked from the burning, but the blaze cannot be stopped."[35]

But the biblical worldview clearly embodies a sense of corporate or structural sin, and it is an essential concept for Christian moral judgments. Psalm 94:20–23 speaks of misery by decrees and laws, Isaiah 10:1–2 of unjust laws and oppressive decrees that deprive the poor of their rights, and Amos 5:10–15 commends justice in the gate, the symbol for the judicial process. In these and many other texts, the actions and character of individuals are certainly involved, but we lose much of the passages' ethical significance if we do not also understand that the laws, policies, and social patterns themselves are unjust and sinful. Personal responsibility is not lessened in these situations, but if the structural dimensions are not addressed, we will not penetrate the full reality of the moral problem. In the Old Testament, one of the primary examples of corporate sin involved the unjust consolidation of the land (i.e., Isa. 5:7–8), which not only led to great accumulation of land by unjust means but also left many without the primary means of economic sustenance in that culture.

In the New Testament, corporate sin is particularly evident in the concepts of "world" and "powers." The term *world (kosmos)* in the classical world meant order, and it was seen as the protectorate of values and life within society. In the New Testament, however, "world" represents the twisted values, patterns, and thinking of the culture and social order. Like many words it can have several meanings: the physical world, people, and a principle of evil that is related to the order of things within culture and society. It is the last usage that applies here, for *kosmos* is "human society insofar as it is organized on wrong principles."[36] Thus, the apostle John wrote: "Do not love the world or the things in the world. The love of the Father is not in those who love the world; for all that is in the world—the desire of the flesh, the desire of the eyes, the pride in riches—comes not from the Father but from the world. And the world and its desire are passing away, but those who do the will of God live forever" (1 John 2:15–17). And the apostle Paul encouraged the Corinthian church to "deal with the world as though they had no dealings with it. For the present form of this world is passing away" (1 Cor. 7:31). Paul and John were describing not the physical universe or merely the actions of individuals but patterns that were embedded in the cultural values and social processes.

The other New Testament concept that speaks of structural sin is "the powers." There are actually at minimum three words that are pertinent and interrelated: rulers *(archai),* powers *(exousia),* and principles of this world *(stoicheia).* In recent years, New Testament scholarship has begun to understand these terms not only as demonic forces or angelic powers but also as forces that are manifest within the patterns of societies and institutions. There are varying interpretations of these concepts, but the general consensus is that in some way the powers, rulers, and principles of this world are related to structural realities within societies. This in no way minimizes the role of Satan or demonic forces within the world. It simply means that forces within the societal and cultural fabrics undermine God's righteousness and goodness.[37] Of course,

Christ has "disarmed the rulers and authorities and made a public example of them, triumphing over them in [the cross]" (Col. 2:15), and believers are called to bear witness to the powers (Eph. 3:10) of that triumph. But their very existence reminds us that sin resides in places of power, institutional realities, and the patterns of social forces. Without a corporate understanding of sin, we cannot address the full reality of ethical problems.

A Christian worldview then understands sin to be the major problem in human and societal life. From a Christian standpoint, the ultimate problems are neither psychological nor political, neither educational nor economic—though sin is always manifest in and through these realities. Humans fail to live up to God's standards, let alone their own standards, because of the fall and sin. Our fallen condition raises the moral specter in many realms of life, though clearly not every dilemma we face involves a direct assent to sin. Rather, sin is the condition of our lives and the world in which we live. The concept of the fall is at the heart of how we as believers understand human life, the societies and cultures in which we live and work, and the cosmos in which we find ourselves.

Sin, as has been shown, is not just the actions and dispositions of individuals; it is also the reverberations of societies, cultures, institutions—the world. Addressing only personal morality will leave much of the world to its own devices and vices. Thus, for example, the evils of slavery should be seen not as the mere actions of individuals stripping others of their freedom and dignity but as a system that subjugated others. Often slavery was sanctioned because many who held slaves were otherwise morally upright citizens of their communities (even Christians) who treated their slaves fairly well. Slavery came to an end only when the institution itself was called into question and made illegal. Individual morality alone was insufficient. Such is the case for a host of issues today ranging from economic injustices to institutional racism to unethical business practices to the legal snuffing out of innocent human life while still in the womb.

Redemption

After the fall and the distortion of God's good world through sin, God the gracious creator began a process of redemption to bring his creatures back to himself and to the designs he originally intended. Sin is still a pervasive reality in all domains of existence, but it does not have the final say (1 Corinthians 15). Redemption was God's solution to the fall, and it is the third part of the biblical drama.

Immediately following the fall there was a kind of *protoevangelium*, or first glimpse of the gospel, as God cursed the serpent: "I will put enmity between you and the woman, and between your offspring and hers; he will strike your head, and you will strike his heel" (Gen. 3:15). The serpent here embodies and symbolizes evil and the ultimate source of evil. Though the forces of sin and evil will wreak havoc in the woman's offspring, there is envisioned a victory through one of the woman's descendants, a victory that will come through the suffering of one who will crush the power of sin and evil.

God's redemption is further seen in the calling of Abraham and the divine promise that through him and his descendants, "All the families of the earth shall be blessed" (Gen. 12:3). Through Abraham and his descendants God began an explicit process not only of revealing himself to humanity but also of calling out for himself a people to live in covenant relationship. This covenant was most powerfully demonstrated in the exodus as God redeemed his people from slavery, guided them toward the Promised Land, and gave them the basic contours of his designs for living, the law (Exodus 20).

Divine redemption is always through grace, but its effects are always moral in nature and most clearly demonstrated in those who accept God's grace. "You have seen what I did to the Egyptians, and how I bore you on eagles' wings and brought you to myself. Now therefore, if you obey my voice and keep my covenant, you shall be my treasured possession out of all the peoples. Indeed, the whole earth is mine, but you shall be for me a priestly kingdom and a holy nation" (Exod. 19:4–6).

The rest of the Old Testament is the story of God's dealing with this covenant people, their moral and spiritual victories and failures, and God's abiding faithfulness. As the story unfolds there is an ever increasing awareness that this covenant offer was being widened to all humanity and that its focus was moving toward an apex of redemption in the person of the Redeemer.

The climax of God's redemptive acts came in the person of Jesus Christ, the eternal Son of God. His life and teachings were the embodiment of God's goodness and designs for humanity, but it was in his death and resurrection that sin and the fall were dealt with most explicitly and forthrightly. The death and resurrection of Christ were not only the means by which humanity was reconciled to God and sins were forgiven but also the means by which new patterns of life were forged. "If anyone is in Christ, there is a new creation: everything old has passed away; see, everything has become new!" (2 Cor. 5:17). Salvation in Christ is through divine grace, experienced by trust and faith in his work and person. God's redemption is not experienced by human moral effort or righteous character; rather, "Just as one man's trespass led to condemnation for all, so one man's act of righteousness leads to justification and life for all. . . . By the one man's obedience the many will be made righteous" (Rom. 5:18–19).

Though salvation does not come through human moral efforts, it clearly manifests itself in ethical character and living. One of the classic statements of justification by faith in the New Testament is Ephesians 2:8–9: "For by grace you have been saved through faith, and this is not your own doing; it is the gift of God—not the result of works, so that no one may boast." But the text then immediately reminds us that justifying faith must always evidence itself in works of righteousness: "For we are what he has made us, created in Christ Jesus for good works, which God prepared beforehand to be our way of life" (2:10). Such works of righteousness are demonstrated not only in personal moral actions but also in social realities, for Paul goes on to address the first great social ethic issue facing the early church, the cultural/racial divide between Jews and Gentiles. Justifying faith is then to be manifest in personal and corporate actions that overturn the effects of sin in cultural, ethnic, and racial divisions, "That he might create in himself one new humanity in place of the two, thus making peace, and might reconcile both groups to God in one body through the cross, thus putting to death that hostility through it" (Eph. 2:15b–16).

The ultimate moral fix in the Christian worldview is God's redemption made possible through the life, death, and resurrection of Christ. All solutions to the problem of sin that bypass this redemption are only partial solutions that never get to the core problem of sin. Thus, when churches offer mere moral reform outside the context of Christ's redemption, they are failing God, the world, and human beings who desperately need that redemption to be both made right with God and made anew morally through Christ. The heart of the gospel is the good news that in Jesus Christ the old alienation between humanity and God has been overcome.

But the gospel, while eminently personal, does not stop there. Those who have experienced redemption are then called to participate in God's cosmic process of redemption, which will ultimately overturn all forms of alienation from the fall—alienation from others, self, and nature. The New Testament envisions that the redemptive work will be cosmically felt, for "the creation itself will be set free from its bondage to decay and will obtain the freedom of the glory of the children of God" (Rom. 8:21). Thus, redemption compels believers to engage in acts of mercy, justice, and stewardship that reflect and participate in God's redemption of all things. As Albert Wolters puts it, "In the name of Christ, distortion must be opposed everywhere—in the kitchen and the bedroom, in city councils and corporate boardrooms, on the stage and on the air. . . . Everywhere humanity's sinfulness disrupts and deforms. Everywhere Christ's victory is pregnant with the defeat of sin and the recovery of creation."[38]

Redemption through Christ then has clear links to ethics. The righteousness of Christ through faith becomes our own righteousness, which is manifest in both moral actions and inward dispositions of the heart. While justification begins that process by establishing a right relationship with God, there is an ongoing process in which righteousness and holiness grow in the lives of believers, transforming them into the likeness of Christ. There have been many understandings of this process, commonly called the doctrine of sanctification,[39] but most understandings encompass both an inner mystical element and an outward behavioral element. While the common stereotype sees sanctification, or the growth in holiness, as a highly individualistic enterprise, the doctrine has historically often embodied strong links to social ethics as well. As John Wesley, probably the person most linked with the idea of holiness, put it, "Solitary religion is not found [in the gospel]. 'Holy solitaries' is a phrase no more consistent with the gospel than 'holy adulterers.' The gospel of Christ knows of no religion but social; no holiness but social holiness."[40] Such sanctification, however, should not be set over against the givens of creation; rather, it should be understood as a renewing of those givens that have been distorted by the fall. Thus, "Marriage should not be avoided by Christians, but sanctified. Emotions should not be repressed, but purified. Sexuality is not simply to be shunned, but redeemed. Politics should not be declared off-limits, but reformed. Art ought not to be pronounced worldly, but claimed for Christ."[41]

Though redemption is to be demonstrated within the world, its most particular demonstration should be in the redeemed community, the church. The most widely used biblical metaphor for the church is the body of Christ, which connotes an extension of the visible reality of Christ on earth. Christ is "head over all things for the church, which is his body, the fullness [i.e., the full expression] of him who fills all in all" (Eph. 1:22b–23). While we may expect the larger world to contain glimpses of God's designs for humanity, made known through reason and experience, the redeemed community is the primary place in which God's covenantal framework is accepted and by grace the primary locus of redeemed empowerment for moral living.

Because Christian ethics is effected by redeeming grace, known by divine revelation, and empowered by a transcendent presence, it is not an ethic for everyone. It is the ethic of the believing church. "Christian ethics is . . . the ethics of the church against the world, it is not a living possession of the unbelieving community, but of the community of faith."[42] The church, therefore, exists within the world as a sign of the ultimate solution to the human predicament and a sign of God's will for humanity. Thus, as the church and Christians live in the midst of a fallen and pluralistic society, they clearly cannot expect their ethical commitments, rooted in a particularistic worldview, to be the prevailing norm.

Consummation

Though Christ brought redemption to the world through his death and resurrection, it is quite clear that redemption of the moral life is not yet fully evident, even in the redeemed community. The realities of sin and the fall are prevalent everywhere, including in those who by grace have received forgiveness and moral empowerment. And though a cosmic redemption is envisioned through the work of Christ, one at times has to look hard to find glimpses of it within a broken world. Thus, the Christian worldview understands that the completion of Christ's redemption awaits the eschaton, when a final consummation will bring all things under his feet. Christians have always understood that history as we now know it will not go on forever. There is movement in history toward God's ultimate reign, when his designs from creation will be brought back to completeness and wholeness. Only then will the effects of the fall be fully overturned and God's moral ideal fully achieved on earth.

Eschatology is not just the domain of Christianity. Almost every religion and ideology has an account of where history is headed and what "the end" will be. For some worldviews, history moves in endless cyclical fashion to which humans must fatefully succumb, while for others history is moving toward a climax. Christianity clearly falls in the latter category and is by no means unique in its linear, climactic understanding. Marxism, for example, embodies a worldview in which history is moving in dialectical fashion toward a climax—a classless society brought on by the salvation of economic transformation, revolution, and the innate forces of history. For Marxists, the ultimate fix is economic. The account one gives of eschatology then has a powerful impact on ethics, for humans live in accordance with their understanding of where history is headed.

Christianity, of course, contains no monolithic understanding of consummation and eschatology, though almost all strands have affirmed the Apostle's Creed: "He [Christ] will come again to judge the quick and the dead." Interpretations of eschatology usually depend on conceptualizations of the kingdom of God and the notion of hope. Some Christian groups envision hope and a future kingdom as an ethereal reality in discontinuity with history and the realities of the created world. In such cases, the eschaton is primarily an escape from an evil world in which there is little temporal hope for change and improvement. Dispensational premillennialists in the late nineteenth and early twentieth centuries reflected this sentiment, for only Christ's second return held out any hope for an end to the moral evils of this world. The kingdom of God was deemed to be a future reign with no relevance to life in the present. Thus, as one critic of such thinking in the early part of the twentieth century put it, they "say that the church has nothing to do with reform in society. Its only business is to preach the gospel, exhibit holy and unspotted lives, and thus bear witness to the grace of God."[43]

Other Christians have emphasized a "fully realized eschatology" that is quite positive about history, because the kingdom of God is becoming more and more a reality on this earth. Here the kingdom is seen to be in continuity with space, time, and history. Often called postmillennialists, these Christians believe that the second return of Christ will come after the kingdom spreads throughout the world. In the early days of American history, many perceived the New World to be the primary locus of God's reign and the primary symbol of hope for the rest of the world. In our own time, this kind of eschatology is evident in the reconstructionist or theonomist movement, which believes that the Old

Testament law is the norm for all societies and that eventually this norm will become a reality on earth as the gospel and its corresponding law reach to all areas. As Rousas Rushdoony, one of the primary leaders, sees it, "The saints must prepare to take over the world's government and its courts,"[44] and then the kingdom will come in its fullness. Such conceptions clearly see a relationship between eschatology and ethics, but they often herald either an optimistic idealism about the forces of history or a triumphalism that fails to comprehend clearly the nature of the kingdom as taught in God's Word and the fallen nature of all social and political endeavors in this world.

There is another way to understand Christian hope and the kingdom of God: "There is a tension between the 'already' and the 'not yet' of the Christian hope, but each is essential to the other. In the language of the seer of Patmos, the Lamb that was slain has by death won the decisive victory (Rev. 5:5), but its final outworking . . . lies in the future (Rev. 22:12)."[45] It is quite clear that Jesus proclaimed the kingdom of God, and thus his reign has a present dimension. At the same time, it is equally clear from Scripture and observations of the world that it has not yet reached its final climax. When Christ returns, the kingdom of God will be consummated and the reign of God will become full and final on earth.

The kingdom climax is not separate from history and this world, for otherwise God would not win "the ball game" of history. This conception of eschatology thus sees continuity between the created world and the eschaton, for the final liberation of this world "cannot occur through its destruction but only through its transformation."[46] As Miroslav Volf has noted, "It makes little sense to affirm the goodness of creation and at the same time expect its eschatological destruction."[47] This affirmation of a real future hope is continuous with God's creation and redemption through Jesus Christ.

According to the Christian worldview, history will not go on in endless fashion, nor is there despair in light of the future forces of history. In contrast to secular utopian hopes or eschatologies of despair, "Hope of a properly transcendent sort (i.e., hope which is invested in something lying beyond the horizons of nature and history . . .) is not only compatible with but actually furnishes the most adequate source of and resources for action designed to transfigure the here-and-now."[48] Eschatology then has great significance for ethics.

David Gill has suggested three primary implications that flow from the Christian understanding of eschatological hope. First, this hope relativizes the world and all present human efforts to change it. "Absolute justice (or equality, peace, etc.) will occur at the return of Christ and only then. This frees us in the present from idolatries, perfectionism, utopian schemes and absolutizing of positions, parties, nations and ideologies. Perfection comes only at the end."[49] Second, hope motivates ethical behavior in the present world. "And all who have this hope in him purify themselves" (1 John 3:3), and, "You ought to live holy and godly lives as you look forward to the day of God" (2 Peter 3:11–12 NIV). Third, notes Gill, hope guides ethical behavior in the present world. "This present world era remains fallen, and only the return of Christ can and will resolve the problems of the world as a whole. Nevertheless, it is our future hope which guides our present particular action. While we are not called upon to purge, reform and manage the world as a whole, we are called to find ways of acting as faithful 'signs' of God's promised future."[50] The consummation is not a theology of escapism and abdication of responsibility within this world; it is a reminder to live now in light of the coming kingdom of God when justice, peace, righteousness, truthfulness, and purity will be made complete.

Conclusion

Christian ethics is ultimately rooted in the nature and actions of the Triune God of the universe. Moral goodness is defined by and flows from the ultimate source of goodness. God is the alpha and the omega, the beginning and the end of all reality including moral reality. But God has been at work in this world, and this work, revealed in Scripture, forms the second foundation for ethics. The Christian worldview is encompassed in the story of creation, fall, redemption, and consummation.

A good God creates a good world with man and woman at the apex of that creation. Humanity, however, chooses its own path, and the good world is infected with sin in every dimension. The gracious God begins a process of restoration to overcome the alienations from the fall, and redemption reaches its apex in the person of Jesus Christ, the eternal Son of God. Christ dies and rises again to bring us to God but also to renew us morally. But that complete renewal of our lives and of the world awaits the final consummation of his kingdom when Christ shall reign as King of Kings and Lord of Lords. That is the heart of the biblical story and the Christian worldview, and along with the ultimate reality of the Triune God, it is the foundation for our moral life in the world today.

PART 2

THE CONTEXTS
OF CHRISTIAN ETHICS

The understanding of ethical foundations, the making of moral decisions, and the application of ethical commitments always occur in a context, or better, a set of contexts. Some people believe context plays no role in ethics. Moral absolutes are the same yesterday, today, and forever, and thus, context is merely the changing scenery in which we apply the non-changing standards of God. The way we discern moral vision and apply ethical convictions is the same in all places and all times.

Others believe context plays a determinative role. According to this perspective, ethics is situational or contextual, in that the norms, virtues, and moral frameworks themselves arise from the context. This means that changing cultures, times, and circumstances preclude any moral absolutes or constants. Hence, we are left with a form of ethical relativism.

A third view is that context plays a mediating role. According to this perspective, there are transcendent realities, known through divine revelation, in which we ground our ethics and moral universals. The context, however, determines how we appeal to these transcultural norms and virtues and how we seek to apply them within the world. If we are honest, we must admit that context even influences our understanding of the norms and virtues themselves. The Bible, the source of a Christian worldview and moral guidelines, is never read in a vacuum.

This latter perspective is the one assumed in this book. It is imperative to understand the way context shapes our perceptions as well as the moral understandings of others. Furthermore, context plays a significant role when we seek to apply our ethical commitments to the cultures and societies in which we live. Indeed, neglecting context is the surest way to be co-opted by it.

There are really two forms of context related to ethics. The first form is a micro-context, a smaller and more immediate setting in which we make moral judgments. Micro-contexts include nations, races, geographic locations, church traditions, communities, and institutions. The other form is a macro-context, which is a larger cultural and historical setting. The next two chapters deal with the macro form by examining broad sweeps of history and culture that have influenced the moral life: modernity (chapter 4) and postmodernity (chapter 5). Each has played a significant role in the way people think about the moral enterprise, and each presents both opportunities and significant challenges as we seek to choose the good in a complex world. These chapters will be primarily sociological in nature as they attempt to explain the impact these contexts have had on Christian ethics and contemporary moral perceptions and actions.

4

MODERNITY AND THE MORAL LIFE

On a recent flight from Chicago to Baltimore, I got into a fascinating discussion with a young scientist who works in one of today's major corporations. I was editing a manuscript on genetic engineering, and upon observing my work, she asked how one could possibly make ethical judgments about an issue in the realm of science. After explaining how my Christian worldview informs the way I think about ethics and an issue such as genetic engineering, she said, "I guess I've always assumed that science carries its own ethical limitations."

The young scientist went on to explain that she believes the world of nature is all we can know for certain, and we are free to explore that world of nature, harness it responsibly, and expand its boundaries as far as it will allow us. As long as we do not hurt human beings and destroy the ecosystem, we are free to do whatever nature allows us to do. Science and reason are the final arbiters of such endeavors, and while we can indeed misuse the natural world, science will lead us to a better and more intelligent existence as human beings. Of course, I raised many questions about such an optimistic view of nature and science. Can science really keep us from destroying ourselves by science's own creations? Could science prevent a holocaust? A nuclear holocaust? And on what basis can we argue that humans and the ecosystem should not be destroyed?

The young scientist reflected what is commonly known as the ethos of modernity. She is perhaps a quintessential modernist, a breed some deem close to extinction. But modernity is far from dead, for though the postmodern extension (see the next chapter) creates another context, we continue to operate within the backdrop of its predecessor.

The modern world began roughly in the seventeenth century with the dawn of new scientific and philosophical understandings about the world and the human ability to control and shape that world. As British sociologist Anthony Giddens sees it, "Modernity refers to modes of social life or organization which emerged in Europe from about the seventeenth century onwards and which subsequently became more or less worldwide in their influence."[1] At the heart of this cultural epoch was a belief that humans could liberate themselves from human traditions and the limits of nature through the utilization of new forms of human thought and new scientific capabilities. Freedom became the hallmark value and progress the ensuing result. As Larry Rasmussen puts it, "Modernity, whose master plan was the plan of mastery itself, had a charged, even fevered, sense of its vocation of progress and control. Its liberation vision burned as constantly as any star in the heavens."[2]

Understandings of modernity are often filtered through ideological commitments and thus sometimes lack clarity. For example, some tend to equate modernity with westernization and assume that the process of modernizing will bear a striking resemblance to the Euro-American experience. Others assume the process was fueled primarily by bourgeois capitalism or by the process of democratization. For some, it was the golden era of human history, and for others, the great "demon" of the world.

The modern world defies simple or monolithic descriptions. It is best understood as a complex of interacting forces and variables. To explain the many nuances of modernity and its implications for Christian ethics, this chapter explores three of its primary components: intellectual, industrial/technological, and sociological.

Intellectual Components

At the heart of the modern world's intellectual agenda was the pursuit of truth, with an anticipation of certainty. Modernists did not always agree on how truth was attained, but they were unified in their relentless pursuit of truth about the world, themselves, society, and transcendence. Truth with certitude would lead to the promised land of progress and freedom; the only barriers lay within ourselves, and they were not insurmountable.

Essentially, there were two schools of thought on how we gain certain knowledge—two epistemological traditions: rationalism and empiricism. The rationalist strand believed that reason alone was sufficient to knowing all there was to discern about the world and life. René Descartes, a seventeenth-century French philosopher and scientist, argued that mathematics was the ideal for all intellectual inquiry. He believed that universal, self-evident truths could be discovered, not primarily through observation of the world but through an innate rationality present in all humans. Reliable knowledge could be attained by beginning with undeniable rational certainties and then building from them arguments that had the same clarity and certainty as mathematics. Anything outside this process was to be doubted. Hence, Descartes could assert certainty of his own thinking—"I think, therefore I am"—and from this certainty move to other rational affirmations.

The rationalists stressed a separation of mind and matter, but all the world could be understood by the ordering of the mind. The world was a rationally ordered whole, and the parts were logically linked to one another. In the Enlightenment of the eighteenth century, reason reigned supreme as the *philosophes* argued for its validity and its application to all spheres of life—the state, religion, knowledge, nature, education, and perceptions of the self. They believed that some truths were self-evident, and all humans could perceive these truths if they were merely enlightened. From such perceptions could come freedom, progress, democracy, and a new world.

The other school of epistemology was empiricism, the view that all knowledge was based on experience and the senses. One garnered truth not through innate reason but through empirical analysis and examination of the world. John Locke and Francis Bacon argued that humans do not come to the world with an ordered cognitive process; rather, the world itself orders minds and cognitive perceptions. This was, of course, the method of the natural sciences. Increasingly, people believed that science could uncover not only the natural world but also the human world, including history, psychology, and sociology. An analysis of the data or facts of this world would result in indubitable knowledge. Isaac Newton, the mathematician/physicist, provided the model, in that his cosmology "seemed to provide an account of everything from the movement of the planets to the falling of an apple, an account that could be, and was to be, developed to cover wider and wider areas of human experience of the world."[3] Through such an enterprise "the darkness of ignorance, superstition, and religion was being banished; the light had come. As Alexander Pope put it in his famous lines: 'Nature and Nature's laws lay hid in night; God said "Let Newton be!" and all was light.'"[4]

While adherents of rationalism and empiricism were at odds with each other over how to perceive truth, they agreed that humans could know truth with certainty and that the intellectual quest would enhance human life, thus creating societies that were superior to those of the past. Both strands agreed that religious authority, such as divine revelation, had to be rejected in favor of newer and better ways of understanding nature, humanity, society, and history. In the early days of modernity, new forms of thought "emerged which questioned all traditional assumptions on the basis of the authority of reason and the senses."[5] Modernity emerged with and continued to herald a suspicion of most traditional forms of authority, including divine revelation. As Lesslie Newbigin writes, "Modernity is distrustful of authority. It was born in a movement of emancipation from what were seen as external authorities, and its appeal was to the freedom and responsibility of the individual reason and conscience to judge between rival claims to truth." Moreover, he notes, "Reliable and therefore authoritative, knowledge of truth is not, in the view of moder-

91

nity, to be found by faith in alleged revelation, but by observation of the facts and rigorously critical reflection on them."[6]

With its intellectual quest for certainty through either reason or empirical inquiry, the modern world fully assumed not only that such knowledge was attainable but also that it would usher in a new world of progress and freedom. It was an optimistic world that believed humans could achieve what had never been achieved before: human liberation from the restraints of "barbaric" religious and moral assumptions, tyrannical governments, and the restraints of nature itself.

What impacts did these intellectual tenets of modernity have on ethics? Clearly, one of the most significant impacts concerned the notion of progress. Heretofore, humans had certainly believed that things could be better in the world, but there was usually a sense of moderation and belief that ultimate hope was divine in nature. While Christian hope was an eschatological concept in the Christian church, some Christians did make links between the hope in God's intervention at the end of time and the role of humans between the times (between the first advent of Christ and the second advent). All of this, however, began to give way to the notion of human progress grounded in human reason, science, and the new technological innovations. At the beginning of the twentieth century, Englishman L. T. Hobhouse spoke confidently of moral progress and opined, "The vaster the social organism, the greater the triumph, when justice, kindled to new life, has again sent purified blood through its arteries."[7]

With such progress and evolution in morals and society, God was no longer needed to deal with social evils and problems. Humans now had at their disposal the means to eradicate the evil and usher in the good. Social progressivism throughout the modern era increasingly meant the development of superior modes of personal and social life compared to earlier times, when God and the church were in control.

The rationalism and empiricism of modernity also meant that divine revelation and transcendent perspectives were insignificant for ethical judgments. In many ways, this followed from the modernist assumption that "God was no longer needed to account for the coherence and meaning of the world."[8] As noted in chapter 1, deontological and utilitarian forms of ethics emerged during this period, based on either rationality or a mathematics-like quantification of consequences. Immanuel Kant used the former approach. Though his primary philosophical assumptions incorporated a synthesis of rationalism and empiricism, his ethics was based on pure reason, independent of religious authority or content. God was needed as a kind of practical necessity to motivate people to ethical living, but Kant's ethical foundation needed neither divine revelation nor God. Similarly, utilitarianism attempted to build on the burgeoning scientific model by calculating consequences, not only without reference to God but also without reference to any intrinsic moral virtues or qualities. Ethics had become mathematics.

In many ways, the dethronement of God and divine revelation in ethics was a main staple of modernity. As Jennifer Herdt has argued, "The so-called modern moral philosophers were divided on many points concerning morality, but they shared a common tendency to eschew sectarian religious premises and to seek a moral vocabulary that all could use. Sincerely religious though most of them were, they contributed to the secularization of moral thought."[9] This was true not only for those doing ethics within the discipline of philosophy but also for those working within a theological framework, Christian ethics. Herdt explains that the Christian worldview was undermined or at least underplayed as it was replaced by scientific assumptions about reality. Before modernity, morality had not "required an explicit justification; it had possessed an implicit justification through its hand-in-glove fit with the Christian worldview."[10] But in modernity, while God in principle was not excluded, ethics increasingly operated on the grounds of autonomy, not heteronomy. Christian ethics and the Christian worldview were separated from each other, and for many Christian thinkers the only recourse was an accommodation to modern impulses.

The challenge facing both secular ethics and Christian ethics today is immense in light of the intellectual forces of the past several centuries. As Herdt sees it:

> The challenge facing secular thinkers is equally daunting, for such thinkers often struggle at the task of erecting an ethics wholly independent of any metaphysical worldview. Committed to the autonomy of ethics from the authority of traditional worldviews, many hold that the only way to escape the appeal to authority is to avoid metaphysics all together, which leaves them with a very thin moral fabric.[11]

And with many Christian ethicists accommodating to the prevailing assumptions of modernity, the fabric is thin for them as well. The mood is well captured by Franklin Gamwell: "Our understanding of reality and ourselves in relation to it cannot be validated or redeemed by appeals to some authoritative expression of tradition or institution. In other words, our understandings can be validated or redeemed only by appeal in some sense to human experience and reason as such."[12] Such is the intellectual legacy of the modern world for Christian ethics and the moral life.

The Industrial Revolution and Technological Components

The modern age was in part ushered in through the Industrial Revolution. With new understandings garnered through modern science, humans became increasingly capable of subduing nature for their own purposes and ends. New scientific discoveries were applied to the production and distribution of goods and services, and a new world of economics began to take shape. The Industrial Revolution began in England during the eighteenth century and continued for the next several hundred years, spreading throughout many parts of the world. It transformed agricultural economies into industrial ones, and goods that traditionally had been made in the home or small shops were now produced in factories that were fueled by new technologies and aided by new modes of efficiency. Because factories brought together large masses of people to work in the production process, cities began to flourish and new social systems emerged. Industrialism transformed not only economies but also politics, religions, everyday ways of life, and human thinking. The modern world was intricately bound up with the Industrial Revolution and its ensuing changes.

The Industrial Revolution emerged as modern science was applied to the development of new tools, machines, and procedures for using them—what is commonly called technology. Technology is not merely the tools we devise but a thinking process that accompanies their development and use. Technology is not science per se but rather the utilization of scientific knowledge in the interplay with the material world. It incorporates a harnessing of that material world and a way of thinking about reality and the human self. As Gabriel Marcel once observed, "To say that man is led to think of himself and of the world in technical terms means first of all that he sees the world as capable of being transformed methodically, by industrious human activity until it should more and more completely satisfy human needs."[13]

Sociologists sometimes describe this transformation through technology as a process of rationalization. Rationality in this sense is not theoretical rationalism or reason, as discussed in the last section, but a functional rationality in which all spheres of human existence are governed by calculation and scrutiny. In traditional societies, custom, habit, and spontaneity were the major marks of social behavior, and personal, rationalized choices were limited. But in the modern world there was, as Max Weber described it, "The methodological attainment of a definitely given and practical end by means of an increasingly precise calculation of adequate means."[14] Rationality in this sense extended far beyond industrial, economic, and bureaucratic spheres to all domains of life, including, as Weber saw it, music, religion, politics, and social life. For sociologist Peter Berger, "Functional rationality means, above all, the imposition of rational controls over the material universe, over social relations and finally over the self."[15] Because means are related to ends with an eye toward efficiency, some fear that "the thrust is towards the eradication of the incidental, the whimsical, the wayward, the poetic, and the traditional."[16]

Modernity, then, was characterized by a technological rationality that emanated from the Industrial Revolution. Its impact was staggering, not only on the economy and everyday way of life but also on human cognition and the moral enterprise. What are the implications for Christian ethics today? Several are important to grasp.

Ethical Issues Tied to Technology

The most obvious ramification of the technological revolution for Christian ethics is that many of the issues we face today arose out of that revolution. Take bioethics. Most of the issues with which we grapple today are a result of the technological means of controlling significant portions of life, death, disease, and the genetic structure of human beings. Issues surrounding abortion, physician-assisted suicide, treatment termination, organ transplants, genetic engineering, stem cell research (and the list could go on) have all emerged in the past few decades because of new technological capabilities. Environmental ethics has emerged from industrialism and its impact on the environment. Ethical reflection on modern warfare has changed substantially because of a technological arsenal that raises serious questions about past understandings and applications. Ethics in the media today faces issues unheard of less than a century ago. For example, a press secretary for one of the United States Senate select committees commented recently that the greatest ethical issue he faces daily is having to put committee news into sound bytes that will get picked up by the media. He is acutely aware that sound bytes distort the complexity of reality and the substance of the actual debates. As a Christian, he fears that integrity and perhaps the common good are at risk through a technology that is now normative.

The common assumption in dealing with technology is that since we as human beings created it, we can control it. Clearly, that is a debatable point. Jacques Ellul in his well-known *Technological Society* argues that technique is not just something we create and control; it is a process that actually comes to control us. Technique has its own inner logic to which we must conform to use it.[17] Edward L. Long sometimes employed an illustration of a bicycle to make the point. When we ride a bike, "Do we ride (control) the bike, or does the bike ride (control) us?" We might at first be prone to say we ride or control the bike. But on further reflection we realize that the bike actually controls us in many ways, because its own inner logic and structure dictate to us what we must do in order to ride it. If we want to stop, we must press the brakes, not peddle forward. Technology then always carries with it a certain kind of control over us. The premise that we can easily control technologies toward moral ends is not at all self-evident. Most of the great ethical issues grappled with today are somehow related to our technological sophistication. Our capabilities to create and manufacture outpace our moral sensibilities.

Human Control over Divine Givens

A second implication for Christian ethics is that humans actually control large amounts of the world that heretofore were outside their control. Before modern technologies, industrialism, and the communication revolution, humans had a much greater sense of dependence on God and divine givens for life in general, including morality. Marcel notes that technological "thinking develops into a practical anthropocentrism—which is to say that man tends more and more to think of himself as the only principle which can give meaning to [the] world."[18] The mastery of the material world gives us the false impression that we are in control, and the many choices now created by our mastery only reinforce our sense of sovereignty. Technology has created a psychological disposition within us that says we must no longer resign ourselves to the divine providence or the taken-for-grantedness of reality. Bryan Wilson describes the process with astute accuracy:

> Perhaps the most significant aspect of our conception of what it means to be modern is the idea that we can consciously change the character of society and the condition of our lives. Most of our present-day concern in economics, politics, public affairs, education, and even in entertainment—is concern with change. . . . We are committed to the idea that we can make the future. . . . Where once we thought that consequences were God's will, we now deliberately program, regulate, and organize our own future.[19]

Perhaps nowhere is this sense of human control more evident than in reproductive technologies. When we combine new technologies with this sense of control, it becomes increasingly difficult to convince people that not all new forms of procreation are morally legitimate within a Christian ethics framework or even wise within any framework. We easily translate "what we can do" into a mind-set of "what we should do." The pulling apart of procreation from the one-flesh, covenant relationship of marriage—which is now reality in artificial insemination by donor, most forms of surrogacy, and donor gametes, and would be the case in cloning—seems to matter little to most modernists. By no means must all reproductive technologies be rejected from a Christian ethics standpoint, but we must be aware of the way in which our thinking patterns are shifting from procreation as "begetting" to a process of "making." "Such a society is incapable of acknowledging the inappropriateness of technical intervention in certain types of activity. When every activity is understood as making, then every situation into which we act is seen as a raw material, waiting to have something made out of it."[20]

When it comes to sexual ethics, our ability to control tends to render outmoded a traditional Christian ethic that calls for sexual relations to be preserved for marriage between a man and a woman. One recent family sociology textbook puts it boldly:

The separation of sexuality from reproduction is in principle complete. Sexuality is for the first time something to be discovered, molded, altered. Sexuality, which used to be defined so strictly in relation to marriage and legitimacy, now has little connection to them at all. We should see the increasing acceptance of homosexuality not just as a tribute to liberal tolerance. It is the logical outcome of the severance of sexuality from reproduction. Sexuality which has no content is by definition no longer dominated by heterosexuality.[21]

In this perspective, sexual behavior is limited only by the consequences that arise from it. Once we have developed the control over consequences deemed detrimental to human happiness or social well-being, the behavioral norms and restrictions can be lifted. In this world of control, the divine givens of a sexual ethic are thrown to the winds.

The Technicization of Morality

In the midst of modern technology and its rationalistic procedures, moral standards came to rest more and more on rationalized, legal, and technical forms of control as opposed to religiously grounded norms and outlooks. Deeply inculcated personal moral virtues gave way to public forms of juris-diction. As David Lyon so vividly put it, "Who then needs public morals . . . to ensure the fair allocation of parking spaces, when the simple installation of meters will do the job?"[22] Public and even personal morality became techni-cized in the sense that they were less dependent on internalized or even local mechanisms of influence and more dependent on external, impersonal mech-anisms such as law, surveillance, and professional ethics codes enforced within each segment of society. All of this was part of the process that Jacques Ellul called technique. He described the transformation it entailed this way:

> Earlier, economic or political inquiries were inextricably bound with ethical inquiry, and men attempted to maintain this union artificially even after they had recognized the inde-pendence of economic technique. Modern society is, in fact, conducted on purely tech-nical considerations. But when men found themselves going counter to the human fac-tor, they introduced . . . all manner of moral theories related to the rights of man, the League of Nations, liberty, justice. . . . When these moral flourishes overly encumber technical progress, they are discarded.[23]

Even if one does not accept Ellul's rather pessimistic account of recent social history, it is clear that the formal roles of public life depended little on moral guidance, let alone the specifics of Christian ethics. With social and geographi-cal mobility in the modern world, individuals became more autonomous, lim-ited primarily by the most overt forms of external control: law, police, electronic eyes, audits, bugging devices, and media pressures. Even law itself was more tech-nical, depending less and less on jurisprudence frameworks, which are usually rooted in a larger narrative or vision of law and morality. As the law became more technical, "It abandon[ed] areas that were traditionally of primarily moral concern."[24] Bryan Wilson notes, for example, that "the widespread use of insurance affects the whole moral principle of fault liability. The insured individual does not himself now pay the consequences of fault."[25] Above all, however, Wilson contends that the demoralization of society (akin to what is here called the technicization of morality) meant less dependence on moral virtues and traditional ethical or metaphysical frameworks. All of this indicated "a shift from reliance on well-defined moral dispositions to dependence on technical and legal provision," and such "may indeed have the paradoxical consequence of absolving individuals from the need to cultivate any sense of personal responsibility."[26]

Sociological Components

In addition to its intellectual and industrial/technological effects, modernity caused a number of shifts within society and its major institutions. These sociological components have had a significant impact on Christian ethics, especially in terms of its interface with the larger society.

Differentiation

In the modern world, especially as a result of the Industrial Revolution, a differentiation (or segmentation, as some sociologists call it) of the various parts of the social order emerged. At the end of the nineteenth century, Emile Durkheim spoke of a division of labor in which jobs were highly specialized and the specific work roles were distinct from one another. People no longer produced for themselves the essentials of life but depended on the specialization of others for their necessities and wants. But the other on whom they depended for these economic goods and services was usually anonymous and hidden—a depersonalized relationship. The same is true today. We do not depend on the benevolence of the mail carrier to have our mail delivered or the personal affections of the farmer to get food on our tables. With a division of labor came a differentiation of roles that characterized interactions with others and defined selfhood.

Durkheim saw this division of labor having ramifications beyond the economic life, for "we can observe its increasing influence in the most diverse sectors of society. Functions, whether political, administrative or judicial are becoming more and more specialized. The same is true in the arts and the sciences."[27] With differentiation, social institutions such as law, economics, politics, education, and religion became distinct from one another, each tending to develop its own set of norms and role expectations. All of this contrasted with premodern, traditional societies in which one encountered a person not primarily within the sphere of a highly specialized role but simply as a whole person. The distinctions between the major institutions of society and their expected roles were minimal. The moral expectations for economics, politics, and work did not differ much from the expectations of home and interpersonal relationships.

The result of differentiation (or segmentation) is that "the world comes to us in pieces, in fragments, lacking an overall pattern."[28] Increasingly, it becomes difficult to find a unifying frame of reference that can guide ethical choices for all spheres of life. Moreover, humans tend to be seized by personal anguish in their search for meaning and identity amid the competing role expectations placed upon them.

The implication of modern differentiation for Christian ethics is quite evident. It is increasingly difficult for one to carry out a singular ethic in every realm of life. Each sphere of society embodies not only its own language and roles but also its own specific rules of behavior. Thus, a religiously based ethic is segmented from politics, education, economics, law, and the workplace. As Agnes Heller states, "There is one ethical minimum for all citizens of a state: to be law-abiding." But, she observes, in the differentiated situation, "The law is not interested in whether someone is a good person, not even whether he or she is a good citizen. The law is not interested in one's actions inside the framework of the law, and even less in one's motivations."[29] As a result, one finds it difficult to apply Christian ethics to the various segmented spheres of society and increasingly challenging to live consistently within the norms of Christian ethics and the framework of a Christian worldview.

Pluralization

It is safe to say that for most of history humans lived in worlds that were fairly homogeneous, and that homogeneity was rooted above all else in a common religious and moral framework. Rarely did one come in contact with people who put their world together in significantly different ways. "For the individual this meant quite simply that the same integrative symbols permeated the various sectors of . . . everyday life. . . . The individual was always in the same world."[30] There were exceptions, of course, such as the pluralistic milieu during the time of the Roman Empire, the period of Christ, and the several centuries following. But for the most part human history has been characterized by homogeneous experiences and worldviews within a given geographical area and time frame.

All of that changed drastically in the modern world. The Industrial Revolution brought geographical mobility with its need for a workforce in a common location. New technologies aided the transportation process, easing the move from one location to another. Recent communication revolutions have created a "global village" and with it a pluralization unparalleled in history. The upshot is not merely a plurality of nationalities, ethnic groups, religions, and races in a common geographical area. More fundamentally, people with discrepant worldviews and moral frameworks now live, work, and play side by side.

Pluralism is a structural reality in today's societies, but it also has vast implications for the way humans think. In particular, divergent worldviews and ideologies challenge one's own views and commitments. As Peter Berger observed, "When an entire society serves as the plausibility structure for a religiously legitimated world, all the important social processes within it serve to confirm and reconfirm the reality of this world."[31] But as pluralization takes place, the multiple worldviews, religions, and moral systems challenge an individual's beliefs and moral foundations.

Chapter 11 explores in-depth the challenges and possible responses to pluralism, since it is such a significant issue in applying Christian ethics to culture and society. But two implications of pluralism are important for this discussion. First, pluralism tends to create a psychological disposition toward moral relativism. With the numerous reality-defining agencies, the plethora of moral frameworks, and the intellectual challenges to traditional notions of authority comes a significant growth in moral relativism. Pluralism by its very nature seems to challenge the idea that universal norms and virtues exist that are right and good for all times and places. The emergence of moral relativism is distinctly tied to the challenges to truth that emerged in the modern world and continue to emerge in the postmodern world.

The second implication of pluralism for Christian ethics is the challenge of how to bring a particularistic ethic to bear on a cultural and societal milieu that does not share the worldview from which Christian ethics emerges. If, as argued in chapter 3, ethics is intimately tied to worldview, then how can we possibly seek to make an impact in a world of competing worldviews, some of which are in direct opposition to a Christian understanding of things? Various approaches have been articulated, and chapter 11 explores them in-depth. Suffice it to say, pluralism raises significant challenges for a Christian ethic that seeks in some way to be relevant to today's world.

Secularization

The differentiation and pluralization of modern societies was accompanied by a secularization of those societies. It is important to distinguish secularization, as a social process, from secularism, as an ideology or worldview commitment. Secularism is a "set of beliefs and practices committed to the abolition of religion in society. Religion is viewed in an uncompromisingly negative light."[32] Secularization, on the other hand, is a process occurring within societies and cultures whereby religion no longer plays the dominant role in shaping major social institutions.

There has been a great deal of debate about the exact nature of secularization, for in recent years it has been quite evident that some of the secularizing projections of sociologists have not come to pass. Some definitions, for example, seemed to imply that religious beliefs and practices were in decline in the modern world, replaced by scientific and modern philosophical outlooks. But we frequently see a resurgence of religiosity in the world today, though not always in the same forms as earlier times. This reemergence of religious vitality has led some to argue that "belief in secularization has been sustained by a deep and abiding antagonism to religious belief and various expressions of organized religion."[33] They would suggest we discard the term.

But it is clear that though religion still plays a significant role in the lives of people and continues to influence societies and cultures, it does not play the same role it once played in relation to major social institutions such as government, economics, education, and law. Thus, as Peter Berger defined it, secularization is the "process by which sectors of society and culture are removed from the domination of religious institutions and symbols."[34] Or as Karel Dobbelaere defines it, "A societal process in which an overarching and transcendent religious system is being reduced to a sub-system of society alongside other sub-systems."[35] Since Berger first wrote about secularization, he has come to qualify and even challenge some of his earlier assumptions about the process, most notably its inevitability and the projected decline of religious belief and vitality. The world, even with structural forms of secularization, has engendered powerful movements of counter-secularization, as many forms of orthodox religion have flourished and new religious movements have emerged.[36] The countervailing "desecularization" expressions, as Berger labels them, are evident not only in personal beliefs and morals. They have also become overtly political, as seen in the Hindu political resurgence in India, Islamic political movements in many countries, and the religious right in the United States.

Despite the counter-secularization movements, secularization has often influenced societies. Religion continues to flourish, and at times religious revival emerges, but within secularized societies, religion tends to have minimal impact on the larger societal institutions and the main contours of cultural life. Religion, therefore, is one social institution alongside the others, no longer providing the overarching framework for the society. Religious practices and vitality may thrive, and religious bodies may even attempt to influence the social and cultural order, but secularization as a process means that the religious worldview and its moral foundations no longer play a significant role in the operation of politics, economics, law, education, the arts, and science. In today's societies, there is, therefore, a tendency for the separation of church and state. Education is disengaged from religious tutelage, and its curriculum functions with minimal recourse to particularistic religious beliefs and values. The legal institution seldom makes reference to God or religiously based norms in sanctioning laws or circumscribing particular behaviors. Economics and business

101

may appeal to professional codes of ethics, but generally they are devoid of religious content, finding legitimacy primarily on pragmatic grounds. And in the arts, while religious themes or symbols may at times find expression, they are for the most part the exception rather than the rule, and the appearances of such expressions are often marked by controversy.

The reality of societal secularization is particularly evident when medieval Europe is contrasted with modern societies. The medieval epoch was religious, not so much in terms of its spiritual devoutness or vitality as in the role the church played in the social and cultural order. "The Church controlled not only the moral fabric of society . . . , but the formal processes of political, juridical, commercial, and social intercourse—the institutional operation of society."[37] In economics, for example, the medieval church extended significant influence in regulating trade, production, and prices, as well as maintaining a ban on usury, the charging of interest rates on loans. The church no longer played that kind of role in the modern world. It still made social, political, and economic pronouncements and gave guidance to its adherents in these domains, but it did not provide the primary foundation or direction for the social and cultural life of the entire society.

In secularized societies, religion and religiously grounded ethics do not disappear. Rather, they tend to be relocated from the public sphere to the private sphere. Hence, the great challenge for Christian ethics today is to find ways of relating a moral framework rooted in a particularistic worldview to a larger society and culture that have been secularized in terms of the role religion plays within them.

Privatization of Religion

Within secularized societies, characterized by pluralization and differentiation, religion continues to play a role, though primarily within the private spheres. As modern societies became highly specialized with specific roles for each domain, a dichotomy emerged between the public arenas and the private arenas of human existence. The public domains included the more impersonal, bureaucratized structures of society such as government, corporations, educational institutions, community associations, and professional or work-related organizations. The private sphere included the world of family, friends, leisure, religion, and voluntary associations. As Robert Bellah observes, "It is an outstanding feature of industrial life that these sectors have become radically discontinuous in the kinds of traits emphasized and the moral understandings that guide individuals within them. Public and private roles often contrast sharply."[38]

Not only was the modern world characterized by a split between the private and the public, but the separation also tended to generate different expectations for the respective spheres. Because the public realm was experienced as an impersonal gathering of role players who placed high demands on one's energy and talents, the private sphere became the haven for solace and intimacy. In the privacy of home, leisure, associations, and church, people often searched for meaning and personal reassurances that they were more than cogs in the public machinery. The rules of the game between the public and the private realms were different. Speaking of modern individuals who experienced this private/public split, Karl Mannheim once remarked, "He [the modern person] lives in two worlds, and he must therefore, so to speak, have two souls."[39]

With the private/public dichotomy, religion continued to function but primarily within the private spheres. This, of course, followed from the process of secularization, which made it increasingly difficult for religiously based ethics to have a significant impact on the directions of public policy or major institutional and cultural life. Religion continued to speak to those spheres, but often its moral directives on matters deemed private—such as sexuality or many issues of bioethics (i.e., abortion, euthanasia, reproductive technologies)—were considered illegitimate for the larger society. The common assumption in modernity was that any ethic informed by religious sentiments was fine as long as it stayed within the private realm. It had no role in the public square.

This privatization of faith and ethics, which continues today, presents a major problem for Christian ethics. The Christian worldview underlying the ethic asserts that all of life is to be lived for God's glory. But precisely because the larger social and cultural framework operates outside the worldview from which Christian ethics emanates, there is a major dilemma. How can the Christian ethic possibly speak to the public realm, when the social ethos and cultural assumptions are fundamentally at odds with Christian conceptions of reality? This situation continues to influence the context in which Christians seek to do Christian ethics and to live out the morality of their worldview commitments.

Conclusion

Modernity, with its intellectual, industrial/technological, and sociological components, created a world of optimism and hope. The common assumption of the past several centuries was that knowledge and technological sophistication would usher in a world of progress, high civilization, and moral maturity. To fulfill this vision, religion was at best unnecessary, at worst an impediment to human and cultural progress. Many were euphoric about the blessings of modernity.

Indeed, the modern world brought much to the human race. The gifts of medicine, psychiatry, modern business growth, technical know-how, and political/social movements toward freedom are all to be welcomed. But the king-

103

dom has not come. Modernity brought us not only scientific and technological progress but also some of the worst evils known in human history.

Of course, the accounts of this modern project vary in accordance with a host of prior beliefs, commitments, and dispositions through which people judge the period. For some observers the modern period was the worst of times. Agnes Heller states, "The legitimating philosophy of modernity was realized; yet, instead of Heaven descending upon Earth, Earth was transformed into Hell. Indeed, the fast trains ran toward their final destination—and the names of the terminal railway stations were Auschwitz and the Gulag—the stations of extermination."[40] The Spanish philosopher Jose Ortega y Gasset saw the primary bane of modernity in a different light, though he was no less scathing in his critique. He believed that the "hyperdemocracy" and the unbridled consumer mentality of industrialism were the major culprits of the modern world in which "mass society" was quickly destroying the individual. Writing in 1932, even before the Holocaust and angst of late twentieth-century life, Ortega y Gasset stated:

We live at a time when man believes himself fabulously capable of creation, but he does not know what to create. Lord of all things, he is not lord of himself. He feels lost amid his own abundance. With more means at his disposal, more knowledge, more technique than ever, it turns out that the world today goes the same way as the worst of worlds that have been; it simply drifts.[41]

Writing from an explicitly Christian framework, Lesslie Newbigin is no less pessimistic in his appraisal of the modern agenda. He believes that in the past several centuries we have seen "the project of enlightenment carried to the furthest parts of the earth, offering a vision for the whole human race of emancipation, justice, material development and human rights. It has, and is, a noble project. Yet it has failed to deliver what was promised. Forces of darkness, irrationality, and violence are perhaps more devastating . . . today than they have ever been."[42]

The problem with modernity is not merely that it failed us but that it carried within itself seeds of moral and spiritual destruction. This does not mean that the modern period was more evil than others. Each epoch carries its own peculiar expressions of fallenness and evil. Christians should never view any period as either the great source of evil or the great embodiment of good, for the origin of those realities lies outside the pale of human historical movements, though always touching historical realities. Nonetheless, the modern period was particularly insidious in its moral effects, precisely because it offered so much and seemed at certain levels to produce so much. Modernists were absorbed in its false consciousness.

This then is the background of the context in which Christians seek to do Christian ethics today. While many believe this modern world has passed, the postmodern world, while a direct affront to modern assumptions, has by no means turned aside much of modernity's forces. Thus, while we are living in a new context, many of the processes of the modern world continue to shape us. What is disappearing is the confidence that we can achieve truth and progress through the great intellectual tenets and technological apparatus of the modern world. But the technological innovations of the modern world are more powerful than ever, and the social processes such as differentiation, pluralization, secularization, and the privatization of religion are far from dead. The context of modernity continues to shape us and presents significant challenges for those seeking to think and live according to a Christian worldview.

5

POSTMODERNITY AND THE MORAL LIFE

One day in an ethics class two students got into a heated exchange on the issue of premarital sexual relations. Jessica was quite convinced that sexual intercourse outside marriage is contrary to God's design and purposes for this good gift to humanity. While the Bible does not explicitly say, "You shall not have sex before marriage," Jessica argued that the meaning and purposes of sex are clear from the Bible, and they preclude premarital sex. She maintained that there are divine givens to which we must conform to ensure the kind of life for which we were made. When we contravene them, we are the losers.

Stephanie was passionate in her opposition to Jessica. She began by asserting, "Who are we to judge someone's private behavior? We may not like what they do, but that's their business. It's arrogant and intolerant to pass judgments on someone's personal decisions." Stephanie went on to argue that there is no inherent meaning in the sexual act. Humans give it meaning, which varies from time to time and place to place. Each community seems to have its own understandings and boundaries about sexual behavior. Stephanie stated that she understood Jessica's desire to look to the Bible regarding issues such as this, but she noted that there are many interpretations of the Bible. If it does not explicitly forbid sexual intercourse before marriage, how can we? "Above all," said Stephanie, "we must cultivate an ethic that seeks the well-being of each individual. If premarital sex actually enriches a couple's relationship and makes them better people, how can we say no to it?"

At issue in this discussion were differences in ethical positions and differences in theology, as well as significant variations in how the two students thought and perceived reality. Their foundational frameworks for looking at the world were at odds with each other. In a sense, they lived in two different worlds. Stephanie lived in a postmodern world, and every argument she employed seemed to reflect that ethos. She may never have read the postmodern thinkers, but because of the culture she imbibed daily, she was a thoroughgoing postmodernist.

As soon as we employ the term *postmodern* to describe the context in which we increasingly find ourselves, we discover that its meaning is far from clear. That is perhaps appropriate given the fact that the postmodern ethos questions traditional conceptions about meaning. The term *postmodern* has been employed by historians, sociologists, artists, architects, philosophers, literary critics, and theologians. If there is one common theme that binds these diverse disciplines together it is a reaction to modernity, to the particular modern expressions in each field of study. In many ways, that is the heart and essence of postmodernity. At the same time, however, postmodernity involves far more than the reactions of intellectuals, for its tenets have reached into the fabric of everyday life, affecting people who have never studied postmodern thought or even heard the term.

Recently, some have described it as a new period of history set apart by its own social, cultural, and intellectual traits. Others see it merely as a phase or extension of modernity. In fact, many of modernity's primary features—a growth in technology, privatization, differentiation, secularization, and pluralization (as outlined in the last chapter)—continue to exist, though not always in the same forms. Sociologist Anthony Giddens writes, "The break with providential views of history, the dissolution of foundationalism, together with the emergence of counterfactual future-oriented thought and the 'emptying out' of progress . . . , are so different from the core perspective of the Enlightenment as to warrant the view that far-reaching transitions have occurred." Yet, he contends, "The disjunctions which have taken place should rather be seen as resulting from the self-clarification of modern thought, as the remnants of tradition and providential outlooks are cleared away. We have not moved beyond modernity but are living precisely through a phase of its radicalization."[1]

Judging periods of history is always fraught with ambiguity and involves complex appraisals regarding social, cultural, intellectual, and technological changes. Whether postmodernity is merely an extension of modernity or a new epoch, it is clear that significant changes have taken place in regard to the main contours of thought and experience. Indeed, the postmodern impulse is a reaction against the rationalism, pursuit of truth, certainty, and confidence in progress that so characterized the past few centuries. It is a questioning of the Enlightenment and the modern scientific agenda that so blithely envisioned a new world free of old bondages and limitations. Postmodern thought assails the unity of all things and questions the modern vision of universal truth. "In a postmodern view all great schemes and systems are socially produced means of some group exercising control over another; that is, all relations are power relations, and suspect. The quest for the good and the true by way of individual access to a universal reason is utterly distrusted."[2]

One of the best ways to understand the broad sweeps of this postmodern reality is to contrast it with modernity. Gene Veith makes the contrasts striking:

> Modernists valued unity; postmodernists value diversity. Modernists looked for universal frameworks of knowledge; postmodernists question all "totalizing" or "foundational" systems. Modernists emphasized the individual; postmodernists emphasize the culture. Modernists sought order; postmodernists prize disorder. Modernists valued science, as a means of finding knowledge about nature; postmodernists care little for scientific knowledge, but they love technology.[3]

These are, of course, broad generalizations, and many who willingly wear the postmodern label defy such simple categorizations. Conversely, many who do not like the label fit the descriptions. Defining any movement of history or cultural trend involves such risks.

There are really two primary ways to examine postmodernity. One is to explore the intellectual thinking of its most influential thinkers, found primarily among philosophers, literary critics, and linguists. The other is to examine general trends that characterize the whole or at least pockets of the culture. It is the latter, the more sociological approach, that this chapter gives significant attention to, but not without looking at some of the key intellectual concepts and thinkers. In the process of examining several major characteristics of postmodern thought and reality, the chapter will reveal their impact on ethics as a discipline and morality as a way of life and character. While the modern context continues on in various ways, there has indeed been a change, particularly in the way people think and envision the world, including the moral world.

Deconstruction and the Assault on Metanarratives

Before the postmodern ethos spread to the broader culture, its ideas first found expression among a group of intellectuals who began to question the modernist enterprise of philosophy, literary interpretation, and confidence in the scientific "illusion." The modern world had operated on the assumption that an objective world exists that can be understood and described with truth and certainty. This basic assumption was questioned in the last several decades of the twentieth century. As Stanley Grenz describes it, "The postmodern understanding of knowledge . . . is built on two foundational assumptions: (1) postmoderns view all explanations of reality as constructions that are useful but not objectively true, and (2) postmoderns deny that we have the ability to step outside our constructions of reality."[4]

One of the first philosophers to employ the term *postmodern* was the French philosopher Jean-François Lyotard. Lyotard, followed by many other postmodern thinkers, questioned the metanarratives, or legitimizing myths, of the Enlightenment experiment and modernity. Metanarratives are the grand ideas or foundational constructs that people use to explain reality and bring coherence to the world. Scientific rationality, with its accompanying notions of certainty and progress, formed the core of the modern metanarrative, but this unified approach to knowledge and reality was coming to an end. Lyotard also believed that the very appeal to metanarratives themselves was coming to an end. Increasingly, local narratives were replacing grand narratives, and appeal to a unifying system to explain reality was fading into history. For Lyotard, these were welcomed events. He wrote, "Simplifying to the extreme, I define postmodern as incredulity toward metanarrative."[5] He and other postmodern thinkers have come to see the postmodern condition as beneficial, "because it heightens our ability to cope with our pluralistic situation. It assists us in the task of living with differences and tolerating things that cannot be brought together into a single whole."[6]

The questioning of metanarratives (and indeed any attempt to find unifying frameworks for either the world at large or specific disciplines) is a major component of postmodern thought. Neither intellectual unity nor cultural unity is possible any longer, for both are a result of misleading attempts to describe the world, attempts that are always bound up with the maintenance of power through ideas and symbols. As Andrew Sullivan, editor of the *New Republic,* put it with a note of celebration, "There is, these days, only subculture. . . . There is no longer any sustaining broader culture to take its place."[7]

Along with the rejection of metanarratives, the concept most often linked to postmodern thought is deconstruction, and the name most often associated with deconstruction is Jacques Derrida. Born to Jewish parents in Algiers in 1930, Derrida eventually moved to France, where he has spent the majority of his life, though he has frequently taught in the United States. Derrida's work focuses primarily on written language, and he believes that the search for meaning in texts and ultimate metaphysical certainty described in texts are an illusion. Drawing on linguistics, psychoanalysis, and the thinking of Friedrich Nietzsche, Derrida argues for a deconstruction of texts that questions the ability of readers to get at the intention of authors, and the ability of authors to uncover any real meaning about the world. Deconstruction is "a mode of analysis that purports to take apart all expressions of objective meaning, showing that everything from a play by Shakespeare to the Declaration of Independence to a scientific experiment is actually unstable linguistic constructions, masks for cultural power, and rationalizations for oppression."[8]

Derrida strongly attacks what he calls "logocentrism," the Western culture's love affair with rationality, meaning, and truth. This privileging of reason to understand the world and written texts is really a form of ethnocentrism, and the entire story of philosophy is "a white mythology which assumes and reflects Western culture: the white man takes his own mythology—his logos—that is the mythos of his idom, for the universal form of that which is still his inescapable desire to call reason."[9]

Derrida believes we must deconstruct or take apart a text, including the author's attempt to make sense of the world. The concept of deconstruction is in many ways an illusive one, but it involves, as Derrida puts it, an "overturning and displacing [of] a conceptual order, as well as the nonconceptual order with which the conceptual order is articulated."[10] Deconstruction is necessary because there is no correspondence between the language we employ and the external world we seek to describe. Thus, as Derrida sees it, "There is nothing outside the text,"[11] for all language and attempts at meaning are ultimately self-referential.

Similar ideas are enunciated by Richard Rorty, a philosopher at the University of Virginia. Rorty questions the privileged status of philosophy as the attempt to discern meaning and truth, and he insists that it is more akin to literary criticism or cultural analysis. He accepts an antirealist understanding of language "which does not view knowledge as a matter of getting reality right, but rather as a matter of acquiring habits of action for coping with reality."[12] While Rorty early on utilized the term *postmodern* to describe his thought, in recent years he has employed the term *neo-pragmatism*. As a pragmatist he believes that the correct question to ask is not, What is right? but rather, What is useful? Philosophy has been wrongheaded in its attempt to discern objective reality and truth, for language simply cannot tell us such things. "For the pragmatist, sentences are true not because they correspond to reality, but because they work—because they perform some useful service."[13] He seeks, therefore, an "edifying philosophy" that focuses on the difference a belief or assertion makes in our personal lives or our life together. There are no philosophical starting points, and no one kind of language (i.e., scientific, philosophical, literary, or moral) has preference over another.

Ideas similar to those of Rorty, Derrida, and Lyotard have also been expressed in literary criticism. In recent years, various schools of criticism have questioned metanarrative as a starting point for thought and also raised questions about the adequacy of language. Not all have gone as far as deconstructionism, but reader-based theories have focused less on the intentionality and context of the author and far more on the reader. For example, Stanley Fish and his reader-response criticism argue that the meaning of literary texts are created, not discovered, by the reader. Interpretation thus lies entirely with the readers, for "the text as an entity independent of interpretation . . . drops out and is replaced by the texts that emerge as the consequence of our interpretive activities."[14] For Fish, this does not result in an individualistic interpretation without boundaries, for the interpreter is always part of an interpretive community, which provides the norms, contexts, and limits for the reader.

All of these postmodern thinkers agree that reality and truth cannot be described using modern assumptions about rationality and science. Moreover, most are in agreement that all metanarratives and attempts at interpretation are social constructs and are ultimately bound up with power expressions. To purport to understand a literary work's meaning or to make a statement declared to be true is a form of social control. French philosopher Michel Foucault most emphatically articulated the role of power in our attempts to understand the world.

Foucault's early work focused on the history of mental illness and society's responses to it, along with the origins of the modern penal system. He came to believe that institutions such as asylums, prisons, and hospitals are societies' means of excluding those who do not fit. With the student uprisings of 1968, Foucault began to focus on power and the way in which knowledge expressions are actual renditions of power. Power is part of all relationships and descriptions and is not necessarily negative in nature. But Foucault was particularly interested in the ways in which power could become coercive and thus at times exclude people rather than include them. What needed to be changed, he argued, was not people's consciousness but rather the "political, economic, institutional regime of the production of truth." Moreover, he noted, "It's not a matter of emancipating truth from every system of power (which would be chimera, for truth is already power), but of detaching the power of truth from the forms of hegemony, social, economic, and cultural, within which it operates at the present time."[15]

The notion that power is tied to ideas is particularly evident in Foucault's understanding of sexuality. With regard to sexual norms, he writes, "Rules are empty in themselves, violent and unfinalized; they are impersonal and can be bent to any purpose. The successes of history belong to those who are capable of seizing these rules, to replace those who have used them, to disguise themselves so as to pervert them, invert their meaning, and redirect them against those who had initially imposed them."[16] Because sexuality has no inherent meaning, any attempt to define its meaning or to establish norms is actually a form of repression and coercive power. Indeed, all expressions of philosophical or theological meaning, including all attempts to define truth, are merely forms of coercion.

Because interpretations and attempts to define reality are intimately linked to power and control, many postmodern advocates call for a hermeneutic of suspicion, meaning that we must be suspicious of the ideological backdrop to all interpretations. Some feminist theorists apply this to biblical studies with the assumption that most biblical texts are products of patriarchy and male domination. Thus, Elisabeth Schüssler Fiorenza contends that the "revelatory canon cannot be derived from the Bible itself but can only be formulated in and through women's struggle for liberation from all patriarchal oppression."[17] As a result, as Kevin Vanhoozer puts it, "Interpretive authority lies outside the text, in those social practices that encourage the liberation of women."[18] The hermeneutic of suspicion then puts the emphasis back on the reader, rather than on the author and his or her attempts to convey meaning.

While the discussion thus far has focused primarily on the intellectual currents of postmodernity, it is clear that the tenets of postmodernity have found their way into popular culture and the consciousness of the average person. What have been the effects on Christian ethics, moral discourse in general, and the moral life of human beings? It is quite evident that postmodern reality, whether of the intellectual or the popular variety, has helped to subjectivize truth and morality. In some quarters, truth as a goal or category has almost completely disappeared, while in others, truth is merely the individual preferences and perspectives of a self that is "socially constructed."

The subjectivization of truth and interpretation is well illustrated by Walter Truett Anderson's story of three baseball umpires discussing their philosophy of calling balls and strikes.[19] The one says, "There's balls and there's strikes and I call 'em the way they are." The second ump is less confident. "There's balls and there's strikes and I call 'em the way I see 'em." The third ump vehemently disagrees with both. "There's balls and there's strikes and they ain't nothin' till I call 'em." If umpire number one reflects the modernist sense of certainty about reality, umpire number three clearly reflects the postmodern ethos: Reality is nothing until we call it. Given such subjectivity regarding reality, is it any wonder that moral thinking has increasingly become subjective in its orientation? Stephanie's perspective in the opening narrative seems to be increasingly prevalent in the postmodern age: "There is no inherent meaning in the sexual act. Humans give it meaning, which varies from time to time and place to place. Each community seems to have its own understandings and boundaries about sexual behavior."

All of this seems to lend credence to the frequent observation that postmodernity is inherently relativistic. Relativism, as noted in the last chapter, gained significant impetus in the modern world through the process of pluralization. The plurality of worldviews and moral frameworks seemed to create a psychological disposition toward the idea that there are no moral universals for all times and places. But in the postmodern context, relativism seems to be the overriding posture given the tenets described thus far. Some postmodernists, such as Stanley Fish and Richard Rorty, resist the label of relativism on the grounds that our interpretations are always part of a community that prevents us from flying off into relativistic subjectivism. But this appears to be merely a reinterpretation of relativism, making ethics stable only within a particular moral community. Even if one is able to control the excesses of subjectivity with appeal to community, clearly this interpretation is still a relativism with regard to the world as a whole, for each community of interpretation can create its own moral frames.

Given the subjectivistic view of truth and morals and the inherent relativism that follows, it would appear difficult to make any claims against some of the worst evils known to humankind. In each case of evil that generally makes everyone's list—the Holocaust, slavery, political totalitarianism, genocide—there is no way to appeal to anything beyond the "community of evil" if we take seriously the postmodern framework. Postmodernists may wish to deny the nihilistic implications that seem to flow from their thought, but the implications are real. As Vanhoozer so astutely observes, with postmodern thinkers

there are no "givens": no eternal truths, no limits on what we can say or on how we can differentiate the world. On the one hand, then, the nihilist believes in nothing; on the other hand, he or she says that humans can invent value and truth. Call it *nihilism with a human face:* there is nothing—in the world, in the text—that is not the creation of some human individual or community. The question is: can such nihilism with a human face preserve humanity and human values?[20]

Fragmentation

The fragmentation of life and experiences began already in the modern world with societal differentiation and segmentation. Due to the Industrial Revolution and division of labor, people began to play particular roles in particular places, and their encounters with others were now defined in relation to the roles they performed. In a differentiated society, people experience fragmentation rather than wholeness. The sense that all things are held together by unified systems and ideals is increasingly challenged as life is divided into segmented parts. Modernity's ideal was to seek universals that would bring wholeness to reality and thought, but the social structures and processes of the modern world played havoc with that ideal.

Fragmentation has been exacerbated in the postmodern world, not only by further social processes but also by the intellectual currents that challenge universals and wholeness. Deconstructionism, the questioning of metanarratives, and subjectivity inevitably lead to a fragmentation of thought. In the postmodern world, "all boundaries and distinctions rapidly fall. Some of the losses associated with the collapse of traditional distinctions have been trivial, but others have been earth-shaking, and there seems to be no way to distinguish between the two in a post-modern context."[21]

In today's world, not only do people lack metanarratives or overtly reject them, but the world is also experienced in fragmentary form. That is, people experience reality in bits and pieces without cohesion or a common reference point. Take, for example, the world of communications. The typical sitcom frequently contains several unrelated scenes, with no sense of movement toward a climax or resolution. In fact, one can start watching a show halfway through and not miss much. Classical forms of communication usually started with a problem or dilemma that was worked out throughout the narrative, and it

113

ended with some sort of resolution or climax. There was a sense of movement and pattern to the thought and experiences. In postmodern communications, there is often no discernable movement or climax but merely episodes, often unrelated to one another. In the communications revolution, description and explanation have been replaced by sound bytes, the catchy phrases that grab the listener but convey little information or understanding.

Today, cyberspace has become the quintessential postmodern experience. There is no coherent tie between one site and another, or sometimes even within a given site. The Internet provides a clear signal that we are moving from a linear thought process, a mainstay of modernity, to image, symbol, and preliterate forms of mental construct. We encounter loosely connected sites and images with no mechanism for discerning the worth of one over the other. We are bombarded with millions of pieces of data but have no way to connect that data, see its significance, or discern its interrelationship. As philosophers Mark Taylor and Esa Saarinen describe the Internet, "The register of the imaginary is anarchic. Images proliferate, the net spreads, the volume rises. No one is in control."[22] The computer and cyberspace revolution may be the single most significant factor in moving us toward fragmentation, despite the instantaneous connections they provide.

Pop culture today is a prime example of fragmentation with its appeal to image, the moment, and episodic portrayals that convey little information. One of the most vivid examples of the "meaning in the moment" is popular music. Simon Frith, a pop music scholar, has noted that when we listen to music today, we experience time in a "fragmented and multilinear" fashion. The traditional sense of movement, coherence, and climax in music has given way, says Frith, to "experience grasped in moments." We focus far more on "sounds," which are immediate, as opposed to "music," as a connected structure of notes.[23]

The fragmentation evidenced in pop art is increasingly found in the fine arts as well. Take architecture, for example. Modernist architecture was shaped by the industrial materials and patterns of the industrial era and focused primarily on principles of coherence, order, or organic unity. In the 1970s, however, a group of "postmodern" architects began to argue that the modern forms were too stifling and lacked creativity. They opted for styles that emphasized a blending of various historical traditions, asymmetry, and incompatibilities of patterns and materials. For a period of time in the 1980s, some architects even referred to their work as deconstructionist, emphasizing local themes, as opposed to universal ones, and arbitrariness of connections.

In this postmodern era, religion has also been significantly influenced by fragmentation and has in turn helped to further engender the fragmentation of thought and experiences. Traditional institutions and forms of religion are on the decline, but in direct contradiction to some modern secularization predictions, religion has by no means passed away. Rather, religion is taking on a different face, moving from "institutional religion" to "spirituality" that is drawn from varying sources and expressed in diverse ways. As one GenXer put it, "My spirituality is drawn from Hinduism, Buddhism, Christian and Muslim mysticism, and Native American religion."[24] Princeton sociologist Robert Wuthnow has found that "growing numbers of Americans piece together their faith like a patch work quilt. Spirituality has become a vastly complex quest in which each person seeks . . . his or her own way."[25] In a fragmented world, people hold to religious beliefs and practice rituals that are from disparate traditions and often conflict with each other.

The religious fragmentation is found not only in new forms of religiosity or heterodox formulations. Many observers of evangelical and more classical versions of Christianity believe that religious ideas and services have become commodities, and churches have become "conveyors of this commodity rather than communities that socialize their members into coherent and comprehensive religious outlooks and forms of life."[26] Church members increasingly focus on experience, as opposed to coherent systems of meaning, and borrow from traditions that are frequently at odds with their own community's tradition.

How has this fragmentation influenced Christian ethics and the moral life? At the general cultural level it has left us without the ability to engage in significant moral discourse. Because of a loss of cultural metanarrative and the ensuing fragmentation of outlooks, we can resort to only individual preferences. Alasdair MacIntyre, in his widely discussed *After Virtue,* refers to our current cultural state of moral discourse as emotivism, "The doctrine that all evaluative judgments and more specifically all moral judgments are nothing but expressions of preference, expressions of attitude or feeling."[27] Such judgments are deemed to be neither true nor false, and we are left with only an emotional appeal that can do nothing to resolve our deepest cultural conflicts. Even confidence in law, the ethical minimum of a society, is being eroded. We are increasingly a litigious society but ironically one that has little confidence that the system of law and the judicial process can render anything other than a biased verdict that reflects someone's self-interest or ideology.

Within the Christian ethics orbit, cultural and societal fragmentation create an ethos in which appeal to the Christian worldview becomes difficult—even for Christians, for they too experience the fragmented world and thus think in fragmented forms. The appeal to a foundation of the Triune God and the Christian worldview of creation, fall, redemption, and eschaton is difficult when people no longer view reality with a sense of coherence and wholeness. The attempt to develop consistency of thought and application within the Christian worldview and ethic is a major challenge. As a result of fragmentation we lack the ability to discern which values and virtues are most significant for the moral life and which ideas and images can truly guide our ethical thinking.

Tolerance, the Great Virtue

In the postmodern context, one virtue is heralded above all others; indeed, for some it is the only virtue: tolerance. The appeal to tolerance began amid the pluralism of the modern world, but today it has become the norm above all norms, the decisive factor in moral issues for large numbers of people. Of course, not all people gladly embrace tolerance, and thus we find ourselves in a culture in which people cannot converse well about controversial issues. As church historian Martin Marty once observed, "One of the real problems in modern life is that the people who are good at being civil often lack strong convictions, and people who have strong convictions often lack civility."[28] One has only to listen to radio talk shows to know Marty is right.

Tolerance is defined in various ways. One definition states, "A fair and objective attitude toward those whose opinions, practices, race, religion, nationality, etc. differ from one's own; freedom from bigotry."[29] It is not at all clear that postmodern tolerance focuses on the "fair and objective" dimension, for postmodernism is skeptical about the possibility of objective assessment. Thus, today tolerance often means simply tolerating any and all views. Ironically, in a culture often driven by political correctness, some beliefs and moral commitments are not tolerated. Postmodern tolerance seems to incorporate the idea that people have a moral right not to be offended; therefore, any worldview or moral stance that some find offensive is not legitimate.

One clear example of this view concerns a 1989 edition of the *Atlantic Monthly*. Political philosopher Glenn Tinder wrote an article titled "Can We Be Good without God?" which elicited the largest outpouring of mail in the magazine's history. "Some of the mail was filled with contempt for the suggestion that biblical notions about the sacrality of the individual were necessary for the sustenance of any humanly decent polity. Religious ideas were neither necessary nor . . . welcome in the discussion of fundamental political values."[30] Tolerance, therefore, is a virtue with limits, and increasingly the postmodern contempt for truth and strong conviction means that tolerance will not be honored for all beliefs and morals, especially those of classical Christianity or those relegated to the private sphere. Indeed, the privatization factor is closely tied to postmodern views of tolerance. Stan Gaede says that today "we choose beliefs the way we choose an entree at a restaurant, taking whatever juicy morsel pleases our palates. This not only puts the self at the center of choice-making activity—thereby erecting a new overarching worldview, with the self playing god—but also puts great pressure on those who are trying to persuade others. . . . The pressure is to make one's beliefs conform to consumer demand."[31]

How did tolerance end up as the supreme virtue—and how did it take its current shape? Gaede believes that the transition from truth to tolerance began with the two great revolutions of the modern world, the French Revolution and the Industrial Revolution. During the French Revolution, truth was separated not just from a particular tradition but from any tradition. The philosophical shapers of the Revolution "conceived of truth as independent of community, and . . . made each individual the captain of his or her own ship of truth. Truth, in other words, was now democratized with a vengeance."[32] With the Industrial Revolution, says Gaede, traditional ties and relationships were severed, and natural forms of community diminished. Choice—not only concerning the purchase of products and places to live but also personal beliefs—became normative. As the individual became more autonomous, the push for tolerance increased. In the postmodern world, with its social construction of reality and subjectivity, tolerance became the reigning virtue.

The primacy of tolerance as a virtue in the postmodern world places the moral emphasis on the individual and one's feelings and choices. It is well illustrated by this statement from Madonna, one of the popular embodiments of the postmodern ethos:

> In all my work, my thing has always been not to be ashamed. . . . People are afraid of their own feelings and I am saying: don't be afraid. It's ok to have whatever feeling you have. . . . If people were comfortable with the way they felt—they didn't feel like they had to play all these different roles for society and other people, if they just could be honest about who they were this world would be a better place.[33]

One of the upshots of tolerance for ethics is that many issues are rendered amoral. Rather than seeing issues as moral in nature, they are seen as matters of personal choice. The language utilized to describe many issues (i.e., abortion, euthanasia, homosexual behavior, reproductive technologies) is no longer the language of morality but rather the language of choice and personal preference. For example, Dr. Panayiotis Zavos, an infertility specialist, has indicated that he and his team want to be the first to produce a human clone. When asked about the ethical implications, Zavos said, "Ethics is a wonderful world, but we need to look beyond the ethical issues here. It's not an ethical issue. It's a medical issue. We have a duty here. Some people need this to complete the life cycle, to reproduce."[34] The most significant element in this statement is Zavos's insistence that cloning is a duty (the traditional language of morality) but that the issue is not ethical in nature. Tolerance as a virtue breeds this outlook.

Of course, as Christians we must be committed to a form of toleration and civility concerning matters of difference in society and among our own communities. Christian history contains ugly moments when truth was made coercive without a spirit of civility and an ability to allow for variations, both in the church and in society. The issue for Christians is not that commitments to truth and conviction are incompatible with tolerance. Rather, the problem is making tolerance the ultimate virtue, the moral trump card. "Adopting tolerance as an end in itself—as a good, as an ethic—is not the only way to achieve forbearance, and in the long run it is self-defeating. For ultimately the ethic of tolerance undermines the reason for one's convictions and renders them nonsensical."[35] Christians must learn the art of civility in church and society, and given the differing worldview assumptions and the nature of human sin, we will need to "tolerate" many things in a fallen order that are inimical to our faith. But the pursuit of such tolerance is never an end in itself or the ultimate virtue. Our commitment to tolerance arises out of our commitments to truth and justice, which are rooted in the nature and actions of God. The foundation makes all the difference in the world.

Ultimately, tolerance as the prime virtue has no way to ground our moral life and prevent the worst abuses imaginable. Such tolerance tends to render God's judgment on moral evil a moot point. As Richard Mouw notes, "It may be that our failure to think and speak about divine judgment is closely related to our refusal to face the reality of human evil. Even more important: it may have something to do with how much we actually feel the reality of human evil."[36] Such is the fruit of tolerance when it is the only or even the supreme virtue.

The Triumph of the Therapeutic

In the postmodern world, men and women increasingly look at the world through a new lens and make their moral judgments within a new framework—the therapeutic. The language employed today for most issues generally focuses on the self: self-actualization, personal well-being, feeling good about oneself, and self-assuredness. It is the language of therapy, and it focuses less on how to conform oneself to moral designs or requirements and more on how to conform the moral demands to one's own personal selfhood.

In 1966, sociologist Philip Rieff wrote his penetrating analysis of shifting, cultural frameworks for moral life, *The Triumph of the Therapeutic*. Written before the onslaught of postmodern thought and experiences, Rieff's work was in many ways prophetic of the direction cultural morality would move over the next decades. Rieff believed that in the modern world morality and religion were being separated. The previous system, which focused largely on a moral culture of commitment, was giving way to a new system in which the cultural center was the self and the symbolic framework for making moral judgments was therapy. Humans were moving away from old conceptions of good and evil and their mechanisms of behavioral control to a cultural system in which the "self, improved, is the ultimate concern of modern culture." We have come "to specialize at last, wittingly, in techniques that are to be called, in the present volume, 'therapeutic,' with nothing at stake beyond a manipulatable sense of well-being. This is the unreligion of the age, and its master science."[37]

Rieff contended that since Sigmund Freud the educated and leisure-oriented classes had come to believe that a "moral demand system" could never again compel inner obedience to moral rules. Affluence had engendered an ethos in which a person's enjoyment of life was a primary goal. People now "feel freer to live their lives with a minimum of pretense to anything more grand than sweetening the time."[38] As Rieff saw it, even religion had acquiesced to the therapeutic model, and there was no turning back. As a result, he was not optimistic about the future of Western culture. With prophetic injunction, Rieff wrote:

> Emancipated from an ethic of hard work, Americans have also grown morally less self-demanding. They have been released from the old system of self-demands by a convergence of doctrines that do not resort to new restrictions but rather propose jointly the superiority of all that money can buy, technology can make, and science can conceive.[39]

An examination of the way moral education is conceived in the United States provides a clear sense that therapy is the *modus operandi* for developing character. James Davison Hunter, a sociologist at the University of Virginia, has clearly demonstrated this in *The Death of Character: Moral Education in an Age without Good or Evil.* Contemporary moral education, argues Hunter, does just the opposite of what it intends; it undermines the very possibility of forming essential ingredients needed for character. "Character is dead. . . . The social and cultural conditions that make character possible are no longer present and no amount of political rhetoric, legal maneuvering, educational policy making, or money can change that reality. Its time has passed."[40] Why the failure of moral education? Hunter believes we have replaced character with a focus on personality; hence, the reigning framework today is the human self with its own ability to develop values steeped in self-esteem.

Hunter analyzes the history of moral education in America and finds that already in the mid-twentieth century personality language was replacing character language, with primary attention given to self-regard and personal happiness. He cites psychologist Gordon Allport, who contended that character was an ethical concept. As such, "The psychologist does not need the term at all; personality alone will serve."[41] By the 1970s, values clarification was being taught in many public schools. Students were encouraged to develop their own values—free from any religion, community, or tradition—with self-esteem or self-actualization as the foundation. Hunter finds that since that time the triumph of the therapeutic has flourished in the numerous character education programs employed in educational and even religious institutions. He attempts to show that "the dominant thrust of psychology has been *affective*. In the field, the centerpiece of this orientation has been the emotions surrounding one's

119

own self-concept and well-being captured in the concept of 'self-esteem.' We are told that children who feel good about themselves . . . are less likely to take drugs, will be sexually responsible, and will be more tolerant of others." Thus, one recent character development program tells students they should be kind because it makes "you feel really good about yourself," and "consideration colors the world in brighter, happier hues."[42] Even the newer forms of moral education that use a more personal-disciplined or religious approach have succumbed to the therapeutic model. One program, *Growing Up Caring,* shows a girl looking at another's answers while taking a test. The caption reads, "Cheating, in any form, is bad for your self-esteem."[43]

Hunter believes these approaches to character and moral development undermine what they attempt to do, precisely because the therapeutic foundation is a wrongheaded approach. In assessing studies that have been done on the effectiveness of the many contemporary programs, he concludes, "There is little or no association, causal or otherwise, between psychological well-being and moral conduct, and psychologically oriented moral education programs have little or no positive effect upon moral behavior."[44] Such approaches are not merely strategies or pedagogies but the heart of a worldview that undermines the development of character by focusing on personal self-esteem.

The triumph of the therapeutic in the postmodern context is by no means only a secular enterprise. It has had a powerful impact on churches and religious institutions. David Wells, in *Losing Our Virtue,* tells a tale of two spiritualities, the classical and the postmodern. "The latter begins, not so much with sin as morally framed, but with sin as psychologically experienced, not so much with sin in relation to God, but with sin in relation to ourselves . . . our anxiety, pain, and disillusionment." As Wells sees it, God in this spirituality is "valued to the extent that he is able to bathe these wounds, assuage these insecurities, calm these fears, restore some sense of internal order."[45] He sees this form of spirituality evident in the preaching and worship of many contemporary churches and denominations.

Such a spirituality has deeply influenced our moral lives. Classical understandings of virtue have given way to a moral life that gives free reign to the desires of a self that seeks to save itself through personal well-being and happiness. Wells believes that therapists have assumed a major role in the postmodern culture with their attempts at enabling people to find meaning and connections in life from within themselves. "This is often done under the language of enhancing the self, of enabling it to transcend itself, rather than of limiting self through moral obligation, service, self-sacrifice, and commitment to others. Self technique thus becomes the new moral nurturing."[46] What is most striking to Wells about this paradigm is its ubiquity throughout culture, including the evangelical church.

The therapeutic has triumphed in a host of moral issues, but its reign is perhaps most visible in sexual ethics. In recent decades, sexual behavior has changed, but so has the way people think about sexual relations. Philip Turner of Yale notes that this fundamental shift hinges on views of the moral self. The "reformists" in matters sexual emphasize primarily loving relationships, wholeness, and fulfillment as the keys to sexual meaning. In this view, says Turner, "It is simply the case that sexual relations are 'natural' to 'embodied' life, and so may be . . . necessary for the wholeness and fulfillment of the individuals no matter what their marital status, sexual orientation, or gender identification may be."[47] The moral acceptability of sexual relations then is not set by divine providence but rather by the motivations and intentions of moral agents and the consequences of their acts. According to the reformist ethic, there is no inherent right or wrong; sexual morality is determined by matters such as commitment, openness, vulnerability, and care.

In this new view of sexual life, Turner sees two primary words that define the moral universe—person and self—words that, as shown, are clearly connected to the triumph of the therapeutic. He utilizes the work of Charles Taylor[48] to probe the meaning of this "moral self" that has become the center of the new sexual philosophies and practices. Taylor notes three assumptions about the self in current moral understanding: The self is defined by inwardness or subjectivity; the self's sphere of activity is everyday life; and the self in everyday life seeks to discover personal abilities that are put into practice. Along with these notions of self, Taylor points to three moral ideas that govern the moral activities of people: benevolence, justice as a guarantee of rights, and suffering as an evil that must by all means be eliminated. Given these basic assumptions, Turner writes, "Neither the person nor the self is now thought to flourish within a providence that directs the undertakings of their lives. Rather, both are said to flourish or not as a result of the intentions and choices that flow from their inner depths." With such an understanding of the moral self, he notes, "It is, therefore, easy to understand why more and more people believe that it is wrong to deny a sexual relation to oneself or to anyone else simply on the basis of marital status, sexual orientation, or gender identification. To do so is tantamount to denial of one's sexuality and so oneself."[49]

While Turner does not use the phrase "triumph of the therapeutic," his analysis of the sexual revolution clearly points in that direction. In contrast to such perceptions of the postmodern self, Turner wisely adds, "If Christians are asked to say 'no' to sexual relations outside the bond of marriage, it is because they are called upon to honor God by saying 'yes' to a providential ordering of life intended both for the glory of God and our individual and common good."[50]

With the triumph of the therapeutic, it is easy to understand why postmodernists confuse ethics with pastoral care, as discussed in the introduction to this book. Increasingly, in regard to a host of issues, people respond on the basis of what will make them feel assuaged of their guilt, grant them a sense of self-esteem, and nurture relationships based on self-actualization. Such is a thin fabric with which to construct our moral lives in a complex society.

Conclusion

Whether viewed as an extension of the modern world or as a new era in its own right, postmodernity signals new modes of thinking and significantly influences the moral life and ethical reflection. The intellectual tenets—such as deconstructionism, the questioning of metanarratives, the social construction of reality, and the coercive power of ideas—combine with the cultural trends—fragmentation, the reign of tolerance, and the triumph of the therapeutic—to transform most traditional conceptions of ethics.

For some, postmodernity is the great liberation from self-assured moral legalism, while for others it is equivalent to "the great whore of Babylon." As noted in the last chapter, Christians should be careful in their assessments of historical movements. Christian hope is never found in the ever changing forces of history. And postmodernity can teach us a thing or two. It reminds us that "we see through a glass darkly" and that all our perceptions of reality transpire within a sociocultural context. The postmodern critique of scientism and technological progress should be welcomed by believers who know there is more to reality than what science can discover and deliver. Moreover, the critique of systems of certainty can in part be accepted, for we must acknowledge that at times we have loved our systems of theology over the God of theology. The drive for certainty can be every bit as much a form of idolatry, erected to dispel our own insecurities, as the idols of the postmodern therapeutic self. And we must acknowledge that the rationalism of Enlightenment modernity, so scathingly critiqued by postmodern philosophers, was rarely a true friend to biblical faith. The postmodernists remind us that humans cannot live by mind alone.

But there are concerns, very real concerns. If we take the postmodern epistemology (or lack thereof) seriously, we seem to be left with a nihilism that undermines much we hold dear as Christians. It is noteworthy that most of the postmodern tenets explored in this chapter fly in the face of almost every approach to ethics known in history, not just Christian ethics. From a Christian standpoint, we must affirm that there is a metanarrative in the Bible, and its story of creation, fall, redemption, and eschaton is unparalleled in its ability both to make sense of reality and to ground our everyday morality. Deconstructionism, the subjectivity of belief, and the commitment to a freedom from all inherent meaning are clearly at odds with the work and teachings of Jesus, who said, "If you continue in my word, you are truly my disciples; and you will know the truth, and the truth will make you free" (John 8:31–32). From the beginning of time, God has spoken, including through the written Word, which guides us to know and do the will of God, albeit with humility and thanksgiving.

Even without the specific critique of the Christian metanarrative, there are concerns. As Kevin Vanhoozer puts it:

Deconstructive ethics amounts to an iconoclastic gesture followed by a shrug of the shoulders: first resistance, then undecidability. There is no escape from context, no escape from a plurality of possible meanings. Yet, at the end of the day, must we not say, decide, *do* something? Or is undoing ultimately a manner of *not* doing? If the responsibilities of the reader are merely negative—"Thou shalt not impose coherence and finality"—then is it ever possible to move beyond the ethics of prohibition to an ethic of love.[51]

And while the modern world was filled with its false gods, pride and holocausts, we must also recognize that the postmodern world is no golden era. "Against the secularizing and cosmopolitan currents of modernity there now arises anew, in frightening degree, old religious passions, buried ethnic nationalism, atavistic loyalties, and venomous worship of the tribe."[52] Replacing universals with parochialisms has not brought justice and mercy.

The context of our times is now clearly a postmodern one, though much of modernity continues. To articulate the gospel, the biblical story, and the Christian ethic that flows from its foundation, we will need to make connections to that postmodern world while not succumbing to its assumptions and agenda. Paul's admonition is more timely than ever: "Do not be conformed to this world, but be transformed by the renewing of your minds, so that you may discern what is the will of God—what is good and acceptable and perfect" (Rom. 12:2).

PART 3

MAKING ETHICAL DECISIONS

Having examined both the foundations of ethics and the contexts in which we do ethics, we now turn to how we make ethical decisions. Many Christians assume that the method we employ is the most salient feature in determining our stance on moral issues. But as demonstrated, decision-making patterns are actually rooted in a larger narrative or worldview that establishes the fabric of the moral decision. Methodology alone is not the crucial issue. Nonetheless, within the foundational framework of a worldview, the actual process of making a decision is extremely important. In an era in which the focus has tilted toward character ethics, decision making is often neglected.

This part of the book begins by exploring in chapter 6 the ways Christians throughout history have made ethical decisions, drawing on a typology from Edward L. Long. Chapter 7 deals with the pivotal issues surrounding the Bible in making ethical decisions: biblical authority, hermeneutics, and the kinds of ethical material in Scripture. Then chapter 8 explores a matter often overlooked in ethical decisions, the empirical judgments, or judgments of facts, that accompany every ethical issue we face. Understanding historical paradigms, God's Word, and contemporary realities are pivotal in choosing the good in a complex world.

6

THREE MOTIFS FOR MAKING
ETHICAL DECISIONS

Bernard Adeney tells the following story from one of his ethics classes at New College in Berkeley, California.

> One of my students excused himself at the break to make a call to Haiti. He was facing a crisis that required an immediate decision. In the hour following the break he shared his story with the class. "James" is a fundraiser for a Christian development organization that provides financial and other resources to indigenous Christian organizations in two-thirds world countries. James had organized a team of physicians, nurses and other health-care professionals to visit Haiti for several weeks and set up rural clinics. The health needs of the poverty-stricken people were extreme, and the clinics were expecting to offer help that in some cases would be life-saving. The team was made up of Christians who had donated their time and expenses. Arrangements for the clinics had been made by local Haitian churches. Airline tickets for the team of twenty-five people had been purchased at a cost of thousands of dollars. They were discounted tickets and could not be refunded or changed. Thousands of dollars' worth of medical supplies had been shipped to Haiti months beforehand. The team was due to fly to Haiti that weekend.
>
> The problem was that the medical supplies had been sitting on the dock in customs for weeks. The main Haitian organizer, a pastor, said customs officials were waiting for a bribe. Appeals had been made to higher officials, but to no avail. Time was running out. Because the stakes were so high, the pastor urged James to authorize a substantial payment immediately. Without the supplies the clinics could not be set up. So much work and so much potential good hung in the balance.[1]

What should James do and why? How should he make this moral decision from a Christian perspective? My own students have grappled with this case study, and their responses have usually fallen into one of three categories.

Some students respond by saying that we must employ reason and common sense to discern the moral good. In this case, it is reasonable to pay the bribe, which is, after all, a cultural custom. There is so much good to be gained and so much to be lost if the medical supplies are not available that it should be clear to any thinking person that in this case a bribe is morally legitimate. Other students respond by appealing to Scripture. They point out that Scripture not only explicitly forbids bribes (i.e., Ps. 26:10; Amos 5:12) but also enjoins us to obey the laws of a country. In most countries, even if bribery is widely practiced, it is nonetheless illegal. Some students, appealing to Scripture, arrive at a different conclusion using essentially the same methodology. They argue that this is a case of two biblical principles in conflict: the principle of repudiating bribes and the principle of doing good to those in need, especially in life-threatening situations. In this case, doing good to those in need is the overriding biblical principle. Still others argue that this is a situation in which Christians must pray, discern the immediate leading of the Holy Spirit, and do what seems to be most in keeping with the Spirit of Christ.

Each of these responses represents a major tradition in Christian ethics. Edward L. Long argues that throughout the history of the Christian church there have been essentially three main ways (or motifs) of formulating ethical norms and making moral decisions. One way involves an appeal to reason, as shown by the first group of students, and is known as the deliberative motif. The second way relies on explicit statements in Scripture, as did the second group of students, and is called the prescriptive motif. The third motif involves the more immediate and direct leading of God, as evidenced by the third group of students, and is called the relational motif. Long states that no one individual or group fits perfectly into a given type, but one of the three motifs tends to be dominant in the ethical decisions of most Christian thinkers.[2] This chapter explores these three motifs, revealed in the thinking of various ethicists and theologians throughout the history of Christianity, and discusses the strengths and weaknesses of each motif.

The Deliberative Motif

In this approach, says Long, reason is seen as synonymous with divine revelation or a supplement to revelation for the task of making ethical decisions. For some Christians, reason is the source of moral judgments, and Christian ethics is "subsumed under the rubrics of philosophy." For others, reason and philosophical reflection are employed to serve theological commitments. "In the first, a rationally autonomous philosophy is the master of Christian judgment; in the second, moral philosophy is the tool of Christian ethics."[3] The first form has been most prominent in Roman Catholic moral theology, while the second form is found among assorted Protestant thinkers.

The deliberative motif rests on the assumption that reason can be a moral guide because God has implanted a natural law within human consciousness that all can comprehend. Many find this approach helpful for several reasons.

First, it speaks to all people, not just Christians who accept divine revelation. Thus, it has the potential to extend Christian ethics beyond the boundaries of the church and those who accept the gospel. Second, it is argued, neither the Bible nor Jesus provides everything we need to know to make ethical decisions in the modern world. Many of the issues we face are not even indirectly addressed in divine revelation; thus, we must supplement with reason. Third, many find it appealing to do ethics in accord with what is natural within the world and human nature. Adherents of the deliberative approach want to recognize the sinfulness of human nature, but they contend that God's will for human life does not run contrary to our essential humanness nor to the essential nature of the created world. There is a natural *telos* or end to the created world, and ethics works toward that naturally known end, not against it.

Thomas Aquinas and the Roman Catholic Tradition

Without doubt, the best examples of the deliberative motif are Thomas Aquinas and the classic Roman Catholic tradition. Aquinas was a thirteenth-century theologian who is best remembered for synthesizing the philosophy of Aristotle with Christian thought. Born in Italy, he eventually taught at the University of Paris, where his thinking had a powerful influence. It is sometimes said that subsequent Roman Catholic theology was basically a footnote to Aquinas's thinking, either in terms of affirming or attempting to correct it. At the heart of his work, in bringing together Christian theology with Aristotle's philosophy, is the belief that the truths of faith and those of sense experience (i.e., Aristotle) are fully compatible and complementary. Some truths, such as the Trinity or incarnation, can be known only through divine revelation, while others, such as the nature of material things, can be known only through experience. Still others, such as the existence of God, are known through both revelation and sense experience.

In moral decisions, as in theology, Aquinas believed humans can be guided by reason because God is ultimate or pure reason and, as beings made in his image, we reflect something of that pure rationality. We may sometimes be faulty in our reasoning, but that is because we do not follow true rationality; it is not the fault of reason itself. Deliberation is not autonomous since it is rooted in God, and thus it can make a contribution to ethics apart from divine revelation. A nonbeliever can therefore gain a partial and yet valid knowledge of God and the divine will. Through natural means a nonbeliever can discover something of the good life that God has ordained. God's grace is imperative for salvation and the ultimate vision of God, yet grace does not destroy nature but rather perfects it; thus, natural reason can serve faith.

The moral life, as Aquinas saw it, revolves around habits or dispositions of the human self. "Habit implies a disposition in relation to a thing's nature, and to its operation or end, by reason of which disposition a thing is well or ill dis-

129

posed thereto."[4] In human behavior, some habits are good and are called virtues, while other habits are bad and are called vices. The knowledge of moral virtues and vices comes from a natural law that all humans can know through reason. The virtues include (as they did for Aristotle) wisdom, justice, temperance, and courage. These basic virtues provide the essential norms necessary for a good society, and Aquinas believed we can expect moral virtue in all human beings and in all societies. This does not imply that all societies will be equally good nor that moral education is nonessential. Indeed, because of the human will and passions, people often resist the virtues they know they ought to seek and form false habits that destroy human goodness and God-ordained patterns. Moreover, these moral virtues are not sufficient for salvation. For salvation we need God's grace and the higher or theological virtues of faith, hope, and charity, which are known only by divine revelation.

The deliberative motif in Aquinas's thinking is particularly evident in his discussion of law. He believed there are four kinds of law that have an intimate relation to one another: eternal law, natural law, human or positive law, and divine law. The eternal law, founded in God's wisdom and very being, is not a law independent of God but is the eternal source of all reality, including all other forms of law. "The end of Divine government is God himself, and his law is not distinct from himself. Wherefore the eternal law is not ordained to another end."[5] While humans can never know the eternal law in its essence, by analogy we can know something of it through the other forms of law.

Natural law, the second form, is the portion of eternal law known by all human beings. Aquinas argued that "all things partake somewhat of the eternal law, in so far as, namely, from its being imprinted on them, they derive their respective inclinations to their proper acts and ends. . . . This participation of the eternal law in the rational creature is called the natural law."[6] From natural law we gain self-evident principles that guide us in the practical realities of everyday life, including the moral life. All things toward which humanity has a natural inclination in accordance with the laws of nature are apprehended by this practical reason. There is in human nature an inclination to know the truth, live in society with others, have offspring, and do good—all of which are reflections of the natural law. This natural law is the same for all human beings, even if they fail to live up to that which they intuitively and rationally know to be the right and the good. Because this law is unchanging and in accordance with the nature of all created things, it forms the first principle from which all other moral principles are drawn.

The third kind of law is human or positive law, the enacted law of a society. Civil laws, according to Aquinas, are to be consistent with natural law, but they are framed "not for any private benefit, but for the common good of all the citizens. Hence human laws should be proportionate to the common good."[7] Human laws, he states, are not to be prescribed for every virtue and vice but only for those virtues and vices pertaining to the common good.

Though these laws are commensurate with and flow from natural law, they can change in accordance with various needs and situations as long as they do not contradict natural law or the natural ends of that law. Aquinas was aware that in a fallen world this ideal is not always met and that at times unjust laws emerge. What then? "That which is not just seems to be no law at all; wherefore the force of a law depends on the extent of its justice. . . . Consequently every human law has just so much of the nature of law, as it is derived from the law of nature. But if in any point it deflects from the law of nature, it is no longer a law but a perversion of law."[8] In such situations, people need not observe the precept.

The final form of law is divine law, the explicit law of God in the Old and New Testaments. This law constitutes the portion of God's designs and truth that cannot be known by reason or natural law. It encompasses salvation and the higher virtues (or theological virtues) of faith, hope, and charity. "Just as the principal intention of human law is to create friendship between man and man; so the chief intention of the Divine law is to establish man in friendship with God."[9] The divine law encompasses some things that are known by reason, such as most of the Ten Commandments, but it goes deeper and further in seeing the law in relation to God and true faith.

Since Christian ethics focuses on virtues and vices that are known naturally through human deliberation, Aquinas believed that ethical issues can be decided by natural reason that is available to all. His deliberative approach to moral decision making can be seen, for example, in his discussion of war. Aquinas made some references to Scripture in his discussion, but he appealed primarily to reason in setting forth three criteria that must be met for war to be legitimate. First, the war must be declared by a legitimate authority. "It is not the business of a private individual to declare war, because he can seek for redress of his rights from the tribunal of his superior."[10] Second, there must be a just cause. A war based on a just cause is not vindictive but "avenges wrongs when a nation or state has to be punished, for refusing to make amends for the wrongs inflicted by its subjects, or to restore what it has seized unjustly."[11] Third, there must be a rightful intention, namely, the advancement of good and the avoidance of evil. Aquinas contended that there is a wrongful use of the sword, and thus not all wars are legitimate. At times, however, war and violence are not only just but morally necessary for the common good. The heart of his moral argument was grounded in reason.

Modern Roman Catholic Thought

Aquinas's use of natural law became a mainstay in Roman Catholic moral theology. All moral decisions could be made on the basis of reason, because all humans could discern both the natural end of any human endeavor and the moral legitimacy of any human action. For this reason, traditional Roman

Catholic thought held the same moral standards for all individuals and all nations. There was no moral dualism that distinguished the ethics of the church from the ethics of the world.

When the papacy sets forth moral instruction for the faithful, it is understood to be instruction for all the world. In the middle of the twentieth century, Pope Pius XII lamented the growing evils of modern culture and appealed to objective standards discerned by reason to combat their effects:

> Before all else, it is certain that the radical and ultimate cause of the evils which We deplore in modern society is the denial and rejection of a universal norm of morality as well for individual and social life as for international relations; We mean the disregard, so common nowadays, for the forgetfulness of the natural law itself, which has its foundation in God, Almighty Creator and Father of all, supreme and absolute Lawgiver, allwise and just judge of human action.[12]

A more contemporary rendition of natural law thinking is reflected in Richard McCormick, long-time professor of moral theology at the University of Notre Dame. McCormick believes that the Christian faith does not offer new content to the ethics that all humans can know by reason, for Christian morality is at heart human morality. He writes, "There is a material identity between Christian moral demands and those perceivable by reason. Whatever is distinct about Christian morality is found essentially in the style of life, the manner of accomplishing the moral tasks common to all men, not in the tasks themselves."[13] The values and principles discerned by reason reflect basic inclinations of human beings and include such things as the "tendency to preserve life; the tendency to mate and raise children; the tendency to seek out other men and obtain their approval—friendship; . . . the tendency to use intelligence in guiding action; the tendency to develop skills and exercise them in play and in the fine arts."[14] It is from these objective values and first principles evident in all humans that we can discern other derivative values and principles and thus choose the highest good in any moral situation.

Protestant Versions of Deliberation

Among Protestant ethicists, the deliberative motif has usually taken the form of placing Christian norms in philosophical categories. Long notes, for example, the work of Adolf Harnack, one of the prime thinkers of modernist or classical liberal theology in the early part of the twentieth century. For Harnack, the Christian moral norms of love and mercy were central and could be expressed in philosophical language such as the phrase "the infinite value of the human soul."[15] Paul Ramsey, one of the noted Christian ethicists in the mid to late twentieth century, set forth an understanding of Christian love that was reminiscent of philosophical idealism. While rejecting a code morality,

Ramsey argued for specific, concrete moral decisions on the basis of "disinterested love for the neighbor."[16] And though he attacked the liberal theology of Harnack, Reinhold Niebuhr utilized categories that were similar to those of Harnack. Employing reason and the broad Christian understanding of sin, Niebuhr argued that the ethical ideal of love could never become a reality on earth, especially in its social and structural dimensions. Christian love is the "impossible possibility" that judges all human actions but can never be used in idealistic fashion to make ethical decisions for corporations, institutions, and nations.[17]

Some deliberative thinkers have employed not reason per se but other forms of human reflection such as scientific understanding, imagination, or even intuition. One of the best contemporary examples of this broader form of deliberation is James Gustafson. He downplays the role of rationality, but as Long notes, "His concept of discernment involves moral reasoning in a broad sense that includes empathy, appreciation, imagination, and sensitivity in approaching issues."[18] Gustafson often begins his moral reflection with a consideration of human experience in general and in recent years has given particular attention to the normative insights of the sciences, both the hard and the behavioral sciences. He believes that the "act of moral discernment is impossible to program and difficult to describe. It involves perceptivity, discrimination, subtlety, sensitivity, clarity, rationality and accuracy. And while some . . . seem to have it as a 'gift of the gods,' others achieve it by experience and training, by learning and acting."[19] Gustafson's broader use of the deliberative motif and particularly his employment of scientific understanding has become increasingly evident among many other ethicists in recent years, as is evidenced in bioethics, discussions about homosexuality, and sexual ethics in general. In this approach, biblical foundations are often supplanted by scientific norms.

Some Christian thinkers, especially those with more classical and evangelical leanings, have seen deliberation primarily as a means to connect explicit Christian moral expectations with modern and postmodern humanity—that is, an apologetic use. C. S. Lewis is a good example of this approach in that he believed there is a natural law that can guide the general behavior of people but has the particular role of pointing them to their own condition before and need of God. Lewis argued that "human beings, all over the earth, have this curious idea that they ought to behave in a certain way, and cannot really get rid of it." But, said Lewis, "They do not in fact behave in that way. . . . These two facts are the foundation of all clear thinking about ourselves and the universe we live in."[20] From this moral knowledge he went on to argue that the source of that knowledge is God. Elsewhere, Lewis wrote:

> For my part, I believe we ought to work not only at spreading the gospel (that certainly) but also at a certain preparation for the gospel. It is necessary to recall many to the Law of Nature before we talk about God. For Christ promises forgiveness of sin: but what is

that to those who since they do not know the law of nature, do not know that they have sinned? Who will take medicine unless he knows he is in the grip of disease? Moral relativity is the enemy we have to overcome before we tackle atheism.[21]

In similar fashion, Kenneth Myers of the Mars Hill tape series argues that a natural law is intrinsic in the moral order of creation. Natural law certainly does not exhaust God's law, but it can play a particularly significant role in commending God's designs to the larger society. Myers notes that telling a contemporary "pagan that he has disobeyed God's Word is likely to have little rhetorical power. Telling him that he has, in C. S. Lewis's terms, gone 'against the grain of the universe' might well pack a bit more rhetorical punch, especially if the inevitability of cosmic splinters is spelled out." Myers finds biblical law language easy to ignore in our postmodern world, but "there does remain some sympathy in our culture, however confused, for the idea that things have an essential nature."[22]

Critique of the Deliberative Motif

How should we assess the deliberative approach in its various forms? First, we must note the Bible's affirmation that God's designs can be known by nature. In Romans 1, the apostle Paul argues that God's wrath against unrighteousness is legitimate, "For what can be known about God is plain to them, because God has shown it to them. Ever since the creation of the world his eternal power and divine nature, invisible though they are, have been understood and seen through the things he has made. So they are without excuse" (Rom. 1:19–20). In the next chapter, Paul speaks of Gentiles, who though not having the law, "Do instinctively what the law requires. . . . They show that what the law requires is written on their hearts, to which their own conscience also bears witness" (2:14–15). These passages clearly show that human beings have at least some knowledge of God and his law; therefore, they bear a responsibility for the knowledge they have. What is less clear is the extent of that knowledge. It is also significant that nowhere does the Bible point to this notion of natural law as a guide for believers. The natural law is explained with reference to unbelievers or at least Gentiles, those without God's direct, special revelation.

A second positive aspect of the deliberative approach is that it rings true to the experience of people throughout history. Human beings seem to have a rational or at least intuitive sense of the reality of transcendence and some cognizance of God's moral designs. Murder, adultery, theft, lying, cheating, and injustice are almost universally condemned as violations of something that is innately precious to men and women. Humans tend by nature to perceive this. As noted above, this kind of moral sense has strong appeal, for it does not depend on a personal commitment to Christ and an acceptance of God's Word as authority.

But while the deliberative motif contains some positive aspects, it also contains some weaknesses and challenges in regard to making ethical decisions. One of the primary critiques is that it overestimates rationality as a guide. Many have suggested that it does not fully appreciate the fallenness of reason and hence its proclivity to mislead in the same way that the will and passions can mislead. After all, "the message about the cross is foolishness to those who are perishing. . . . For since, in the wisdom of God, the world did not know God through wisdom, God decided, through the foolishness of our proclamation, to save those who believe" (1 Cor. 1:18, 21). Of course, one might argue that while knowledge of Christ and salvation are antithetical to natural wisdom, human morality is not. But in the New Testament, ethical teachings are always set in the context of the gospel, the message of the cross and the resurrection.

This then leads to a second major concern regarding the deliberative approach: It tends to divorce ethics from larger worldview foundations (chapter 3). While appeal to natural law is a means for making ethical decisions, it often breeds an autonomous ethics that is separated from the nature and actions of God and the biblical drama of creation, fall, redemption, and consummation. Biblical morality, however, is always a response to God's grace and is understood in light of the larger story. Christian ethics can never be a mere following of law, whether that be natural or biblical law. Such is to miss the depth, motivation, and larger framework (narrative) needed to follow Christ in everyday life.

There is then a third problem with this approach, namely, the lack of clear agreement concerning the content of natural law. Even if we postulate that there is a natural law and find some advantage in this approach as an apologetic tool, we are faced with the difficulty of finding agreement on the norms and virtues that can be discerned by nature. It is therefore easy to end up with a minimalist ethic. Such an ethic stands in stark contrast to the rigorous ethic of the New Testament, which compels believers to take up their crosses and follow Christ. Clearly, we may employ reason as we sort out the options, norms, and virtues relevant to a given ethical situation and discern how to apply them. But that is different from a pure deliberative ethic that rests solely or primarily on reason for its norms and moral guidance.

The Prescriptive Motif

In this approach to ethical decisions, one looks to explicit rules, principles, or moral actions that are derived from divine revelation. One appeals to the statements of Scripture or the life and teachings of Jesus as concrete guidance in prescribing ethical behavior. Long sees two forms of the prescriptive approach: adherence to principles, such as "Love your neighbor as yourself," and adherence to codes, such as "Give a cup of cold water to whomever asks."

Long notes that the first "sets forth a principle; the second specifies a type of expected behavior; the first invites deliberation about the means necessary to express love for the neighbor; the second states how the neighbor is to be treated."[23]

The principle approach has been the primary expression of this motif throughout the history of the church, but there has often been a desire to codify moral behavior or at least to engage in moral casuistry—the "if . . . then" approach to Christian ethics. One of the best examples of a thoughtful code approach is the Puritan writer Richard Baxter. Contrary to common stereotypes, Baxter and the Puritans were not legalists who feared human freedom and enjoyment. Rather, they believed that all of life was to be lived under the sovereignty of God. As the Westminster Shorter Catechism put it, in answering the question concerning the chief purpose of humanity on earth, "To glorify God and enjoy him forever."[24] In that vein, Baxter set out in his multivolume *Christian Directory* to engage in moral casuistry for every domain of life. The moral and spiritual directories are corollaries of God's law and prescribe directives against pride and for humility, directives for dealing with money, time, speech, and sleep, and directives for relating to the church and the government. Baxter attempted to spell out in explicit form what he believed the moral law required in specific cases. For example, in dealing with money matters, he asked the question, "If I find money or any thing lost, am I bound to seek out the owner, if he seek not after me? and how far am I bound to seek him?" In code fashion, Baxter stated, "You are bound to use such reasonable means as the nature of the case requireth, that the true owner may have his own again. . . . Finding gives you no property, if the owner can be found."[25]

Most forms of prescription by theologians and ethicists have focused less on codes and more on principles. Some biblical scholars, such as C. H. Dodd, have argued that this principle variety was essentially the ethic of Jesus and Paul. While Dodd believes that ethical action is a response to the acts of God in redemption through Jesus Christ, the biblical pattern of moral action is basically prescriptive in nature. The Sermon on the Mount can be understood as law, and Paul's moral exhortations are "perfectly straightforward general maxims which you could transfer directly to the field of conduct."[26]

John Calvin

Next to Martin Luther, John Calvin was the most influential of the sixteenth-century Protestant Reformers. A native Frenchman, Calvin turned from the study of law to theology and was drawn immediately to the ideas of Luther and the burgeoning Reformation. By the age of twenty-five, Calvin had written the first edition of his *Institutes of the Christian Religion*, a work that profoundly influenced the Protestant movement. Eventually, he moved to Geneva,

Switzerland, where he gave pastoral and theological leadership to the reformation of the area.

Calvin's thinking is often seen as the prime example of the prescriptive approach with its strong emphasis on moral decisions flowing directly from the law of God. The law in itself is not the foundation of ethics; that rests in the character of the sovereign God. But the law is an expression of God's character and the primary arbiter in all human decisions. For Calvin:

> Everything relating to a perfect rule of life the Lord has so comprehended in his law, that he has left nothing for men to add to the summary there given. His object in doing this was, first, that . . . in regulating all our actions by his will as a standard, he alone should be regarded as the master and guide of our life; and secondly . . . [to] show that there is nothing which he more requires of us than obedience.[27]

Calvin saw no contradiction between the Old Testament law and the law of Christ, for both point to the manner in which obedience to God is expressed. Following the law is not an end in itself (i.e., legalism) but the means by which we glorify God and reflect gratitude to our maker and redeemer.

Unlike Luther, Calvin saw three primary uses of the law. The first was the pedagogical use—to show us our sin and hence our need for Christ. Second, through its civil use, the law functions as a restraint in society. Third, the law functions as a guide to believers, the dimension that Luther rejected for fear that it would engender works righteousness. Calvin wrote, "The third use of the Law (being also the principal use, and more closely connected with its proper end) has respect to believers in whose hearts the Spirit of God already flourishes and reigns." Though the law is written on all human hearts by the finger of God, and though believers are motivated to obey God primarily through the Holy Spirit, the law still plays a significant role in the Christian life. "It is the best instrument for enabling them daily to learn with greater truth and certainty what that will of the Lord is," and further, "by frequently meditating upon it, he will be excited to obedience . . . and so drawn away from the slippery paths of sin."[28] The way in which Calvin carried out his understanding in both civil and ecclesiastical life in Geneva reveals that for him Christian ethics involved applying the principles of God's law to every domain of life. Though the law may not have directly touched on every moral issue faced, it was sufficient to apply to all moral questions.

Carl F. H. Henry

Carl Henry has been one of the leading theologians of the contemporary evangelical movement in America, through both his prodigious writings and his editorial leadership of *Christianity Today* in its early days. Henry wrote several books on ethics, and many of his editorials addressed current situations in society and the church.

Ethics for Henry is essentially doing the will of God, known through divine revelation. While reason and human experience can provide glimpses of God's will, they are always distorted as a result of the fall and human sin. Thus, we need God's self-disclosure, for "only the ethics of special revelation dares stand in judgment upon much that passes for the 'highest morality' of the age."[29] Ethics, however, is not a mere repetition of divine commands. Following the pattern of Jesus, it can be summarized in one word: love. But Henry, in contrast to some of his contemporaries, reminds us that "love, as the Bible exposits it, is not something as nebulous as moderns would have us think. The New Testament knows nothing of lawless believers in Christ. No believer is left to work out his moral solutions by the principle of love alone. . . . The content of love must be defined by Divine revelation."[30] Love in the Bible is a particularization of the will of God and finds its most explicit expression in Jesus Christ. Christ is our great moral example, but his example can never be divorced from the larger work of redemption. Such disconnection, Henry believes, was the failure of liberalism and the social gospel.

Henry's approach is prescriptive with a principle orientation. Because Christian ethics is rooted in God's will and known through divine revelation, it is not an ethic for everyone. It is primarily the ethic for the redeemed community. "Christian ethics is . . . then the ethics of the church against the world, it is not a living possession of the unbelieving community, but of the community of faith."[31] The principles drawn from Scripture are not, however, only for personal life, for Christians are called to seek a "transformation by supernatural impulse in individual lives whereby the social scene is renewed through a divine spiritual motivation."[32] In regard to work, politics, community, and culture, prescribed principles from God's Word can guide believers and through them influence the larger social order.

Richard Mouw

Richard Mouw is a leader in contemporary evangelicalism through his writings, teaching, and presidency at Fuller Theological Seminary. Mouw is from the Reformed tradition ecclesiastically and theologically and thus like John Calvin sees Christian ethics as following the command of God. Like Carl Henry and most evangelicals, he believes this command is most visibly evidenced in the Bible. Mouw, however, argues that the command of God comes in much broader forms than is traditionally perceived, and therefore the application of divine command ethics is broader than the mere command statements of Scripture.

Mouw believes there is a sense "in which a divine command morality is coextensive with all systems of thought that view God as the supreme moral authority. In this more comprehensive sense, virtue ethics and agapism and an emphasis on a divinely implanted sense of justice can all be seen—along with the ethics of 'external law'—as diverse proposed strategies for exhibiting a pattern of moral surrender to the divine will."[33] He sees this broader understanding of God's command in the Bible itself and believes we will overlook many divine commands if we look only to grammatical imperatives. "The Bible is much more than a compendium of imperatives: the sacred writings contain historical narratives, prayers, sagas, songs, parables, letters, complaints, pleadings, visions, and so on. The moral relevance of the divine commandments found in the Scriptures can only be understood by viewing them in their interrelatedness with these other types of writings."[34]

One of the ways Mouw applies the broader notion of divine command is through the use of biblical worldview. The Bible gives us not only direct statements but also a larger story of creation, fall, redemption, and eschaton (see chapter 3), which can provide significant guidance for contemporary ethical issues. He particularly works this out with reference to political life, arguing that "the Bible has spoken to us in the 'wholeness' of our lives, including our political lives. We must attempt to speak about political matters out of minds and hearts disciplined by the word from God. Our political thoughts must be developed to the point where they are fitting ones for people who confess obedience to the will of God."[35]

John Howard Yoder

The late John Howard Yoder wrote one of the most provocative works in twentieth-century Christian ethics, *The Politics of Jesus*. Writing from an Anabaptist-Mennonite perspective, Yoder attempted to counteract the mainstream assumption of Christian ethics: "That Jesus is simply not relevant in any sense to the questions of social ethics."[36] While some may not think Yoder demonstrated a prescriptive approach to ethics, his work has clear affinities with this motif in that he appealed to the norm of Jesus as a prescription for life, not just personal but social life.

Yoder believed we can gain substantial moral guidance from the life and teachings of Jesus. Because Christ is the apex of God's self-disclosure, we can look to him as the key to hermeneutical understanding of Scripture. Thus, through a Christocentric focus, Yoder attempted to show how the Old Testament and the teaching of Paul can be harmonized with the "politics of Jesus." In contrast to those who asserted the moral irrelevance of Jesus, Yoder set forth the thesis "that the ministry and claims of Jesus are best understood as presenting . . . not the avoidance of political options, but one particular social-political-ethical option." That option sees Jesus "to be not only relevant but also normative for a contemporary Christian social ethic."[37] While Yoder's work is clearly at one level a defense of biblical pacifism, his intention was much broader. He believed that Jesus' life, teachings, and very personhood form a paradigm for all moral and social life, for "Jesus was in his divinely mandated . . . prophethood, priesthood, and kingship, the bearer of a new possibility of human, social, and therefore political relationships. His baptism is the inauguration and his cross is the culmination of that new regime in which his disciples are called to share."[38] This was a radical application of Jesus as a paradigm for ethics and therefore a form of the prescriptive motif.

Critique of the Prescriptive Motif

Of the three motifs, the prescriptive form clearly gives the greatest weight to the authority and relevance of the Bible. It is no accident that this approach has found its greatest acceptance in the more classical Protestant and evangelical traditions, in which the inspiration and unique authority of the Bible as God's Word are given priority.[39] Clearly, this motif attempts to take Scripture seriously not only as a theological commitment but as a practical means to making ethical choices. For those with a high view of the Bible and its authority, this is its most compelling asset.

The prescriptive motif also has much to commend in its concrete accessibility to the populace of the church. The very nature of the prescriptive format helps the average Christian understand God's designs for living in clear and specific ways. Some expressions of Christian ethics are so complex and intellectual that their applications have been limited.

At the same time, however, the prescriptive approach also faces some challenges. For example, historically, prescriptive ethics has tended toward a legalism in which the rules and principles become ends in themselves—rules for rules' sake. This, of course, was strongly condemned by Jesus in his evaluation of the Pharisees' approach to morality. Legalism, in part, is related to another problem of this approach: its tendency to overlook the larger theological foundations for the prescriptions. As contended throughout this work, the heart and foundation of Christian ethics are not rules, principles, or virtues. We need their moral guidance, but one can follow them in a wooden, mechanistic manner and be far from the mark of true Christian discipleship and morality. The biblical guidelines in whatever form are rooted in the nature and actions of the Triune God and secondarily in the biblical worldview of creation, fall, redemption, and consummation. Thus, for example, we do not follow the biblical injunctions toward sexual purity and marital faithfulness simply because they are stated. The injunctions themselves flow from God's own nature of purity and faithfulness and from the larger story of a good creation and God's redeeming work of fallen nature. While we look to the biblical guidelines as an epistemological necessity, the foundation and motivation for the moral life must always go much deeper.

140

Furthermore, the prescriptive approach does not solve all our moral problems. Ethical issues are sometimes very complex, and a simplistic prescriptive paradigm can lull us into thinking they are easily resolved by appeal to a principle. Often there may be multiple biblical principles or paradigms applicable to a given situation. Moreover, the biblical prescriptions themselves must undergo the careful hermeneutical processing that is always part of our use of Scripture. While most prescriptive ethicists and theologians clearly recognize such challenges, the populace is not always quite so careful.

The Relational Motif

Using the relational motif, ethical decisions are made as a direct response to the leading of God and in a somewhat spontaneous fashion. As Long describes it, "In relational ethics the direction of action is shaped by the sense of excitement or gratitude which arises from a live, dynamic, and compelling encounter with the source of moral guidance."[40] As will be seen shortly, this type encompasses a broad range of moral thinking, but its adherents find agreement in a common rejection of prescriptive ethics and natural law formulations. Ethics is conceived to be relational in the sense that even the content and direction of moral decisions flow from an immediate relationship with God and relationships with others. Rather than establishing norms to which humans must aspire, "It understands an ethos in which they live."[41]

In the relational motif, the Bible does not offer specific direction but a general orientation for the moral life. Biblical commands or principles are essentially illustrations of how God has led in the past and how he will likely lead in the present. This relational perspective on the Bible is clearly articulated by Bruce Birch and Larry Rasmussen in *Bible and Ethics in the Christian Life.* They contend that "the question of biblical authority is not properly focused in the inherent character of the Bible itself. The question is more fruitfully focused on God who is active in the world and whose will is disclosed to persons in and through this activity."[42] Biblical texts such as the Ten Commandments, the Sermon on the Mount, or the Pauline exhortations are not comprehensive instruction but exemplary guidance. "The Scriptures were not so much a *fixed moral deposit* for these communities as they were precious community records to try to *be* Israel or to try to *be* a Christian people of God."[43] Thus, "The Bible acts as a shaper of Christian identity"[44] but not as explicit direction.

Long sees at least partial expression of the relational motif in several major historic thinkers—namely, Augustine, Martin Luther, and Jonathan Edwards. In each case, Long associates them with this type because the motivating factor in their ethics was relational.[45] For Augustine, moral action was primarily a result of the will and what one loves; for Luther, it was a spontaneous overflow of justifying faith; and for Edwards, it was a "benevolent propensity of heart to being in general, and a temper or disposition to love God supremely," which "are in effect the same thing."[46] While ethics for all three was clearly rooted in relationship with God, and while all three emphasized this relational dimension as essential for moral living, the actual way each tended to make ethical decisions was more prescriptive in nature.

This can be seen, for example, in Luther, who as noted earlier rejected the third use of the law as a guide for Christian life. At first glance, therefore, he would appear to be anything but prescriptive. But despite his emphasis on good works flowing from justifying faith, and despite his rejection of the third use of the law, when he dealt with a broad array of issues—including war, marriage, work, and politics—he made use of biblical and theological prescriptions that differed little from those of Calvin. Augustine, Luther, and Edwards demonstrated a relational perspective in the motive and context for ethics but a prescriptive orientation (with principles and theological understandings) in the actual approach to ethical issues.

Karl Barth and the Neoorthodoxy Movement

Many would argue that Karl Barth was the most influential theologian of the twentieth century. The Swiss-born theologian was nurtured and educated in the context of rational, historicist liberalism, or as he termed it, cultural Protestantism. Through his first pastoral experience (in a working-class town) and a fresh reading of the Epistle to the Romans, Barth experienced and then began a revolution that sent tremors through the optimistic, humanistic assumptions of the religious landscape. He argued that Christians must return to the classical understandings of God's sovereignty, human sin, and divine grace. Shocked at the capitulation of many of his former theological teachers to German National Socialism (Nazism), Barth believed the sellout was due to the loss of transcendence in theology and the church.

Just as he chastised the theological currents of his day, so Barth attacked the ethical thinking of his contemporaries. Indeed, he implied that ethics was the original sin. "When the serpent promised Adam and Eve that they would become as God, what he had in mind, according to Karl Barth was 'the establishment of ethics.'"[47] Barth stands in opposition to all forms of ethics that seek to formulate moral decisions on the basis of natural law (deliberative motif) or moral rules and principles (the prescriptive motif). Such attempts are autonomous ethics in which humans attempt to answer the ethical questions apart from God's grace and redemption in Jesus Christ. Even the attempts to do moral casuistry from prescribed biblical texts were rejected by Barth, for the moralist treats God's command as a universal rule apart from God, and the prescription destroys the mystery and freedom of God.

For Barth, ethics was a gift of divine grace, not a burden, and thus could never exist apart from God's redemption and direct, gracious command. Moral decisions could never be autonomous, for "theological ethics is itself dogmatics [theology], not an independent discipline along side it."[48] At its heart, true Christian ethics was the command of God. But for Barth, God's command was not prescribed in a text; it was an event in which God speaks and commands at the moment of the decision. As Barth put it:

> The command of God is the event in which God commands. It is a specific command of God in each specific form of his dealing with man, in each specific time. . . . Thus the command of God is not a principle of action revealed to man and imposed upon him. It is not a collection of such principles . . . [to] expound and apply to the best of his knowledge and conscience. . . . God in his command, however, tells him very concretely what he is to do here and now in these or those very particular circumstances.[49]

Because theological ethics in its truest sense is God's immediate, concrete command, ethics as a discipline "can only indicate that in the here and now the obedience or disobedience of man has also taken place and does and will do so, in relation to God's command. Ethics, then, cannot itself give direction. It can only give instruction, teaching us how to put that question relevantly and how to look forward . . . to the answer that God alone can and does give."[50]

What role does the Bible play in God's commands? For Barth, the Bible gives indications of how the command came in the past and will likely come in the future. Texts such as the Decalogue and the Sermon on the Mount are ordinances with which one "must be familiar in order to be able to hear, and actually to hear, the decrees of God which concern . . . actual life. . . . They prepare the way for that openness of heart which . . . has to be demonstrated and realized in a specific obedience which is always new."[51] This understanding of God's command flowed from Barth's view of Scripture as a witness to God's Word, rather than being God's Word itself. For Barth, the Bible becomes the Word and divine revelation as God speaks through it and humans respond to it. To respond to the Word and the divine command was not simply a matter of right interpretation of the text but of being predisposed to hearing God speak through it.

Interestingly, when dealing with specific ethical issues, Barth made direct use of the Bible, in both its broad pictures and specific injunctions, and engaged in something similar to moral casuistry. But for Barth, this ethical engagement was in itself not the command of God but preparation for the command. We can see the form of his engagement with Scripture in his discussion of issues surrounding the taking of human life: war, abortion, and euthanasia. On the issue of war, Barth believed that God's command would usually be on the side of peace and a rejection of violence, but there could always be exceptions. Barth's one noted exception would be resistance to an "attack on the independence, neutrality and territoriality of the Swiss Confederation."[52] On the issue of euthanasia, Barth wrote:

When these points are fully weighed, it can hardly be said of this form of deliberate killing that it can ever seem to be really commanded in any emergency, and therefore to be anything but murder. It must be remembered that not only the patient but his relatives and the doctor are all dying men . . . who . . . will have to bear sufferings which might make the shortening of this period seem desirable to them. . . . What will the end be, therefore, and what will become of our relationship to God and the commanded protection of life, if there is to be constant reflection and discussion concerning the fulfilment of arbitrary desires of this kind.[53]

While these engagements with specific issues seem not unlike the forms of ethics he so strongly critiqued, Barth insisted that such analysis was only preparatory for the actual command. Ethical decisions then were essentially relational, for they came directly from relationship with God and God's immediate, concrete command.

A similar rendition is given by fellow Swiss theologian Emil Brunner. Though the two theologians had a parting of the ways over the issue of natural theology (Barth rejecting it, and Brunner accepting it), Brunner's understanding of how we make ethical decisions was very close to Barth's. Faith is essential to Christian ethics, and no moral principles or statements of law can ever encompass the will of God. Christian morality is a matter of responding to God's will as made known in each concrete situation by the Holy Spirit. Brunner asserted that "the divine command . . . can only be perceived by him to whom God Himself speaks His Word, in faith. . . . Hence I cannot know beforehand the content of the Command as I can know that of the Law; I can only receive it afresh each time through the voice of the Spirit."[54] The Bible provides intimations of how God usually guides in similar situations, but God speaks through the Bible at the moment; he does not prescribe ahead of time.

Stanley Hauerwas and the Ethics of Character

Chapter 2 explored the thinking of Stanley Hauerwas and character as a foundation for ethics. Such a view focuses not on moral decisions but on character formation. Virtue, nurtured through a community's narratives, is the primary framework for ethics. Long does not place character or virtue ethics in the category of relational ethics; rather, in his *Survey of Recent Christian Ethics,* he devotes an entire chapter to this emphasis as a separate category. Character ethics, however, and Hauerwas in particular, share many affinities with the relational motif: a rejection of deliberative and prescriptive ethics, a focus on the moral life as a response to relationship, and an emphasis on the natural overflow of the moral decision from character.

Hauerwas believes that the key issue is not the moral decision itself but the kind of person someone is. "The moral life is not first a life of choice—decision is not king—but is rather woven from the notions that we use to see and to form the situations we confront. Moral life involves learning to see the world through an imaginative ordering of our basic symbols and notions."[55] Through learning to see the world in a different way, informed not by principles but by narrative, we learn to do the right thing in life because of who we have become.

Traditional formulations of ethics in both Protestant and Roman Catholic circles have failed, says Hauerwas, because "they confirm modernity's presumption that God is, at best, something added on to the moral life."[56] Rather, we must see an interrelationship between God and morality so that our conception of and experience with God have a profound effect on our character and hence our actions, and in turn, so that our morality has a profound impact on our experience of God. As Hauerwas puts it, "Only a community that has properly learned to honor mothers and fathers, to share rather than steal, to speak truthfully and to respect what rightfully belongs to one another, . . . only a community so formed is capable of, and . . . desires to worship the one true God truly."[57] Moral decisions then are tied to relationship—relationship with God, the Christian community, and the confessing stories that shape its identity, purpose, and moral virtue.

Rosemary Radford Ruether, an Eco-Feminist Ethic

A different rendering of the relational motif is seen in the thinking of Rosemary Radford Ruether, a feminist Roman Catholic theologian who teaches at Garret Theological Seminary near Chicago. A critic of traditional formulations of theology and ethics, Ruether emphasizes that God is constantly shattering our idolatrous worship of conventional religiosity, and the church is God's agent for such iconoclastic endeavors, which she calls revolution. Her most recent work blends feminist thought and environmentalism, "ecofeminism," and in it she calls for a restructuring of social relations from systems of "domination exploitation" to "biophilic [i.e., earth-friendly] mutuality."[58] To achieve such mutuality between humans and the earth and among races, nations, and sexes, she commends an understanding of the essential interrelatedness of all things and the affirmation of two motifs, God and Gaia. Gaia, the Greek earth goddess, is a symbol for the "immanent voice of the divine—'the personal center of the universal process,' 'the Great Self' or 'the Matrix of life'—beckoning us into communion."[59]

Our concern here is not so much with Ruether's social ethic perspectives as with her formulations for making ethical judgments. How are we to discern God's shattering actions against the conventional moral wisdom that needs to be revolutionized? Ruether believes that neither Jesus nor the Bible provides the final voice for moral judgments. In the Christian tradition, she asserts, there is no "absolute point of reference" for values and moral guidance. Jesus, for example, points beyond himself to the ever re-creating function of the Holy Spirit, who is the final arbiter. It is in the personal encounter with the Spirit that we discern guidance and judgments.[60] Scripture, like Christ, is part of the tradition to which we appeal, but "the world of the Hebrew Bible or New Testament falls short of values which we must affirm." She sees in their pages "tribalistic triumphalism, sectarian rancour, justifications of slavery and sexism. . . . The text then becomes a document of human collective moral failure, rather than a prescriptive norm. These judgments are not foreign to scripture itself, because, at these points one can also judge scripture by scripture."[61] Ruether's formulations for ethical decisions are clearly different from those of Barth or Hauerwas (both of whom would likely reject both the content of her social ethics and much of her methodology), but her rejection of prescriptive approaches and her emphasis on the immediate leading of the Spirit reflect another expression of the relational motif.

Critique of the Relational Motif

It is somewhat difficult to give a general critique of the relational motif, since there are such widely varying approaches within it. Thus, the following evaluation may not apply equally to all expressions. First, the relational motif is certainly correct in terms of moral motivation: Decisions and character should be shaped by a dynamic encounter with God. An ethic that does not flow from God's initiating grace will indeed turn into a legalism of rules as ends in themselves. In the Bible, grace, not law, is the primary motivation for Christian life and discipleship. Second, the relational motif (at least in some of its expressions) is correct in that Christian ethics must be theological. An ethic divorced from a larger narrative and from a particular way of seeing the world will become an autonomous ethic in which God is unnecessary. Barth's model of ethics set in the context of his *Church Dogmatics* is laudatory. Third, the emphasis on ethics flowing from both divine reality and inward character is consistent with biblical Christianity.

The relational motif, however, faces some challenges and reflects some significant weaknesses. Its greatest problem is its propensity for subjectivism and relativism. Clearly, Barth attempts to guard against these problems by insisting that the command of God cannot be divorced from the Bible and is always set in the context of a listening community, the church. But it is not as clear that his followers were able to maintain this balance, and some critics have seen a link between the neoorthodox undermining of moral prescription and the rise of situational ethics. The relativistic and subjectivistic orientation is clearly seen in Ruether's thinking, which leaves us with only the "Spirit" and some notion of "Gaia" to guide us; Christ and Scripture are simply among the various possible sources. If there is a Word from God for Christian ethics, then it will surely embody a degree of objectivity that transcends the subjectivity of the moral interpreter.

A further weakness of at least parts of the relational camp is its overemphasis on community as the source of moral direction. As noted in chapter 2, character ethics can easily make the community the final arbiter of ethics, as when it is asserted that "community is the chief architect of character."[62] But what do we do when the community and its narratives are unjust or unrighteous? How is transcendence and divine guidance mediated when the community itself is the chief architect of moral character and action?

Conclusion

Throughout Christian history, believers have made moral decisions through deliberation, prescription, and relational impulses. How are we to evaluate them and see their possible interrelationship? All three have a place in making ethical decisions but within a priority of modified prescriptivism. The prescriptive motif rests on assumptions about theology and divine revelation, namely, that there are divine designs for human life and that God has spoken in his written and incarnate Word relative to those designs. But a prescriptive motif must be modified in two ways. First, as contended earlier, prescriptions are not the foundations and motives of Christian ethics. The moral life is rooted in the nature and actions of the Triune God and in our worldview as Christians. It derives from a particular way of seeing the world and from an experience of divine grace in Jesus Christ, our Lord and Savior. The biblical principles, laws, narratives, and paradigms are then understood in light of a much bigger picture. Second, a prescriptive motif must be modified in that the prescriptions are much broader than just the biblical imperatives. God has spoken in multiple forms, and the directions from Scripture and Christ are broader than merely the genre of moral law and principle.

Within a prescriptive approach to decision making, however, there is also a place for deliberation. First, when reason is employed in ethical judgments, we should recognize both the foundations of the moral life and the directives from divine revelation. This is different from building ethics from reason or natural law, but it does recognize that deliberation plays a role in understanding moral designs and even in providing some rationale for them. Second, reason plays a role in understanding the nature of the issue. As will be shown in chapter 8, ethical decisions in part hinge on how we interpret the empirical situation surrounding a given issue, and we certainly employ reason and other forms of judgment in that assessment. Third, there is a place for reason in those moral decisions in which no clear revelational prescriptions exist, of either the specific or more indirect variety. In the midst of highly complex issues, we sometimes have to rely on reason within the framework of our Christian worldview to discern the moral good. Fourth, there is a place for the deliberative motif in making moral appeal in a pluralistic world that does not share our worldview assumptions and acceptance of revelational authority (more on that in chapter 11).

Along with the deliberative motif, the relational perspective also has a place within a modified prescriptive motif. Certainly the motive and experiential context for carrying out a Christian calling and moral directives stem from a dynamic, personal relationship with God. Ethics in experience ought to be an overflow of justifying grace, the empowerment of the Holy Spirit, the reflection or imitation of Christ within us, and the moral enablement of the Christian community. Moreover, the relational approach also has a place in those complex moral situations in which the moral direction remains unclear after biblical and theological guidance has been sought. Prayer, the discernment of fellow Christians, and the leading of the Holy Spirit must play a role in moral discernment amid the complexities of the world and our life together as Christians. But such discernment must always be made in light of the overarching biblical story and revelational perspectives—not over against them.

7

THE BIBLE IN ETHICAL DECISIONS

While teaching at a seminary in India, I was approached one day by a student in my Christian ethics class seeking advice regarding a moral quandary. Ruam, my student's friend, lived in one of the northeastern states of India, where levirate marriages were practiced.[1] The practice meant that if a married male died, the next brother was to take the widowed wife as his own, provided he was not married. Ruam's brother had just died, leaving a young wife but no children, and it now fell to Ruam to take her as his spouse. The problem? She was a nonbeliever who practiced a traditional tribal religion, and Ruam was a deeply committed Christian. My student wanted to know, "What should I advise Ruam to do?" After we talked and prayed about the situation, I asked my student if we might discuss this in class, and he assented. I knew that wisdom and insights of those closer to the culture would be more valuable than my own.

When I presented the situation in class, the first response from a number of students was unequivocal—he cannot marry the woman on the basis of 2 Corinthians 6:14: "Do not be mismatched with unbelievers. For what partnership is there between righteousness and lawlessness? Or what fellowship is there between light and darkness?" Initially, this principle seemed to resolve the situation in the minds of the students. Then one woman in the class said, "Are we sure that this text really relates to marriage? In the context, marriage is not mentioned. Perhaps it relates more to a church setting than to a family context." Another student (from northeast India) chimed in, "And besides, in the Old Testament levirate laws were practiced (Gen. 38:8–10; Deut. 25:5–10), and Onan lost his life for not fulfilling the obligation. The understanding of marriage and family in Ruam's tribal region is much closer to the understanding of marriage and family in the Old Testament than to the kind of romantic marriages you have in the West. Maybe the Old Testament law takes precedence in this case." Now the discussion was heating up. Others argued that this is a case in which there are two conflicting biblical principles:

149

the unequal yoke principle, on the one hand, and the principle of caring for one's family, on the other (1 Tim. 5:8: "And whoever does not provide for relatives, and especially for family members, has denied the faith and is worse than an unbeliever"). The question is, Which biblical principle takes priority for this decision?

All of the students were deeply committed to the authority of Scripture and desired to seek biblical guidance in ethical decisions. It quickly became clear, however, that this right and laudable dependence on the Bible did not immediately solve all moral dilemmas. Christians, of course, are a people of the Book. But how should it function as authority for us, especially when many contemporary issues are not directly addressed, or when a number of biblical principles are at work? How do we interpret Scripture given that the contexts of then and now are so different? And just what portions of Scripture or kinds of biblical texts have relevance to modern ethical questions? These are the issues we immediately confront in applying the Bible to our day.

The Nature of Biblical Authority for Christian Ethics

Most Christians throughout church history have appealed to the Bible in some manner in responding to moral dilemmas. Moreover, they have seen the Bible as central in the formation of Christian character in believers and the collective life of the church. But just how does the Bible function as authority? What is the essential nature of Scripture that gives it significance and relevance to ethical decisions and character?

Some Christians see the Bible as a book of moral codes or an ethics textbook. They look to the Bible for specific direction in every specific situation. As a song, popular in some Christian circles, put it, "God said it, I believe it, that settles it for me." With this perspective, Ruam would go to the Bible to find the rule that applies to his need, most likely, "Be not unequally yoked," and make his decision. He would not process the nature of his dilemma or look at the full range of biblical teaching, and he certainly would not appeal to any other source as his moral authority.

The problem with this approach to authority is that the Bible is not primarily a book of moral codes, nor is it an ethics textbook. It contains a few codes and some ethical principles, but these do not make up a majority of the biblical material. Moreover, many of the ethical issues we face today are nowhere addressed in Scripture. Christians who employ this notion of biblical authority will find little information about the complex issues related to business, politics, medicine, environment, and law. Generally, this approach to the Bible tends to overlook the contextual nature of biblical teaching and the hermeneutical processing that always needs to take place in our use of the Bible for theology and ethics. God did not send us a theology or ethics text but a compendium of letters, poetry, narratives, visions, discourses, prayers, and laments—all directed to particular situations and times. To treat the Bible in textbook fashion is to dishonor its very nature and the process God utilized in graciously revealing his Word to us. Such an approach to biblical authority often actually undermines the breadth and sustaining power that the Word can have in our moral decisions and Christian character.

Others see the Bible as one among many authorities for Christian ethics or perhaps distantly relevant for today's complex issues. As one proponent put it, "What we need is a new understanding of the role of the Bible in the church today that acknowledges the actual reality of our situation—an understanding that takes the Bible as a foundational document but not as authoritative."[2] Some in this camp argue that because the canon of Scripture contains such ideological and moral diversity, it can never function as the final authority for today's ethical issues. Wayne Meeks, for example, argues that when we look to early Christianity, we find "only a record of experimentation, of trial and error, of tradition creatively misread and innovation wedged craftily into the cracks of custom . . . of disputes and confrontation, of fervent assertions of unity amid distressing signs of schism. . . . There has not ever been a purely Christian morality, unalloyed with the experience and traditions of others."[3] In the midst of such diversity, he claims, we are left with only the church's common sense in conjunction with its memory and tradition for making ethical judgments.

Those who hold this view of the Bible and its authority explain that the gap between the biblical world and our world is simply too great for the Bible's teachings and models to be relevant. We cannot apply the norms from a simple agrarian society to our complex world. Thus, Jack Sanders concludes, "The ethical positions of the New Testament are the children of their own times and places, alien and foreign to this day and age. Amidst the ethical dilemmas which confront us, we are now at least relieved of the need or temptation to begin with Jesus, or the early church, or the New Testament, if we wish to develop coherent ethical positions. We are freed from bondage to that tradition."[4]

There are, of course, many who do not want to go as far as Sanders's radical perspective and yet are reticent to believe Scripture has direct relevance for Christian ethics. Paul Jersild, for example, argues for the authority of Scripture in moral decisions insofar as it "finds its center in Jesus Christ as Lord who summons believers to a life of repentance and faith." However, the nature of the Bible itself and the contextual nature of the moral life mean that it is "impossible and inappropriate to understand the Bible's authority for the Christian life in terms of specific directives for moral action."[5] He believes the ethical message of the New Testament cannot be "identified primarily with imperatives relating to issues of our time." Rather, we must understand that in specific moral decisions "it is generally the case that the ethical witness of the Bible is neither sufficiently clear nor consistent to give it a blanket hemeneutical primacy."[6]

151

For many adherents of this general perspective, the Bible is one among various authorities including tradition, reason, human experience, and scientific understandings. Authority does not reside in the Bible per se but in the transforming encounters that the Bible mediates. As Sallie McFague puts it, "If we wish to take Scripture seriously and see it as normative, we should take it on its own terms as a model of how theology should be done, rather than as the authority dictating the terms in which it is done. . . . [It is] not so much a content as a form."[7] If Ruam accepts this understanding of biblical authority, he will certainly look to Scripture as one of the prime sources for his decision, but he will not be limited to the biblical mandates. He will understand them as examples of how people in the past encountered God, and he will seek to find God's immediate leading in the dilemma he faces. More than likely he will see Scripture as the source of his faith and the general pattern of his character, but he will not expect to find a clear directive from God for his decision.

In contrast to the textbook approach and the approach that sees the Bible as distantly or moderately relevant, there is a third way to understand both the nature of the Bible and its authority for ethical decisions. In the classical view, the Bible is the inspired Word of God that though addressed to particular contexts, people, and issues of a given time, nonetheless speaks to contexts, people, and issues of another time. "All scripture is inspired by God and is useful for teaching, for reproof, for correction, and for training in righteousness" (2 Tim. 3:16). This classic view rests on the assumption that "the God of the Bible is a God who acts and talks. He is personal. The Christian's view of the Bible is tied to the doctrine of God, who discloses himself in deeds and words."[8] The inspiration of Scripture was not a dictation from heaven but embodied both divine and human elements. Nonetheless, God was providentially at work in both the revelatory events and the spoken or written word in such a way that what we have is what God intended. Thus, "you must understand this, that no prophecy of scripture is a matter of one's own interpretation, because no prophecy ever came by human will, but men and women moved by the Holy Spirit spoke from God" (2 Peter 1:20–21).

Biblical authority ultimately rests not on the Bible's ability to move or instruct followers but on its very nature as the Word of God. Thus, as Richard Hays states, "The Bible's perspective is privileged, not ours."[9] In a postmodern world that tends to be reader-based rather than text-based, such notions of authority are often rejected, to the peril of Christians and the church. Of course, we must recognize that an interpretive process is necessary so that the biblical authority can become operative for Christian thought, life, and character. Hays reminds us that "these texts were not written in the first instance for Americans at the end of the twentieth century. When we read Paul's letters to his churches, we are reading the mail of people who have been dead for nineteen hundred years; when we read the gospels, we are reading stories told for the benefit of ancient communities whose customs and problems differed vastly from ours."[10] But the nature of Scripture is such that it has the ability to transcend the particular situations of the original hearers to provide truthful guidance for hearers in other circumstances. Though we may face many ethical issues and situations that are vastly different from those the Bible addresses, our task is to move from the particular situations in Scripture to those that now confront us.

Such a move entails a number of interpretative issues that will be addressed momentarily. But the assumption here is that God's providential work in both the writing and assembling of the Bible ensures its unique ability to address and guide us today in the midst of highly complex issues that the biblical writers never imagined. Stephen Mott captures the process and task well when he writes:

> This much can be affirmed without making the Bible either into an ethical code or a book of systematic ethics, a fear which many students of the hermeneutics of biblical ethics possess. The transcendent ideas are addressed to concrete situations of another time. This fact affirms the importance of history but also creates difficulties in understanding both their transcendent character and their application to a different age. The problem in interpreting a particular command is not that it is inappropriate to the nature of Scripture that God's revelation takes such a concrete form. The problem, rather is to understand the meaning for another period of that very concreteness which makes God's Word relevant to a particular moment of history.[11]

If Ruam operates from this perspective of biblical authority, he will look to Scripture as his ultimate authority, believing that he will find either direct or indirect guidance for his dilemma as well as his character. He will not overlook the interpretive process in examining biblical texts, nor the complexity and competing moral claims concerning his situation. But through the process of understanding his own dilemma and understanding the meaning and impetus of varying relevant texts, he will make a biblically informed decision. The rest of this chapter works from this assumption, that the Bible is the inspired Word of God that continues to function as moral authority today because of its very nature of concreteness.

Hermeneutical Issues in Ethical Decisions

A strong affirmation of biblical inspiration and authority does not solve all problems related to Christian ethics. In many ways, it creates a number of problems as we seek to interpret the Bible and relate it to the complexities often inherent in contemporary situations. A high view of Scripture calls for honest engagement with the hermeneutical issues and the difficulties we face. The following five hermeneutical issues are not exhaustive, but they are the key ones confronted when using the Bible in ethical decisions.

The Bible Does Not Address Many Contemporary Issues

The first issue is that many of the pressing issues of our time are not addressed in the Bible. One will not find a discussion of genetic engineering, treatment termination, nuclear war, human rights, corporate ethics, the allocation of scarce medical resources, contraception, abortion—and the list could go on. As a result, one possible option is simply to ignore these issues, which of course a small number of Christians choose to do in their attempts to withdraw from society. Another option is to engage the issues without recourse to Scripture. But if we accept the working assumptions of the Bible just outlined, then we will attempt to address these pressing issues within the confines of biblical authority. To do so we will need to employ the larger contours of Scripture—teaching that provides the basic framework, assumptions, and outlooks for the discussion—as well as broad principles that can be applied to the moral dilemmas.

Most biblical engagements with issues such as those listed above will draw from biblical paradigms and principles that were not directed to the subject at hand. The hermeneutical task is to make sure that the biblical material utilized is a legitimate application. Because the Bible provides a large overarching story of creation, fall, redemption, and consummation, there is a clear framework from which to start. Contained in that story and in the various other biblical teachings are understandings about life, death, human nature, the natural world, structural realities of society, the state, work, justice, order, and a host of other topics. The test is always to ensure that the particular text of Scripture being used can be applied with integrity to the issue at hand.

A good issue with which to test the relevance of Scripture is abortion. Christians have drawn on a wide arsenal of biblical texts to support the case that life in the womb is human life and calls for the same moral protection as human life outside the womb. The question we must ask is whether the texts are legitimate for dealing with the issue. Take, for example, Psalm 51:5, in which David confesses, "Indeed, I was born guilty, a sinner when my mother conceived me." Some take this as proof that David was a person, a living soul from the moment of conception. But an examination of the passage in its context reveals that David, in this psalm of confession, is using poetic parallelism to describe his utter sinfulness. The reference to conception is not making a metaphysical or ontological statement about life in the womb; rather, David is poetically describing his condition before God. He is not making a theological statement as to when sin began in his very being. Another text sometimes used for the same purpose is Jeremiah 1:5: "Before I formed you in the womb I knew you, and before you were born I consecrated you; I appointed you a prophet to the nations." If one attempts to use this verse to support personhood before birth, that person would also have to assert personhood before conception because this verse affirms God's personal knowledge of Jeremiah before he was formed in the womb. But the notion of the preexistence of the soul has long been rejected by a majority of the Christian church. Moreover, the point of the passage is related not to Jeremiah's personhood but to God's omniscience, which, of course, does exist before the emergence of a human being.

While these particular texts may not be applicable to abortion, other passages can be applied legitimately even though not addressing the issue per se. Psalm 139, for example, focuses on divine knowledge and care for the psalmist and includes God's work and care in the womb:

> For it was you who formed my inward parts;
>> you knit me together in my mother's womb.
> I praise you, for I am fearfully and wonderfully made.
>> Wonderful are your works;
> that I know very well.
>> My frame was not hidden from you,
> when I was being made in secret,
>> intricately woven in the depths of the earth.
> Your eyes beheld my unformed substance.
> In your book were written
>> all the days that were formed for me,
>> when none of them as yet existed.

vv. 13–16

Though the psalmist is not engaged in a metaphysical or theological discussion about personhood, the passage encompasses an explicit understanding that God treats life in the womb with special care and protection. Another text with similar relevance is Luke 1:41, regarding the visit of Mary to Elizabeth: "When Elizabeth heard Mary's greeting, the child leaped in her womb. And Elizabeth was filled with the Holy Spirit." The significant issue here is not the baby's movement in the womb but rather the text's use of the word "baby" (brephos), a term that is also used of an older child.[12] A number of other biblical texts refer to conception as a gift of God. None of these texts explain the exact moment when a person or living soul begins to exist, but clearly they provide strong evidence that life in the womb is always God's special gift that warrants protection and care.

For many ethical issues, we need to use biblical material in this way, attempting to make sure that while passages may not address an issue directly, their focus in application is broad enough and close enough in content to be legitimate. The biblical material employed will not simply be commands and principles but the broad array of Scripture that helps to give frameworks and paradigms for ethical decisions.

Issues Addressed in Scripture Are Not Always Identical to Today

A second issue encountered when interpreting the Bible for Christian ethics is that issues in Scripture are inevitably tied to particular situations and contexts. Because circumstances and contexts change over time, current issues may not be exactly the same as those faced in the Bible. Several examples make this clear.

The Old Testament prohibits usury, the charging of interest on loans (Exod. 22:25; Lev. 25:35–38; Deut. 23:19). Does this then translate into a moral denunciation of the banking industry today? Ronald Sider has argued that a close look at this biblical prohibition reveals that loans then and banking loans today are not identical.[13] In the Hebraic world, they were personal loans between family and kin, and the intent was to protect the poor and relieve distress. Today, commercial loans exist in an economy in which loans are used for the development of an industry or the procurement of an economic essential, which will then eventually bring economic assets to the person borrowing. Hence, an interest charge seems just and reasonable. The principle of the passage, justice for the poor, surely continues but not necessarily the explicit prohibition, for the nature of the issue then and now are not the same.

Or take the example of Paul's statement in Romans 13 that governing authorities are God's servants to do good and that rulers "are not a terror to good conduct, but to bad" (v. 3). Therefore, believers are to submit to the God-ordained authorities. But is Paul here speaking of all governing authorities? Does this text apply to a Hitler, a Stalin, or a Pol Pot? Many commentators have suggested that Paul was directing his thought to the Roman government of that particular time, which at that moment was less than tyrannical. However, a full biblical teaching on the nature of the state and Christians' responses to it requires a look at other biblical teachings in different contexts. Revelation 13 paints the state not as a servant but as a beast and an enemy of the church, and such it was when the book was likely written. Moreover, in the Book of Acts, the apostles engaged in civil disobedience in response to the government's prohibition of evangelism (Acts 5:27–29). Thus, what Paul faced in Romans 13 was not the same issue that John faced in Revelation 13 or what the Christians faced in Nazi Germany in the 1940s.

Many issues today are not the same as those the Bible addresses. To discern whether and how a given text should be used today requires both exegetical and historical/cultural analysis of the biblical text and a thorough understanding of the ethical quandary facing us.

Moving from the Old Testament to the New Testament

Another hermeneutical issue encountered in Christian ethics is one central to all biblical interpretation and theology: the relationship of the Old Testament to the New Testament. This, of course, is part of a larger theological issue, namely, the relationship between law and grace, though we should understand that there is grace in the Old Testament and law in the New. Nonetheless, the Old Testament contains a number of narratives, directives, and practices that give us pause. Are these unfamiliar and troublesome practices normative today? For example, as noted earlier in this chapter, the Old Testament encourages the practice of the levirate law, and Onan is judged for not carrying it out. How do we evaluate its normativity for Christian ethics? Capital punishment is commanded for sixteen offenses, including persistent disobedience to parents. While capital punishment for murder is a hotly debated issue in society and even among Christians, hardly anyone would encourage its use for all the offenses listed in the Old Testament.[14] And though polygamy was never commanded, it was widely practiced among the patriarchs and their contemporaries, seemingly without explicit moral judgment. Then there are, of course, all those "savage" wars, most of which would not survive a just war critique. If we want to be guided in our ethics by the Bible, what are we to make of these Old Testament texts?

At the same time, of course, many Old Testament texts are praiseworthy and resourceful for preaching and moral exhortations. Many Christians are prone to see the Jubilee year of Leviticus 25, the land use regulations (Lev. 19:9–10; Deut. 24:19–22), and the sabbatical laws (Exod. 23:10–11) as embodying relevant principles for economic justice, though the particular expressions or forms are not applicable in a non-agrarian society. We are quick to utilize the teachings of Amos, Jeremiah, and Micah for encouraging honesty, righteousness, and justice. Almost all Christians look to the moral law of the Decalogue as relevant and applicable to a host of issues today, and most find the wisdom teachings of Proverbs significant in shaping moral character. So how are we to sort through the Old Testament without falling into the trap of using texts that fit our preconceived moral framework and rejecting those that do not?

First, we must recognize that many of the troubling incidences in the Old Testament are reported but not necessarily condoned. For example, the narratives of Judges 18–21 include blatant idolatry, theft, rape, murder, bodily dismemberment after murder, and the near wiping out of an entire tribe. In the immediate texts, there is little moral condemnation; it comes at the end of the book: "All the people did what was right in their own eyes" (21:25). The narratives of the Old Testament report morally grievous events, but as Walter Kaiser reminds us, we "need to distinguish between what the Bible records and what it teaches." Moreover, "Divine approval of an individual in one aspect or area of his life does not entail and must not be extended to mean there is a divine approval of that individual in all aspects of . . . character or conduct."[15]

We must also understand that the relationship of the Old Testament to the New Testament is linked to progressive revelation, the continual unfolding of

157

God's plan and designs that reach their apex in the death and resurrection of Christ. The Old Testament even contains a growing disclosure of God's moral designs for his people and all humanity. In the process of this self-disclosure, God, being deeply personal, often begins where people are in their understanding of his will and plan. This forms a kind of missiological pattern that many have found fruitful when taking the gospel to cultures that have little understanding of the Bible and its moral framework. Peter Craigie explains how this idea of meeting humans where they are is helpful in dealing with the issue of war in the Old Testament:

> If God is to meet man in history and act on his behalf, it must be in the world as it is. But the world which is, is a world which is sinful, for God has given to man a certain freedom. Therefore, if God is to work on behalf of man in the world, He must give the appearance to man of using sinful means—He must seem to be unethical in his behavior. . . . War cannot be looked at apart from man. . . . To say that God uses war is to say in effect that God uses sinful man in His purposes. In the Old Testament, if we were to expect to see God working only in what we might call an absolutely "ethical" manner, we would in effect be denying the possibility of seeing His work at all.[16]

This understanding does not solve all the problems related to war in the Old Testament, but it is a helpful perspective for assessing this complex problem.

God's act of beginning where people are is also evident in the *lex talionis,* which declared "eye for eye, tooth for tooth" (Exod. 21:24; Lev. 24:20; Deut. 19:21). This civil law regulation at the time was a vast moral advance over the clan practices of "a life for a tooth." In the fullness of God's revelation, Jesus, of course, would call for believers to go beyond the *lex talionis:* "You have heard that it was said, 'An eye for an eye and a tooth for a tooth.' But I say to you, Do not resist an evildoer. But if anyone strikes you on the right cheek, turn the other also" (Matt. 5:38–39). Jesus called his followers to go beyond the practice of the Old Testament (which was originally intended as a legal practice of restitution), in the way they lived their lives.

Polygamy was clearly accepted by a number of the patriarchs and kings, but throughout the Old Testament it seems to decline in practice as God's design from creation becomes more readily understood in the light of his fuller revelation. In the New Testament, the creation design is clearly normative, not only in its call for one spouse but also in its rejection of serial polygamy, multiple spouses over a period of time through divorce.[17] As we view the continual unfolding of the Old Testament, the fullness of revelation in Christ (Heb. 1:1–2), and the apostolic teaching, we detect that the moral demands actually increase with fuller understanding and fuller moral empowerment through redemption in Christ and the presence of the Holy Spirit. The New Testament teaching on marriage, divorce, and the forgiveness of an enemy (which follows Christ's example in the atonement) are cases in point.

A large segment of Old Testament law is commonly called civic law and ceremonial law, in contrast to the moral law (i.e., the Decalogue). While many Old Testament scholars insist that the Hebrew people did not have the distinctions and designations we employ today, Oliver O'Donovan has suggested that the threefold designation for the law was not formulated as "an account of the way Israel itself interpreted its obligations. It was an attempt to analyze from a Christian point of view what the constituent elements of those obligations were."[18] Nonetheless, the distinction goes back in history, and even the rabbis during the early Christian era made distinctions between "light" and "heavy" commandments and seem familiar with the designations "moral law" and "ceremonial law," with the former considered more important.[19] Many of the laws clearly had a social and political purpose that set them apart from the more general moral laws that were educative in nature. Clearly, the New Testament writers and Jesus himself understood differences between the types of law, in terms of their claim on our lives. Thus, with regard to circumcision, there were grounds within the gospel itself for rejecting it as a normative practice within the Christian church. Jesus made a distinction between the lesser and more important aspects of the law (Matt. 23:23–24), and the apostles and biblical writers understood that Jesus' own death and resurrection embodied much of what the ceremonial laws foreshadowed. Therefore, their moral claim was no longer binding.

Given the progressive revelation in which the full intent of God's moral designs becomes clearer and more possible through Christ and the Spirit, the safest principle is to interpret the Old Testament in light of the fuller New Testament. When the Old Testament directives are clearly affirmed in the New Testament, we must affirm them as normative for our moral actions and character (i.e., homosexual behavior). When practices and directives go contrary to the New Testament, the latter clearly takes precedence (i.e., circumcision). When practices in the Old Testament are not explicitly contrary or affirmed in the New Testament, we must weigh the moral teaching or example in light of the larger contours of biblical teaching. This should in no way imply an inferiority of the Old Testament or an evolutionary stance on moral development. Rather, the notion of progressive revelation is tied only to the process of God's self-disclosure.

In relating the Old Testament to Christian ethics, it is helpful to distinguish the social structures and cultural practices of biblical times from their primary intent. "The commandments of the Old Testament and New Testament do not assume an ideal social structure for all time. Rather they assume the social structure of their own time and outline ways in which Israel, or the church, was to be different."[20] Thus, we find the existence of slavery, agrarian economic structures, levirate marriages, a monarchial political system, and a host of other social patterns common to the period. The intent of divine law was not immediately to destroy those structures or patterns but to call the people to righteousness and justice within them. The seeds for transformation of those structures were embedded in the teaching of the law and then the gospel, though the seeds were likely beyond the perceptions of the biblical writers themselves. With regard to Old Testament social structures, therefore, Bernard Adeney writes:

> With the ancient law God offered Israel an opportunity to be different from the surrounding nations. Within the context of a social structure based on slavery, Israel was to free all slaves and give them a nest egg every seven years (Deuteronomy 15). Within the context of a political system of monarchy, Israel was to know that monarchy would become a vehicle of oppression (1 Samuel 8) and that even its greatest king was not above the law of God (2 Samuel 12). Within the context of an agricultural economy, Israel was to ensure that everyone had a fair share of land and that both land and animals would be respected (Leviticus 25). Within the context of patriarchy and polygamy, Israel was to protect the rights of women (Deuteronomy 21:10–14; 22:13–29).[21]

The Relationship between Particularity of the Text and Universality

Scripture was given in a specific context and often addressed particular pastoral, theological, spiritual, and ethical issues. The working assumption in this chapter is that we can move from the particular to other situations. However, sometimes when interpreting Scripture we have reason to believe that the particular injunctions or example of a given text were for a particular situation and context and are not applicable to other settings in the same manner. The challenge, of course, is not to turn uncomfortable texts into particularistic texts that do not apply today simply on the grounds that they are "hard passages." The key here is finding reasons in the text, context, or other biblical texts that warrant a limit of its application. In some ways, this entails the last two hermeneutical issues discussed: Some issues addressed in Scripture are not identical to issues today, and moving from the Old Testament to the New Testament. Some cases, however, are distinct from these two issues.

One of the most obvious examples involves commands given to individuals that were clearly meant for those individuals alone. God's direction to Abraham to "Go from your country and your kindred and your father's house to the land that I will show you" (Gen. 12:1) was obviously not a universal directive. The focus of the text is God's special dealing with the patriarch so that through him all the world would be blessed. Clearly, we can learn something about divine leading and human response from this passage, but the specific injunction is not normative for all Old Testament saints or Christians.

There are, of course, many biblical injunctions that go beyond individuals but are nonetheless time-conditioned and not necessarily directly applicable today. One of the clearest examples from the Old Testament involves legislative or case laws, such as in Exodus 21–23. Through examining the laws themselves, the biblical context, and the sociocultural context, we can conclude that they played a function different from the more general moral law or Ten Commandments. They fulfilled a social and political function tied directly to the context in which they were given. "To recognize this judicial function is to acknowledge that the laws are context-dependent in a special sense: that they have a task to perform within the community institutions which is other than that of moral education."[22] Furthermore, these laws were given to a covenant community, which was significantly different from the secular, pluralistic society in which we find ourselves. This does not mean there are no moral lessons to be learned, but the nature and the context of these laws reveal that they are not immediately applicable to modern politics, the church, or individual believers.

In the New Testament, an example of a particularity that limits universality is teaching regarding women in the church.[23] Most ecclesiastical traditions today accept that Paul's teaching that women should pray and prophesy with their heads covered was a time-bound injunction (1 Cor. 11:3–16). Women without veils in that culture were morally suspect, and freedom in Christ did not negate a cultural form of propriety. Similarly, the two passages in the New Testament that would seem to limit women's roles in the church (1 Cor. 14:34–35; 1 Tim. 2:11–15) were directed to specific problems that had emerged in the churches of Ephesus and Corinth. Ephesian Christians had to contend with a broad array of religious forces that included worship of the goddess Artemis. The passage may well be dealing with abuses in the church that emerged from the pagan practices centered in the local cult. And while Paul in the 1 Corinthians text seems to limit women's gifts and roles within the church, he also recognizes their involvement in public ministry with his commendation of women prophesying (i.e., preaching) and praying with their heads covered. Moreover, the New Testament recognizes other women in ministry such as Priscilla, part of the husband-wife church-planting team (note, she is mentioned first), and Junia, "prominent among the apostles" (Rom. 16:7). Therefore, the two texts that would seem to limit women's roles in ministry were particular in their address and not universal.

The Handling of Complex Issues with Multiple Biblical Principles and Paradigms

The story of Ruam, which began this chapter, created a situation in which two biblical principles are at play—the unequal yoke principle and the injunction to care for family. Both are valid ethical principles drawn from Scripture, but in this and similar cases, it is necessary to decide which takes precedence. As noted in chapter 1, the classic example of competing moral claims is the situation faced by those hiding Jews during World War II. When confronted by authorities, should they protect human life (implied in the sixth commandment) or tell the truth (the ninth commandment)? Or take the example of a

161

physician in an emergency room with a patient who needs a blood transfusion or faces certain death. The family members, who are Jehovah's Witnesses, object to the transfusion on the grounds of their religious convictions. The physician and hospital are faced with a conflict of ethical principles: the protection of human life and the protection of religious conscience.

In dealing with complex ethical issues today, we are often confronted with these kinds of situations, especially in the social arenas of politics, business, law, education, and the environment. While a conflict may not relate to direct biblical statements, it may embody conflicts between principles, paradigms, or narratives that are ultimately rooted in the Bible. For example, many issues surrounding environmental ethics hinge on a complex mix of stewardship of the natural environment, freedom of human beings, and the production of goods and services to meet human need—all of which are rooted in biblical teaching.

How do we resolve this kind of hermeneutical issue? Some ethicists have argued that the Bible itself gives us a hierarchy of values or principles.[24] While it is true that from direct and indirect biblical teachings we may be able to determine some priorities, such as human life over human property, we should not make the Bible say more than it says. Difficult cases must be decided within the broad contours of biblical teaching, but sometimes we may have to appeal to the leading of the Holy Spirit and the discernment of the Christian community. This does not mean that one moral response is as good as another, but it does mean we must use humility in the decision-making process. We need to make clear what is at stake biblically and theologically and then seek the moral good through the Spirit's leading, sanctified reasoning, and the collective wisdom of the church, both past and present.

Forms of Ethical Guidance in the Bible

Having established the authority of the Word for ethical decisions and having surveyed the various hermeneutical issues, we now turn to the forms of guidance found in the Bible. The tendency is to limit ethical materials to laws or imperative principles, but Scripture contains far more guidance and perspective than mere commands. There have been various attempts to determine the kinds of ethical material in the Bible,[25] but this section focuses on five forms of moral guidance. Clearly, there may be some overlap between the forms, which must be understood as generalized types for clarity and understanding.

Casuistic Law

Casuistic law is the most specific form of direction in the Bible. Typically, using an "if . . . then" form, these laws mandate explicit behavior for specific situations. In the Bible, the best-known casuistic law section is the book of the covenant in Exodus 21–23. Here we find laws such as:

> If someone leaves a pit open, or digs a pit and does not cover it, and an ox or a donkey falls into it, the owner of the pit shall make restitution, giving money to its owner, but keeping the dead animal. If someone's ox hurts the ox of another, so that it dies, then they shall sell the live ox and divide the price of it; and the dead animal they shall also divide. But if it was known that the ox was accustomed to gore in the past, and its owner has not restrained it, the owner shall restore ox for ox.
>
> 21:33–36

> For six years you shall sow your land and gather in its yield; but the seventh year you shall let it rest and lie fallow, so that the poor of your people may eat; and what they leave the wild animals may eat. You shall do the same with your vineyard, and with your olive orchard.
>
> 23:10–11

As noted in the last section, these are case laws used to adjudicate conflicts and problems in the civic life of the Hebrew people.[26] They can also be understood as applications of the primary moral law rather than the heart of God's moral designs. In the Old Testament, similar laws are found in the Holiness Code (Leviticus 17–26) and the Deuteronomic Code (Deuteronomy 12–25). Few such laws are found in the rest of Scripture. In the New Testament, Paul does occasionally address specific problems and commend specific forms of response, as in his admonition regarding the immoral man in the Corinthian church (1 Corinthians 5). However, his instruction is not set forth in casuistic form and seems to address an already existing issue in personal fashion. James's treatment of favoritism in the church (2:1–11) sets forth a hypothetical situation that has similarities to casuistry, but his primary intent is to illustrate the principle of loving one's neighbor. Similarly, Jesus' statements in the Sermon on the Mount regarding turning the other cheek if struck by another (Matt. 5:38–42) seem to be an application and illustration of a principle rather than a casuistic injunction. The bottom line is that the Bible contains little casuistic law, and most of it is civil case law.

Many Christians seem to wish that God had simply deposited divine commands in casuistic fashion so that we knew exactly what to do in every ethical dilemma. It is highly significant that God did not choose that path. One of the problems with casuistic law is that it does not apply broadly, only to the specific situation addressed. If Jesus and the apostles had spoken casuistically, we would find most of their teachings irrelevant for our world, or the Bible, in attempting to address every conceivable situation of every era, would be enormous. We should also note that when moral casuistry has been practiced in the Christian church, it has tended toward legalism—law for law's sake.

163

Ethics then becomes a burden rather than a gift of God. Furthermore, if all biblical guidance was in casuistic form, there would be little development in maturity in the lives of disciples, who grow in grace and understanding through the process of moral reflection and application in the midst of complexity.

Biblical casuistic law, however, is not entirely irrelevant for Christian ethics. Often underlying the casuistic injunctions are intentions or principles that provide moral guidance and perspective. For example, the edict, "You shall not boil a kid in its mother's milk" (Exod. 23:19b) is neither irrelevant nor a mandate for animal rights activists. The text refers to a Canaanite fertility practice, and its primary aim was to forbid syncretism with foreign religion and gods. The intentionality of the text has great relevance today. Similarly, the sabbatical laws and directives for harvesting (leaving the corners of the field for the poor) has application, not in its original form but in its goal of procuring justice for the poor.

Apodictic Law

Apodictic laws are straightforward regulations in the form of divine commands. These laws contain some specificity of action, but both the setting and the behavior elicited are much broader than casuistic law. Thus, apodictic laws entail some form of human deliberation in application to real-life issues. The commands may be in either negative or positive form, but the "negative moral principles include affirmatives and affirmatives include negatives so that when any sin is forbidden, the opposite duty is urged upon us and when any duty is encouraged, its opposite sin is forbidden."[27]

The best-known example of apodictic law in the Bible is the Decalogue, the Ten Commandments (Exod. 20:1–17; Deut. 5:6–21). As noted in chapter 3, these are not universal, abstract laws isolated from a larger context. They were given in the context of the exodus and God's initiative to establish a covenant relationship with the Hebrew people. The relationship between faith and ethics in the Decalogue is evident in its structure. The commands are generally divided into two groups: The first four commands are vertically directed toward God, and the last six are horizontally directed toward fellow humans. Thus, flowing out of exclusive worship of God (shunning idolatry and honoring God's name and day) comes a regard for human life, parents, marriage, property, and the reputation of others. The Decalogue constitutes the primary law of God.

An examination of apodictic law and specifically the Ten Commandments reveals much more than first meets the eye. Underlying the commandments are broader understandings about reality and God's dealings with humanity. For example, the fourth commandment, "Remember the sabbath day, and keep it holy" (Exod. 20:8) is far broader in meaning and ethical content than simply requiring one not to do anything on Sundays.

The foundation of this apodictic law is God's own activity: "For in six days the LORD made heaven and the earth, the sea, all that is in them, but rested the seventh day" (20:11). The primary principles are twofold: First, we should set aside a day to stop making the world and remember that God has already made it (i.e., worship); second, we should rest from our work to be rejuvenated and care for our body, soul, and mind. Scripture also applies the meaning of this commandment to stewardship of the land, care for the poor, and economic justice (Exod. 23:10–13). As we consider the fourth commandment, we begin to see that it calls forth a way of life that reflects a God-ordained rhythm incorporating worship, work, and play. Finding balance between these three dimensions is an application of the command to our world. As Gordon Dahl once put it, we middle-class Americans tend "to worship our work, work at our play, and play at our worship."[28] Thus, the meaning and application of the Sabbath law has far greater depth than we might imagine. Its recovery is crucial for our own moral life and the health of society.

The sixth command is quite simple and straightforward: "You shall not murder" (Exod. 20:13). But it too carries much greater depth of meaning and application than the statement itself. The foundation of the command is God's creation of humanity in his own image. Why is murder wrong? Because it desecrates the very image of God in a person. It destroys that person's inherent dignity, value, and worth. But the application of the command goes even further. Jesus himself extended it to anger toward and broken relationship with another individual (Matt. 5:21–26). The heart of the command is to protect the God-given dignity of another person, and therefore, it is relevant in a wide scope of arenas including race/ethnic relations, treatment of employees in the workplace, and a host of bioethical issues such as abortion, euthanasia, genetic engineering, and organ transplants.

The commandments, therefore, carry with them far greater depth and meaning than we might think at first glance. Their application extends to many contemporary issues that were not yet in view at Mount Sinai.[29]

There are, of course, other examples of the apodictic law form throughout Scripture. The Ten Commandments themselves are often articulated directly or indirectly in various places throughout both Testaments. The New Testament contains statements akin to apodictic law form in Jesus' teaching in the Sermon on the Mount and other texts:

Everyone who looks at a woman with lust has already committed adultery with her in his heart.

Matthew 5:28

Do not swear at all.

Matthew 5:34

Love your enemies and pray for those who persecute you.

Matthew 5:44

Whoever divorces his wife and marries another commits adultery against her; and if she divorces her husband and marries another, she commits adultery.

Mark 10:11–12

Paul, while not frequently using the commandment form, provides the same specific directives, as in Colossians 3:5: "Put to death, therefore, whatever in you is earthly: fornication, impurity, passion, evil desire, and greed (which is idolatry)."

Principles

Principles are general foundational perspectives and guidelines for human behavior. They are duties, ideals, responsibilities, and life orientations that are set forth in broad terms. The specific form of behavior elicited is less specific than with apodictic laws, though clearly these two categories overlap. Principles can be imperatives or indicatives, and often they contain a breadth of application because of their more general nature.

In recent years, especially among character or virtue ethicists, there has been resistance to the use of principles in Christian ethics for fear that they might become empty universal norms devoid of a larger grounding and context. Stanley Hauerwas writes, "Indeed when biblical ethics is so construed one wonders why appeals need to be made to Scripture at all, since one treats it as a source of general principles or images that once in hand need no longer acknowledge their origins."[30] But principles need not be understood in this way. They should always be understood in light of the overarching biblical story and the context or narrative of a given text. Principles are not necessarily antithetical to virtues. While a principle guides human behavior, the virtue side of a principle focuses on character and internal disposition.

One of the most obvious sources of principles in the Old Testament is the Book of Proverbs. Set mostly in the form of indicative wisdom sayings that were widespread in the ancient Near East, the proverbs are broad generalized principles that apply to practical everyday life. They are often short pithy sayings that provide guidelines for happiness, success, and the morally good life.

Whoever walks in integrity walks securely,
but whoever follows perverse ways will be found out.

10:9

Those who guard their mouths preserve their lives;
those who open wide their lips come to ruin.

13:3

> Without counsel, plans go wrong,
> but with many advisers they succeed.
>
> 15:22

> Pride goes before destruction,
> and a haughty spirit before a fall.
>
> 16:18

Various other principles are found in the Old Testament, particularly in the prophets. Speaking in light of the evils of their own day, the prophets called the people back to God and divine designs for living. In enunciating principles, the prophets were essentially applying the more specific forms of the apodictic or primary law. Isaiah used the genre of principle as an application of the moral law when he cried out, "Ah, you who make iniquitous decrees, who write oppressive statutes, to turn aside the needy from justice and to rob the poor of my people of their right, that widows may be your spoil, and that you may make the orphans your prey!" (10:1–2). Principles of righteousness, justice, mercy, integrity, and holiness were continually on the lips of the prophets. Thus, Micah answered his own question: "And what does the LORD require of you but to do justice, and to love kindness, and to walk humbly with your God?" (6:8). Micah, like the other prophets, clarified the ways in which the people had subverted God's requirements in their worship and their actions. Amos in similar fashion proclaimed, "Hate evil and love good, and establish justice in the gate; it may be that the LORD, the God of hosts, will be gracious to the remnant of Joseph" (5:15).

The New Testament also contains principles that have broad application but are clearly not divorced from their worldview context or God's grace. Jesus spoke in principle form when he summed up the Old Testament law: "'You shall love the Lord your God with all your heart, and with all your soul, and with all your mind'. . . . And a second is like it: 'You shall love your neighbor as yourself'" (Matt. 22:37, 39). In the Golden Rule, Jesus gave not a specific form of behavior but a generalized principle to guide both action and motivation. "In everything do to others as you would have them do to you" (Matt. 7:12).

Paul laid out a principle when he said, "Do not be mismatched with unbelievers. For what partnership is there between righteousness and lawlessness?" (2 Cor. 6:14). His commendation of generosity and love in the face of others' needs (2 Corinthians 8–9) was also set forth with principles, yet he never lost sight of the larger theological grounding for such action: "For you know the generous act of our Lord Jesus Christ, that though he was rich, yet for your sakes he became poor, so that by his poverty you might become rich" (8:9). And in dealing with weaker brothers and sisters on issues of conscience (i.e., eating meat offered to idols), Paul, in the midst of his discourse, laid out a number of principles to guide believers:

Welcome those who are weak in faith, but not for the purpose of quarreling over opinions.

Romans 14:1

Why do you despise your brother or sister? For we will all stand before the judgment seat of God.

14:10

Nothing is unclean in itself; but it is unclean for anyone who thinks it unclean.

14:14

Do not let what you eat cause the ruin of one for whom Christ died.

14:15

For the kingdom of God is not food and drink but righteousness and peace and joy in the Holy Spirit. . . . Let us then pursue what makes for peace and for mutual upbuilding.

14:17, 19

Paul clearly hoped that the weaker Christians would see the light and not make an issue of meat offered to idols. Nonetheless, he laid out principles, within a theological and ecclesiastical context, to guide the stronger believers in their actions and attitudes toward the weaker.

Richard Longenecker has argued that principles really form the heart of New Testament ethics, for "what we have in the New Testament is a declaration of the gospel and the ethical principles that derive from the gospel, and a description of how that proclamation and its principles were put into practice in various situations during the apostolic period." He believes that the "proclamation and principles . . . are to be taken as normative. The way . . . [they] are put into practice in the first century, however, should be understood as signposts at the beginning of a journey."[31]

Longenecker sees the central principles of the New Testament in Galatians 3:28: "There is no longer Jew or Greek, there is no longer slave or free, there is no longer male and female; for all of you are one in Christ Jesus." This forms what he calls the cultural mandate (Jew nor Greek), the societal mandate (slave nor free), and the sexual mandate (male nor female). While these key principles are from the New Testament, their full development in practice did not occur during the New Testament period. Just as theology developed throughout church history, so Longenecker sees a developmental hermeneutic at work in the application of New Testament social ethic principles. "The recorded practices [in the early church] are meant to show how these principles were applied in that day and to point the direction in which we as Christians should be moving in reapplying those same norms in fuller and more significant ways in our day."[32] Thus, the principles carry the seeds for more than what the texts themselves say.

An examination of biblical principles in light of the larger biblical narrative and the immediate context in which they were given reveals a richness of moral insight and guidance. This is well illustrated in the New Testament principle of showing hospitality. Hospitality is both a principle to guide actions and a virtue to be manifest in character. Today we think of hospitality as "having family and friends over for a pleasant meal. Or we think of the 'hospitality industry,' of hotels and restaurants."[33] But as Christine Pohl has so ably demonstrated, hospitality is central to the gospel in the New Testament: "The distinctive quality of Christian hospitality is that it offers a generous welcome to the 'least,' without concern for advantage or benefit to the host. Such hospitality reflects God's greater hospitality that welcomes the undeserving, provides the lonely with a home, and sets a banquet table for the hungry."[34]

In the New Testament, hospitality is a prerequisite for leadership in the church (1 Tim. 3:2; Titus 1:8), believers are called to practice it (Rom. 12:13; 1 Tim. 5:9–10; Heb. 13:2; 1 Peter 4:9), and Jesus, while not using the term per se, calls his disciples to hospitality with these words: "When you give a banquet, invite the poor, the crippled, the lame, and the blind. And you will be blessed, because they cannot repay you" (Luke 14:13–14). Pohl gives not only a biblical foundation for hospitality but also a historic overview of its practice, an analysis of the places of hospitality, and a portrayal of the spiritual rhythms of hospitality. This is an example of the way in which biblical principles can provide rich moral guidance without being divorced from God's grace, the biblical story, and the enduring real-life needs of human beings.

Biblical Paradigms with Implied Ethical Guidance

Biblical paradigms are basic understandings of life and theology that contain within them implied directions for ethics. They are broad understandings of reality drawn from throughout Scripture or a given text. In and of themselves, paradigms are not ethical mandates, but as indicative statements pointing to worldview understandings, they embody moral direction. At their heart, paradigms are theological teachings. Theology is rooted in Scripture but is a kind of analysis in which biblical teaching is synthesized to create paradigmatic understandings about Christian faith and life. For example, the word Trinity does not appear in the Bible, but the Christian church declared a trinitarian understanding of God based on the teachings of Scripture concerning the relationship of Father, Son, and Holy Spirit. Thus, the doctrine of the Trinity is

169

biblical, but it is deduced from biblical statements rather than being explicitly stated.

Many biblically based paradigms carry with them ethical import. Chapter 3 developed this notion (under the category of Christian worldview) as a foundation for Christian ethics. It explored the overarching biblical story of creation, fall, redemption, and consummation as the heart of the Christian worldview and a foundation for the moral life. This paradigm, however, not only serves as a foundation but also actually guides us in ethical decisions. When faced with many contemporary ethical issues, about which we lack direct forms of biblical guidance, we often need to look to paradigms to guide us.

Take, for example, the paradigm of the lordship of Christ. This paradigm is based on various texts in the New Testament that when put together form a theological affirmation that in thought and life Christ is the ruler of everything. For ethics, this implies that no other kingdom, institution, or person can claim allegiance over Christ. Human and institutional claims certainly have a rightful place in the moral lives of believers, but the allegiance to Christ's kingdom has priority. At times, therefore, we should say no to certain claims, not because they have no legitimate place in life but because nothing can ultimately supplant the lordship of Christ.

Or take the understanding of human beings outlined in chapter 3. Christians simultaneously affirm the paradigms of human sinfulness and the creation of humans in the image of God. Thus, when considering politics and public policy, we will be skeptical of utopian schemes built on humanistic assumptions of human goodness; likewise, we will reject policies that degrade human dignity. Reinhold Niebuhr's famous phrase about human nature was built on a biblical paradigm: "Man's capacity for justice makes democracy possible; man's capacity for injustice makes democracy necessary."[35] Democratic government is certainly not explicitly advocated in Scripture, but biblical paradigms point in its direction.

Many of the bioethics issues today are perhaps best approached using biblical paradigm sources. For example, when we think as Christians about death and dying issues (i.e., treatment termination, euthanasia, physician-assisted suicide, etc.), it is helpful to reflect paradigmatically. Theologically, the Bible affirms death as both friend and foe, suffering as both a challenge to persevere and an opportunity to overcome, and human action as both under divine providence and an act of human stewardship.[36] These paradigmatic tensions need to be held together and thus will preclude any radical answer to the pressing ethical questions. On the basis of these paradigms, we can infer an ethical rejection of euthanasia, which insists on taking life when it becomes burdensome, as well as medical vitalism, which insists on keeping a person alive at all costs. "These theological assertions do not solve every dilemma. . . . But they do provide a framework that can guide us to make wise decisions amidst the complexity and ambiguity we often face in death and dying issues. On the one hand they preserve us from playing God in ethics, but on the other hand they also prevent us from abdicating our responsibilities as human stewards made in the very image of an all-powerful God."[37]

Christopher Wright has attempted to demonstrate the usefulness of a paradigmatic approach when applying the Old Testament to contemporary ethical issues. While he believes that "we cannot simply lift the social laws of an ancient people and transplant them into our vastly changed modern world," the biblical paradigms allow us to make "imaginative reflection on what modern realities correspond in principle to realities addressed by Israel."[38] Israel was called to be an example of a particular constellation of beliefs, demonstrated in the way they used the land, cared for one another, and lived with justice and personal righteousness. As Wright sees it, the relevance of the Old Testament for contemporary ethics is its larger vision that is demonstrated within the "parameters of ancient Near Eastern macro-culture," whereby "God brought into being a society through whom he both revealed a new paradigm of understanding God, the world and humanity, and actually modeled a framework of laws, institutions, conventions, and customs, which experimentally demonstrated the truth of that revelation."[39] Though Israel frequently failed to embody the new paradigm morally, the paradigm provides significant guidance for us in terms of its vision and intent.

Richard Hays, in *The Moral Vision of the New Testament,* uses essentially a paradigm approach in his analysis of the unity of New Testament ethics. He sees three "focal images" that summarize the ethical teaching in the New Testament and can be used normatively in contemporary moral judgments: community, cross, and new creation. In regard to the community image (paradigm), he writes, "The church is a countercultural community of discipleship, and this community is the primary addressee of God's imperatives." As for the cross, "Jesus' death on a cross is the paradigm for faithfulness to God in this world." And as to new creation, "The church embodies the power of the resurrection in the midst of a not-yet-redeemed world."[40] Such images provide insight in understanding the broad paradigms of the New Testament and can be helpful when grappling with contemporary issues, as Hays does in the last section of his book. Such broad images, however, should not be used to negate specific directives found in the Bible. As Hays acknowledges, "These images are not principles that can be applied generally to moral issues apart from any particular New Testament texts. Rather, they are guides for our interpretation and placement of specific texts within a wider canonical perspective."[41]

Moral Examples and Narratives

The Bible is full of stories and narratives about real-life people facing spiritual, theological, moral, and practical issues. In recent years, narrative has been the rage in biblical interpretation, theology, preaching, and ethics, and we

171

should not neglect it as a source of moral guidance, perspective, and motivation, despite its sometimes faddish tendency. Stories and narratives contain a richness in their human touch, imaginary appeal, and relevance to life. "We discover our human self more effectively through . . . stories."[42]

When we examine the narratives and examples in the Bible, however, we face an immediate problem: Many stories are about moral failures. Jesus' parables are one thing, but what are we to do with Abraham's lie about his wife (Gen. 12:10–20), David's adultery and murder plot (2 Samuel 11), Tamar's deceit and adultery with her father-in-law (Genesis 38), or Ananias and Sapphira's economic deceit (Acts 5)? How are we to separate the moral virtue from the moral vice in the narratives of Scripture?

First, we must interpret them in light of the overarching story of the Bible. Richard Bauckham reminds us, "A key place within this overarching story is occupied by the gospel story of Jesus, but the gospel story is incomplete and lacks its fully biblical meaning apart from the more comprehensive story in which the Bible places it."[43] Thus, a particular story should be understood in light of the entire biblical story, which culminates in the gospel of Jesus Christ.

Second, as we examine an individual narrative, we may find clues to its moral assessment in the text itself or in a nearby text. Thus, while Genesis 12 offers no evaluation of Abraham's lie about Sarah (calling her his sister, which was technically correct but terribly misleading), Genesis 20 renders his action morally blameworthy, for Abimelech, the King of Gerar, discovers Abraham's actions, cries out to God about the wrong, and calls Abraham in for an accountability session. Similarly, David's actions with Bathsheba and her husband, Uriah, receive a stinging condemnation from Nathan the prophet by means of a parable, through which David sees his immorality (2 Samuel 12). And the immediate context is quite clear in the story of Ananias and Sapphira, for their lying and economic stinginess result in the judgment of God.

Third, when assessing the moral narratives of Scripture, we should examine the outcomes of the stories. At times a verdict is not given within a story, but reverberations reveal that the designs of God have been circumvented. A good example is the story of Abraham taking Hagar as a kind of surrogate mother to have a child (Genesis 16). Both Sarah and Abraham agreed to the plan, but the long-term results were devastating.

Fourth, we should assess the story in light of other forms of moral guidance, such as biblical laws, principles, paradigms, and other narratives in which ethical norms are clearly affirmed. Thus, we can render a negative moral verdict on the various incidents of polygamy in the Old Testament in light of the creation paradigm, the seventh commandment, Jesus' own affirmation of the creation paradigm, and other New Testament texts.

172

Finally, as we examine biblical narratives, we should give hermeneutical and normative priority to the narratives of Jesus—both his own examples and the many stories he told. Because God has spoken ultimately in redemption history through his Son (Heb. 1:1–3), we should readily accept the moral guidance of his teachings. Hence, the story of the poor widow's offering (Luke 21:1–4), the parable of the rich fool (Luke 12:13–21), the story of the Good Samaritan (Luke 10:25–37), the parable of the talents (Matt. 25:14–30), and many others should guide Christian character and actions. Other New Testament writers look to the example of Jesus' life as the ultimate norm for the Christian life:

> Let the same mind be in you that was in Christ Jesus, who, though he was in the form of God, did not regard equality with God as something to be exploited, but emptied himself, taking the form of a slave, being born in human likeness. And being found in human form, he humbled himself and became obedient to the point of death—even death on a cross.
>
> Philippians 2:5–8

The Bible contains rich material ranging from specific laws to more general principles, paradigms, and narratives that can guide moral decision making. As finite creatures we will need to grapple with which biblical material takes priority. The safest approach is to look first to direct or clear guidance on an issue and then bring together the other forms of ethical guidance with an understanding that Scripture interprets Scripture. We must interpret the part in light of the whole, with special attention to the fuller revelation in Christ and the apostolic witness of the New Testament.

Conclusion

Christians look to the Bible for making moral decisions, not merely because they have done so for hundreds of years but because it is God's Word written. It "is useful for teaching, for reproof, for correction, and for training in righteousness" (2 Tim. 3:16b). Scripture, however, was written in particular cultural and historical contexts. The biblical authors, under the providence of God, used various genres to address the issues of their day. The hermeneutical task we face in our own cultural and historic contexts, which influence our perceptions and interpretations, is to move from then to now with integrity and openness to biblical guidance. As shown in this chapter, the ethical materials of the Bible are rich and varied: casuistic law, apodictic law, principles, paradigms, and narratives. From the biblical texts of long ago, we find guidance and comfort in the midst of our own moral journeys.

8

EMPIRICAL JUDGMENTS
IN ETHICAL DECISIONS

A number of years ago I served as an interim pastor at a Chinese church in the heart of Chinatown, New York City. Very quickly I learned that these ardent believers were not of one mind on an issue I had never personally encountered. It is a moral quandary faced not only among the Chinese but also among believers in many parts of the world and within varying cultures. The issue involves their ancestors, and the debates become intense on those special days when all are expected to go to the cemeteries and perform rituals that have long been practiced by their respective families and cultures.

Some of my Chinese friends were quite convinced that merely showing up at the cemetery was nothing short of pagan idolatry. Burning paper money and placing rice before the tombstone were rituals they had left behind when they had become Christians. They believed even a token appearance at the cemetery was a compromise and morally wrong. Others were not so sure. They agreed that ancestor worship was forbidden in their Christian faith, but the rituals were not in themselves necessarily ancestor worship and hence idolatrous. They argued that going to the cemetery did not mean they were buying into the religious worldviews from which these practices came. Most on this side of the debate would not participate in all the rituals, but they would attend, show respect, and in the end interpret their actions as family solidarity and appreciation.

As I listened to the debates of these equally committed Christians, it became clear that their differences were not over theology, principles, or commitment to the authority of Scripture. Both sides rejected idolatry, believed that compromise must be eschewed, and believed the Bible to be the final authority. Their differences resided in an interpretation of the facts, in their rendition of what was actually going on at the cemetery on those special days. For one side, the empirical judgment was rendered idolatry, for the other side, it was rendered respect.

When we think about Christian ethics, we normally think of the application of principles, virtues, and theological understandings to realities of everyday life, as has been discussed in previous chapters. But ethics also involves judgments of another sort—namely, judgments about the facts or empirical realities surrounding the issues faced. As Alan Geyer states, "Ethics is not simply an argument about what ought to be; it is an almost uninterrupted argument about what is, what has been, and what will be . . . whose reading of history, . . . which social analysis . . . which intelligence data shall we choose as being empirically sound?"[1] Every ethical issue has a factual side to it. Often differences in ethical decisions are due to differing accounts of what is happening in a given situation. The particular way we portray the reality may well determine, at least in part, the ethical outcome.

Some of the empirical judgments we accept are based on a selection of the facts or data. At times the hard sciences (biology, chemistry, physics) and quite often the social sciences contain different sets of data regarding a particular issue. Which set one accepts will greatly affect one's ethical judgment. Then too at times there are differences of interpretation of given data. That is, people may look at the same data but end up with different interpretations of its significance or what it means. For example, the scientific data regarding life in the womb is fairly straightforward, but people give differing interpretations of what it means and how significant it is for the abortion debate. Beyond selection and interpretation of data, there are also more impressionistic renditions of empirical realities. These include the particular ways in which we construct the reality being interpreted. This appears to be the case with the differing judgments about ancestor veneration. The particular renditions given as to what happens when descendants visit a cemetery on those special days are based primarily on impressionistic accounts of the situation. Therefore, whether a selection of data, interpretation of data, or impressionistic rendition of a situation, empirical judgments play a significant role in moral decisions.

Examples of Empirical Judgments in Ethics

Just War

One of the most vexing ethical issues faced by the Christian church has been the issue of war. Over the centuries, Christians have essentially responded in one of three ways: pacifism, a rejection of participation in violence; holy war, an enthusiastic participation without moral scruples and with divine blessing; and just war, a selective participation that attempts to place moral parameters around warfare.[2] Since the fourth century, the majority of Christians, at least

175

theoretically, have adhered to the just war tradition. Just war advocates over the years have developed criteria to discern both when it is just to go to war *(jus ad bellum)* and what actions are just or unjust within the war itself *(jus in bello)*. Wars, in this tradition, are deemed just when the criteria are met, and nations and Christians within the nation are then allowed to participate.

First, in this tradition, a war is just when it is the last resort. All other means of resolving the conflict must first be tried, and only then can violent resistence be employed. Of course, such a criterion involves an empirical judgment, a judgment as to whether in fact all other means of resolution have been tried. During the Gulf War of 1991, this was one of the issues surrounding military deployment by the United States. Had all possible means been employed in an attempt to thwart the aggression of Saddam Hussein? The intelligence experts disagreed. Some argued that nothing was left but force; others argued that mechanisms such as economic embargos could be implemented. When intelligence experts themselves differ over which data to accept, it is difficult for the average person to make a judgment and take a moral stand in the midst of a conflict. Much of the moral debate surrounding that war (at least for those in the just war tradition) was not over principles but over the facts.

Another criterion used by just war advocates is proportionality, the notion that the good gained by entering the conflict must outweigh the evil that is sustained and meted out within the conflict. That is, if a country had to sacrifice half its population to win a war, the good gained would be disproportional to the evil sustained to garner victory; hence, the war would be unjust. Of course, the application of this principle again hinges on empirical judgments, and in this case, they apply not so much to what is as to what will be. Indeed, "such calculation must properly seek to take account not only of specific deeds that one is immediately aware of choosing, but also of the potential for escalation and proliferation of the violent effects."[3]

Proportionality has become a significant issue in ethical debates surrounding the use of nuclear weapons. The potential damage not only to soldiers but also to noncombatants and the environment forces modern society to wrestle with unthinkable consequences and hence the issue of proportionality. Many have argued that nuclear warfare could never be just because of the disproportional negative effects, while others have argued for at least a limited use of nuclear weapons. Still others have contended that the presence of nuclear weapons acts as a deterrence against their use and thus they constitute a mechanism for peace.[4] But, of course, these views hang on judgments of fact, and projected fact at that. It is the difficulty of gathering this kind of empirical knowledge that has made the application of just war theory so complicated in the modern world and why some have even argued that given modern weaponry it is no longer a viable ethical framework.

Environmental Ethics

During the past several decades, Christians have gained a new awareness of the physical environment in which they live and their ethical responsibilities therein. Drawing on the creation accounts of Genesis 1–2 and texts such as Psalm 8 or Romans 8:19–22, believers have come to understand the role that the physical earth plays in God's economy and the stewardship that has been granted to humans for its care. The ecological mandate of the Bible has become fairly common in the thinking of many. However, Christians are not of one accord on the environmental crisis and how to carry out the mandate. Some portray the environmental situation in almost catastrophic language, with the assumption that we are headed for disaster unless there is immediate intervention, based not on volunteerism but on state-mandated action. Others use milder language, and they support less radical action based on moderate structural interventions.

What is behind these differing ethical responses? In part, they are related to different judgments about the state and its role in such issues, but clearly differing empirical judgments play a significant role. To understand the nature of the issue, the average person relies on media reports, which in turn draw their information from the technical experts. When it comes to the intricacies of the environment, however, scientists do not always agree on either the data or the interpretation of the data.

One of the major environmental issues of our time is global warming. While there is general agreement among experts that global warming is a reality with potentially dire consequences, there is a fair amount of variation on many of the particulars. Two researchers at Carnegie Mellon University have written:

> The extent to which greenhouse gas emissions will change climate is highly uncertain. Many resources are being invested in atmospheric science research. . . . Some investigators use historical analogies to explore periods when there was more CO_2 in the atmosphere and the earth was warmer. Other atmospheric scientists depend on relatively simple models to investigate these issues. In addition, there are more than a dozen general circulation models-computer simulations. . . . These three methods do not produce identical results; indeed, there is no agreement even on predictions such as temperature increase.[5]

These researchers go on to argue that public policy formulations are based on varying scenarios that have less to do with hard scientific data than with prior beliefs. For example, some judgments are based on whether one is an optimist, a pessimist, or a moderate in outlook. In similar fashion, S. George Philander, writing on global warming, states, "If we can distinguish clearly between the scientific and political aspects of the problem, we can focus on reaching a solution that is acceptable to all. Unfortunately, the distinction between science and politics can easily become blurred. This invariably happens when the scientific results have uncertainties."[6]

The role of empirical judgments in environmental ethics was highlighted in a 1997 United States Senate subcommittee hearing regarding proposals to tighten standards for clean air. While all sides appealed to scientific data, there were clear differences in both the data to which they appealed and their interpretation of the data. For example, some senators were dismayed that in one study only 265 out of 28,000 asthma sufferers (less than 1 percent) in New York City experienced a decrease in asthma-related hospitalizations under newly proposed standards for ozone. Senator John Chafee asked, "Am I missing something here? Or are we dealing with very minor health improvements here?" George Thurston, a New York University scientist who has written extensively on pollution epidemiology, replied, "I guess it comes down to whether you're one of those people." But as the *Washington Post* reporter put it, "No one succeeded in accomplishing what 15 senators and scientists purportedly set out to do yesterday; resolving the scientific questions behind the federal government's latest proposed clean air standards."[7]

Another dimension of environmental concern is population and its impact on the capacity of the earth. While the data is fairly clear regarding population trends (the world will have ten billion people by the middle of the twenty-first century), wide variations exist concerning the interpretation or meaning of that data. Lester Brown, president of the Worldwatch Institute, says that the "day of reckoning" has already arrived. "I personally do not think we are ever going to get close to a world population of 10 billion. . . . Ecosystems are already starting to break down."[8] But others read the data quite differently. Many experts believe that the earth's vast resources can feed ten billion people as long as we learn how to increase food production, limit environmental damage, and develop good mechanisms of resource distribution. The differences between these two scenarios are well captured in a debate between Norman Myers and Julian Simon. Myers is an ecological doomsayer who believes that "our planetary ecosystem faces unparalleled threats" that we cannot escape unless we adopt "an entirely new mode of Earthling existence . . . a shift in our attitudes, our goals, our values . . . a basic redesigning of our societies."[9] But Simon rejects both the statistics and overall scenario painted by Myers. As an economist he sets forth his own graphs and data showing "steadily improving trends in U.S. environmental quality rather than the deterioration claimed by environmentalists."[10]

The point is clear. Many differences in ethical judgments about the environment are not the result of varying theology or ethical principles but of divergent sets of data or interpretations of the data. When experts in the field offer varying empirical renditions, all supposedly based on scientific data, the task for the average Christian seeking to make sound ethical judgments and pursue an accompanying lifestyle is not easy.

Poverty and Economic Justice

Christians have no option regarding care for the economically disenfranchised and victims of economic injustice within the world. Scripture is clear in its mandate to pursue justice, to love mercy, and to respond with care to those in economic need. As 1 John 3:17 puts it, "If anyone has material possessions and sees his brother in need but has no pity on him, how can the love of God be in him?" (NIV). But when it comes to the particulars of economic justice, Christians do not always agree. They do not always agree on the causes of poverty, the best ways to alleviate poverty, or even what economic justice would look like in real life.

One scenario regarding poverty and economic justice goes like this. Poverty is a result of exploitation by the powerful in this world. Economic justice will never become a reality until there is a redistribution of the world's goods, a change in economic structures, and a diffusion of economic power to the masses. Poverty is a result of unjust economic arrangements and economic dependency, factors that can be rectified only by a liberation from those arrangements. Enrique Dussel, a proponent of liberation theology and a critic of reliance on the market, states, "The norms, actions, institutions or ethical systems that are the unintentional fruit of the market . . . contain the evil and injustice proper to those who kill." Thus, a commitment to liberation "obliges us to deconstruct the negativities—or norms, actions, institutions or ethical systems—and practically construct the new bodies needed— the complex stages of a liberation process."[11]

Another scenario paints a different picture. Poverty is a result of inadequate development within a country or a given area due to a lack of education, sufficient technological know-how, and adequate infrastructures needed to maintain a viable economy (such as transportation, communication systems, etc.). The answer to poverty and economic injustice is adequate education, stable political systems, adequate capital formation, and a relatively free market that encourages growth and creativity.

In still another scenario, poverty is a result of worldview, moral systems, and lifestyles. The cause of poverty clearly rests on the shoulders of the poor and their societies, for it is related to the characteristics and circumstances of those suffering poverty. Only shifts in ways of living, patterns of culture, and basic beliefs will result in adequate systems to overcome poverty.[12]

And in still another scenario, poverty is a result of one or more of the above factors, with causes varying according to context. Poverty can be overcome only by addressing all the issues that are pertinent to the particular nation, geographical area, or society. As David Landes in *The Wealth and Poverty of Nations* puts it, "Economic analysis cherishes the illusion that one good reason should be enough, but the determinants of complex process are invariably plural and inter-related."[13]

179

It is possible, therefore, for Christians to operate from the same ethical principles or theological commitments but still end up with different approaches to economic justice and poverty. Certainly, numerous assumptions account for this, but one of them clearly has to do with the data. Which data we accept, how we interpret the data, and the overall empirical scenarios we use go a long way in our understanding of and approach to economic ethics.

Factors Influencing Empirical Judgments

Why do Christians differ in empirical judgments? Why do people who may hold to the same view of the Bible, have similar theological beliefs and compatible ethical principles or virtues, and belong to the same denomination accept different judgments about the nature of given issues? To answer those questions we must recognize first the fallenness and finiteness of humanity. But it is also helpful to understand a number of factors that influence fallen, finite thinking. A selection of particular data, an interpretation of data, and impressionistic renditions of the ethical situation are largely dependent on one or more of the following influences.

Social Mores

Every society contains a normative structure of rules and regulations that govern the behavior of that society. The normative structure ranges from reflective ethics (such as philosophical or religious ethics) to laws (regulations enforced by power) to social mores (traditions in a culture that are rarely spelled out in textbooks or law codes but nonetheless convey a great sense of authority). In traditional, folk societies, these three dimensions of the normative structure are not highly differentiated from one another, but as societies become more complex and modern, the dimensions become distinct. The legal regulations are usually the ethical minimum in a society, and reflective ethics the ethical maxim. But the mores are often the most stubborn of the three because they are firmly embedded in the culture and thinking of a people.

The concept of social mores goes back to the work of William Graham Sumner nearly a century ago. This Yale professor described the difference between "folkways" and "mores." Folkways, said Sumner, are relatively durable, standardized practices in a society that have to do with etiquette or the way things are done. They involve such things as food, eating practices, and style of dress. Mores are also traditions passed on from generation to generation, but they pertain to more serious matters and carry with them a sense of moral authority by embodying a sense of oughtness. For example, style of clothing is a folkway, but wearing clothes (at least in most societies) is part of the mores. Sumner noted several characteristics of social mores: They are nonrational and merely accepted; they are always right and are not to be challenged; they function to maintain the status quo, perpetuating the way things are; they carry with them a sense of sacredness; they change but stubbornly so.[14]

Social mores influence not only the values we bring to ethics but also our perceptions of the way things are, our empirical judgments. Cultural mores, for example, likely play a role in economic ethics. If one's cultural mores include freedom, individualism, and hard work, that person's empirical judgment may emphasize personal responsibility as a causal agent and cure for poverty. Many Americans, influenced by the social mores of freedom and self-determination, similarly accept a particular set of data regarding the issue of gun control.

Social mores are also significant in national differences over public policy positions and policy making processes. Yasuko Kawashima examined the different approaches that Japan and the United States have taken toward global environmental problems. He found the variations to be rooted in national characteristics, including characteristics of the people. Kawashima noted that in Japan "a village community was once the fundamental unit of group activity. Although the structure of Japanese society has changed, this community culture remains a characteristic of the government's policy-making process, in that, decisions are made through a process of consensus building." The United States has a different set of mores and thus different approaches to decision making. "Freedom and privacy are highly respected, and the people are reluctant to be controlled by the government." Moreover, in the United States, "they tend to prefer claims or assertions which can be supported by scientific or numerical evidence. The scientific uncertainty of global warning may have had much to do with the people's indifference in relation to efforts to tackle the problem."[15]

Social mores then play a significant role in making empirical judgments regarding a host of ethical issues. Subsequently, they also influence public policy formulations. At times social mores are even intertwined with a religious outlook so that they become part of religious understanding and expression, though their origin is cultural and not endemic to the faith.

Ideologies

Ideology often determines which facts are accepted or how they are interpreted. The notion of ideology goes back to Karl Marx and Friedrich Engels in the mid-nineteenth century. Their definition of ideology was economic in nature. Ideology was false consciousness and involved the ideas of the ruling class that distort facts and are used to justify their position in society. Later sociologists broadened the concept to include more than economics. Talcott Parsons, for example, defined ideology as "an empirical belief system held in common by the members of any collective"; it is a system of ideas used to interpret the social realities in which people find themselves and to provide goals

181

and actions for the particular collective.[16] Another definition states, "It presents a picture of the world that gives legitimacy to the cultural values and goals it holds most dear. While its focus is on social-empirical reality . . . it colors one's understanding of every aspect of life."[17]

Ideologies are often seen as deviations from scientific objectivity as they seek to bend truth toward particular ends. Parsons noted two ways in which objectivity is lost in ideological thinking: (1) a selectivity in the issues treated (hence, ideologies are often oriented toward one issue or at least interpret all reality through the lens of one issue), and (2) a distortion of the problems and issues treated.[18] Ideologies tend to paint the world in rather simplistic terms with either/or analysis that sometimes overlooks ambiguity and complexity.

A good example can be seen in Marxist analysis of social problems. With its assumption of economic determinism, Marxism boils all social issues down to economic realities—namely, the class conflict between the owners and the workers. At least in its classical formulation, the ideology does not take account of other dimensions of reality as primary causal agents. Radical feminist ideology paints the empirical world through the lens of male domination over females. All social problems and even many personal problems are attributed to disproportionate male power. This perspective then forms the lense through which the world is viewed and hence the framework for ethical judgments.

Nationalistic ideologies often oversimplify by seeing a particular group within society as the major culprit for social ills. Ideological assumptions about a nation's history and often its ethnic or racial heritage lead to empirical judgments about other people within the country and hence a corporate blame for all that is wrong with society. Such ideologies tend to be highly racist and ethnocentric.

Whenever Christians and churches have begun to think about social responsibilities and social ethics, they have faced a temptation in the form of ideological thinking. Some Christians, rather than bringing their Christian assumptions to bear on issues, have grabbed hold of preexisting ideological constructs that informed the nature of the problem as well as possible solutions. This has happened particularly in regard to economic and political issues and in relation to ideologies of both the left and the right.

Some Christian movements have been upfront and unabashed in their ideological commitments. A number of liberation theologians, for example, are quite explicit about their use of ideologies, as long as they are not divorced from religious faith. As one writer put it, the church must "abandon its so-called objectivity and . . . become partisan,"[19] coming down on the side of the poor and oppressed. Liberation theology tends to use a modified Marxist ideology in its construal of economic realities, emphasizing that the real cause of poverty is exploitation by the wealthy and power brokers. They then set forth a theology that calls for liberation from those unjust structures, a reshuffling of the economic arrangements within societies and in the international economic networks. Their acceptance of this ideological framework provides both their understanding of the nature of poverty as well as means for eradicating it.

Another Christian movement with explicit ideological commitments is the Christian Coalition. Its empirical assumptions about society and its ills differ vastly from the liberationist paradigm. The planks of the Christian Coalition are drawn rather directly from the political platform of the most conservative element in the Republican Party. Adherents' commitments to conservative economics and politics embody not only issues that are specifically related to religion (such as their support of family values, religious symbols in public places, and voluntary prayer in public schools) but also perspectives that would seem less explicitly linked to religious commitments (such as tax cuts and a balanced budget).[20]

When Christians make ethical judgments, particularly those of a social nature, it is easy for them to be captured by ideological thinking. Even many who would argue against the use of ideologies unwittingly fall prey to their assumptions and goals. When people differ in their empirical judgments about an issue, it is often because particular ideologies have provided the lense through which they understand both the nature of the issue and its solution.

Vested Interests

Vested interests are often associated with ideologies. It is possible, however, to hold to ideologies without a vested interest, and it is certainly possible to be influenced by vested interests without ideological commitments. Vested interests can best be defined as benefits received from existing arrangements in society or within an institution. We usually think of vested interests as primarily economic in nature, but they can also be based on power or even convenience.

Perhaps the clearest example of a vested interest is when a person votes for a particular candidate who will represent that person's greatest economic advantage, whether related to taxation policy or certain positions taken on business and economic life. When this happens, the voter is not driven by principle or virtue but by what gain he or she will receive from a particular societal arrangement.

Vested interests influence not only values and goals but also empirical judgments. One of the most obvious examples involves the tobacco industry's scientific studies on the effects of nicotine. In the throes of attempts to clamp down on tobacco companies through taxation or changes in advertising, the industry has for years attempted to downplay the effects of nicotine on cigarette users. Their own scientists have produced "scientific data" to minimize its effects or even to deny them. In fact, one document from the British-American Tobacco Company stated boldly, "Chronic intake of nicotine tends to restore the normal physiological functioning of the endocrine system, so that ever-increasing dose levels of nicotine are necessary to maintain the desired action."[21]

When Christians in the eighteenth and nineteenth century supported slavery, their ethical position was likely fueled by various factors, but clearly vested interests had a powerful influence on their empirical judgments and ethical stance. Slavery was an economic boon. Similarly, Christians in South Africa who supported the apartheid system, which held the majority of the population in economic and political subjugation, did so because of vested interests. They developed vast empirical scenarios as to why this was a legitimate societal arrangement.

In conflicts between labor and management, labor usually provides vast amounts of data to show that workers are underpaid, that the company is experiencing a windfall, or that company policies are damaging to their work environment. On the other side, management produces its own data or interpretation of the data to demonstrate that it is faced with significant hardship and will not be viable in the marketplace if it gives in to labor's demands. Both sides set forth empirical judgments fueled by potential benefits.

When it comes to differences in ethical judgments, Christians at times give differing renditions of the empirical situation because they are influenced by vested interests.

Personal Dispositions

Perceptions of reality are also influenced by personalities, temperaments, or dispositions. While to some degree these may be influenced by sociocultural factors (such as those discussed above), personal dispositions are more innate tendencies that inform outlooks. Personality types may have propensities not only toward particular values and beliefs but even toward particular understandings of empirical reality. Social psychologists in particular are interested in the perceptions, motivations, and behaviors of people relative to social justice and social movements, focusing primarily on social factors as the primary agents of these perceptions, motivations, and behaviors.[22]

Some psychologists, however, focus primarily on personality types for understanding human behavior and perceptions about the world. One such model is reversal theory, as set forth by the British psychologist Michael J. Apter. Reversal theory attempts to set forth a grand, comprehensive theory of human beings that emphasizes the changeability of human nature and human complexity but within the framework of certain universals. This theory is centered in the mental life and understands perceptions, actions, and behavior with reference to a person's own subjective meanings. There are in this paradigm fundamental states of perception and motivation that function in pairs of opposites "so that change consists of movements between members of each pair, only one of them being operative at a given time."[23] One set of pairs is the conformist style, which

184

focuses on maintaining rules, routines, and obligation, versus the challenging (or negativistic) style, which focuses on personal freedom and even a breaking of conventional rules. In this paradigm and others in the field of psychology, perceptions about reality, motivations, and actions are related to personality.

By general observation, we all know some people who are by nature conservative and slow to change from the status quo. This disposition tends to engender an acceptance of empirical scenarios that emphasize sameness and stability. Others are by nature radical, loving to upset the fruit cart and change the status quo. They tend to accept empirical scenarios that are more cataclysmic in nature. Still others are predisposed to remaining in the middle. The facts they accept or the interpretation of the facts are moderate, never extreme, and they tend to position themselves squarely in the middle in regard to social issues. In each of these cases, a personality factor is at work, not only in ethical positions taken but in perceptions of reality and the facts.

A good example of this is the earlier cited study on climate change by the researchers from Carnegie Mellon University. Because of uncertainties in the basic science of global warming, they note that "individuals and interest groups have a range of views on the economic and environmental losses from anthropogenic climate change."[24] They categorize these groups and individuals into three main types: optimist, moderate, and pessimist. That is, the dispositional outlook of people plays a significant role in which data they accept and how they interpret the data. Though environmental science attempts to garner precision in its portrayal of the situation, uncertainties exist, and within the uncertainties personality plays a key role. The same is true for many other issues.

Conclusion

How should we respond to the complexities of empirical judgments when making ethical decisions? One possible response is moral cynicism. This is a popular retort in the postmodern world that tends to undermine the possibility of ever discovering the true, the good, and the right. Moral cynicists argue that it is impossible not only to discern true moral principles or virtues but also to gain an impartial and valid understanding of the empirical situation. Truth in empirical renditions, therefore, is impossible, and one choice is as valid as another. All reality is socially constructed, and the pursuit of clear and decisive knowledge is a misguided dream.

The temptation toward moral cynicism is particularly strong today when the public is bombarded by conflicting polls and scientific studies. While many are still wowed by data, the possibility of "lying with numbers" engenders a great deal of mistrust and cynicism about data and quantitative studies.[25] Moreover, we are often hounded by what Robert J. Samuelson calls "psycho-facts: beliefs that, though not supported by hard evidence, are taken as real because their constant repetition changes the way we experience life. We feel assaulted by rising crime, increasing health hazards, falling living standards and a worsening environment. These are all psycho-facts. The underlying conditions aren't true, but we feel they are and, therefore, they become so."[26]

Christians, however, need not and should not fall prey to the "psycho-facts" or the moral cynicism of our culture. As we approach ethical issues, we are morally obligated to discern the empirical situation with unbiased integrity. Because we are committed to the truth of the gospel and our ethics is rooted in the truthful reality of the Triune God, we are to be committed to truth in all areas of life. This commitment should carry over to pursuing truthfulness in the way we understand social and ethical realities. Even if the truth flies in the face of our cherished biases, we must lay them aside for the sake of integrity. We need to be aware of the social mores, ideologies, vested interests, and personal dispositions that tend to inform our empirical judgments in ways that distort our understanding of the reality surrounding an issue.

Of course, our pursuit of truth must always be bathed in humility. As the apostle Paul said, "We see through a glass, darkly" (1 Cor. 13:12 KJV), and that is true in matters spiritual as well as empirical. Or as T. S. Eliot in his memorable words put it:

> Between the idea
> and the reality
> Between the motion
> and the act
> Falls the shadow.[27]

None of our empirical judgments is ever fully truthful, clear, or unbiased. But the fact that our judgments are finite, fallen, and influenced by the social milieu in which we make them does not render such judgments totally misguided. We can see in part, and as Christians rooted in and committed to the truth, we must pursue all truth wherever it is found. Of course, our Christian worldview will influence the way we perceive reality, but there is reality within the world that can be grasped (in part) by all human beings if they seek it with integrity, self-awareness, and a bracketing of their own biases.

Christians will not always see eye to eye on all ethical issues, and often such situations will result not just from variations in theology or ethical methodology but from differing empirical judgments about the issues. As people committed to the truth of the gospel, however, we must seek to render the facts with precision, clarity, integrity, and yes, humility.

PART 4

APPLYING CHRISTIAN ETHICS IN CULTURE AND SOCIETY

Ethical decisions are never made in a vacuum. We live our moral lives, of both character and decision making, in the midst of cultures, societies, institutions, and social groups to which we belong. These social realities influence us, but as Christians we often seek to influence them as well. The journey is not easy, for the sentiments of the world we inhabit are often inimical to the commitments and beliefs of our Christian faith. Thus, we face a number of crucial issues as we seek to live and apply our faith in the midst of a complex, secular, pluralistic world. The final part of this book explores these crucial issues.

Chapter 9 examines what H. Richard Niebuhr called the Christ-culture issue, exploring the ways Christians throughout history have linked their faith with society, or the kingdom of God with the kingdoms of this world. Chapter 10 ventures into the difficult issue of justice, what is owed people in this complex world. How do we define justice and seek to implement it? Chapter 11 discusses the crucial issue of Christian ethics and pluralism, seeking to discern how we can connect a Christian ethic to a world that does not share our worldview assumptions. Chapter 12 explores a number of models that Christians and the church can use as they seek to influence the world around them for the sake of God's kingdom. Almost every ethical issue we face incorporates these themes. How we relate our worldview and moral commitments to the societies and cultures in which we live is pivotal in Christian ethics.

9

CHRIST AND CULTURE

During the past few years, I have taught several seminary courses in Russia and Ukraine. After a long period of forced sectarianism (the Soviet era) in which the church played virtually no role in society and culture, Christians in these countries now have the opportunity to help shape the future of their countries. The seminary students I taught grappled with tough questions: What should their society look like in the days ahead? What role should Christians and the church play in the transformation? What should they do when faced with issues that conflict with their Christian beliefs and moral commitments?

Inevitably in our discussions, the students would raise issues related to business practices in these countries. Given the common practices of bribery, payoffs to the mafia to stay in business, an underground economy to avoid taxes, and a tax system that demands more tax payment than net income, how can Christians possibly be ethical in business? Many students were convinced that Christians simply have to stay out of the business world. To engage in business would invariably mean compromises with one's faith commitment and an enmeshment in unethical practices. Other students were not so sure. They argued that God has called us to live in the midst of the world and that will mean getting our hands dirty. The moral ideals of the Bible are our goal, they contended, but we can never live them out purely because of the nature of sinful societies and economies. Others argued that believers must enter into the business world in order to transform it. Because Christians in these countries have opportunities for the first time in almost a century to influence their societies, they need to be in the midst of them as salt and light. If they do not take part, the unethical practices will never change. A few students contended that though some Christians must work in the rough and tumble world of economics, there is a higher calling—to the ministry or to missions.

These students in Russia and Ukraine were grappling with issues related to what H. Richard Niebuhr called "Christ and culture."[1] They recognized that

189

it is not enough to know the foundations of ethics and the way we make decisions. We must also come to terms with how we relate these ethical commitments to the society and culture in which we live.

How we answer the Christ-culture question affects a number of important issues. First, it influences what we expect of society relative to Christian ethics. Our understanding of faith and culture influences whether we think society can be transformed into the kingdom of God, whether it will always be a long way from God's ideal, or whether it will be somewhere in between. Second, our Christ-culture view affects our general stance toward society, whether we seek to flee from, fight against, reform, or ignore the social order and its institutions. All strands of Christianity have incorporated general understandings of the world, and these perceptions invariably lead to a particular positioning within that world.

Third, our Christ-culture perspective influences how we seek to evoke change, if indeed we believe we are called to be change agents. It shapes the methods we employ in attempting to use kingdom ethics to influence the larger society and its institutions. Christians throughout the ages have employed everything from personal persuasion to the development of alternative communities to political reform to revolution. The Christ-culture stance has always influenced the methods used.

Finally, our Christ-culture perspective affects what we draw from culture and society in our attempts to live and proclaim the Christian message. As the Christian church exists within the world, it continually faces questions regarding the extent to which it can borrow from the culture in its forms of worship, church structure, styles of communication, and theology. Can we use societal management models in the church? How much can we borrow from secular music in our hymnody? What thought forms from secular disciplines (i.e., psychology, sociology, philosophy) are appropriate in explaining our faith or enunciating our theology?

Clearly, our faith and our world make claims on our lives. Simultaneously, we experience expectations associated with being members of the kingdom of God and with being members of the sociocultural arenas: state, workplace, communities, educational institutions, and voluntary associations. The central issue then is how do we relate the kingdom of God to the kingdoms of this world?

The classic work that probes these issues is Niebuhr's *Christ and Culture,* in which he describes and evaluates five approaches to the enduring problem. A few other scholars have developed typologies to describe the relationship between Christianity or Christian ethics and society, but Niebuhr's work continues to be the most widespread.[2] In recent years, a number of scholars have critiqued Niebuhr's strategy. They have pointed out the woodenness of his typologies, his own lack of self-criticalness toward the approach he favors, questions concerning the placement of certain individuals and movements, the neglect of power in his treatment of culture, and an obscuring of other ways to frame the question.[3] This chapter uses Niebuhr's typology as he himself intended—namely, a heuristic device to help us find our way through the maze of various thinkers and movements. Any typology contains inherent weaknesses, and thus, the categorizations cannot be pushed too far.

For Niebuhr, one type emphasizes opposition between Christian faith and the world—Christ against culture—while another emphasizes essential agreement between the two—Christ of culture. Three positions that attempt unity fall between the poles: Christ above culture, Christ and culture in paradox, and Christ the transformer of culture. As we explore these five types and representative people and movements, we need to heed Niebuhr's reminder that "a type is a mental construct to which no individual wholly conforms."[4] A type is a broad categorization that helps us make sense of the complexity in a given field of study. The following sections follow Niebuhr's work in terms of representative figures and critiques, while also incorporating a few additional individuals or movements and critiques. The conclusion sets forth an alternative type for Christian ethics.

Christ against Culture

The Christ against culture approach "uncompromisingly affirms the sole authority of Christ over the Christian and resolutely rejects culture's claims to loyalty."[5] Christians who adhere to this approach draw a sharp line between the redeemed people of God and fallen society and culture. The world is so evil that believers must withdraw from it or in some way reject it. Christ against culture advocates often reject numerous aspects of the sociocultural order, including war, property, politics, sports, amusements, the arts, secular business, educational institutions, science, and philosophy. In this perspective, there is a clear demarcation between the claims of Christian ethics and the claims of the world. Thus, Christian moral commitments find expression primarily in the church, Christian institutions, or individual lives. Adherents have few expectations about influencing the world.

Tertullian

Tertullian was an early church theologian (155–220 A.D.) from North Africa. Raised in a pagan family that provided him with a strong education in grammar, rhetoric, literature, philosophy, and law, Tertullian became a Christian as an adult after studying in Rome. He was apparently drawn to the faith by the endurance and witness of Christians facing persecution and martyrdom. Tertullian went on to be a prolific writer in the church, addressing themes in theology, apologetics, devotional writings, and morality. He was not without controversy, for in the later part of his life he joined the Montanists, a sect that emphasized rigorous morality and church discipline and had a propensity toward ecstatic experiences and prophetic manifestations. Tertullian's own assessment of moral laxity in the church seems to have pushed him in that direction.

Though Tertullian believed God had created a good world, he concluded that many parts of that world (i.e., society) needed to be questioned and rejected. He saw two theological foundations for his view of culture and Christians' relationship to it: the lordship of Christ and the prohibition of idolatry. Tertullian argued that because Christ is Lord, nothing should supplant Christ and his law. Yet much of culture and society begged for prominence in life and ran contrary to Christ. Hence, he believed that many aspects of the culture needed to be rejected. Christians, for example, were to refrain from political life because it involved emperor worship; from being a soldier, for "the Lord in disarming Peter disarmed every believer";[6] and from any occupation that involved idolatry, such as the building trade, which inevitably incorporated idolatry in its use of pagan icons and images.

Tertullian opposed Christian involvement in many amusements of his day, including attendance at the amphitheater shows (gladiator fights and wild beast fights), the most famous form of amusement in the Roman Empire. He rejected the shows on the grounds that they were idolatrous in origin and practice, that it was impossible to maintain thoughts of God in such a setting, and that Christians were killed in them.[7]

Despite a strong academic background, he opposed the arts, philosophy, and literature. Unlike many fellow Christian thinkers who attempted to make positive connections between Greek philosophy and Christian ideals, Tertullian asked, "What has Athens to do with Jerusalem?"[8] When it came to literature, he believed that the study of pagan writers was legitimate, since it helped one in the propagation of the faith, but the teaching of literature was suspect: "Learning literature is allowable for believers, rather than teaching; for the principle of learning and teaching is different. If a believer teaches literature, while he is teaching doubtless he commends, while he delivers he affirms, while he recalls he bears testimony to, the praises of idols interspersed therein."[9]

While Niebuhr sees Tertullian as the classic example of Christ against culture, George Forell raises questions about that assessment. He believes that Tertullian did not reject culture per se; rather, his commitment to the lordship of Christ and the prohibition of idolatry led him to a selective rejection of culture. "It appears that Tertullian was not the vaunted representative of the Christ-against-culture pattern but rather a proud Roman citizen who anticipated Christ above a culture cleansed from worthless and powerless idolatry."[10] But even if Tertullian's stance was a selective one, clearly his overall posture raised questions about much of what happened in society, and he called believers to make a radical break from those patterns.

192

Medieval Monasticism and Mysticism

Monasticism and mysticism are not always given as examples of Christ against culture, primarily because they were not monolithic movements. Some have interpreted monasticism primarily as a movement to renounce the world, others as a movement seeking the vision of God, and still others as a protest against the laxity of the church.[11] There is probably some validity in all three interpretations, depending on the time, place, and particular strand of monasticism. But clearly part of the movement had world-denying impulses that reflected a Christ against culture stance. "Some of the earliest monks, such as Anthony of Egypt and Simeon Stylites, withdrew as individuals from ordinary society in order to purge themselves of contamination from worldly idolatries and attain personal holiness."[12] These and later monastics were highly ascetic in their ethic and were fed by Neoplatonic notions that the material world and bodily impulses were suspect or even evil.

All monks and nuns took the vows of poverty, chastity, and obedience, and inherent within those promises was a renunciation of life outside the monastery. Their way of life was deemed to be the true embodiment of the Christian ethic, the means by which loyalty to Christ was best expressed. Though Francis of Assisi in the thirteenth century began the Franciscan order in part to serve the world, he continued to reflect anti-world sentiments. In one of his writings, a man living within the world asks Brother Giles if he should enter the monastery or continue to do good works within the world. Brother Giles, reflecting Francis's thinking, responds:

> My brother, it is certain that if a man knew of a great treasure lying hidden in a common field, he would not ask counsel of any one to ascertain whether or not he should take possession of it and carry it to his own house: how much more ought a man to strive and hasten with all care and diligence to possess himself of that heavenly treasure which is to be found in holy religious orders and spiritual congregations, without stopping to ask counsel of so many![13]

Though such statements to some degree reflect this first of Niebuhr's types, monasticism also reflects the Christ above culture type, which Niebuhr sees as the predominant motif of the medieval church.

Mysticism was closely aligned with monasticism, for most mystics were monks or nuns. Mystics sought a direct apprehension of and communion with God. At the heart of the mystic experience was the *via negativa,* the elimination of temporal distractions. This did not necessarily entail a full rejection of the world but an attempt to place strong controls on one's mind and passions to experience the vision of God.

Women made perhaps their strongest contribution to the medieval church from within the mystic movement. Catherine of Siena in the fourteenth century was a Dominican nun who lived during the outbreak of the plague. In the midst of this devastation to human life and society, Catherine wrote passionately of human love rooted in divine love. To experience God's love, Catherine commended a life in which self-will was negated through setting aside the distractions and impediments of this world. As she put it, "So the soul who follows your truth's teachings in love becomes through love another you. Disposed of her own will, she is so well clothed in yours that she neither seeks nor desires anything but what you seek and will for her."[14] Some mystics went much further in their apprehension about the world around them. Meister Eckhart, for example, so emphasized absorption of the physical and mental self with God that he bordered on pantheism. He contended that the goal was that the human soul "might look at God without anything in between . . . unconscious of the knowing process, or love, or anything else."[15] In such a conception of mysticism, the spiritual realm tended to negate the physical-material realm and the social order.

Anabaptist Movements

In the sixteenth century, the Anabaptists wanted to extend the Reformation beyond the theological and lifestyle boundaries of the magisterial Reformers. They wanted a believers' church, defined not by geography but by radical discipleship. Believers' baptism (as opposed to infant baptism), nondependence on the state, the church as community, and a rejection of warfare became the hallmarks of the movement, which was quickly perceived as a threat to the existing political and ecclesiastical systems. The result? Thousands of Anabaptists were persecuted, martyred, or pushed to the hinterlands.

The primary Anabaptist expression is the Mennonite Church, and of them Niebuhr writes, "The Mennonites have come to represent the attitude [Christ against] most purely, since they not only renounce all participation in politics and refuse to be drawn into military service, but follow their own distinctive customs and regulations in economics and education."[16] Niebuhr here shows a lack of familiarity with the Mennonites, for he is describing just a portion of this multifaceted movement, namely, the Amish or one of the old order or conservative Mennonite groups. Moreover, John Howard Yoder has taken great exception with Niebuhr's designation, arguing that the issue is not about being against culture but about devotion to the way of Christ, which at points conflicts with culture and society.[17]

Nonetheless, some strands of Anabaptism in the past and present have evidenced a strong suspicion of society and its institutions. The first Anabaptist Confession from 1527, the Schleitheim Confession, set the tone:

We are agreed . . . on separation: A separation shall be made from the evil and from the wickedness which the devil planted in the world; in this manner, simply that we shall not have fellowship with them [the wicked] and not run with them in the multitude of their abominations. . . . He further admonishes us to withdraw from Babylon and the earthly Egypt that we may not be partakers of the pain and suffering which the Lord will bring upon them. . . . Finally it will be observed that it is not appropriate for a Christian to serve as a magistrate because of these points: the government magistracy is according to the flesh, but the Christian's is according to the Spirit.[18]

Many Mennonites today do not adhere to the Schleitheim sentiment, but a Christ against culture view has been accepted among many in the Anabaptist movement.

Leo Tolstoy

Next to Tertullian, Niebuhr sees the Russian writer Leo Tolstoy (1828–1910) as the one who most explicitly expressed the Christ against culture type. "Noble by birth, wealthy by inheritance, famous by his own achievements as the author of *War and Peace* and *Anna Karenina,* he . . . found himself threatened in his own life by the meaninglessness of existence and the tawdriness of all the values that his society esteemed."[19] Out of his personal crisis he turned to Christianity, but a very austere and unorthodox version. Tolstoy rejected the doctrine of the Trinity, miracles, the sacraments, and the immortality of the soul on the assumption that they obscured true faith, which he believed was found primarily in the Sermon on the Mount. Christianity was in essence the law of Christ, not the person of Christ. Maxim Gorky, who had the dubious distinction of being the father of Soviet literature, once remarked that when Tolstoy spoke of Christ, there was "no enthusiasm, no feeling in his words, and no spark of real fire."[20]

Tolstoy's faith emphasized nonviolence and a rejection of oaths, property, the state, and the institutional church. He believed that property was based on theft and maintained by violence, and thus he gave away most of his money and lived much like the peasants. He believed that the state was built entirely on violence and power in contrast to Christian love. For Tolstoy, there was no such thing as a good government. "The revolutionaries say: 'the government organization is bad in this and that respect; it must be destroyed and replaced by this and that.' But a Christian says: 'I know nothing about the governmental organization'. . . . All the state obligations are against the conscience of a Christian."[21] In similar fashion, he argued that the church must be repudiated as a servant of the state and violence. Furthermore, Christ never founded churches. Tolstoy's version of faith led him to turn his back on culture, literature, and even his own writings. In his understanding of "the man Jesus," as he preferred to call him, there was a call to live against virtually everything that society offered.

There are, of course, other figures and movements that could be added to the list of those who held the Christ against culture posture. American fundamentalism in the early to mid-twentieth century contained elements of this type, though at times it also attempted to transform society. In recent years, some Christians have attempted to build their own educational and social institutions in an attempt to maintain moral and theological purity. In some parts of the world, as was the case for the Russian and Ukranian students mentioned at the beginning of the chapter, the stance was not voluntary but forced on the church by a political philosophy.

Evaluation

Niebuhr's verdict on the Christ against culture stance is that it is a necessary but inadequate position. He recognizes that the "sectarians" have at times made an unintended impact on the world and are certainly to be lauded for their strong devotion to Christ, but he is quite strong in his rejection of the type as an abdication of "responsible engagement in cultural tasks." Moreover, he chides them for being inconsistent in that "the radical Christians are always making use of the culture, or parts of the culture, which ostensibly they reject."[22] But certainly John Howard Yoder and other critics are right to challenge Niebuhr at this point. The thrust of the sectarian stance is not fueled primarily by a rejection of culture but by a commitment to faithfulness, and the sectarians' rejection of parts of culture is not necessarily inconsistent but an attempt to apply their radical commitment to Christ.

Despite this laudatory commitment, there are several weaknesses within this approach. For one, it too easily sets aside the incarnational imperative to live in the midst of a fallen, confused world. Jesus gave the Great Commission to make disciples of all nations (Matt. 28:19–20), which followers of this type have sometimes managed to do, but also to call his followers to be salt and light in the world (Matt. 5:13–16). A withdrawal approach that does not engage the world can hardly be faithful to this mandate.

Second, the Christ against culture approach has a tendency to overlook the need for discernment. It too easily opts for a total rejection of "worldly" patterns that look suspect or contain particular elements that need to be rejected. Rather than seeking a discerning ethical stance amid the complexities of life, these Christians seek the easier path—all or nothing.

Finally, this approach to culture and society reflects a theological imbalance in its denial of creation theology. Chapter 3 noted that a Christian worldview should incorporate creation, fall, redemption, and consummation. The sectarian stance slights the first and sometimes even the last. It fails to acknowledge that God created a good world and that though fallen and corrupt, it still manages under the providence of God to be a place where God is at work, even to some extent in its most fallen recesses. These believers are certainly right to emphasize the special and distinct work of God within the believing community, the church, but God has not and will not abdicate divine reign over the good world he created. Christians are called to reflect that reign, not away from society but in the midst of it.

Christ of Culture

In the Christ of culture type, Christian faith is merged with the heights of human insights and civilization. Adherents see no tension between the best of culture and the heart of Christian thought and values, for both are expressions of God's goodness. Hence, one can simultaneously embrace faith and many societal and cultural norms with a minimal sense of dissonance. These Christians are thoroughly at home in the world and its institutions. In theology, this means one can wrap the faith in the language of science, psychology, philosophy, or sociology without tension. In social ethics, one can embrace societal structures as vehicles for expressing or inducing the kingdom of God.

As Niebuhr sees it, these people "interpret culture through Christ, regarding those elements in it as most important which are most accordant with his work and person: on the other hand they understand Christ through culture, selecting from his teaching and action . . . such points as seem to agree with what is best in civilization."[23] Jesus is, therefore, often seen as the great reformer, philosopher, and educator whose teaching and life are commensurate with the larger world.

Peter Abelard

Peter Abelard was a theologian from Brittany (in France) in the twelfth century. He is perhaps best known for his love affair with a woman named Heloise, with whom he bore a son out of wedlock and to whom he was then secretly married. Abelard eventually deviated from many of the classical theological formulations of the Christian church in his attempts to make the faith more palatable to human and cultural sensibilities. Niebuhr describes him this way: "In stating the faith, its beliefs about God and Christ and its demands on conduct, he reduces it to what conforms with the best in culture."[24]

The Christ of culture orientation was particularly evidenced in two ways in Abelard's thinking: his view of secular philosophers and his view of Christ's atonement. In regard to the philosophers, Abelard saw significant continuity between their teachings, especially in morals, and the teachings of Jesus. Regarding philosophers such as Socrates and Plato, he wrote, "In their care for the state and its citizens . . . in life and doctrine, they give evidence of an evangelic and apostolic perfection and come little or nothing short of the Christian religion. They are, in fact, joined to us by the common zeal for moral achievement."[25]

As to the atonement, Abelard set forth what is commonly called the moral example theory. Jesus' death on the cross was, for Abelard, not a substitutionary death for the sins of humanity (the view of his teacher Anselm) or a ransom paid for sin but a moral example that rekindles within humans a love for God and others. Rejecting both original sin and the notion that sin resides in personal actions, Anselm argued that what counts with God is human intention. Sin is the acquiescence of the mind to what it clearly knows to be wrong, and thus, intention determines morality. In light of this assumption, Abelard taught that Jesus' death was an example of love that shapes human designs and actions. "Every man . . . becomes more loving to the Lord after the passion of Christ . . . because a benefit kindles the soul into love."[26] Thus, Niebuhr concludes about Abelard: "What is offered here is kindly and liberal guidance for good people who want to do right. . . . All conflict between Christ and culture is gone."[27]

Cultural Protestantism (Classical Liberalism)

In the nineteenth and early twentieth century, the movement of theological liberalism sought to make Christianity acceptable to the modern mind. Adherents saw themselves as the "saviors" of Christianity, for classical Christianity with its transcendent and supernatural underpinning was out of step with modern assumptions about reality. As Harry Emerson Fosdick, one of the movement's premier preachers, often quipped, "It's not a question of a new theology or old, but a question of a new theology or no theology."[28] Thus, Christians had to accept the new philosophical and scientific understandings about human nature and society and welcome those insights into the faith.

The modernists, as they were sometimes called, stressed the immanence of God in the world, working hand in hand with human efforts to make a better world. They emphasized, therefore, the "fatherhood of God and the brotherhood of man." Culture and society had not escaped sin, but there was great potential in their ideals and institutions that merely needed direction and prodding. Theologians such as Friedrich Schleiermacher and Albrecht Ritschl emphasized the continuity between heaven and earth. "This Christ of religion does not call upon men to leave homes and kindred for his sake; he enters into their homes and all their associations as the gracious presence that adds an aura of infinite meaning to all temporal tasks."[29]

A prime example of cultural Protestantism is Ernst Troeltsch, author of the classic work *The Social Teachings of the Christian Churches*. Troeltsch was a historicist, believing that religious ideas are powerless apart from cultural forms. Religion is so closely tied to the processes of history that one can scarcely speak of transcendence. He contended that "the great religions might indeed be described as crystallizations of the various biological and anthropological forms."[30] Because he believed there are no norms outside culture and the social

198

context, a number of critics see a tie between Troeltsch's thought and his zealous patriotism during World War I, when he said of the German military, "The army is flesh from our flesh and spirit from our spirit; our salvation lies in its hands."[31]

Contemporary Expressions

Contemporary manifestations of the Christ of culture approach usually display a selectivity in their embrace of culture. Few theologians or ethicists would give a full-orbed embrace, but at various levels or on specific issues they merge faith and culture. For example, many attempting to forge a social ethic embrace a particular political or economic stance in such a way that their view seems to mirror a social ideology. In the United States, the religious right's political views are often a reflection of the conservative wing of the Republican Party, and the religious left's views are often a reflection of the liberal wing of the Democratic Party. These movements reflect not a full acceptance of the larger cultural ethos and its institutions but a selective acceptance of a portion of culture. Whenever Christians attempt to equate their faith with a particular political or economic system, remnants of this type exist.

Some reflect a Christ of culture position in their approach to particular issues. This seems to be particularly true in regard to sexual ethics, an area in which the cultural ethos seems to have made a significant impact in more "liberal" Christian circles. The traditional stance of sexual intercourse reserved only for a marriage between a man and a woman is increasingly called into question in light of both societal trends and alleged social-scientific understandings.[32]

This type of faith-culture stance can also be seen in some Christians' attempts to influence culture. Evangelicals have been quick to reject modernist and postmodernist thought in their theology but have been in the vanguard of those who accept modern technology to spread the gospel, often without serious reflection on the way it might affect their faith. Some have so emphasized identification with culture in evangelism that the culture has shaped their theology. Robert Schuller, pastor of the Crystal Cathedral in California, has argued that in method and in thought Christians must move to where people are today. Hence, Schuller is reluctant to use the traditional language of sin and instead focuses on self-esteem that the gospel can bring to people.[33]

Evaluation

Clearly, one of the positive contributions of the Christ of culture position is its willingness to deal with cultural realities and to demonstrate the universal meaning of the faith. While there are limits to contextualization, all forms of Christianity are contextualized, and this approach recognizes such. Moreover, this approach has allowed its adherents to make contact with the prime movers of culture and society in their attempts to show the relevance of the faith to the arts, education, politics, science, economics, philosophy, and business.

There are, however, significant problems with the Christ of culture stance. Niebuhr points out that in this embrace of culture and society, the Christian faith is distorted and the specter of false gods emerges. "Loyalty to contemporary culture has so far qualified the loyalty to Christ that he has been abandoned in favor of an idol called by name."[34] This happens because the finite dimensions of society tend to become infinite in the attempts to link social systems and ideals with transcendence. The Christian faith at its core becomes easily distorted, for too close an alignment of Christianity with culture engenders a situation in which the latter masters the former. In a critique of cultural Protestantism and its easy alignment of the kingdom of God with cultural attainments, Niebuhr writes, "A God without wrath brought men without sin into a kingdom with judgment through the ministrations of a Christ without a cross."[35]

The Christ of culture approach also faces another sobering problem: the inability to critique culture from a reality beyond the culture. When faith is closely aligned with sociocultural realities, transcendent judgment is diminished. Thus, Karl Barth and other critics saw a link between the theology of cultural Protestantism and the acquiescence of its theologians to the menacing ideology of the Third Reich in Germany. Barth was appalled that many of his former teachers, steeped in a theological liberalism without transcendence, lacked the ethical framework and moral power to stand against the evils of Nazism. Indeed, whenever Christians and the church become too closely tied to a social or political system, they face the same threat.

Christ above Culture

The Christ above culture approach affirms Christ but also culture as a good gift from God. Adherents contend that there is a life within society and its institutions that is good and needs to be affirmed, for after all, God ordained the sociocultural order. Simultaneously, however, there is a dimension of reality that is beyond culture and society. This realm does not negate the temporal realms nor stand against them. It merely goes beyond the sociocultural realm to new heights. Cultural elements are both holy and sinful, in a way that reminds Christians that there is more to reality than politics, law, economics, education, and cultural aspirations. Yet the divine ideal does not contradict this world. Some are called to live in the world with its mix of good and evil; others are called to leave it for the sake of the kingdom and the world itself. This approach has been most visibly expressed in the Roman Catholic tradition.

Clement of Alexandria

By the second century A.D., Alexandria, Egypt, was becoming the new Athens of the world, a center of intellectualism, the arts, and commerce. In this context, people from the center of society were coming to faith in Jesus Christ. Clement of Alexandria (150–215 A.D.) was a teacher there in what was essentially one of the first theological seminaries in the Christian church. He wanted these new believers to feel at ease in becoming Christians and to understand that their newfound faith did not necessitate a repudiation of intellect, prosperity, or power. The church was moving into society and making an impact, but simultaneously, the world was moving into the church in thought forms and church structures. This reality was at the heart of Clement's ethical dilemma and subsequent reflection.

Clement embodied a Christ above culture perspective in several ways. First, it was demonstrated in his use of philosophy to argue for and uphold the Christian faith. It is sometimes said that Christianity was never so Greek as in Clement, for "by using philosophy, Clement believed he would be able to demonstrate to the cultured despisers of Christianity in his time the intellectual and moral superiority of the Christian world-view."[36] Clement did not attempt to reduce Christian thought and morals to philosophy, as is sometimes the case with the Christ of culture perspective. Rather, he attempted to show that philosophy was a kind of preparation for the gospel and divine revelation. For Clement, philosophy was to the Greeks what the law was to Israel—a schoolmaster to bring people to Christ. Moreover, philosophy and sound reason were conducive to piety, not enemies of faithful and ethical living.

Clement of Alexandria also reflected a Christ above culture posture in his teaching on wealth. As wealthy people came into the church, Clement struggled with the hard sayings of Jesus such as, "Go, sell what you own, and give the money to the poor, and you will have treasure in heaven" (Mark 10:21). Did Jesus' statement to the rich young ruler mean that wealthy Alexandrians who became Christians needed to sell everything and give the money to the poor? Clement wrestled with this question in *The Rich Man's Salvation* and came to the conclusion that the selling of possessions Jesus calls for is an internal selling—a banishing of wealth from one's soul. Property is justified, and wealth in itself is legitimate, for often those who despise material things and relinquish their property actually find their passion for material things intensified. Moreover, said Clement, if one abandons all wealth, that person has no means left for giving to those in need, for "how could one give food to the hungry, and drink to the thirsty, clothe the naked, and shelter the houseless . . . if each man first divested himself of all these things?"[37]

However, said Clement, for some there is a higher way—selling possessions and living a life of ethical rigor. Clement, therefore, implied two levels of the Christian life: a lower way of plain, simple faith lived in the world with wealth, and a higher way motivated by love and true knowledge of God. But the two were not contradictory. As Niebuhr puts it in summarizing Clement's teaching on economics, "There are two motives, then that should guide the Christian in his economic action; and two stages of life in economic society. Stoic detachment and Christian love are not contradictory, but they are distinct and lead to different, though not contradictory actions; life among possessions by which one is not possessed and life without possessions are not identical, though not in disagreement with each other."[38]

Thomas Aquinas

Thomas Aquinas, in the thirteenth century, set forth the most explicit example of this type. He established a model that included a full acceptance of social institutions and cultural expressions such as art, philosophy, and law, yet he argued that there is a way beyond the cultural that is higher, without being antithetical. "Thomas . . . answer[ed] the question about Christ and culture with a 'both-and,'" and his view was thoroughly demonstrated in both his life and thought. "He is a monk, faithful to the vows of poverty, celibacy, and obedience. With the radical Christians he has rejected the secular world. But he is a monk in the church which has become the guardian of culture, the fosterer of learning, the judge of the nations, the protector of the family, the governor of social religion."[39]

Christ above culture was manifested at various levels of his thinking. First, we can see the motif in his understanding of the universal end of humanity—happiness. Through gifts of nature and culture, Aquinas argued, one can gain a basic happiness. It is, however, an imperfect happiness, for perfect happiness is found only by grace in the vision of God. The natural forms of happiness do not contradict the higher forms but are partial images of the full reality.

Second, the Christ above culture perspective is evident in his understanding of law. Aquinas saw four kinds of law: eternal, natural, civil, and divine. All humans can know something of the eternal law through the natural law, for it has been imprinted on them in creation. By reason and reflection on the nature of things, humanity can gain a valid though incomplete understanding of God's moral designs. As a result, we can expect the civil laws of countries to be built on the natural law known by all. The divine law, the Old and New Testaments, is in part coincident with natural law and in part goes beyond it. Some things, such as salvation, are known only by divine revelation, but such revelation never negates the natural law. Once again this thinking reveals the "both-and" pattern in Aquinas's theology.

Third, the motif is seen in his understanding of the virtues. The natural or cardinal virtues—wisdom, justice, temperance, and courage—are evident by nature to all. Through these virtues humans can achieve a decent moral life, and society a sense of equilibrium and order. But there are higher virtues beyond the natural ones. The theological virtues—faith, hope, charity—do not negate the cardinal virtues but are necessary for true salvation. Aquinas asserted that "man's natural principles which enable him to act well according to his capacity, do not suffice to direct man to this same [ultimate] happiness. Hence it is necessary for man to receive from God some additional principles whereby he may be directed to supernatural happiness. . . . Such . . . principles are called theological virtues."[40]

Finally, his view of calling reveals the Christ above culture approach. The way of life within the world is a good way. Working, governing, raising a family, and educating are all legitimate expressions within society. But there is a higher way, the calling to the monastery and the religious orders. For Aquinas and the medieval church, only the "religious" have a calling from God. This higher way does not contradict the lower way but is clearly a form of life above the society and its good but fallen institutions.

Contemporary Expressions

Roman Catholic thought since Aquinas has continued the Christ above culture approach in various forms. In our own time, it is evident in the theology of Richard McBrien and his widely used text, *Catholicism*. In contrast to Protestant theology, which emphasizes opposition between realities such as nature and grace, McBrien asserts that Roman Catholic thought emphasizes the analogical: "Realities are more similar than different." He believes divine grace and nature (human existence apart from God's self-communication) do not stand in opposition to each other but work in harmony, since human existence itself is "graced" by God. "The Catholic tradition has always been insistent that the grace of God is given to us, not to make up for something lacking to us as human persons, but as a free gift that elevates us to a new and unmerited level of existence."[41]

In a different form, the Christ above culture approach has been manifest in some pietistic and evangelical Protestant circles. Many have heard sermons and challenges that emphasize two ways of Christian life: a life lived in the secular professions and a higher calling to the ministry, especially the mission field. While being a teacher, lawyer, or business person is legitimate, the strongly committed will sacrifice all to heed "the call."

Evaluation

Many people have found an appeal in this "synthesis" approach, as Niebuhr sometimes dubs it, because of its stress on harmony and unity. "There is an appealing greatness in the synthesists' resolute proclamation that the God, who is to rule now rules and has ruled, that His rule is established in the nature of things, and that man must build on the established foundations."[42] In this approach, life is not carved up into separate compartments, for all reality finds a place under the reign of God. Moreover, cultures and societies are indebted to this type, for it has provided a framework in which science, art, philosophy, law, politics, business, and education can flourish within the sphere of God's influence.

There are, however, some significant challenges to the Christ above culture type. Because the above-noted cultural realities are affirmed as from God, there is a tendency to absolutize them. As Niebuhr puts it, "The effort to bring Christ and culture, God's work and man's, the temporal and the eternal, law and grace, into one system of thought and practice tends, perhaps inevitably, to the absolutizing of what is relative, the reduction of the infinite to a finite form."[43] Cultural and societal activities are then too easily equated with God's activity. Related to this concern is the tendency toward a cultural "conservatism" that assumes that what is, is right. Moreover, many have questioned whether this type adequately appreciates the pervasiveness of sin within social institutions and cultural values, let alone human nature. There has always been an assumption among its adherents that humanity and culture, while fallen, retain great moral capacity. It was this assumption, in part, that contributed to the rise of the Protestant Reformation.

A final problem with this faith-culture stance is its dualistic conception of the Christian life. The lower way and the higher way embody grades of perfection in the Christian faith that lack biblical justification. Moreover, in practice a two-tiered system of spirituality and morality tends to let most Christians off the hook too easily. It does not generate a strong commitment among all believers that they are called by God to live for God's glory and to be involved in the mission of the church.

Christ and Culture in Paradox

The Christ and culture in paradox approach emphasizes the fact that sin pervades all that humanity does, for even our most righteous acts are tainted by sin. Because all human works are corrupt, culture itself is badly askew. The solution to sinful society, however, is not withdrawal; the solution is God's grace in the midst of fallen society. Dualists (as Niebuhr sometimes calls them) know that they belong to the world and that there is no escape from its corruption. Grace forgives, but we are as Martin Luther put it, *simul justus et peccator,* simultaneously just and sinner. Living in the midst of the fallen world without the possibility of moral perfection, these Christians accept the paradox of being simultaneously committed to Christ and to the fallen structures of society. In their particular spheres, each has authority, and one must live with the tension therein. The vision of a heaven on earth nurtured through religious idealism is, for the dualist, a misguided aspiration.

Martin Luther

Martin Luther, a sixteenth-century Reformer, is without a doubt the classic example of the Christ and culture in paradox position. He dealt with many of the ethical and societal issues of his day from both theological and practical standpoints. Underlying Luther's approach was an understanding of natural orders and the two kingdoms. The natural orders, which essentially make up the kingdom of the world, include realities of society such as state, economy, law, marriage, and sometimes even the institutional church.[44] One cannot apply the gospel and its ethic to the kingdom of the world. The kingdom of God, by contrast, is composed of all true believers in Christ, who is its King and Lord. The divine kingdom is ruled not by the sword but by the Word of God. Here the gospel ethic, such as the Sermon on the Mount, guides behavior.

For Luther, the kingdom of the world is not the realm of Satan, for he is at work in both kingdoms. The kingdom of the world is ordered by God and under his control but through divinely appointed offices within the natural orders. Here God rules in a different way than he does in the divine kingdom, at times with coercion and even the sword, because of human sin. Because the earthly kingdom is not the realm of redemption, it embodies all people. Hence, marriage is a natural order of creation that embraces all human beings; its benefits and ethical restraints are not dependent on the divine kingdom or faith. The kingdom of God, in contrast, is ruled by faith and the Word and applies primarily to the more private and "spiritual realms" of life. Here one must live by the Sermon on the Mount, loving one's enemies and not retaliating with force. But when a Christian carries out responsibilities in an office of the natural orders (i.e., judge, ruler, soldier), that person must be willing to use force and violence, for in that role he or she is operating under the kingdom of the world.

Luther contended that "if all the world were composed of real Christians . . . there would be no need for or benefits from prince, king, lord, sword, or law." But because of evil in the world, "If any one attempted to rule the world by the Gospel and to abolish all temporal law and sword . . . he would be loosing the ropes and chains of the savage wild beasts."[45] The two kingdoms are not to be confused and are essentially not at odds with each other. Rather, they point to separate spheres of life in which humans operate. Luther in his flamboyant style once stated in the midst of peasant uprisings, "Now he who would confuse these two kingdoms—as our false fanatics do—would put wrath into God's kingdom and mercy into the world's kingdom; and that is the same as putting the devil in heaven and God in hell."[46]

For Luther, God rules both kingdoms (but in a twofold way), and a Christian belongs to both. While the kingdoms operate in different avenues, they are not in conflict, for they point to differing spheres of life and call for differing ethical responses. Luther believed that one must live with the tension inherent in being a member of these two kingdoms; there is no escape to a land of moral perfection. Nor can one expect to transform the earthly kingdom into the kingdom of God. The solution to the paradox is God's grace.

Reinhold Niebuhr

Reinhold Niebuhr (1892–1971) was the older brother of H. Richard Niebuhr and is often viewed as one of the most influential American theologians of the twentieth century. In *Christ and Culture,* the younger Niebuhr does not mention his brother as an example of the Christ and culture in paradox position,[47] but clearly his Christian social realism is representative of this type.

After seminary, Reinhold Niebuhr began his ministry as a theological liberal with a social gospel bent in a Detroit parish. Over time his ministry with auto industry workers in the city engendered doubts about the progressive reformism of the social gospel, the idea that one could apply Jesus' ethics directly to society. He became dubious of the notion that moral education could change society, that pacifism could ensure world peace, and that there was a Christian social order—all tenets of his earlier theological training. Niebuhr first went through a modified Marxist phase in which he viewed social reality through class struggle, but eventually he moved to what many have termed Christian social realism.

Niebuhr's insistence on the reality of sin and the ambiguities of human history became primary motifs in his social ethics. In one of his earlier works, *Moral Man and Immoral Society,* he argued that in collective social reality, power struggles between groups are so great that we cannot apply personal ethical norms directly. The thesis of his work was "that a sharp distinction must be drawn between the moral and social behavior of individuals and of social groups, national, racial, and economic; and that this distinction justifies and necessitates political policies which a purely individualistic ethic must always find embarrassing."[48] Moral idealism, of both religious and rational strands, have tended to misunderstand "the brutal character of the behavior of all human collectives, and the power of self-interest and collective egoism in all intergroup relations." Thus, said Niebuhr, "The relations between groups must . . . always be predominantly political rather than ethical, that is, they will be determined by the proportion of power which each group possesses at least as much as by any rational and moral appraisal of the comparative needs and claims of each group."[49] The most that can be hoped for in social life is a reasonable balance of power between the competing groups.

For Niebuhr, Jesus' ethic was therefore not directly applicable to social ethics. It is an ethic of perfectionism that even individuals fail to achieve, let alone institutions and societies. "Surely this is not an ethic which can give us specific guidance in the detailed problems of social morality where the relative claims of family, community, class, and nation must be constantly weighed."[50] The ethic of Jesus may offer valuable insights but no direct social ethic. Niebuhr often spoke of the relevance of an "impossible possibility," in that Jesus' ethic constantly judges all human and social actions, but we can never believe we have arrived at a pure ethic in social life. The most we can hope for in politics, economics, and international affairs is a relative justice, a tolerable harmony between the interests and claims of the various groups. Yet, said Niebuhr, we can never be content with the status quo, for the ideals of Jesus always press down on our endeavors, reminding us that we can do better, but within a realistic recognition that we can never arrive.

Thus, for Niebuhr, the paradoxes—relevant and not relevant, good and evil, realism and judgment—are bound up with all we do. His thinking had a profound effect on an entire generation of Christian ethicists who accepted the Christian realism label. His thought and writings, which emphasized the balance of powers, even found their way to the corridors of Washington, D.C., especially in the fray of mid-twentieth-century Cold War politics. Indeed, many today, from a broad theological spectrum, continue to imbibe directly or indirectly at the waters of Niebuhrian realism.

Evaluation

Clearly, Christ and culture in paradox proponents take seriously the pervasiveness of sin in human culture and society. They recognize that because of sin the kingdoms of this world will not become heaven on earth by human effort, moral education, or social engineering; the fullness of God's kingdom awaits the eschaton. As H. Richard Niebuhr puts it, the dualist motif "mirrors the actual struggles of the Christian who lives 'between the times,' and who in the midst of this conflict in the time of grace cannot presume to live by the ethics of that time of glory for which he ardently hopes."[51] Also embodied within this approach is a distinction between the kingdom of God and the earthly kingdoms. While this type separates them too far, it nonetheless is correct to distinguish the reign of God from the temporal rule of human beings, even though the temporal rule has been ordered by God. Thus, there is a healthy suspicion about even our most worthy and idealistic efforts, a suspicion that prevents us from too easily claiming God for our endeavors. All of this is clearly consistent with a Christian worldview.

But there are also significant challenges to the dualist position. First, adherents tend to dichotomize life into the sacred and the secular and thus force Christian faith into the private realm. Luther's view of the two kingdoms and Niebuhr's insistence on the irrelevance of the particulars of Christian ethics for social life separate the faith from culture and society, and the Christian's life therein. This only plays into the privatization of faith so common in our world today.

Second, this type in practice tends toward a cultural status-quoism that accepts things the way they are. Niebuhr's dialectic tensions helped him avoid this problem, but such an avoidance is not always evident in his followers. Further, Luther's two kingdom theory allows the state, economics, education, and culture to remain unchallenged by the ethics of God's kingdom. Some critics have suggested that this static formulation of the two kingdoms may have contributed to the rise of Hitler's Nazism, for large segments of the German Church were unable to stand against its evils. Too much realism and too great a separation of the two kingdoms can easily precondition people merely to accept the way things are.[52]

A third issue concerning the Christ and culture in paradox position is its failure to incorporate redemption and the subsequent work of holiness in the lives of believers and their engagement with society. Adherents are correct to emphasize grace as the answer to the human dilemma and to remind us that even in redemption we are still sinners. But a theology of redemption cannot remain content with the way things are, individually or collectively. Christian holiness, an extension of redemption in Christ, is an integral part of Christian ethics. It calls individuals to move beyond the way things are and challenges the unrighteousness and injustice of culture. Such ethical holiness is a missing ingredient in the dualist framework.

Christ the Transformer of Culture

Christ the transformer of culture approach to faith and culture recognizes the sinfulness of humanity and culture but is more hopeful than the last type in believing that something can be done to transform society into a desired religious ideal. Because God is over all and active in all the works of humans and cultures, the world can be changed. Adherents emphasize that God the creator and God the redeemer are one, and thus redemption is not a move away from the world but a transformation of the world that God created and still rules. History is the story of God's mighty deeds within cultures and societies and humanity's responses to them. This approach has "a view of history that holds that to God all things are possible in a history that is fundamentally not a course of merely human events, but always a dramatic interaction between God and men."[53]

Niebuhr does not spell out exactly how this transformation takes place, but he seems to focus primarily on a social conversion rather than on individual conversion. This approach for Niebuhr is not primarily about evangelism of people but of an entrance into the structures and institutions of society to evoke change. Since God is at work in all parts of culture and society, Christians should not fear engaging those dimensions and seeking to bring them into conformity with the ways of God. Niebuhr sees the "conversionist" motif in a number of individuals throughout history, including St. Augustine. Augustine is not included here, for he best fits, I believe, in the paradox type, though clearly there are also conversionist motifs in his thought.

John Calvin

In many ways, John Calvin, a sixteenth-century leader of the Reformed movement, is the classic example of this type. The transformation of culture approach is evident in both his theology of culture and government and his pastoral leadership in Geneva. While many know Calvin primarily for his views of election and predestination, he clearly addresses issues of this world more than the next one, though always from a theocentric perspective.

In Calvin's *Institutes of the Christian Religion* and other writings, we get a clear sense of his acceptance of the created world and the call for Christians to work in and transform that world. Linking creation and human activity, Calvin wrote:

> It becomes man seriously to employ his eyes considering the works of God, since a place has been assigned him in this most glorious theatre that he may be a spectator of them. . . . Sculpture and painting are gifts of God. . . . Intelligence in some particular art [is] a special gift of God. . . . In reading profane authors, the admirable light of truth displayed should remind us that the human mind . . . is still adorned and invested with admirable gifts. . . . We will be careful . . . not to reject truth wherever it appears. In despising the gifts we insult the Giver.[54]

The transforming role of faith is particularly seen in his treatise on government. Like Luther, Calvin accepted the idea of two kingdoms, but the earthly kingdom was never far removed from the divine kingdom and was much more closely tied to "spiritual" and "moral" matters. While the work of Christ begins "the heavenly kingdom in us even now upon earth," Calvin also insisted that the earthly kingdom has responsibility "to foster and maintain the external worship of God, to defend sound doctrine and the condition of the Church, to adapt our conduct to human society, to form our manners to civil justice, to conciliate us to each other, to cherish common peace and tranquility."[55] The role of government is far more than the restraint of evil in society; it extends to both tables of God's law and to the promotion of the general welfare of men and women.

> Its object is not merely . . . to enable men to breathe, eat, drink, and be warmed (though it certainly includes all these); . . . it is [also] that no idolatry, no blasphemy against the name of God, no calumnies against his truth . . . be disseminated among the people; that the public quiet be not disturbed, that every man's property be kept secure, that men may carry on innocent commerce with each other, that honesty and modesty be culti-

vated; in short that a public form of religion may exist among Christians and humanity among men.[56]

Calvin believed that a nation should be built on the law of God, which is imprinted on the consciousness of the people but also needs to be taught publicly within a society. He contended that if civil laws are barbarous and savage, they should not be called laws, and if a magistrate commands anything against God, "Let us not pay the least regard to it."[57] He even went so far as to say that the popular magistrates are appointed to curb and subdue the tyranny of kings, thus opening the door for just revolutions.

Calvin did not develop his theology in a vacuum. What he declared theologically found life in the city of Geneva. In the local canton, not only were church and state closely tied together (the norm of the day) but most civil regulations were also rooted in divine law, and many sins were deemed civil offenses. Calvin and other religious leaders gave directions on economic matters (including lifting the ban on usury), education, and politics. His sermons "do not speak very much of another world and happiness there. They speak of this world—of the necessity of serving God here. They cry scorn against all injustice, whether it be ecclesiastical, bureaucratic, legal, or in the marketplace."[58] It is no accident that Calvin's Geneva is often called a theocracy, for the aim was that all society be conformed to the law of God.

Wherever the Reformed faith went, it was always accompanied by a strong transformation emphasis, not only of the person through faith in Christ but also of the entire society. Today's expressions of Reformed theology usually do not seek complete conformity of pluralistic societies to God's law, but they do emphasize that Christians have a responsibility to change the culture in a direction of God's righteousness and justice.[59]

The Social Gospel

Niebuhr places the social gospel movement in the Christ of culture category, perhaps because he was trained in its idealistic norms and found it wanting. While the social gospel has some tendencies in that direction, with its close association of God's kingdom and earthly structures, the movement is best understood as a Christ the transformer type. The social gospel emerged in the late nineteenth and early twentieth century in the context of growing industrialism, urbanization, and the social problems that ensued. While the movement was not entirely modernist in its theology, it did have a fairly optimistic outlook on history and the possibilities of human culture. At its core the social gospel emphasized that God wants to save not only individuals but also society and its structures. This salvation was most needed in the realm of economics and could be effected through an extension of kingdom ideals.

One of the best-known proponents of the social gospel was the Baptist minister-theologian Walter Rauschenbusch (1861–1918), who is often regarded as the great systematizer of the movement. Rauschenbusch was brought up in the pietistic tradition and began to incorporate social gospel ideas during a pastorate in Hell's Kitchen on New York City's west side. Facing firsthand the effects of poverty, disease, crime, unemployment, and malnutrition, the Baptist minister reflected on the meaning of the kingdom for social life. "The saving of the lost, the teaching of the young, the pastoral care of the poor and frail, the quickening of starved intellects, political reform, the reorganization of the industrial system, international peace—it was all covered by the one aim of the reign of God on earth . . . the divine transformation of all human life."[60] For Rauschenbusch, "Christianizing the social order means bringing it into harmony with the ethical convictions which we identify with Christ."[61]

Rauschenbusch believed society contained five main parts: family, church, education, politics, and economics. The first four were well on their way to attaining the kingdom ideal, evidenced by their democratization. The realm of economics needed to be converted. Rauschenbusch and most other adherents of the social gospel decried self-interest and the profit motif, called for the rights of labor, and spoke of a democratic socialism, which today would be labeled social welfare economics. These social reformers were not utopian in their visions, but they clearly affirmed that the kingdom of God could become more a reality on earth through the transformation of both individuals and social structures.

Recent Movements

There is great variety in the specific goals and ideals of adherents to the transformer motif, and nowhere is that more evident than in the contrast between two recent expressions: liberation theology and the political activities of what is commonly called the religious right. Liberation theology emerged in Latin America in the context of poverty and oppression of the 1970s. Eventually, it found expression in a wide variety of geographical and social groupings as an attempt to bring theology to the world, with the goal of social and economic liberation. Thus, during the last couple decades of the twentieth century, black, feminist, Asian, African, and other liberation theologies emerged.

Drawing on Marxist social analysis, liberationists argue that God has a preferential love for the poor and socially oppressed. Developmentalism, with its focus on economic cultivation from the top down, is deemed too timid and a continuation of unjust social structures. What is needed is a "radical break from the status quo, that is, a profound transformation of the private property system, access to power of the exploited class, and a social revolution that would break this dependence, would allow for the change to a new society, a socialist society—or at least allow that such a society might be possible."[62] The key paradigm theologically is liberation, drawn from the exodus story. Social liberation does not fully exhaust the meaning of salvation, but it must always be part of the salvific process. It must also focus primarily on the temporal world, not the next world. Gustavo Gutierrez, who wrote what many believe to be the most significant systematic theology of liberationism, argued that Latin American societies cannot remain under the economic dominance of Western capitalism, especially that of the United States. Rather, there must be "a profound transformation, a social revolution, which will radically and qualitatively change the conditions in which they now live."[63]

There could hardly be a more striking contrast with liberation theology than the now defunct Moral Majority and the more recent Christian Coalition. These movements, made up of conservative Christians, propose a different set of core issues: humanism in public schools, the sanctity of human life, family life, homosexuality, pornography, a strong national defense, and freedom of religion. Jerry Falwell, who began the Moral Majority in 1979, wrote:

> As a pastor, I kept waiting for someone to come to the forefront of the American religious scene to lead the way out of the wilderness. . . . Finally I realized that we had to act ourselves. Something had to be done now. The government was encroaching upon the sovereignty of both the church and the family. The Supreme Court had legalized abortion on demand. The Equal Rights Amendment, with its vague language, threatened damage to the traditional family, as did the rising sentiment toward so-called homosexual rights.[64]

Falwell and the Moral Majority mobilized the conservative religious masses to vote, speak out, and enter the political process.

A decade later the Christian Coalition and Pat Robertson picked up the mantle along with the likes of James Dobson, founder of Focus on the Family. As they assessed the culture, they concluded that the threats "came not from without but from within. Families are disintegrating, fathers are abandoning their children, abortion is the most common medical procedure in the nation, and young people attend schools that are not safe and in which they do not learn."[65] Though the Christian Coalition initially focused on national elections, it soon turned toward a more grassroots movement at the local level. As Ralph Reed, the Coalition's executive director, put it, "Our goal was to transform the religious conservative community from a political pressure group to a broad social reform movement based in local communities."[66] Though this ideological agenda differs greatly from that of liberation theology, the two movements are one when it comes to their basic stance toward culture—Christ the transformer.

Evaluation

It is highly significant that H. Richard Niebuhr offers no critique of the "conversionist" approach; no doubt because this reflects his own view. It is an approach to society and culture that takes seriously the call of Jesus to influence the world. Affirming creation as a good gift of God, these individuals and movements attempt to overcome the sacred/secular dichotomy that has too often plagued Christian thinking and action. They understand that the faith addresses not just individuals—speaking to individual motives, character, and behavior—but also culture, society, and its institutions. Moreover, Christ the transformer motif recognizes that sin is lodged not only in human hearts but in the structural dimensions of life. Adherents of this approach rightly want to do something about the injustices, unrighteousness, and sociocultural problems that plague society.

But as with each of the other types, the transformer type faces some challenges. First, this approach fails to do justice to the covenantal nature of biblical ethics. That is, it fails to appreciate that while biblical ethics has a potential role outside the faith and the acceptance of divine revelation, its primary focus is those who believe. To expect that a nonbelieving world or secular society can live by the moral expectations of the Christian faith is to expect far too much.

Second, the "transformers" have tended to use the world's means to change the world. Adherents enter into the fabric of social institutions, including politics, to accomplish desired transformation. Often they fail to recognize the irony of needing to employ societal strategies in their attempts to change society. Ernst Troeltsch once observed that the church type of Christianity "dominates the world and is therefore dominated by the world."[67] For Troeltsch, this was not a pejorative statement but a mere observation of reality. Using the world's means to effect change may not in and of itself be a problem, but clearly Christians must be aware of the potential tension this creates.

A final challenge for the Christ the transformer of culture approach is its tendency to equate particular social and political agendas with God's kingdom. In their attempts to effect change for righteousness and justice, the varied expressions of this approach historically have fallen into this trap, thus pushing them toward a Christ of culture stance. Effectiveness has preceded faithfulness, and in the process, the unique contribution of Christian ethics has been lost. Cal Thomas and Ed Dobson were once leaders in the Moral Majority. Over the years they came to question its too easy alliance with the kingdoms of this world in its attempts to transform society. Thus, they wrote, "Christians are deluded if we think we will change our culture solely through political power. One of the major reasons the Religious Right failed is that they were seduced by one of the oldest temptations known to man."[68]

Conclusion

213

The relationship between Christ and culture is one of the most significant elements in Christian moral discernment. How we answer the Christ-culture question will invariably affect the way we seek to implement and live out the Christian ethic within society. This chapter surveyed and critiqued H. Richard Niebuhr's five types of relationships, which have existed throughout the history of the Christian church. All have made significant contributions to Christian thinking about life in the world, but all face profound challenges from the perspective of a Christian worldview.

How then should we think about the relationship between Christ and culture? Growing up in evangelical Christianity, I remember many sermons and youth group discussions about how Christians were to be in the world but not of the world. The nomenclature of any Christ-culture proposal will likely always have its limitations, and certainly the nuances of the slogan I remember from my youthful years were not always spelled out with clarity, depth, or care. But as the years have passed I have found myself coming back to the phrase, "Christ in but not of culture."

Certainly the preposition "in" can too easily portray a static role for Christians in culture and society, but it points us in the direction of an incarnational model that seeks to be faithful to both the paradigm of creation, fall, redemption, and consummation and the model of Jesus himself.

In the incarnation, Jesus, the eternal son of God, took on human flesh and lived among us in the midst of fallen culture. In doing so, Jesus was not only acting to procure salvation but also affirming that God's created world is a good place and should not be abandoned despite the sinfulness of humanity, culture, and social institutions. Moreover, Jesus clearly calls his followers to be in the world and to influence it. The Great Commission (Matt. 28:18–20) compels us to a ministry of proclamation in which we herald the gospel of Jesus Christ to make disciples of all nations. Simultaneously, his metaphors of salt, light, and leaven compel us to a ministry of presence whereby our individual and corporate actions, characters, and prophetic voices serve both to negate the excesses of a fallen world and to evoke change toward righteousness, justice, and goodness.

But the Christian mission should never be change at all costs. One of the most insightful texts for understanding our role of being in but not of culture is Jesus' high priestly prayer in John 17:14–19:

> I have given them your word, and the world has hated them because they do not belong to the world, just as I do not belong to the world. I am not asking you take them out of the world, but I ask you to protect them from the evil one. They do not belong to the world, just as I do not belong to the world. Sanctify them in the truth; your word is truth. As you have sent me into the world, so I have sent them into the world. And for their sakes I sanctify myself, so that they also may be sanctified in truth.

Because the world is ultimately God's and the result of a good creation, Jesus calls us to live within the world. But because that world is fallen, there is the constant threat that God's redemptive work will be thwarted, even within those who have embraced redemption in Christ. Therefore, Jesus calls believers to a sanctified life within the world, to a character and pattern of behavior that is distinct. Christians will not reach perfection in this world, and we cannot escape the moral ambiguities and complexities that inevitably face us in a broken, sinful society. But within that world, we are called by God to a life of holiness and faithfulness that seeks to bear witness to God's created order, the redemptive work in Christ, and Christ's coming kingdom, when all things will be made new.

10

PURSUING JUSTICE

Mickey Mantle was a baseball superstar. During the 1950s and 1960s, Mantle was known for his unusual combination of speed and power, as he led the New York Yankees to twelve American League pennants and seven World Series championships. Three times he was the league's most valuable player, and many considered him the greatest all-around player in baseball history. "With a telegenic, boyish grin, an aw-shucks Oklahoma drawl and a big No. 7 across his muscular back, he became everyone's idea of what a great baseball player should look and sound like."[1]

But there was a dark side to Mantle's life, for off the field he was known for his high living, carousing, and consumption of alcohol. Mantle was an alcoholic and in 1995 received a liver transplant as a result of cirrhosis and hepatitis C. But unbeknown to the transplant physicians, cancer was present in other parts of his body, and in August of that same year he died. At a news conference several weeks before his death, Mantle expressed remorse for his years of abusing his body, declaring to young people that he was not a true role model. On his deathbed Mantle is reported to have had a spiritual conversion to Christ through the influence of his former teammate, Bobby Richardson.

Though sports fans mourned the passing of Mantle, his reception of a new liver just before his death set off a wave of controversy regarding organ transplants. The quickness with which Mantle received his liver caused some to ask whether celebrities were receiving preferential treatment. Would he have received the organ so soon had he not been Mickey Mantle? Moreover, should the former baseball great have been a recipient given his decades of careless living and drinking? Should lifestyle be a factor in deciding who gets the medical goods when there are not enough to go around?

The Southwest Organ Bank officials and Mantle's doctors denied that Mantle's celebrity status was a factor in his quick reception of an organ. The chief of transplant surgery at the hospital said Mantle received priority "because he was sicker than anybody else."[2] One's position on the waiting list is determined by the degree of sickness and length of time on the waiting list, combined with other factors of compatibility. But given the fact that in 2001 there were 77,000 people waiting for transplants and in 2000 fewer than 23,000 transplants were performed,[3] many continue to wonder whether the Mantle transplant was just.

Justice is an issue in all societies, and it is a central theme in Christian ethics. It emerges in regard to organ transplants, race and ethnic group relations, economics, environmental issues, business transactions, and gender issues. At the heart of justice is the question, What is due a person? in relationship to certain actions performed or by virtue of being a member of a particular group, including the human race. While justice according to the ancient philosophers and medieval theologians was a virtue (along with wisdom, fortitude, and temperance), today justice is also viewed as a principle or even a social vision to guide humans and societies in ordering their relationships. The topic of justice is included in part 4 because it involves social relationships and the way we seek to carry out the Christian worldview in relation to the larger communities and societies in which we live.

There are actually several spheres of justice, but essentially they can be broken down into two main categories: retributive and distributive. Retributive justice focuses on what is due a person when that person has perpetrated wrong. The issue involves the sorts of punishments and liabilities that are just in light of the suffering or damage that person has caused. A perennial issue has been whether capital punishment is a just or unjust retribution for murder. Recently, another debate has emerged in retributive justice: whether it is just for judges to order "deadbeat dads" to abstain from procreating or face imprisonment. Some have even proposed mandatory sterilization as a punishment for failure to take care of one's children.

Distributive justice is positive in nature, focusing on the kinds of rewards, rights, opportunities, services, and treatments due a person because of who that person is, what he or she has done, or even the group to which he or she belongs. Distributive justice "concerns a wide variety of goods and services distributed (such as money, health care, honors, educational opportunities, and protection from threats to life . . .) by a wide variety of agents (such as . . . [family], employers in a business, civil government, and even God . . .) to an equally wide variety of recipients (such as children . . . , employees, citizens, and businesses)."[4] Distributive justice involves some of the toughest justice issues as we attempt in a complex society to decide what is owed people in given circumstances and by whom it is owed. The Mickey Mantle transplant fits in the sphere of distributive justice. How do we decide a just way of allocating resources when there are not enough for everyone?

This chapter focuses on distributive justice as we seek to grasp what the Christian worldview can contribute to the complex issues we face as individuals, institutions, and societies. A number of significant theological and philosophical issues attend to this matter, and ultimately, we must decide on a definition of justice. From the outset, we must recognize that debates concerning justice have often been skewed by the vested interests of particular groups, ideological commitments, and the general "rightsism" ethos so prevalent in our time. This chapter will attempt to clarify what is at stake in the justice debates and the way justice fits within the larger framework of Christian understandings and normative commitments.

The Biblical Teachings on Justice

The Bible contains much teaching on justice. As the foundation for human justice, God is portrayed as just in both character and action:

> God . . . who is not partial and takes no bribe, who executes justice for the orphan and the widow, and who loves the strangers, providing them food and clothing.
>
> Deuteronomy 10:17–18

> The LORD works vindication
> and justice for all who are oppressed.
>
> Psalm 103:6

> The LORD maintains the cause of the needy,
> and executes justice for the poor.
>
> Psalm 140:12

> For I the LORD love justice.
>
> Isaiah 61:8

> I am the LORD; I act with steadfast love, justice, and righteousness in the earth, for in these things I delight.
>
> Jeremiah 9:24

> Here is my servant, whom I have chosen. . . . I will put my Spirit upon him, and he will proclaim justice to the Gentiles . . . He brings justice to victory.
>
> Matthew 12:18, 20

> And will not God grant justice to the chosen ones who cry to him day and night?
>
> Luke 18:7

218

> If our injustice serves to confirm the justice of God, what should we say?
>
> Romans 3:5

He scatters abroad, he gives to the poor; his righteousness [justice] endures forever. He . . . will . . . increase the harvest of your righteousness [justice].

2 Corinthians 9:9–10

Because God, the foundation of Christian ethics, is just, God's people are called to just actions and character:

Justice, and only justice, you shall pursue, so that you may live and occupy the land that the LORD your God is giving you.

Deuteronomy 16:20

Maintain justice, and do what is right.

Isaiah 56:1

Let justice roll down like waters,
  and righteousness like an ever-flowing stream.

Amos 5:24

What does the LORD require of you
but to do justice, and to love kindness,
and to walk humbly with your God.

Micah 6:8

Blessed are those who hunger and thirst for righteousness [justice], for they will be filled.

Matthew 5:6

Woe to you, scribes and Pharisees, hypocrites! For you tithe mint, dill, and cummin, and have neglected the weightier matters of the law: justice and mercy and faith.

Matthew 23:23

. . . Who through faith conquered kingdoms, administered justice.

Hebrews 11:33

The above texts are, of course, only a sampling of the many biblical references to justice, and beyond those references are many allusions to actions that correspond to justice, without mention of the term.

An examination of the Hebrew and Greek words used for justice reveals that they are sometimes translated "judgment" and "righteousness." The main Hebrew words are *mishpat* (justice, judgment) and *tsedaqah* (righteousness, justice). The primary Greek words are *dikaiosune* (justice, righteousness), *krima* (judgment, justice), and *krisis* (judgment, decision, justice).

When we probe the meaning and usage of these words throughout Scripture, we find that they are used in different ways, with the same word carrying various meanings in different contexts. For example, at times justice refers to God's retributive justice or judgment, which is closely linked to God's holiness. At other times God's righteousness/justice *(tsedaqah, dikaiosune)* is what meets the demands of God's holiness and retributive justice, thereby procuring human salvation through Christ's death on the cross. Thus, the apostle Paul states that through Christ's atoning death God shows his righteousness "to prove at the present time that he himself is righteous *[dikaiosune]* and that he justifies the one who has faith in Jesus" (Rom. 3:26). Through God's saving work in Christ, recipients of divine grace are now declared righteous or just, in the sense that Christ's own righteousness/justice becomes our own before our maker (Rom. 4:24; Gal. 3:6). But this righteousness is not merely a forensic declaration; it is also a way of life to be pursued by those who by faith have experienced God's justifying work of grace through Christ.

The striking feature of many biblical texts is the way righteousness and justice, in terms of human character and actions, go hand in hand and are intimately related. What are we to make of this? Righteousness (as both God's declaration through justification and the resulting outworking in our moral lives) can never be far removed from justice. Thus, to be a righteous person because of the work of Christ is also to be a just person. While we tend to think of righteousness primarily in terms of character or personal actions, its link to justice demonstrates that it invariably has a social dimension, a reality sometimes obscured by particular translations of the Bible. How do we discern whether the Hebrew and Greek words should be translated "righteousness" or "justice"? "A rule of thumb is that when one sees *righteousness* or *judgment* in the context of social responsibility or oppression, one can assume that *justice* would be a better translation."[5] And yet human justice in the social arena is ultimately rooted in God's own justice, made possible through his own righteousness, which then overflows to us. If God's work of righteousness does not result in both personal righteousness and social justice, then we can say with James that faith without works is dead (James 2:17, 26).

Though the Bible contains much teaching on justice, it is not always clear as to what justice actually entails. In other words, what is due human beings from the biblical perspective? To answer that question we need to move beyond the mere statements of the biblical texts to see them in their contexts and in relationship to the entire biblical narrative. That is, we need to develop a theology of justice (we will return to this in a later section). From a cursory overview of the texts themselves, however, several things stand out about the content of justice. First, justice is associated with fairness and integrity, as in fair trials (Lev. 19:15; Deut. 16:18–20) and just weights or measures (Lev. 19:35–36). Second, justice is right living in all areas of life (Isa. 1:16–17; 26:7). In the biblical understanding, one cannot be just in relation to social issues and lack personal character, or have personal character and lack social justice. This follows not only from texts that combine the two but also from the interchangeability of the various words translated "justice" and "righteousness." Third, as evidenced in many of the texts cited earlier, justice is clearly associated with a special concern for the oppressed, the poor, and those who lack the means of self-sufficiency. This stands in contrast to many historic conceptions of justice. As Nicholas Wolterstorff notes, "By contrast, when Plato in *The Republic* spoke of the just society, widows, orphans, aliens and the impoverished were nowhere in view. The fundamental contour of justice was identified by Plato with a certain kind of 'law and order.'"[6]

As we attempt to work out the biblical concept of justice amid the complexities of life, we are faced with some immediate questions: What is the relationship between justice and love? What is the relationship between justice and freedom? Which understanding of justice (i.e., what is due people) best reflects the Christian worldview? From whom or what is justice owed? How we seek to relate Christian ethics to the cultures and societies in which we live is related to these questions.

Love and Justice

People often speak of justice and love as if they go hand in hand and are virtually the same. The Bible sometimes proclaims them in the same breath, as when Micah says that the Lord requires justice and mercy (6:8), or Hosea admonishes, "Sow for yourselves righteousness [or justice, *tsedaqah*]; reap steadfast love" (10:12). But an examination of the issues relative to these two moral norms reveals that things are not so simple. For example, the opening narrative about Mickey Mantle shows that love will not solve the moral quandary surrounding organ transplants. Or take the example of racial justice. Love alone did not end slavery or procure the necessary civil rights laws to facilitate justice in the United States. In fact, during the slavery era, some owners no doubt showed a kind of love to their slaves, treating them with compassion and mercy, but such love never got to the fundamental issue of what was owed the slaves as human beings created in the image of God. Justice, as a moral concept, was needed to bring an end to slavery, for love alone (at least thought of in terms of personal mercy and compassion) was insufficient.

What is the relationship between love and justice? Theologians and ethicists have long debated this issue, and there are several views. Emil Brunner, the twentieth-century neoorthodox theologian from Switzerland, argued that love and justice are two different things. Love, which ultimately is comprehended only by faith, is most visibly revealed in Jesus Christ. Love, according to Brunner, is always personal in nature, as it seeks to respond to a particular person in his or her uniqueness. But "justice is a totally different thing. When we are just, and deal justly, we render to the other what is his due. Justice makes no free gift; it gives precisely what is due to the other, no more and no less. Its basis is strictly realistic, sober and rational."[7] While love always regards a person in light of his or her particular context and needs, justice is always in a sense blind.

Brunner saw justice related to the world of systems and institutions, a realm in which love cannot sufficiently operate. A person of love, acting in institutions, must turn his or her love into justice or run the risk of ruining institutional life. "Love which is not just in the world of institutions is sentimentality. And sentimentality, feeling for feeling's sake, is the poison, the solvent that destroys all just institutions."[8] Thus, within the world of institutions, we must essentially change our mode of operation from love to justice in order that people receive their due. Love can certainly do more than justice within the personal realm, but Brunner believed that justice is always the precondition of love, and love can never render justice void. In essence then, for Brunner, love is the operating virtue in personal relationships patterned after the *agape* love of Christ. Justice, known by reason, is the operating virtue in the institutions of society. Both are needed, each in its own sphere.

Some who follow Brunner's lead of separating justice and love emphasize that because the state cannot love, it has no role in meeting economic welfare needs. Responding to the needs of humans in their economic deprivation is a responsibility of individuals and is motivated by love. Because the state is the sphere of justice and not love, it cannot respond to specific human need; it can only establish just or fair procedures in economics and carry out retributive justice.[9]

There is, of course, a sense in which Brunner's separation of love and justice for differing spheres of life is correct. Frequently, love is more personal in nature, and justice more related to institutions. We can love people, but it is quite difficult to love institutional patterns and processes. But the problem with this view is twofold. First, it does not accord with Scripture, in which love and justice are interrelated and closely held together. Second, separating love and justice too far allows institutional life and the state to boil justice down to a few basic rights. This form of justice misses its full biblical understanding. When love, as virtue and principle, is removed from the person effecting justice, that person will likely lack the sensitivities needed to render justice.

Another view of love and justice is seen in the thinking of Reinhold Niebuhr. For Niebuhr, love and justice are not only distinct, as in Brunner's view, but are also often in tension with each other. As shown in the last chapter, Niebuhr, as a social realist, believed that the ethics of Jesus (with its emphasis on love and the kingdom of God) could never be a guide in the rough and tumble of societal life. It could not be a guide amid the competing claims and interests of institutions, societies, and nations. In fact, in such spheres love could actually do harm. In those spheres, only justice is applicable, and its demands are at times in tension with *agape* love. Moreover, the justice that is applicable in societal spheres is not ideal justice but a balance of power among the competing interests. As Niebuhr once described it:

> The New Testament never guarantees the historical success of the "strategy" of the cross [love]. . . . Since this possibility does not exist, it is not even right to insist that every action of the Christian must conform to *agape*, rather than to the norms of relative justice. . . . For as soon as the life and interest of others than the agent are involved in an action or policy, the sacrifice of those interests ceases to be "self-sacrifice." It may actually become an unjust betrayal of their interests.[10]

The sinfulness of humanity and the inability of social life to transcend the forces of history send love and justice in opposite directions, according to Niebuhr. Love is an "impossible possibility" that hovers over all we do and judges even the best intentions. It is never achievable. Justice is all we can hope for within the confines of historic contingency, and it will by necessity be a justice that seeks to balance the competing powers, though always with an eye toward increasing power for the victims of injustice. Justice for Niebuhr was a relative justice, a tolerable harmony between the competing claims of a sinful world. This means that "society must strive for justice even if it is forced to use means, such as self-assertion, resistance, coercion and even resentment, which cannot gain the moral sanction of the most sensitive moral spirit."[11]

Niebuhr was perhaps correct that tension can exist between love and justice in the midst of a fallen world. But are the Christian conceptions of justice and love defined primarily by the contingencies and complexities of history or by the transcendent beckoning of a God beyond us? The tension between individual and social morality is significant, but pulling them apart too far allows "morally upright" people too much latitude in the administration of justice. Niebuhr allowed "industrial groups, societies and governments a disturbing amount of license"[12] in the name of justice.

How then should we think about love and justice? Richard Higginson has wisely suggested that love and justice mutually supplement each other. Love needs justice, and justice needs love. While love tends to be personal and justice institutional, separating them into distinct spheres (Brunner) or setting them in tension (Niebuhr) is not only contrary to biblical teaching but also fails to appreciate their mutual reinforcement in the midst of historic situations. As Higginson notes, love must provide a supplement to the verdict of justice:

> Where justice makes life hard for someone, love remains attentive to the individual's needs, and seeks to mitigate the harshness of the verdict. If justice does dictate that long-term considerations take priority over short-term ones, love does its utmost to make those immediate consequences bearable. If society was ever to adopt a stricter abortion law,

then it is vital that compassion be awakened for many thousands of unhappy women who will be expected to go through pregnancies against their will.[13]

At the same time, justice must be a supplement to love, for "awe-inspiring though love is as an ethical principle, it requires direction and in some cases correction from the principle of justice."[14] As Higginson sees it, justice has the ability to look beyond the immediate needs calling for love to the long-term commitments. Similarly, "Love tends to respond to the most eye-catching and desperate types of need, whereas justice demands that one spreads one's gaze rather more widely." Thus, "A just ordering of medical resources is sensitive to the whole gamut of human need,"[15] not merely the glaring needs that catch us emotionally. Justice also directs love by exposing the structural dimensions of social or ethical issues, thus requiring not just charity but actual changes in the way things operate.

The mutual supplementing of love and justice is evident in issues of race relations. Justice calls for policies and procedures that ensure races and ethnic groups equal access to jobs, education, and power in society. Justice is sensitive to past wrongs and seeks to overcome them, addressing issues of institutional racism. But such justice may not improve actual relations among the various races or ethnic groups. Love calls for personal engagement among the groups so that prejudices are overcome and reconciliation occurs. Stopping at racial reconciliation will not complete the divine task in racial relations, for justice ensures that policies, laws, and structures render to people their due, simply because they are made in the image of God. But to stop at just policies, laws, and structures will not achieve God's vision for humanity either, for God desires that in our differences we learn empathy, understanding, and mercy. Justice and love must walk together. When they do, they nurture each other and guard against the excesses of a single principle or virtue pursued alone.

Freedom and Justice

Often freedom and justice are seen as going hand in hand or even as the same thing. In this common assumption, to pursue justice is to pursue freedom and vice versa. Freedom was particularly the cry of the Enlightenment philosophers as they sought to build societies free from tyranny, oppression, and external obstacles to human aspirations and desire. Life, liberty, and the pursuit of happiness (or wealth in the original version) was the mantra, often built on the assumption of human autonomy. Thus, a just society was a free society.

John Stuart Mill was a utilitarian who believed that justice was determined by maximizing good for the greatest number of people. But he believed that the most fundamental principle of society and the key to its justice was freedom. Mill wrote, "The only freedom which deserves the name is that of pursuing our own good in our own way, so long as we do not attempt to deprive others of theirs, or impede their efforts to obtain it."[16] For Mill and many other proponents of the supremacy of freedom, a good and just society is a free society.

But justice and freedom in real life do not always reside together so easily. The reality is that justice in some manner always limits freedom. This, of course, is obvious within the sphere of retributive justice, but it is also true concerning distributive justice. To grant someone his or her due invariably places limits on someone else's freedom to act as he or she sees fit. Conversely, a pursuit of freedom alone will never result in justice, though some argue for such.[17]

Take the example of abuses stemming from the work conditions during the burgeoning Industrial Revolution. As industrialism spread and market economies flourished, economic prosperity emerged, but often at the expense of many workers. Women and children were initially used in the coal mines because of their short stature, often for long periods of time and to the detriment of their health. There were virtually no safety regulations in factories, and it was quite common for workers to lose fingers and limbs or to be maimed for life. Employees had no rights, pay was poor, conditions were unhealthy, and six days of work for twelve hours a day took its toll on men, women, and children. The cries for justice, first heard in England, came from Christians such as Lord Shaftesbury, who led the way in championing labor laws to procure justice and dignity in the workplace.[18] The pleas for justice were countered by cries for freedom. Many of the industrialists argued that workers were free to come and go as they pleased; they did not have to work in the factories. Moreover, factory owners believed that because they owned the factories, they should have the freedom to run them as they saw fit. If freedom in the workplace was not honored, they would go out of business. Freedom was essential to the economic market.

Justice in these situations clearly meant a limitation on entrepreneurs' freedom. Laws that limited working hours, required safety devices on the machines, and stipulated ventilation in the factories limited the freedom of some for the justice of others. Of course, debates have ensued since those days as to the limits of both labor and management claims, but the point is that freedom for some is curtailed for the sake of justice.

A similar example can be seen with regard to ecological justice. Many have argued that justice is about how we treat not only humans but also the environment, which in turn affects human beings. As seen earlier in this book, there is a biblical mandate for caring for the earth and its resources, but it is clear that demands of justice with regard to the environment place limits on the pursuits of humans. Some today argue that economic freedom and the need to meet human needs call for limits to environmental justice, while others argue that economic freedom and prosperity must be limited for the sake of environmental justice and ultimately human health. Environmental debates invariably come down to debates about freedom versus justice.

As Christians, what are we to make of the tension between the two? True Christian freedom is found in relationship with God through Christ and the way of life that follows: "If you continue in my word, you are truly my disciples; and you will know the truth, and the truth will make you free" (John 8:31). But political freedom can also be argued from several biblical and theological sources: human creation in the image of God, the story and paradigm of the exodus, and the existence of the church as a distinct entity apart from the government's jurisdiction.

Perhaps the kind of society that best reflects the Christian worldview is one that maintains a tension between justice, freedom, and order.[19] A society that has a singular focus on justice will lack freedom and overly accentuate order, as witnessed by Marxist or communist governments of the twentieth century. A society with a singular focus on freedom will lack justice and order, tending toward anarchy. And a society that focuses solely on order will lack justice and freedom, tending toward totalitarianism. Holding the three together will not solve all public policy debates and certainly will not inevitably lead to one specific political ideology. But it does provide a framework for Christians seeking to apply their moral commitment to a complex, fallen world. It is, moreover, a framework that Christians can appeal to in a pluralistic world in which people do not share the Christian worldview assumptions.

What Is Due? Definitions of Justice

Most of the debates about justice today ultimately boil down to the definitions employed: What do we actually owe people in given situations of life? The varying definitions lead to divergent views regarding a host of issues. Essentially, there are three primary theories or paradigms for defining distributive justice: merit, equality, and need.[20]

Meritorious Justice

Justice understood as merit focuses on what is owed a person by virtue of his or her actions, efforts, and impact. In this version, there is impartiality in rewarding human effort, with a minimal focus on actual outcomes. Justice is best achieved by establishing fair procedures within a given sphere of activity and then rewarding people according to what they merit. As long as just mechanisms are in place, merit is deemed the best way to reward people, even though the rewards for merit will often vary significantly even for similar kinds of activities. Generally this view has espoused a minimal role for government in distributive justice. Merit is not understood in terms of a person's role or position in life but in terms of what that person actually performs within his or her role or position.

If this definition of justice is used to decide who gets an organ transplant, an immediate answer will not be found. The question will remain, What form of merit? Ability to pay, one's efforts to procure an organ, or one's contribution to society and the immediate community? Many who espouse this definition would argue that it is not an approach for issues such as scarce medical resources, in which merit is difficult to define, but it is a good approach for areas such as economics and education.

A number of Christian scholars have argued for this view of distributive justice on the grounds that the Bible calls for a limited state and thus precludes federal actions to ensure egalitarian outcomes or appeals to human need as the basis for public policy. Ronald Nash believes that unbridled "statism" is the result of egalitarian or need-based theories of justice. He argues that "the widespread tendency to connect moral and economic merit ought to be avoided. Because many people are offended by the fact that someone who is less deserving in a moral sense is worth more economically, they believe steps should be taken to alter the situation through statist action."[21] What justice calls for, says Nash, are just procedures that ensure that there is no way of knowing ahead of time what the results will be. Nash does not use the term merit justice, but that is clearly the sentiment of his theory once just procedures are in place. Merit is clearly evidenced in his assertion that "while each person should be given an equal chance to enjoy the best possible life, it is sometimes necessary to give extra attention to the especially gifted. Since the gifted are often people who lead society, aiding them helps all within society. At the very least, society should place no obstacle in the path of the more gifted."[22] Similarly, Calvin Beisner argues for a minimalist, procedural justice that prevents fraud, theft, and violence. The Christian conception of justice in economics "requires that people be permitted to exchange and use what they own . . . freely so long as in so doing they do not violate others' rights."[23] Beisner believes, therefore, that minimum wage laws, racial quotas for employment, laws requiring equal pay for equal work, and legal restrictions on imports and exports are all unjust.

Both Beisner and Nash seem to reflect the philosophical influence of Robert Nozick. Writing from a purely rational framework, Nozick argues for a minimal state with a few basic rights: the right to freely choose our course of action in life, the right to own property, and the right against injury by others. Following Kant, he believes that we should treat people as ends, not merely as means, and grant them natural rights that are inherent within their nature. The state's only responsibility is to protect those basic rights and ensure fair mechanisms for pursuing them. Nozick's basic principle is that whatever happens from a just situation by just procedures is just. He believes that "past circumstances or actions of people can create . . . differential deserts to things,"[24] and it is clearly unjust for the state to reverse those outcomes. The minimal state allows people the freedom to pursue their own goals, limited only by harm to others. "Treating us with respect by respecting our rights, it allows us . . . to choose our life and to realize our ends . . . aided by the voluntary cooperation of other individuals possessing the same dignity."[25] While Nozick says he rejects any formula of "to each according to . . . , " including merit, once his procedures are in place, his theory is closest to the merit view.

What are Christians to make of the merit view of justice? Clearly, there are spheres of life in which what people are owed ought to reflect their effort and expertise. Most people agree that grades in the academic arena ought to reflect merit—the effort and quality of work from the student. Moreover, it also seems just that in economic exchanges merit should be significant in what is owed. If two people—doing the same job—reflect differences in energy, expertise, and output, they should be rewarded according to merit. Indeed, when people in the marketplace are not rewarded for the amount and quality of their work, not only are they demoralized but society itself also suffers. Furthermore, there are biblical grounds for merit. Second Thessalonians 3:10 states, "Anyone unwilling to work should not eat," and Jesus said, "Laborers deserve their food" (Matt. 10:10; cf. Luke 10:7). In the parable of the talents told by Jesus in Matthew 25:14–30, there is reward for those who wisely invested and demerit for the one who wasted his resource.

But is the merit understanding of justice sufficient for all circumstances of life? Do we want to settle the organ transplant issue on the basis of some form of merit? Many believe that if people received organs based on their creative efforts to get an organ or their ability to pay, only the wealthy and powerful would ever receive transplants. There seems to be something about the nature of organ transplants, with human life in the balance, that calls for a different approach. Even the idea that Mickey Mantle should not have received a liver on the basis of his lifestyle (a demerit) seems problematic in practice. Do we really want finite, sinful creatures to decide who lives and who dies on the basis of issues related to lifestyle? Certainly, lifestyle might be weighed as a medical factor, but that is different from making it a decisive element of justice. Wisely, the transplant system in the United States has not employed the merit definition of justice.

But what about economic life, the realm most talked about by the defenders of this definition? Do we really want merit alone to determine how mentally handicapped people are compensated economically? Are they owed a meager existence because their mental capacity precludes them from ever meriting economic rewards? If we allow merit alone to determine all of economic life, we will find it difficult to meet the biblical challenge to care for the least of our brothers and sisters. Of course, one can argue that caring for them is the work of compassion or love, to be meted out by individuals and the church. But in a complex, fallen world, in which injustices abound and many are outside the reach of compassionate communities, we are still left with the question as to whether government has a role in procuring justice for the economically disenfranchised.

Merit clearly must be part of the picture in regard to justice, but taken alone it can never achieve God's designs and standards of justice.

Egalitarian Justice

Egalitarian justice encompasses two forms: equal outcomes and equal access. In the first form, justice is defined by the actual outcome of reaching some type of equality. Since all humans in their very being are of equal value, they ought to be compensated in the various spheres of life in basically the same way. Various forms of socialism have tended toward the equal outcome definition, and some feminists have pursued this course as well. The most obvious problem is that in history this egalitarian utopianism has not worked. Such a system treats people unfairly in order to produce equal outcomes (thereby nullifying both merit and need), and it tends toward an all-encompassing political structure to achieve them.

The more popular form of egalitarianism has been the equal access approach, whereby all people are ensured equal access to jobs, rights, housing, and pay. This does not mean that all people will get the jobs they want or entrance into the schools they desire, but no personal or external factors will prevent people from fairly competing for the rights and goods available in a given society. Within this definition, "Justice can be understood to mean similar treatment for similar cases. . . . All those who are in a comparable situation should be treated equally."[26] Egalitarian justice generally calls for a more activistic government than does merit justice to ensure that people have equal access to the rights, goods, and privileges within society and that they are treated similarly in similar situations.

If we employ this definition of justice to decide who gets the organs when there are not enough to go around, we will emphasize a procedure that ensures that all people have an equal opportunity to receive an organ. Clearly, there will not be equal outcomes, which this definition never ensures, but each person will have the same opportunity to receive an organ. In its pure form, this approach does not consider need or merit.

The name most often associated with egalitarian justice is John Rawls, the moral and political philosopher who taught for many years at Harvard and authored *A Theory of Justice,* deemed by some to be one of the most pivotal works on the topic. For Rawls, justice is the first virtue of social institutions, as it relates to the fitting allocation of duties, rights, and benefits to people who participate freely and equally in political society. Justice is particularly relevant in those social situations in which there may be disagreements over entitlements or a scarcity of resources. The heart of justice in these situations is fairness, achieved by a "veil of ignorance" that precludes certain kinds of knowledge that could make the distribution unfair.

Within this general framework, Rawls sets forth two primary principles to determine justice.[27] The first is the principle of equal liberty in which "each person is to have an equal right to the most extensive total system of equal basic liberties compatible with a similar system of liberty for all."[28] Given the reality that society is never a "zero sum game," there will not be equal outcomes, but theoretically equality would be the outcome if society started from that reality. Because there will be differences of outcome in the competition for scarce resources and in the disagreements over rights, Rawls proposes a second principle for achieving justice: maximize the minimum. Rawls states, "Social and economic inequalities, for example inequalities of wealth and authority, are just only if they result in compensating benefits for everyone, and in particular for the least advantaged members of society."[29] In the allocation of rights and goods, the only social and economic inequalities in the distribution must be aimed at advantaging the least advantaged. Rawls's two principles are focused primarily on the macro-level in society, not the micro-level. That is, they "are geared toward the basic structure of society, not toward every act of every level where justice is a concern."[30]

How should we assess egalitarian justice? The theme of equality has been central to modern democracies. It has given people hope that no matter what their background, color, or status in society, they will have in principle an equal access to its rights, goods, and liberties. While this, of course, is never fully achieved, it nonetheless grants to all human beings a vision of fairness and a confidence that in principle the social system will not treat them according to external characteristics such as race, gender, ethnicity, or religion. Egalitarian justice has been the foundation of basic human rights.

While equality as we speak of it today is primarily a child of the Enlightenment, there are biblical and theological foundations for the concept. Creation in the image of God means that every human being bears an equal dignity and value before God that ought to be honored by society. That is the ultimate foundation for any concept of human rights, sense of fairness, or vision of equality. The Old Testament law mandated equality in the judicial procedures: "You shall not render an unjust judgment; you shall not be partial to the poor or defer to the great: with justice you shall judge your neighbor" (Lev. 19:15). Jesus echoed an egalitarian note when he said that the Father in heaven "makes his sun rise on the evil and on the good, and sends rain on the righteous and on the unrighteous" (Matt. 5:45).

But the egalitarian definition of justice also faces some challenges. A practical problem is determining what equal access or fairness looks like in real life. A few years ago a rather humorous but nonetheless serious issue emerged in the state legislature of Virginia—the debate over "potty parity." As the news reported it, "A legislator decided to go against the flow when he noticed how much more time women spent in restrooms than men, so he penned a 'potty parity' resolution to help relieve the situation."[31] The legislator contended that the state plumbing code, which called for a 50-50 ratio of space for men's and women's restrooms, was essentially discriminatory. The equal space code did not take into consideration the fact that urinals occupy less space than toilet stalls, and hence, men's restrooms have more facilities. Moreover, elderly people take longer in restrooms, and there are more elderly women than men. Beyond that, women often have children with them. The result, contended the legislator, is that women's restrooms should be larger than men's. This story makes the point well: Equality does not take into consideration the contextual factors or specific needs concerning an issue.

Some have critiqued equality on the grounds that it will not redress past injustices. That is, if unjust procedures and actions have existed in the past, there may need to be some form of redress, or equal access can never become a reality.[32] Others have argued that equality too easily negates the role of merit, the effort and quality of individuals in their pursuit of the goods and privileges of society. For example, Rawls's second principle seems to assume an equal effort by the least advantaged of society. There are, of course, many reasons for being disadvantaged in a society, but surely one of them has to do with effort. Still others have been concerned with the way in which egalitarian justice seems to proliferate the state's entrance into domains of life in which it should not play a role. Obviously, at this point, one's understanding of the nature and role of the state plays a significant role in one's definition of justice.

Need Justice

In need justice, what individuals are owed is based primarily on their concrete needs in a given sphere. The defenders of this approach believe that at times equality must be laid aside to respond to the specific needs of individuals or groups of people within society. Frequently, adherents focus on redressing past injustices that the principle of equality is not able to reverse. They believe that the merit approach too easily allows for rewards that are inevitably tied up with status and privilege in society, and they generally call for an activistic government to address the concrete needs of individuals and groups who have not shared adequately in society's rights and resources. The approach is captured by Marx's famous statement, "From each according to his ability, to each according to his need."[33]

If we take this approach in determining who gets an organ for transplant, we will focus on the greatest need at the moment. Decisions will not be made based on who merits the organ or on an egalitarian principle such as a lottery method. If taken alone, this definition calls for the sickest person at the moment to receive the scarce medical resource.

To some extent we have already been introduced to this definition of justice in John Rawls's second principle, acting for the benefit of the least advantaged in society. While Rawls's approach is fundamentally egalitarian in nature, he employs a kind of need justice in giving special attention to those who are at the bottom of economic society.

From a Christian perspective, this definition of justice has been clearly articulated by Stephen Mott and Ronald Sider. Mott believes that justice must be attentive to the unique needs of those to whom God has shown special care, the poor and disenfranchised. He believes that equality alone will not address the needs of those who cannot compete successfully in the world. Thus, "The equal provision of basic rights requires unequal response to unequal needs. Justice must be partial in order to be impartial."[34] Mott argues that biblical justice is dominated by the idea of redress, which means attempts must be made to correct the inequalities of the past and hence to allow for more equitable justice to take over. "The goal of redress is to return people to a normal level of advantage and satisfaction in the community, particularly with respect to the capacity to earn a living." He sees the Year of Jubilee in Leviticus 25 as a clear indication that God desires redress, meaning justice as response to need, especially needs created by past injustices. Thus, Mott contends, "When the number of sufferers becomes too large, private charity cannot cope with the ills of society; love then requires structural measures to achieve social justice."[35]

Sider joins Mott in heralding need as the essential biblical understanding of justice. In an article written together, they rehearse the numerous biblical texts that speak of God lifting up the poor and oppressed, tearing down the rich and powerful, and inviting his people to share in that divine action. They note, "Hundreds of biblical verses show that God is especially attentive to the poor and needy. God is not biased. But because of unequal needs, however, equal provision of basic rights requires justice to be partial in order to be impartial. . . . Partiality to the weak is the most striking characteristic of biblical justice."[36]

It is quite clear that this view has generated some of the strongest heat in the debates about justice, in part because of its affinity to Marx's dictum quoted earlier: "From each according to his ability, to each according to his need." But this view does not necessarily entail a Marxist understanding of reality or economics. The view has appeal in its contention that love and justice must be held closely together; what love begins, justice must complete. Unlike the merit and egalitarian understandings, this approach wants "blindfolded" fairness, along with a clear vision of human and historical realities. It argues that the other understandings of justice are not as attuned to what is happening in the world.

In Scripture, justice and human need are often held together. The texts listed near the beginning of this chapter reveal God's special concern for the weak and least in society and the call for God's people to respond. Some might contend that these texts do not call for government but the covenant people to respond. But clearly we cannot get around the biblical teaching that "the LORD maintains the cause of the needy, and executes justice for the poor" (Ps. 140:12). As Mary put it in the Magnificat, "He has brought down the powerful from their thrones, and lifted up the lowly; he has filled the hungry with good things, and sent the rich away empty" (Luke 1:52–53).

While need justice has strong biblical and emotional appeal (i.e., compassion), it also faces some challenges. One of the major challenges is in discerning the need of a person or group. It is easy to respond to a visible and immediate need and not touch the deeper, long-term need. For example, slowly American society is awakening to the reality that welfare or aid to the poor does not really address the most fundamental needs of the poor: the need for dignity, self-worth, opportunity, and skills, whereby they could enter into the economic realm with new possibilities. A system that focuses purely on the need of the moment does not address these more fundamental human needs, which are at the heart of a Christian understanding of reality. Work in the biblical framework is a creation mandate and a significant means not only of livelihood but of self-worth and camaraderie with others. Clearly, many government programs that attempt to be compassionate and achieve justice have frequently worked against these more fundamental needs. Thus, a just government is one that allows work to flourish and people to participate in the economic arena. At the same time, we must recognize that there will always be some who are not able to participate adequately in the economic realm because of physical, emotional, or contextual limitations. Need justice must come into play in these situations, though in a way that does not demean these individuals or severely limit economic opportunity within society.

There is a second danger associated with need justice: Human need can move one to sentimentality and away from the dimension of justice as fairness. As we have seen, justice in the biblical sense is not only a response to human need but a pursuit of fairness in treatment. Historically, justice has often been signified by a blindfold, which symbolizes its transcendence of historical realities that at times can easily distort vision and perspective.

For example, people are often moved by feelings of compassion at the sight of human need, but in reality the most visible form of compassion is sometimes not the ethical or just course of action. There are times when a person might, for the sake of justice, have to let someone go from a job because that person has not performed the work or is a detriment to the functioning of others. Such an act may seem cold and compassionless, but at the same time it is the most just action for the other workers, for the company as a whole, and perhaps even for the worker.

Similarly, if we look to need justice alone regarding the issue of abortion, we may get caught up in the singular appeal of compassion for the mother's plight or the "need" to use embryonic stem cells for research. In such situations, human need and appeals to compassion overlook justice and what is owed those human lives that are most vulnerable to the designs and "needs" of others. Need justice, by itself, can easily turn into sentimentality.

Need justice is one dimension of just actions and a just society, but taken alone it is inadequate. It does not sufficiently allow for merit, in places where merit should count, and it does not give adequate due to fairness and equality.

An Evaluation of Definitions

It is evident that there is theological and biblical support for all three definitions of justice. As a result, it may be helpful to recognize that the different definitions of justice apply to different activities and spheres of reality. As William Werpehowski puts it, "Specification of justice requires specification of criteria appropriate to the nature of the relationship in question."[37] In some spheres of life, the various definitions need to be held together in a creative tension.

In the economic realm, merit must play a significant role to do justice to one's effort, expertise, and responsibility and to maintain productivity for the entire society. Without productivity human need is not met, and justice is not rendered. At the same time, people need equal opportunity when applying for jobs or seeking advancement. Simultaneously, there must be provisions for those who are poor and those who find it difficult to enter into the economic rewards of society. This does not entail a particular commitment to political ideology, for justice in principle transcends ideology. Ethically sensitive Christians must be committed to such areas of justice regardless of their political persuasion.

Other realms of life require differing scenarios of justice. Currently, the United States transplant system uses a combination of need (i.e., sickest patients) and egalitarian considerations. The complex system is not without its problems, but in principle a combination of these two definitions seems to best fit that sphere of life.

When it comes to political rights, housing, and educational opportunities, an egalitarian justice seems to be most appropriate. We should not allow one group a disproportionate amount of political power for the sake of securing that group's interests. Such an approach clearly stereotypes a given group in society as having only one set of perspectives or interests and hence destroys the dignity of each individual.

Obviously, defining justice is no easy matter. Attempting to discern the appropriate definition or combination of definitions for the various spheres of human activity is a challenge that calls for clear thinking and analysis that moves beyond ideological commitments.

From Whom or What Is Justice Owed?

One more issue often divides people today in discussions about justice. Who or what is responsible for justice? The state, citizens, the Christian church, or Christian individuals? Most Christians would argue that the Bible means what it says when it speaks of God's compassion for the poor and the need for a commitment to justice on their behalf. But some people do not think this is primarily the role of the state. Others believe that when the Bible speaks of social justice the primary mediator is government. In these debates, the issue is not always different definitions of justice or even variant interpretations of biblical texts. Sometimes the debate hinges on differing understandings about the nature and role of the state.

The central question here is whether the state has the responsibility to ensure justice or whether justice is the domain of individuals and the church. If both have a role, which spheres of justice reside with the government and which spheres reside with individuals and the church? Most Christians agree that the Bible is clear on the issue of retributive justice—the punishment meted out for breaking the law, harming others, and violating other people's rights. As Romans 13 indicates, this sphere of justice is not in the hands of individuals or the church but the state. The larger debates involve distributive justice, particularly in the realm of economic life. While it seems clear that government ought to have laws that protect basic rights, property, and ensure equal opportunity for all, it is not immediately clear how far government should go in seeking distributive justice economically.

When we look to Scripture and theological paradigms, we do not find immediate answers to these issues, but we can garner some basic understandings that give us perspective and general direction. First, it is certainly clear that justice is a responsibility of individuals. While it always has a social dimension, justice ought to be deeply entrenched in a Christian's personal character and a firmly held principle for making judgments in a complex world. The fact that the Bible uses the same words for righteousness and justice and holds the two together in various texts implies that individual believers are responsible for justice in all the spheres of life into which God places them.

Second, Christians should maintain some caution regarding the extent to which the state regulates and carries out distributive justice. If the state holds justice, freedom, and order together, it will invariably be limited in its efforts at achieving justice. A society focused exclusively on distributive justice will not be a free society; a society fixated on freedom will not be ordered or just. Christian ambivalence about the state can also be argued from biblical teaching in which the state is described as both servant and beast. In Romans 13, the state is a servant for good and is to be obeyed and not rendered inoperative by the Christian church (cf. 1 Peter 2:13–17). Revelation 13, however, portrays the state as a beast and an enemy of the church. In similar fashion, Jesus refers to Herod, a government official, in derogatory fashion as a fox (Luke 13:32), and in Acts, the early apostles engage in civil disobedience by not heeding the government's policy forbidding evangelism. They proclaim in the court, "We must obey God rather than any human authority" (5:29). Similar ambivalence about government is also found in the Old Testament. Queen

Esther comes to the halls of power in Persia for "such a time as this" (Esther 4:14), but at the same time there is grave concern about Israel having a king like the governments of surrounding nations (1 Samuel 8).

Thus, biblical and theological understandings of the state preclude us from giving a carte blanche to human governments, even if we see the state as ordained by God from creation and not merely a result of the fall.[38] Christians should be predisposed to question a state that becomes so expansive that it limits both individual initiative and the significant role that other mediating institutions (i.e., family, church, voluntary organizations) can play in society.

Third, there is biblical support for the role of government in distributive justice, amid caution about government and instruction concerning the role that individuals and mediating institutions should play. In a petition for the king of Israel, the psalmist prays, "Give the king your justice, O God, and your righteousness to a king's son. May he judge your people with righteousness, and your poor with justice. . . . May he defend the cause of the poor . . . give deliverance to the needy" (Ps. 72:1–2, 4). Similar passages calling for governmental action are Psalm 45:4, Jeremiah 21:12, and Amos 5:12, 15. One might object to this view, stating that Israel's government at the time was more akin to the church today than to secular, human governments. In one sense that is true, for Israel was called to be God's people, just as the church is today. Nonetheless, Israel, unlike the church, was also a nation and with its own sinful proclivities was given mandates for justice, not only of a retributive nature. Moreover, throughout the Old Testament, not only Hebrew kings were called to justice; even the pagan kings were expected to rule with justice (Prov. 8:15–18; 31:8–9; Dan. 4:27).

Thus, while individuals and churches must play a role in distributive justice, and while Christians must be cautious regarding an all-encompassing state, the state has a significant role to play in effecting justice in society. At the same time, we need to realize that in the personal-rights-oriented society of today, many negate personal responsibility when it comes to issues of justice. Perhaps one of the most neglected arenas is the role that family breakdown plays in poverty. The impact of divorce on families is staggering in terms of poverty, and most children born outside marriage live in households that are extremely poor.[39] Justice can never be too far removed from the choices people make and the lifestyles people live. To make justice the domain of government alone is to negate personal responsibility and to expect too much of this necessary but fallen institution.

Conclusion

236

Justice is always a concern in human societies. And justice is a major theme of the Bible. As this chapter has shown, however, justice is a complex issue.

The biblical understandings of justice relative to merit, equality, need, love, and freedom do not render a clear picture of exactly how justice should be accomplished in society. The government certainly has a role in distributive justice, but it should not negate or overwhelm the unique role that individuals and mediating institutions can and should play. Moreover, Christians have reason to be concerned about an expansive state that dominates and controls spheres of life that are not intended for the impersonal, bureaucratic rule of government agencies.

Clearly, then, Christians and all peoples will continue to debate what justice should look like in society and how it should be effected. What Christians cannot evade is the biblical mandate to "let justice roll down like waters, and righteousness like an ever-flowing stream" (Amos 5:24).

11

PLURALISM AND CHRISTIAN ETHICS

Dr. Jones was a deeply committed Christian, attempting to apply the faith to her work as a physician. As a member of her hospital's ethics committee, she one day found herself in a heated discussion on the topic of physician-assisted suicide. Several bills were pending in the state legislature, and while assisting in suicide was illegal, having been rejected (as a constitutional right) by the Supreme Court, the committee was engaged in a "what if" discussion. Dr. Jones's opposition to euthanasia in any form was clearly rooted in her personal faith and biblical principles, and on this day she became acutely aware of the gap between herself and her colleagues. As she listened to the discourse, she realized that her assumptions about life, death, suffering, God, and human nature were fundamentally at odds with the assumptions of many who sat around the table that day.

One social worker on the ethics committee, who declared himself a nominal Protestant, argued that he could in no way give ethical sanction to undue suffering, hence his support of euthanasia in some cases. A fellow physician and a native of India said that he did not believe assisted suicide was ultimately at odds with his Hindu beliefs. An administrator, who declared herself a secularist, argued that religious beliefs had to be kept out of the discussion because the hospital was a public hospital. Another physician, a practicing Roman Catholic, voiced opposition to physician-assisted suicide, not on the basis of biblical teaching but because it was contrary to the very nature of medicine, which aims to heal. Such an act was also contrary to the laws of nature, which are always on the side of preserving life rather than destroying it by human initiative.

During the ethics committee discussion, Dr. Jones did not encounter merely diverse views on moral quandaries. She came face to face with pluralism, one of the major realities of the modern world. As Max Stackhouse of Princeton Theological Seminary puts it, "Perhaps no societies in the history of humanity have been as pluralistic and dynamic as modern ones. Indeed, the terms pluralistic and dynamic have become not only descriptive of the way things are, but prescriptive of the way things ought to be."[1] The prescriptive dimensions of pluralism concern us in this chapter, as we explore the relationship between a particularistic Christian ethic and a pluralistic culture.

Pluralism in this sense does not primarily refer to differing races, ethnic groups, nationalities, and cultures living side by side within given communities or society as a whole. That, of course, is a given reality within modern pluralistic societies. Within this matrix something more profound occurs: There is the sociocultural reality of discrepant worldviews, ideologies, and moral frameworks existing side by side. A person living 150 years ago in rural America would rarely have encountered someone whose religious and ethical frameworks were widely divergent from his or her own. Today, that is not the case. We rub elbows with people not only who are different culturally and ethnically but more significantly who have varying perspectives regarding reality, moral frameworks, and the nature of a good society. In pluralistic societies, humans live, work, and attempt civic responsibilities with people whose fundamental outlooks on reality are at odds with their own.

The primary ethical issue with regard to pluralism is not its basic existence. One who takes that stance can easily fall prey to ethnocentrism or racism. At the same time, however, pluralism raises dilemmas for Christians who seek to be faithful to their calling as followers of Christ. In particular, the pluralistic context raises two apparent dilemmas: the truth dilemma and the social dilemma. This chapter seeks to demonstrate that these are not genuine dilemmas, as is often assumed by both secularists and Christians. One can be committed to truth while at the same time affirm a sociocultural pluralism, albeit one in which Christianity is a voice of influence.

The Dilemmas of Pluralism

The Truth Dilemma

In the midst of sociocultural pluralism, there is a tendency to relativize all claims to truth. The wide variation of worldviews and moral frameworks tends to create a climate in which people are suspicious of assertions about the truthfulness of one religion or ethical system. Claims to truth of an ultimate nature are called into question and deemed to be merely preferences, not unlike one's personal aesthetic tastes.

While pluralism is a characteristic of both modernity and postmodernity, the postmodern world has virtually rendered obsolete the very notion of truth, as discussed in part 2. The pursuit of truth and truth commitments are rapidly declining, especially insofar as they pertain to worldview and

239

moral frameworks. The commonly heard phrase on the street is, "One religion is as good as another," or "One set of values and virtues is as valid as another." In a more sophisticated vein, philosopher Richard Rorty argues that "there is nothing to be said about truth save that each of us will commend as true those beliefs which he or she finds good to believe."[2] Pluralism as a descriptive phenomenon quickly becomes a prescriptive enterprise in which particularistic claims to truth are put on the defensive and judged to be arrogant, brash, and narrow.

Thus, Jesus' statement, "I am the way, and the truth, and the life. No one comes to the Father except through me" (John 14:6), runs contrary to the prevailing mood of prescriptive pluralism. This cultural climate pushes human thinking toward an inclusive universalism in which all paths are equally valid in their rendition of God, salvation, and the moral life. Universals in theology and in ethics are commonly questioned. All of this raises a dilemma for Christians who believe not only that there is truth[3] but also that truth has been revealed in the incarnate and written Word of God.

The Social Dilemma

The social dilemma involves two issues: first, how a religiously informed ethic can relate to the pluralistic milieu, and second, how society itself can exist given the broad mix of worldviews and moral outlooks. From a Christian standpoint, the question concerns how to connect a highly particularistic framework to a pluralistic world that does not accept Christian assumptions and foundations. From society's standpoint, the issue is how to allow religion to play a role when there are so many competing voices.

The Christian moral framework arises from specific commitments and beliefs. It emerges from a commitment to Christ as Savior and Lord, an acceptance of the Bible as the authority for belief and action, and an understanding of a particular story that accounts for the world and its condition—namely, the story of creation, fall, redemption, and consummation. Given the particularistic nature of the Christian worldview, how can we connect Christian ethics to a context in which many or even a majority do not share the same commitments and worldview? And what should we expect of a pluralistic society bombarded by competing voices, some of which are religious in nature and some of which are secular?

This social dilemma of pluralism is compounded by the fact that many Christians believe the Christian framework is the best possible way for human beings to live and the most adequate foundation for both personal and social life. But if we accept the Christian framework by faith, how can we justify it to a pluralistic culture? How can we seek to translate the great insights, visions, and perspectives of our faith to a society that does not share the faith or the many assumptions in which our ethical commitments reside?

The social dilemma is further compounded by the fact that at least some sociological traditions (namely, those influenced by Emile Durkheim)[4] believe that religion forms the basis for culture and society. Like Durkheim, adherents of these traditions contend that religion is the glue that holds a culture together by providing a coherent sense of what is good or bad and which virtues are worthy of the greatest pursuits in life. Religion provides a larger guiding vision that transcends the personal whims and wishes of individuals. While secular social and political ideals may attempt to play that role, people will ultimately give themselves in a meaningful way only to moral and social ideals that have a transcendent focus. Religion, it is argued, is needed to compel moral and social compliance and to provide an overarching narrative for society and its institutions.

But if religion is the foundation of culture, which religion? And if Christianity, though ultimately true, is embraced by personal faith rather than by fiat from a social or governmental power, how can it possibly form the grounding for a pluralistic society? More modestly, how can it seek merely to be an influence? These questions are at the heart of the social dilemma.

Many people today assume that the two dilemmas (the truth dilemma and the social dilemma) are intricately related. They conclude that if a person is a particularist at the truth level, he or she will invariably reject pluralism and tolerance at the social level. A commitment to truth in faith and morals is seen to be at odds with a pluralistic society that truly guarantees the rights and freedoms of all peoples. To put it simply, they contend that truth commitments of an ultimate nature are contrary to the principles of democracy. As Ian Markham puts it, "The choice for the secularist is simple; either an intolerant society with religion in the saddle or a tolerant secular society with religion taking its place alongside other opinions and life styles."[5]

The perceived incompatibility of Christian truth and plurality is clearly articulated by Tom Driver of Union Theological Seminary. Driver has argued that we have no hope of getting rid of political Constantinianism (the notion of mandating a religious state and a particular religion to ensure moral standards) unless we give up theological Constantinianism, by which he means, "The old habit of supposing that in matters of salvation and liberation there is only one true way."[6] For Driver and a host of contemporaries, a commitment to the truth claims of the Christian faith is incompatible with a pluralistic society. For a democratic pluralism to exist, people must minimize their commitments to religious and moral truth, or at the very least, they must leave them at the door when entering civic and cultural engagement.

But is this the only recourse Christians have? How can we relate our particularistic, truth-claiming faith to the culture and the social institutions in which we live, work, and play? The rest of this chapter exlores several options for connecting our Christian faith with the pluralistic milieu. One approach makes it possible to be committed to truth while simultaneously affirming

241

societal plurality, albeit a plurality in which Christianity is a legitimate voice. The so-called dilemmas raised by pluralism are not genuine dilemmas that call for an abandonment of either the truth claims of Christianity or its influence in a pluralistic culture.

Christian Ethics Options in the Midst of Pluralism

The Privatization of Religion

In the opening narrative, Dr. Jones encountered the privatization option in the discussion about physician-assisted suicide. The hospital administrator who declared herself a secularist argued that religion was fine as long as it did not enter into discussions pertaining to societal and institutional life. Since assisted suicide was a social and political issue, arguments arising from religious sentiments were ruled out. Privatization has become perhaps the most pronounced perspective on religion in our time. Religion is a means of personal enhancement or individual meaning, but it can play no role in the public square amid the competing voices of a pluralistic and secularized society.

Curiously, privatization has both a Christian and a secular version. In the Christian version, faith is privatized primarily because the world is too evil for Christian engagement. These believers have an individualistic faith that affects personal meaning, habits, and behavior but does not translate into the social arena. Indeed, social involvement is not the role of the church and the Christian community. Modern fundamentalism and some parts of evangelicalism have reflected this individualism, resulting in a passionate personal ethic but a minimal social ethic.[7] For most contemporary evangelical Christians, however, privatized faith is no longer an option. They have shifted from a sectarian stance at the periphery of society to a more engaged stance in society.

The primary version of privatization today is a secular one. Proponents argue that the nature of a pluralistic society makes it impossible for religion to have a public role. While some advocates have an antipathy toward religion, much privatization is fueled by an overriding commitment to a secular society in which religion plays a role only in personal or at most interpersonal existence. Appeal to a religiously grounded moral position for public policy or institutional life is suspect. As Charles Krauthammer put it in a *Time* article:

> Every manner of political argument is ruled legitimate in our democratic discourse. But invoke the Bible as grounding for your politics, and the First Amendment police will charge you with breaching the sacred wall separating church and state. . . . Should someone stand up and oppose abortion for reasons of faith, he is accused of trying to impose his religious beliefs on others. Call on Timothy Leary or Chairman Mao, fine. Call on St. Paul, and all hell breaks loose.[8]

The privatization approach is clearly implied in the works of John Rawls when he argues that "no comprehensive doctrine is appropriate as a political conception for a constitutional regime." By comprehensive doctrine Rawls means religious, moral, as well as philosophical frameworks that provide an overarching perspective for the social order. Such "a reasonable comprehensive doctrine cannot secure the basis of social unity, nor can it provide the content of public reason on fundamental political questions."[9] Rawls envisions a good, just, and stable society that is built on popular consensus in which the principles are independent of religious and moral motivation or content. For Rawls, as discussed in the last chapter, justice is the first virtue of social institutions, but it must be established on procedural grounds, not epistemological grounds that appeal to a comprehensive moral view. Citizens "should be ready to explain the basis of their actions to another in terms each could reasonably expect that others might endorse as consistent with their freedom and equality."[10]

This privatization of religious belief is particularly evident in debates concerning abortion, euthanasia, homosexuality, family life, and sexual morality. One can maintain personal beliefs about these issues and apply strictures to oneself, but personal beliefs rooted in religion have no role in public discourse or in shaping institutional or public life. In the field of bioethics, this was clearly articulated for a number of years by Tristram Engelhardt, who said the discipline in its entirety must be secular in nature as it seeks a consensus across the broad spectrum of moral communities. As he put it, "A secular bioethics is unlikely to develop convincing arguments for forbidding many actions that our Western Christian societies have taken to be wrong, such as 'unnatural sexual activities,' suicide, or the active euthanasia of severely defective newborns."[11] Particular moral communities, noted Englehardt, can achieve "a contentful understanding of the good life," but such can never inform the public domain, for their moral frameworks "require accepting certain basic premises that cannot be secured by argument."[12] Only a secular bioethic can speak to the public square. Engelhardt, however, had a profound conversion to orthodox Christianity, and in a later work, *The Foundations of Christian Bioethics,* he offered a scathing critique of the hollowness of secular bioethics and much that passes for "Christian" bioethics. Engelhardt now believes that only a "bioethics grounded in the recognition or experience of a transcendent God and in one's obligations to that God offers the possibility of a deep anchor for a content-full morality."[13]

The result of this privatization approach, as Rabbi Arthur Hertzberg notes, is that the contemporary American experiment is asking "something previously unknown and almost unthinkable of the religions," namely, that "each sect is to remain the one true and revealed faith for itself and in private, but each must behave in the public arena as if its truth were as tentative as an aesthetic opinion."[14]

Underlying the privatization option is moral relativism. That is, many proponents believe not only that pluralism makes religiously grounded ethics impossible but also that all religious and moral frameworks themselves are relative. There is no final truth, and there are no ultimate moral guidelines or narratives that are right for all places and all times. All religious and ethical claims are relative to a particular setting and context; there are no universals other than tolerance.[15]

But privatization is not a viable option for Christians who seek to be faithful to their calling and consistent with their beliefs. Privatization forces them to bifurcate themselves, to be different people in different spheres. It forces them into an existence in which the lordship of Christ is muted and relegated to one small sphere of life. Most of their waking hours (filled with work, community, and civic responsibilities) are then subject to a situation in which their true selves must be negated and denied. Such an approach to life would appear to be not only unhealthy psychologically but also contrary to the very nature of faith, in which every dimension of reality is to be captive to Christ and lived for the glory of God.

Privatization is also contrary to the Christian mandate. Jesus called his followers to be salt and light within the world (Matt. 5:13–14) and to be leaven in the midst of an unleavened culture (Luke 13:21). Clearly, Jesus wanted the faith of his followers to make a difference in the world. His metaphors assumed a darkness and decadence in culture that needed the light and influence of a Christian community rooted in a transcendent worldview and ethic. If we as Christians mute our transcendent foundations in our roles in the world, we fail to give the world something it desperately needs. Moreover, Christian thought in such an approach loses its distinct voice and perspective. Its message and moral obligations are watered down to the common denominator of pluralism. As moral philosopher Jeffrey Stout notes, theology of this kind "has often assumed a voice not its own and found itself merely repeating the bromides of secular intellectuals in transparently figurative speech."[16] With such an agenda, both the church and the world lose.

The Theocratic or Constantinian Approach

A second approach in relating Christian ethics to pluralism seeks to mandate a religiously based ethic for the entire society. The argument is that since societies need a moral and religious base, and since biblical faith is universal and true, Christianity (or perhaps Judeo-Christianity) should be the foundation for cultural and public life. In the United States, this is often buttressed by a historical argument—namely, that the country was founded as a Christian nation or at least built on Judeo-Christian principles. Now in the midst of modern cultural decadence, we need to return to those historic roots to preserve our moral sanity and prevent our society from further deterioration. While the particulars may change from country to country, wherever the Constantinian or theocratic[17] model is heralded, proponents appeal to historical analysis—namely, religion's loss of a privileged position—and point to the moral and cultural deterioration that is sure to follow. Only when society is rooted in clear ideals with a religious base, and thus shares a common moral heritage, can it maintain its equilibrium and survive.

Cardinal Spellman in the mid-twentieth century is an example of the theocratic approach to pluralism. As a Roman Catholic, he worked from a natural law tradition, believing that the laws of nature are so evident that they must be the laws of the land. Spellman was particularly fond of arguing that error has no rights. That is, neither the government nor public institutions have a moral obligation to protect views and actions that are contrary to the self-evident truths of God. When the philosopher Bertrand Russell was hounded out of a job at City College of New York in 1940 because of his atheism and unconventional beliefs, Spellman applauded, for "falsehood has no more legitimate claim to be freely disseminated than have the germs of a disease a right to formal cultivation in the bloodstream of the individual."[18]

Another example of this approach is the Christendom Group found in England during the early to mid-twentieth century. These Christian thinkers and leaders (such as V. A. Demant and T. S. Eliot) were firmly established in the Anglo-Catholic tradition. They claimed that the modern post-Enlightenment secular culture was primarily responsible for the rise of twentieth-century totalitarianism as well as the many moral and cultural degradations of the epoch. Society needed to recover a theistic foundation, clearly evident through natural theology and natural law, which all humans could perceive. This was the framework that made the medieval period such a stable society, they argued, and it was an ideal toward which British society again needed to return. The liberalism of modern democracy, the self-centered greed of capitalism, and the wrongheaded reaction to social ills by socialism were the results of a culture that had lost its moorings.

T. S. Eliot, in *The Idea of a Christian Society*, envisioned a Christendom-oriented society "in which the natural end of man—virtue and well-being in community—is acknowledged for all, and the supernatural end—beatitude [happiness]—for those who have eyes to see it." Furthermore, said Eliot, "A Christian community is one in which there is a unified religious-social code of behavior."[19] Eliot called for a "plurality" in which even non-Christian political leaders and educators would seek to protect an essentially Christian ethos. The state was to ensure basic Christian virtues, and the establishment of religion (the Anglican Church in England) was essential toward this end. "For the Christendom Group the choice was simple: sinful secularism or Christianity. And in deciding between these options our culture must opt for the truth."[20]

In the throes of an American pluralistic culture that seems to have lost its way amid the cacophony of moral voices, many are now clamoring for a similar restoration. Two types of theocratic responses currently exist in the United States: hard theocracy and soft theocracy. Hard theocracy is particularly evident in the movement known as theonomy, or reconstructionism. Unlike the Christendom Group, which sought to build a society on natural law, the reconstructionists want to build a society directly on the law of God revealed in the Old Testament and reaffirmed in the New Testament. Rousas John Rushdoony, often called the father of the movement, believes that every state and social order is a "laworder," for laws always represent some form of enacted morality. Pluralism is therefore not a neutral order but itself a religious order, built on secular humanistic religion. For Rushdoony, the great problem of our time is that "the state as a religious establishment has progressively disestablished Christianity as its law foundation, and while professing neutrality, has in fact established humanism as the religion of the state."[21] Rushdoony and his cohorts believe that democracy as practiced is really a heresy because it is a carte blanche for unbridled pluralism that disregards the law of God.

Greg Bahnsen, another theonomist leader, argues that the Old Testament laws are binding in the New Testament unless they are clearly modified or rescinded by further revelation. These laws, including the civil ones, are a reflection of "God's immutable character and, as such, are absolute in the sense of being non-arbitrary, objective, universal, and established in advance of particular circumstance."[22] As a result, any Christian involvement in political life must recognize these laws as the standard for all social and political life. Civil magistrates in all times and places are obligated to conduct their affairs under the meticulous laws of God. For some theonomists, these laws even include the capital punishment laws of the Old Testament (including the stoning of adulterers), and some have even called for a modified restoration of slavery in the form of indentured servanthood to pay off debts and obligations. The movement as a whole is not overtly political in the sense of creating political parties, but adherents believe that by continually making people aware of the dangers of secular pluralism, the triumphant reign of God's law will become a reality. For Bahnsen, the dangers of pluralism are clear, for "by contending that civil polity should not be based upon or favor any one distinctive religion or philosophy of life . . . , pluralism ultimately takes its political stand with secularism."[23]

Soft theocrats call for a foundation that is rooted in the Judeo-Christian tradition but without some of the specific formulations found in reconstructionism. Recent examples of this perspective include the Christian Coalition and Pat Robertson, the now defunct Moral Majority of Jerry Falwell, and Focus on the Family and its founder, James Dobson.

Soft theocrats agree with the reconstructionists that pluralism as practiced today has been the downfall of the United States. It has established a religion of humanism that seeks to negate or minimize the moral and religious traditions that they believe have guided this nation for many years. But they would not attempt to build a society on the explicit laws of the Old and New Testaments. Nor would they seek to demolish all forms of pluralism. Rather, soft theocrats insist that the fundamental direction of public life must be guided by moral principles that emanate from the Bible but can be found in other religious traditions and in chastened human reason. Therefore, its leaders have been willing to work alongside Mormons, Jews, and other concerned American religious players in attempts to negate the negative impacts of secular, pluralistic morality. They do not want to establish Christianity as the official religion or establish a state church, but they do want to give judicial and legislative recognition to a moral heritage that flows from the Judeo-Christian framework and to seek to restore that heritage as the foundation of public life.

Certainly, these jeremiads are right to lament the passing of significant virtues, self-restraint, and moral commitments that long flourished in Western cultures. Modernity ushered in great technological advances and new options for human choice, but with these benefits came cultural disintegration, a loss of collective virtue, and moral practices that were unthinkable a generation or two ago. Even secular analysts have begun to lament a culture that has lost its way. Indeed, the great appeal of contemporary theocrats is their prophetic injunctions against the malaise of our time. But are these theocratic and Constantinian solutions viable, practically and theologically?

From a practical standpoint, we can easily see the problems raised by this approach. Constantinianism ultimately favors one religious tradition over others in public life, thereby not only raising constitutional issues but engendering hostility and conflict in the process. One only has to go back in history to recognize the problems that emerged from a Christendom type approach. It was fine for those who were in the majority, but it was clearly discriminatory toward those who were not, as evidenced in nineteenth-century American Protestant attitudes toward Roman Catholic immigrants. It is one thing to say that Christianity must have a legitimate voice at the table of public debate (something that has often been denied by secularists in recent decades and has fueled much of the theocratic reaction), but it is quite another to say that Christianity must have the privileged voice. The contention that America must be built on the principles of Judeo-Christianity clearly favors that tradition politically over others, thereby denying equal rights for all.

Moreover, we cannot forget the historic results of such favoritism, when varying religions and frameworks were competing for power. The Thirty Years' War (1618–1648) is a case in point. At the heart of the conflict was profound religious antagonism that emerged in the pluralistic context following the Protestant Reformation. Though other issues, such as dynastic rivalries, eventually became part of the war, the main issue was the inability to live with religious differences. The result was one of the most destructive wars in European history.

But Christians have an even more profound and theological reason for rejecting theocracy in any form. It runs contrary to the nature of Christianity, which is based on faith, not public or cultural inducements. The Christian ethic is primarily a covenantal ethic, arising out of a personal relationship with the Triune God of the Bible. The Ten Commandments, as argued throughout this work, are not in essence universal principles known by reason (though many can be deduced by human reason and experience) but responses to a God who has redeemed his people and now calls them to live in faithfulness to his own character and actions. The theocratic response rightly wants to see changes in the culture, but to make Christianity a privileged voice is to rely on political and legal inducements to engender a Christian type of morality. Such runs contrary to the very nature of Christian ethics.

Constantinianism, of the hard and soft varieties, places far too much hope in political elections, public policy positions, and judicial actions with the hope of ensuring godly morals in human lives and in culture. Frequently, this agenda has been far too self-serving, for as Carl Henry notes in critiquing the contemporary efforts:

> The Religious Right eagerly appealed to religious liberty and increasingly declared it to be basic to all other human freedoms. Yet it specially invoked religious liberty to protest encroachments on evangelical freedom, and to advance legitimate evangelical concerns. But a disciplined public philosophy would stress religious freedom for all persons of whatever faith, as at the same time the best guarantee of religious liberty for Christians.[24]

The Civil Religion Response

Proponents of civil religion agree with the theocrats that a religious basis for society is imperative. But in a pluralistic world, they contend, it is impossible for any of the traditional religions to play that role. Pluralism calls for a broad religion around which the entire society can unite. Civil religion, therefore, refers to a broad religion that transcends particular religions, yet one to which particular religions can adhere without a sense of contradiction, and provides coherence and foundation for a nation.

The notion of a civil religion is quite old. St. Augustine spoke of a civic religion that was present in the Greek and Roman Empires. He strongly castigated these religious expressions but noted that each city tended to have its own gods, around which the *civitas* gathered.[25] In the eighteenth century, Jean Jacques Rousseau, a French philosopher, spoke of a civil religion that was essential for French society. In the midst of the Enlightenment, Rousseau felt that the Roman Catholic Church could no longer be the glue that held the social order together. He saw a need for a broader religion, a civil religion, that would provide the nation with a sense of identity, responsibility, and moral values. Rousseau envisioned four elements in this civil religion: the existence of a benevolent sovereign, reward or punishment in future life, moral responsibility for the collective, and exclusion of religious intolerance. He contended that one could hold to a particular religion as long as those commitments did not conflict with the premises of civil religion, but the social contract could be maintained only by a broader civic religion.[26]

In the United States, the language of civil religion began to emerge in the 1950s. Will Herberg, in his significant work on American religious expressions, *Protestant, Catholic, Jew,* described the American way of life as constituting a kind of common folk or cultural religion. Herberg believed the American way of life embodied everything from democracy to Coca Cola, from free enterprise to a belief that God is particularly fond of America. He wrote, "This American culture-religion is the religious aspect of Americanism, conceived either as the common ground of the three 'faiths' or as a kind of super-religion embracing them."[27]

But the name most associated with civil religion is sociologist Robert Bellah. In a widely circulated article in 1967, Bellah stated that "there actually exists alongside of and rather clearly differentiated from the churches an elaborate and well-institutionalized civil religion in America."[28] Bellah was a student of Japanese religion and noted the parallels between Shintoism in that country and civil religion in the United States. The Japanese practice particular religions such as Buddhism, but the religious ceremonies for weddings, national holidays, and community events follow Shintoism. In similar fashion, in America religious rituals, beliefs, documents, and saints are utilized by the entire society but are clearly differentiated from particular religions and denominations. For example, at presidential inaugurations God-language and religious images are frequently invoked, but the language and imagery are always general in nature. God is not defined in a specific way, there is no reference to Jesus Christ or the Holy Spirit, and there is no appeal to specific doctrines. The religious motifs are generic enough that all Americans of whatever faith, or no faith, are able to be caught up in the religious fervor of the moment. The same is true at Memorial Day parades and Independence Day celebrations. While Bellah has analyzed American civil religion, it is much wider in its scope. Civil religion is "that religious dimension found . . . in the life of every people, through which it interprets its historical experience in the light of transcendent reality."[29]

For Bellah, this is not just sociological observation. He has sometimes been described as a prophet of civil religion, believing that in modern pluralistic societies, civil religion has the ability to challenge societies to greater moral heights, judge their shortcomings, and provide collective meaning. National times of trial may challenge the civil religion underpinnings, but according to Bellah, this quasi-religious phenomenon has the potential to sustain a society and provide a foundation in a pluralistic world.

Harold Berman, a prominent professor of law and jurisprudence, does not use the language of civil religion, but the idea is implicit in his writings. Berman contends that democracy and fundamental legal principles cannot survive without a religious or quasi-religious foundation. "People will not give their allegiance to a political and economic system, and even less to a philosophy, unless it represents for them a higher, sacred truth."[30] He believes that some elements of a common religion are necessary for a society to have direction and cohesion. "The world needs a radical vision of a common destiny, and common convictions for which people of different nations, races, and classes are willing to make sacrifices; and it needs common rituals and traditions that embody its vision and its convictions."[31] Though he does not spell it out explicitly, Berman seems to envision a common religious basis that, while not antithetical to particular religions, transcends specific religions in providing a foundation for law and society.

How should Christians evaluate the civil religion option as a response to pluralism? Certainly, one of its appeals is that it supports a religious basis for society and culture that is inclusive enough to embody all or most of the religious and worldview perspectives. It also takes seriously the Durkheimian notion that societies need a religious grounding to give them cohesion and a framework for moral and cultural life. At first glance, therefore, the civil religion approach appears to be an ideal solution to the social dilemma raised by pluralism.

However, it is not quite that simple. From a practical standpoint, the ideals of civil religion are not as coherent and cohesive as advocates would like to believe. Ten years after his groundbreaking article, Bellah himself acknowledged that the covenant of American civil religion is broken, for the previously agreed-upon ideals are now challenged and up for grabs.[32] Thus, while civil religion would appear to be a solution to the dilemma of pluralism, the very reality of pluralism itself undermines commonly held tenets of civil religion. The broad strokes of this religious expression, transcending the particularities of traditional religions, no longer find agreement and adherence in pluralistic societies.

Christians face some serious theological issues in regard to civil religion. One problem of civil religion is its propensity to legitimize a nation's endeavors rather than to play a prophetic role in calling society to moral accountability. Bellah was aware of this problem but felt that civil religion had great prophetic possibilities if allowed to act as a standard of collective judgment. In practice, however, civil religion tends to legitimize a nation's practices as it merges God and country. Civil religious expressions easily become ways of absolving oneself (individually and corporately) of baser impulses or naively protecting the self from life's most difficult challenges and realities. This misuse of religion is especially pronounced in civil religion because of the nature of this "faith" and because of its link to patriotic impulses. In civil religion, there is a strong temptation to identify the cause of God with the cause of the nation.

In American history, this was evident in the notion of manifest destiny. The nation believed it had special favor granted by God among the nations and a significant, divinely mandated role within the world. This easily led to unbridled nationalism, racism, and ethnocentrism. The following statement by Dale Evans Rogers demonstrates the way in which civil religion has historically tended to legitimize the ways of a nation:

> It was never in the destiny of 400,000 red men to have and hold dominion over a land promised to greatness and power in the world. Its vastness was too much for one race. Yet the Indian did represent a long step forward in the divine purpose; he was a vast improvement upon the beast. . . .
>
> But even their Great Spirit could not save them from the relentless attack of a new brand of man who came against them. . . . The white man brought weapons of iron and gunpowder, axes that leveled their forests, ploughs that cut deep into the earth—and Bibles. The scattered, wandering tribes fought desperately to stem the tide but they could not possibly win. They were forced out, in the words of Jesse Hays Baird "by cosmic forces beyond the control of any man or nation."[33]

Even if civil religion does not fall prey to such jingoistic impulses that overly legitimize a society's actions, it still faces another problem from a Christian perspective. It is the same issue noted by St. Augustine in his critique of civic religion in the Roman Empire: the problem of idolatry. To have any other gods before the Triune God of the universe is to break the first of the Ten Commandments: "You shall have no other Gods before me" (Exod. 20:3). This commandment does not forbid proper patriotic expressions or lauding a nation's history, legacy, and accomplishments. But when those expressions become religious in nature, when they are couched in the language of transcendence, they fall prey to idolatry. This is even more evident in the way in which civil religion waters down the notion of God. As Herberg noted:

> In this kind of religion there is no sense of transcendence, no sense of the nothingness of man and his works before a holy God; in this kind of religion the values of life, and life itself, are not submitted to Almighty God to judge, to shatter, and to reconstruct. . . . In this kind of religion it is not man who serves God, but God who is mobilized and made to serve man and his purposes—whether these purposes be economic prosperity, free enterprise, social reform, democracy, happiness, security, or "peace of mind." God is conceived as man's "omnipotent servant," faith as a sure-fire device to get what we want.[34]

Though written nearly a half century ago, Herberg's indictment is pertinent to today's religiosity, including the fragmented remnants of American civil religion.

Civil religion, with its broad religious expressions that transcend the particular religions, may at first glance seem a viable response to pluralism, but Christians must take the issues of legitimation and idolatry seriously. It is perhaps even fair to say that civil religion may at times be good for the nation, from the standpoint of societal coherence and unity, but it is bad for the church in that it runs contrary to cherished Christian principles and commitments.

Christian Influence within Pluralism

There is another and better way to respond to the dilemmas of pluralism: a Christian influence within pluralistic contexts. This approach contains a commitment to truth. By this I do not mean that our own personal understandings or expressions of faith and morals are ultimate and infallible. Rather, there is ultimate divine reality that can be experienced by God's grace, and that reality can be spoken of, lived out, and understood, albeit always in ways that are far less than the reality itself.

This approach to the dilemmas of pluralism, therefore, does not capitulate to pluralism at the truth level by appealing to tolerance as the only virtue. G. K. Chesterton was on to something when he observed that "tolerance is the virtue of the man without convictions,"[35] an apt description of our postmodern world. For Christians, the driving motivation for personal morality and the impulse for influencing society come from the truth framework. The claims of Christ and the Word are the basis for all of life, including our desire to be salt and light within secular, pluralistic societies.

But while being committed to and operating from a framework of truth, believers today need to accept and even defend pluralism within society. A commitment to truth and a commitment to a pluralistic society need not be in opposition to each other. In fact, many would claim that it is only within a framework committed to truth that tolerance and plurality can really be maintained.[36] When tolerance is an end in itself and the only virtue, there is no larger framework to undergird, critique, and guide. As Stan Gaede so aptly states, "It is our commitment to truth and justice that compels us to affirm such tolerance, not our commitment to the modern value of tolerance or the need to be inoffensive."[37]

The simultaneous commitment to truth and pluralism needs some qualifications. First, we should insist (on the basis of theology and societal need) that religion, including particularistic brands of Christianity, ought to be a voice within the public arena. This differs drastically from the secular privatization approach, which argues that religion must remain private and must have no role in the public square. But it also differs from the theocratic approach by insisting on the right of all religious traditions and worldviews to have a legitimate public voice. Adherents of Islam, Mormonism, or the religion of secular humanism have as much "political" right to speak their convictions within society and institutions as evangelical Christians. A legitimate political right is not, however, the same as truthfulness. We can defend the right of any group or movement to both exist and speak its mind within society without sanctioning its beliefs. Thus, a number of years ago I served as an expert witness in a court trial to defend the Father Divine movement concerning an issue of taxation. In no way do I sanction the beliefs and claims of this small, dwindling sect, which has what I would call some rather bizarre ideas. But as an evangelical Christian I was willing to help defend this movement's right to practice its bizarre ideas because I cherish human freedom and human rights, which stem from an understanding that all people are created in the image of God.

We as Christians have a theological obligation and a civil right to speak our ethical convictions within the pluralistic milieu. We are right to reject the privatization option and the social hegemony of secularism, which as Stephen Carter has argued treats religion as merely a hobby with no social relevance.[38] But as we speak our voice, we must simultaneously extend the same courtesy and rights to all groups. Such does not mean that all ideas are of equal ultimate value, nor even of civic value. But the right to the public arena and basic human rights must always be guaranteed. At times in this setting our ideas will have influence and even prevail as the norm; at other times they will lose.

That leads to a second qualification of this approach: Christians must learn the limits of political action within the pluralistic society. We must recognize that not all Christian behaviors and ideals will, can, or should be enforced by law or public policy. Because Christian morality is ultimately grounded in a Christian worldview and motivated by God's grace manifested in Christ, most Christian virtues and sentiments flow from within, from the heart of human beings. Clearly, it would be difficult to legislate commands such as avoiding covetousness, inward prejudice, or materialism. Even legislating all forms of sexual immorality would likely be self-defeating and create an oppressive, totalitarian society due to invasions of privacy. We must learn that a significant part of the way we evoke social and individual change lies outside the parameters of law and public policy. Within a pluralistic society there are ways beyond those of politics to be salt and light and engender justice and righteousness. Many Christians today are perhaps too eager to attempt public policy solutions to our most grievous sociocultural ills. In the midst of pluralism, we need to recall that Christian morality flows from the heart and is most effected by divine power from within. That dimension of our social responsibility cannot be negated by any secular, pluralistic agendas.

At the same time, however, Christians should seek to influence public policy on some issues. At times it is imperative to change laws, influence judicial procedures, and redirect institutional policies, which leads to a third qualification of Christian influence within a pluralistic society. Though the motivation and drive to evoke change in a secularized culture come from the particularities of the Christian faith, we will at times need to speak with a new voice.

Dr. Jones quickly learned in the discussions about physician-assisted suicide that appealing to the Bible carried little weight in the pluralistic setting. Clearly, her own convictions were rooted in the Bible and in theological understandings derived from the Bible, but in attempting to convince others of her moral convictions, she had other options available besides appeal to Scripture and theology. Christians can appeal to a remnant of God's design that is often still embedded in the hearts and minds of even fallen humanity. To be sure, this type of natural law approach has its own difficulties (see chapter 6), such as its lessened appeal in a secularized culture. But using rational arguments, examples from history, and the coherence of viewpoints are still possible ways of attempting to influence individuals and even public policy. Moreover, as Nicholas Wolterstorff has argued, in a pluralistic society, "we do not for the most part aim at achieving agreement concerning a political basis; rather we aim at agreement concerning the particular policy, law, or constitutional provision under consideration."[39]

In using this approach, Christians will need to learn to be bilingual, at times speaking the language of Zion, which undergirds the specifics of our ethics, and at times also speaking a broader language that is not dependent on the particularities of the biblical faith.[40] Such is not a compromise of one's faith but rather an attempt to make points of contact with a pluralistic society and push it at least somewhat closer to the designs of the Creator. Thus, Dr. Jones could ground her opposition to euthanasia in the specifics of her Protestant Christian faith but voice opposition with arguments similar to those used by her Roman Catholic colleague: It is contrary to the nature of medicine; it is contrary to our commitment to preserve human dignity; it could never be adequately controlled; it is ultimately rooted in an autonomy that works against the human good. These arguments are not the foundation of Dr. Jones's position (which is ultimately grounded in her worldview), but they might carry some weight amid the competing voices of a secular, pluralistic setting.

The Christian influence within pluralism does not seek a privileged place within public policy or the law. Christianity's privileged status is secured by God and will always be most explicitly manifested within the church and other Christian institutions. Still, Christians should strive to be an influence, yet without seeking to establish either a theocratic state or one girded in the idolatries of civil religion. Our ethic should be rooted in Christian commitments, but we should not seek to rule the world or its moral sentiments by mechanisms that will ultimately undermine or contradict those very commitments. And as Richard Mouw and Sander Griffioen have noted, "The conflict is real [between truth and societal realities]: truth and righteousness must someday vanquish all falsehood and oppression. The triumph, however, will belong to God. Our appropriate creaturely response to that victory will be one of humble gratitude and not smug vindication."[41]

Conclusion

In the midst of pluralistic societies, Christians sometimes feel like a beleaguered minority. We sense that our ethical virtues and commitments seem to make little difference. Indeed, our faith and ethic are at times opposed and even ridiculed. We likely feel much like the saints of Israel (Judea) after being taken captive to Babylon. There they asked the question, "How could we sing the LORD's song in a foreign land?" (Ps. 137:4). In many ways, the ethical task before us is similar to that of the early Christians living in the pluralistic Roman Empire. They were a small voice among many and like Israel attempting to sing the Lord's song in a foreign land. But by commitment to the truth of the gospel, deep convictions, and consistent living, and by commending to others the "good life" that flows from God, they turned the world upside down. The culture of pluralism we face in the postmodern world may be a challenge to Christian ethics, but it is also a great opportunity.

12

MODELS OF CHRISTIAN INFLUENCE

In his widely read *Rich Christians in an Age of Hunger,* Ronald Sider tells the following parable:

> A group of devout Christians once lived in a small village at the foot of a mountain. A winding slippery road with hairpin curves and steep precipices without guard rails wound its way up one side of the mountain and down the other. There were frequent fatal accidents. Deeply saddened by the injured people who were pulled from the wrecked cars, the Christians in the village's three churches decided to act. They pooled their resources and purchased an ambulance so that they could rush the injured to the hospital in the next town. Week after week church volunteers gave faithfully, even sacrificially, of their time to operate the ambulance twenty-four hours a day. They saved many lives, although some victims remained crippled for life.
>
> One day a visitor came to town. Puzzled, he asked why they did not close the road over the mountain and build a tunnel instead. Startled at first, the ambulance volunteers quickly pointed out that this approach, although technically quite possible, was not realistic or advisable. After all, the narrow mountain road had been there for a long time. Besides, the mayor would bitterly oppose the idea. (He owned a large restaurant and service station halfway up the mountain.)
>
> The visitor was shocked that the mayor's economic interests mattered more to these Christians than the many human casualties. Somewhat hesitantly, he suggested that perhaps the churches ought to speak to the mayor. After all, he was an elder in the oldest church in town. Perhaps they should even elect a different mayor if he proved stubborn and unconcerned. Now the Christians were shocked. With rising indignation and righteous conviction they informed the young radical that the church dare not become involved in politics. The church is called to preach the gospel and give its cup of cold water. Its mission is not to dabble in worldly things like changing social and political structures.[1]

This parable illustrates, among other things, that Christians can appeal to the same ethical principles, or the same biblical texts, and still end up with different strategies for applying their moral and ethical commitments to societal issues. Many Christians, for example, have developed an environmental ethic that seeks to preserve the ecological integrity of the earth. When it comes to translating their concerns into action within the world, however, varying models emerge: voluntary plans for stewardship of individuals, political strategies to elect "green" candidates, social pressure on corporations, or consciousness raising through the media. In similar fashion, ethical concerns over abortion have elicited a broad response concerning ways to protect life in the womb: civil disobedience at abortion clinics, the use of mass media advertising, legal procedures to change laws, and crisis pregnancy centers that provide counseling and support for women with unwanted pregnancies.

The various models employed to carry out ethical concerns are dependent on a number of factors. Certainly, context plays a role. Christians living in an oppressive regime in which the church has few freedoms will not have at their disposal the same models as do Christians living in a democracy with unbounded freedom. Indeed, the attempts at influence by oppressed Christians will be severely limited and will call for creative responses. The models used also depend on the Christ-culture perspectives espoused. Advocates of a Christ against culture approach will not use public policy or structural mechanisms for change. For example, in Sider's parable about the village, those of a Christ against culture stance are more likely to opt for ambulances, while those with a Christ the transformer approach are more likely to push for structural changes. The models employed also depend on the issue being addressed. Some issues by their very nature may call for more personal interventions and others for more structural approaches to evoking change.

Nine Models for Implementation

The models explored in this chapter fit on two continuums. The first ranges from remedial to preventative actions. A remedial model attempts to address an already existing evil, unethical practice, injustice, or social problem. In responding to hunger and poverty, economic relief would be a remedial approach addressing an existing situation. At the other end of the pole are preventative actions, which in regard to hunger and poverty would include economic development programs that seek not just a remedy for the moment but a prevention for the future.

The second continuum ranges from personal to structural actions. The personal models focus on individual needs and seek to bring about changes at the individual level. In regard to the issue of racism, for example, personal models would include strategies that seek to change attitudes or heal personal relations by working at racial reconciliation. Structural models would seek to change laws and institutional practices within society.

It is evident that correlations sometimes exist between the remedial and the personal or between the preventative and the structural.

Christian Relief

Christian relief focuses on bringing social and physical relief when the need arises. It may take the form of personal responses to neighbors and acquaintances or specific programs operated by churches and Christian agencies. The church has historically often employed this model through shelters for the homeless, food pantries for the poor, funds for the unemployed, medical help in times of crisis, refugee resettlement in times of oppression, or hunger relief in times of famine. The Christian relief model is a straightforward and simple response to various needs as they emerge and involves practicing Christian virtues in relation to immediate and concrete situations.

The strengths of this model are its highly personal nature and its attention to specific and immediate needs. It is clearly Christian love in action. But this is also its major weakness: love devoid of justice. While these actions are needed, they usually do not solve a problem long-term or touch the institutional dimension of issues. The old Chinese proverb is certainly appropriate: "Give a man a fish and he eats today; teach a man to fish and he eats for a lifetime."

Christian Alternative Institutions

In the model that uses Christian alternative institutions, ethical commitments are implemented through the development of institutions created to address a particular need or issue. While these alternative institutions often have a personal dimension to them, they are also structural and preventative in nature, in that they provide ongoing mechanisms for dealing with situations that evoke ethical concern.

Historically, one of the classic examples of this model is the development of hospitals and medical clinics by missionaries in the developing world, usually where health care was lacking, inadequate, or not affordable. Even in the European world, most of the early hospitals were established by the church or religious orders. "Until the late Middle Ages, religious personnel remained in leadership positions [in hospitals or healing facilities]. . . . Spiritual care remained in the hands of priests, while physical nurturing became mostly the responsibility of religious and lay women."[2] In the United States as late as 1904, the hospital census reported that there were 831 nonsectarian benevolent hospitals, 442 "ecclesiastical" hospitals, and 220 public hospitals under federal, state, or local government control.[3] Today, some Christian or church-related hospitals clearly function as an alternative form of health care in which their mission, values, and practices stand in contrast to the prevailing norms of societal medical practices.

Another example of this model involves alternative educational institutions. The Christian church has long been involved in the development of educational programs, but recently there have been some efforts, especially in inner-city settings, to provide quality private education where public institutions are perceived to have failed. Of course, Christian schools have been established for a host of other reasons, some honorable and some less than honorable (i.e., escape from the realities of this world). But this model refers to those established to provide options where good choices have not existed or to provide alternative forms of character development in light of the perceived failures of public schools.[4] Moreover, some have contended that alternative institutions provide competition for public schools and thus help to improve the larger social system of education and ultimately the culture.[5]

There are a host of other alternative institutions. Legal clinics developed by churches and Christian organizations provide legal aid at moderate costs. Drug and alcohol rehabilitation centers, including many "old-time" rescue missions, provide institutional mechanisms for dealing with chemical dependency. Job training programs provide people with necessary know-how or start-up capital for small business development. Housing programs, such as the highly successful Habitat for Humanity, and programs that offer housing loans help people enter the housing market and create stable environments for families. Recently, these types of church-based social agencies have flourished with the adoption of the private-public ventures initiative supported by the United States federal government.

In issues of life and death, two developments stand out: crisis pregnancy centers and the hospice movement. The crisis pregnancy center movement began in part because of a realization that public policy alone cannot deal with the abortion crisis in the United States. Centers have sprung up in hundreds of communities to provide not only medical information but also legal, economic, and personal support for women who decide not to abort. These centers have flourished in part because of a realization that abortions are often chosen not based on ideological commitments but because women have the perception that there are no other alternatives for dealing with the personal crisis.[6]

The modern hospice movement began in 1967 through the initiative of physician and social worker Cicily Saunders in London. Hospices use trained health professionals and volunteers to offer relief of pain and emotional support for terminally ill patients and their families. While the hospice movement did not begin as an ethical response to physician-assisted suicide or euthanasia, many today see it as a significant vehicle for addressing needs that often propel people to support euthanasia.

All of these endeavors, which involve the creation of alternative institutions to carry out ethical commitments, often embody both structural and personal dimensions and have the capacity to be both preventative as well as remedial.

Evangelism

Some may think it odd that evangelism is a model for implementing Christian ethics and change in the world. After all, many forms of evangelism and portrayals of salvation have tended to be "pie in the sky" versions with seemingly little relevance to the moral and social complexities of the modern world. But as noted in chapter 3, salvation is central to the biblical drama, which is a significant foundation for ethical engagement in the world. Thus, many Christians have understood evangelism, as the proclamation of the gospel and the invitation to respond personally to it, as a method of changing the world and addressing ethical issues.

In this model, evangelism is done with the intent of bringing people into relationship with God through faith in Christ, with the subsequent result that they will become more loving, just, caring, and honest people. At first glance, this appears to be only a personal model with little relevance for the structural dimensions of society. But, says Richard Mouw, "It would be wrong to understand the individual who is being evangelized as completely isolated from social, political and economic contexts."[7] Personal conversion in this understanding is intimately related to racism, sexism, economic exploitation, business integrity, and the denigration of human dignity.

Christians have understood the relationship between evangelism and ethical or social concern in various ways.[8] Some have understood evangelism as social concern, so that it is the Christian's only mechanism for change. Others have seen social concern as the prelude to evangelism, as a means of getting people to listen to the gospel. Some have viewed social concern itself as evangelism, so that the actions of justice are themselves the gospel. Still others have seen evangelism and social concern as distinct yet partners in the mission of the church.

The Lausanne Conference of 1974, which drew together evangelical Christians from around the world, began to hammer out the relationship between evangelism and social concern. In a follow-up consultation nearly a decade later, leaders argued for three equally valid relationships, and for many evangelical Christians, the resulting statement now captures their understanding. First, "Social activity is a consequence of evangelism. That is, evangelism is the means by which God brings people to new birth, and their new life manifests itself in the service of others."[9] Second, social action can be a bridge to evangelism. That is, "It can break down prejudice and suspicion, open closed doors and gain a hearing for the Gospel. Jesus himself sometimes performed works of mercy before proclaiming the Good News of the Kingdom."[10] Third, social concern is a partner with evangelism in the church's mission. "They are like the two blades of a pair of scissors or the two wings of a bird. This partnership is clearly seen in the public ministry of Jesus, who not only preached the Gospel but fed the hungry and healed the sick. In his ministry, *kerygma* (proclamation) and *diakonia* (service) went hand in hand."[11]

Evangelism as a model of Christian influence emphasizes that the gospel itself is the most compelling means of changing the hearts of human beings and subsequently their involvements within the institutions of society. Repentance, the prelude to personally appropriating the gospel, will embody not only personal sins but also social sins and personal entanglements with structural evil.[12] William Booth, the founder of the Salvation Army in the nineteenth century and the promoter of numerous social ministries, addressing the issues of his day stated, "And insoluble it [social evil] is, I am absolutely convinced, unless it is possible to bring new moral life into the soul of these people. This should be the first object of every social reformer, whose work will only last if it is built on the solid foundation of a new birth, to cry 'You must be born again.'"[13]

Prophetic Pronouncements

The prophetic pronouncement model for implementing change involves the voice of the church or Christian groups speaking to the world to challenge existing values, policies, structural arrangements, and cultural practices and to commend new forms in their place. This model sees itself in the tradition of the Old Testament prophets who challenged kings, religious leaders, and society as a whole with reference to their moral failures and evil. In the words of Frederick Buechner, "Nobody before or since has ever used words to express more powerfully than they our injustice and unrighteousness, our hardness of heart, our pride, our complacency, our hypocrisy, our idolatry."[14] Jesus continued that prophetic tradition as he embodied within himself the fullness of the Old Testament offices of prophet, priest, and king.

The prophetic voice to evoke change can come from various sources. Clearly, preachers in their proclamation of the Word call into question existing personal, cultural, and societal practices and beckon righteousness and justice in their place. David Gushee writes, "The gospel—rightly understood—addresses human communities and human societies with its word of redemption. Thus, it is fair to assert that proclaimers of the gospel should regularly address all dimensions of human personhood and human community."[15] The prophetic model is also found in congregational pronouncements or local congregations who come together to raise awareness regarding a particular issue. For example, when I was a pastor a number of years ago, the local ministerial group along with the individual congregations issued a statement that was printed in the local newspaper protesting the possibility of legalizing gambling in the state.

The most widely known form of prophetic pronouncement is at the denominational level. Denominations in their conventions or assemblies often issue statements on a range of issues such as racism, abortion, war, euthanasia, economic justice, the environment, or the family. These statements are usually intended as mechanisms for educating the constituency and influencing the larger society. Among the most in-depth prophetic pronouncements have been letters from the American Catholic Bishops on economics and war. Drawing on expert analysis, the bishops issued lengthy statements intended to guide the faithful in their own moral understandings and to evoke change within the culture at large.[16]

A recent example of prophetic pronouncement came from the Jubilee 2000 movement, an international movement calling for the cancellation of all debts for the world's poorest countries. The Pontifical Council for Justice and Peace in Rome (composed of representatives from bishops' conferences from twenty of the most impoverished countries) ended their consultation with a prophetic statement supporting Jubilee 2000:

> We call on the leaders of the world's largest economies meeting at the G8 Summit in Genoa in July 2001 to reduce further the debts of poor countries . . . and to address the problems of highly indebted middle income countries. Deeper cancellation is required. This should result in a 100 percent cancellation of unpayable debts including those owed to the international financial institutions.[17]

Prophetic pronouncements by religious bodies can vary significantly in their level of specificity. One level involves general principles. Biblical or theological principles are enunciated relative to a given issue, but the application remains broad in nature. Thus, rather than specifically calling for nations and international agencies to cancel the debts of poor nations, this approach would enunciate principles of economic justice, mercy, and jubilee without specifying the exact direction the principles should take. A second level of specificity involves middle axioms. The term was first employed by J. H. Oldham in 1937 when he proposed:

> Between purely general statements of the ethical demands of the gospel and the decisions that have to be made in concrete situations, there is need for what may be described as middle axioms. . . . They are attempts to define the directions in which, in a particular state of society, Christian faith must express itself. They are not binding for all time, but are provisional definitions of the type of behavior required of Christians at a given period and in given circumstances.[18]

Middle axioms clearly go a step beyond the norms themselves to indicate directions the norms might take in society, but they stop short of specific policy positions or strategies.

A third level of specificity involves technical solutions. In this approach, the church or religious body offers specific directions for public policy or specific strategies for dealing with a given issue. The churches' commendation of Jubilee

2000 is clearly of this nature, for it specifies a particular strategy for nations and international agencies in dealing with world economic poverty. Technical solutions have often generated the greatest amount of controversy among Christians, for they do not always reflect the sentiments of the populace. Moreover, many have contended that the church lacks the expertise to offer technical solutions and thus should go no further than to offer middle axioms. The late Archbishop of Canterbury William Temple argued that "the Church must announce Christian principles and point out where the existing social order at any time is in conflict with them," but it must stop short of advocating particular policies that are dependent on technical knowledge. If a bridge is to be built, said Temple, "The Church may remind the engineer that it is his obligation to provide a really safe bridge; but it is not entitled to tell him whether, in fact, his design meets this requirement." In the same manner, "The Church may tell the politician what ends the social order should promote; but it must leave to the politician the devising of the precise means to those ends."[19] Temple, along with other critics, believed that many Christian social pronouncements were misguided and self-defeating because they did not sufficiently come to terms with the complex technicalities of social problems.[20]

Lobbying

Lobbying has long been a vehicle for social change, especially in the United States, as various interest groups seek to influence the commitments and contours of public policy. There are really two types of lobbying: inside lobbying, which involves contact with public officials to influence voting or basic commitments on given issues, and outside lobbying, "defined as attempts by interest group leaders to mobilize citizens outside the policymaking community to contact or pressure public officials inside the policymaking community." Indeed, behind "most telephone calls, letters, faxes, and E-mails to members of Congress, behind marches down the Mall in Washington, D.C., and behind the bus caravans to the Capitol, there are coordinating leaders, usually interest group leaders, mobilizing a select group of citizens to unite behind a common message."[21] The number of interest groups involved in the various forms of lobbying has proliferated, as "the number of national associations has grown from approximately five thousand in 1955 to over twenty-three thousand at the end of the twentieth century."[22]

Among these special interest lobbying groups are religious bodies and denominations. This is not a new concept among Christian groups seeking to evoke public policy changes. In nineteenth-century America, for example, the Anti-Saloon League and the National Woman's Christian Temperance Union both had offices in Washington, D.C., to facilitate access to policy makers.[23] By the 1960s many religious bodies had Washington offices, including various Baptist denominations, Roman Catholics, Methodists, Seventh-Day

263

Adventists, Lutherans, the African Methodist Episcopal Zion Church, Disciples of Christ, Presbyterians, Jewish groups, Unitarian-Universalists, the United Church of Christ, the Mennonite Central Committee, the National Council of Churches, and the National Association of Evangelicals.[24] The religious lobby groups have two primary missions: educating their constituencies regarding issues and influencing legislators and public policy.

Religious lobbying is clearly a structural approach to social and ethical issues in that it seeks changes in laws and public policy through the legislative and judicial processes. It has frequently come under fire, however, for not adequately representing the grass roots of denominations. This has been an issue particularly for the mainline Protestant denominations and has sometimes led to what Jeffrey Hadden once called the "gathering storm in the churches."[25]

Political Parties/Political Groups

The relationship between church and state has been a source of major debate throughout Christian history. Some have eschewed the state and political processes, while others have embraced them in varying forms and with differing motivations. Since the fourth century, when Constantine gave legal sanction to the church, some Christians have seen the political process as a means of carrying out churchly concerns, including ethical commitments. Since the state is ordained by God, it is argued, the political process can be a legitimate means for carrying out God's purposes on earth, especially in relationship to human behavior. Those who view the state in this fashion have by no means been monolithic in their vision for state-aided ethics, but overall they have believed that the state rightly ordered can be a force for freedom, justice, peace, and even personal righteousness.

From Constantine until modern times, many have assumed that the state could be a significant vehicle for shaping moral sensibilities. Throughout the Middle Ages, the church and state were so closely intertwined that it was simply assumed that the state would help reinforce a moral order. As noted in chapter 9, the model continued with the Protestant Reformation, particularly in Calvin's Geneva. The church in Geneva made strong pronouncements and exerted considerable force on matters such as health care, education, welfare, and political life in the canton. Christians assumed that if the state followed these mandates, the culture as a whole would be closer to God's moral designs. Only smaller sect groups, such as the Anabaptists, questioned the arrangement.

In the modern world, the church and state began to become unhinged, beginning with the American experiment and continuing with the process of secularization, which became pervasive throughout much of modernity (see chapter 4). Whether the intention was to preserve religious integrity or to engender state autonomy, the result was the same. Nonetheless, old patterns die hard, and many Christians and churches continued to hang on to the notion that the political process, including the state, could be a vehicle for carrying out ethical commitments.

In nineteenth-century Europe, Christian Democratic Parties emerged in a number of countries as vehicles for churchly influence on society. In Italy, for example, the *Democrazia Cristiana,* which dominated government from 1945 to 1994, when it divided into two parties, set limits that reflected clerical influence on matters such as divorce and contraception.

Outside Europe the political model has been less oriented toward political parties and more toward political influence and coalitions. For example, in 1972, during the Vietnam War, a coalition of mainline denominational members formed a significant backing for George McGovern in his presidential bid against Richard Nixon. A major dimension of the coalition was religious opposition to the war and support for a politically liberal social agenda. As noted earlier, the Moral Majority and the Christian Coalition emerged in the past several decades in an attempt not only to support given public policy positions but also to exert influence in particular political races. Perhaps the most noted vehicle of these coalitions has been the voter's score card, which grades Congress members and senators relative to various social issues.

In Great Britain in the 1990s, a rather interesting cross-party, nondenominational political movement emerged called the Movement for Christian Democracy. With membership from all three political parties in its rank—Labor, Conservative, and Liberal Democratic—the MCD focuses on principles that can draw disparate groups together, even if they differ on specific policy formulations. Members are willing to relativize policies but not principles, which they derive from their Christian faith. The MCD believes that "Christianity gives a vision for the whole of politics—through principles, policies, peacemaking, economic policy, and ethics."[26] The primary principles of the movement, set forth in the Westminster Declaration, are social justice, reconciliation, active compassion, wise stewardship, empowerment, and respect for life. The MCD stands out as a fascinating attempt at carrying out ethical commitments through politics, though without partisan political commitments. Whether it is able to succeed in this endeavor remains to be seen.[27]

The political party/political group model is a clear example of a structural approach that can be both remedial and preventative. It also remains one of the most controversial models both within the church and within secular society. Secularists believe it encroaches on political freedom and separation of church and state, while many Christians contend that it tends to destroy the unique contributions of the Christian message. Stephen Carter seems to offer sage advice on this matter when he argues, "There is nothing wrong, and much right, with the robust participation of the nation's many religious voices in debates of matters of public moment." At the same time, says Carter, "Religions . . . will almost always lose their best, most spiritual selves when they choose to be involved in the partisan, electoral side of American politics."[28]

Nonviolent Resistance

Another model that emerged in the middle of the twentieth century was nonviolent resistance, the use of pressure tactics to change society by peaceful means. Outside of Christianity, the best-known example is Mahatma Gandhi, whose calls for boycotts and peaceful resistance led to India's independence from British rule. This model has used marches, sit-down strikes, boycotts of certain products, the blocking of entrances to certain institutions, and a refusal to pay taxes as means of evoking change toward a desired moral ideal. At times the resistance has also employed civil disobedience, though clearly not all forms of nonviolent resistance are against the law. Stephen Mott refers to this approach as strategic noncooperation, which "seeks justice through selective, socially potent forms of nonconformity. Although it is brought to bear when the fallen nature of society denies normal channels of political decision-making to those who work for justice, it is carried out under the self-discipline of respect for the order of society."[29]

Without doubt the best-known example of this model from within a Christian ethics tradition is Martin Luther King Jr. As King dealt with the racial injustices and barriers of American society, he came to believe that nonviolent strategies of coercion could persuade humans to do what neither the law nor moral persuasion could do. Faced with the enormous challenges to civil rights and economic justice for his people, Dr. King during his college and seminary days began to reflect on how transformation could occur. Through a sermon by Mordecai Johnson, who spoke of the nonviolent teachings and methods of Gandhi, King began his journey toward this approach. He came to believe that the "love ethic of Jesus" could actually be a method of resistance to evoke social change. For the civil rights leader, however, "Nonviolence . . . was more than a strategy or a method for addressing racial issues; it was a personal and social ethic."[30]

King's ethic and model for implementing his ethic was an amalgamation of black religion, evangelical Christianity, the theology/philosophy of personalism, and the teaching of Gandhi. He contended that nonviolence

can touch men where the law cannot reach them. When the law regulates behavior it plays an indirect part in molding public sentiment. The enforcement of the law is itself a form of peaceful persuasion. But the law needs help. The courts can order desegregation of the public schools. But what can be done to mitigate the fears, to disperse the hatred, violence and irrationality around school integration, to take the initiative out of the hands of the racial demagogues, to release respect for the law? . . .

Here nonviolence comes in as the ultimate form of persuasion. It is the method which seeks to implement the just law by appealing to the conscience of the great decent majority who through blindness, fear, pride, and irrationality have allowed their consciences to sleep.[31]

King is by no means alone in employing this model, and the ethical issues to which it has been applied have been many and varied. Dorothy Day's Catholic workers movement used it to evoke change regarding war and poverty, and the Southern Baptist denomination used it when it boycotted Disney over immoral content. It has been the method of abortion protestors blocking abortion clinics, of Cesar Chavez boycotting grapes to empower farm workers, and of Morality in the Media boycotting certain products that sponsored morally questionable television shows. It is an approach that is particularly remedial in nature and focused primarily on structural change, though King argued its significance for personal change as well. The primary controversy surrounding this model is whether it indeed persuades the thinking of the masses or conversely builds resistance to a given cause.[32]

Christian Embodiment

Another model for implementing ethical commitments involves the church and Christian institutions embodying Christian moral ideals within their own structures and patterns of interaction. The focus here is on the church as a counter community within society through its character, actions, and vision. Adherents believe that "for the church to have a corrective impact on culture it must maintain a separate and distinct identity from the surrounding society and any new society that it may help to create."[33] Thus, the church—as individual congregations, denominations, and para-church organizations seeks to embody racial reconciliation, economic justice, business integrity, respect for human life, and authentic personal and corporate character. Most Christians agree that this is the starting point for any Christian ethic, but adherents emphasize that embodiment is the primary model through which God wants to work in culture. Because the norms of secular society and its institutions are at odds with the commitments of Christian ethics, the church's primary calling is to be a counter community through its very being and actions.

One of the main adherents of this model was the late John Howard Yoder. As shown in chapter 6, Yoder, in contrast to mainstream Christian ethicists, argued that the ethics and politics of Jesus are relevant for social life, but the ethics of Jesus will not find its primary expression within fallen society. It is primarily in the church where we can expect to find Jesus' politics manifest. Yoder believed that we cannot "deny the powerful . . . impact on society of the creation of an alternative social group, and . . . overrate both the power and the manageability of those particular social structures identified as 'political.'"[34] The fundamental responsibility of the church is not to manage society or be effective therein but faithfully to embody the way of Christ. Indeed, said Yoder, "The very existence of the church is her primary task. It is in itself a proclamation of the Lordship of Christ to the powers from whose dominion the church has begun to be liberated."[35]

The other primary advocate of this model is Stanley Hauerwas. As shown in chapter 2, Hauerwas advocates an ethic of character shaped by the Christian community. The church is a counter community by embodying within itself the character of Christ. Thus, Hauerwas contends that the church does not *have* a social ethic but *is* a social ethic. "The church is not directly God's agent for the realization of the kingdom, but rather it is God's harbinger of the kingdom by being the fellowship in which the reality of the kingdom is manifest."[36] Hauerwas and Yoder have had a powerful impact on many Christian groups by emphasizing this unique role of the church within culture. As the charismatic leader Larry Christenson put it, "The church's value to the world is not so much in what she does for the world as in what she is in the world." He believes that over the long haul the greatest service of the church to the world "is to be the household of faith which, by its example, demonstrates a better way of life."[37]

The Christian embodiment model is both structural and personal in nature, though its structural dimension is focused primarily on Christian structures, not societal structures. Because of its antipathy toward controlling society and its problems, the model tends to lie somewhat outside the polar types of preventative and remedial action, though advocates emphasize its unique role in society simply by being there. Most Christians would agree that this is a necessary model, but the debate comes as to whether it should be the exclusive or even primary model. Many critics believe that this model by itself cannot give sufficient attention to social justice and cultural righteousness. As one critic put it, "The demonstration of Christian community is a facet of social change, but as the single expression of social justice it is inadequate."[38]

Individual Impact

The final model for implementing Christian ethics in society focuses on the role of individual Christians in their jobs, communities, and civic responsibilities. Individual impact is not necessarily individualistic but rather emphasizes that Christians can make a difference in society and its institutions through their character, actions, articulation of Christian moral ideals, and personal persuasion in the natural spheres of responsibility into which God places them. This model draws on the notion of vocation as articulated by the Protestant Reformers Martin Luther and John Calvin that emphasized that every believer has a calling from God in life. Vocation, as they understood it, is not a profession but rather the primary place to which God calls us and works through us in the world.

Carl Henry, the first editor of *Christianity Today*, has been quite skeptical of a politicized approach to social ethics in which the church as a body espouses specific public policy positions. But he believes that individual Christians in their specific callings and areas of expertise can be used to influence the direction of Christian ideals. Henry writes:

> The development of Christian character comes by applying all time and all talent with a sense of responsibility to God and neighbor. Responsibility for God-given time includes the Christian's work and leisure and sleep, his use of weekdays and the Lord's day; responsibility for God-given talent includes his trusteeship of special skills and his stewardship of possessions.... One's work [is] a divine vocational penetration of the social order.... Wherever his life touches human need, the believer is to respond.[39]

For Henry, this involves one's job, civic responsibilities, and other opportunities into which God guides.

This model in its current form does not minimize the complexity of modern social life found in government, business, and other institutions, but it emphasizes that Christians should not allow the complexity to overshadow the roles they can play in their spheres of influence. Moreover, adherents emphasize that Christians need to have a grand vision of how God can use them to move society toward Christian ideals in these spheres. As N. T. (Tom) Wright, the Canon of Westminster Cathedral in London, frames it:

> We need Christian people to work as healers: as healing judges and prison staff, as healing teachers and administrators, as healing shopkeepers and bankers, as healing musicians and artists, as healing writers and scientists, as healing diplomats and politicians. We need people who will hold on to Christ firmly with one hand and reach out with the other, with wit and skill and cheerfulness, with compassion and sorrow and tenderness, to the places where our world is in pain. We need people who will use all their God-given skills ... to analyze where things have gone wrong, to come to the place of pain, and to hold over the wound the only medicine which will really heal, which is the love of Christ made incarnate once more, the strange love of God turned into your flesh and mine, your smile and mine, your tears and mine, ... and your joy and mine.[40]

The individual impact model is clearly personal in nature and seeks to be institutional within a personal context. Some are skeptical as to how significant the institutional dimension can be because of its personal nature. This model can be both preventative and remedial. Like many of the other models, it is not mutually exclusive and certainly must always be the intention and vision of all Christians.

Wisdom in Seeking a Model

As noted earlier, the choice of models for implementing Christian ethical commitments likely depends on context, the nature of the issue, and one's Christ-culture stance. Beyond these factors, there is the need for wisdom and discernment. Christians always need to give careful attention to how their efforts are communicating the moral vision and analyze any secondary, unintended consequences of the methods employed.

Take the example of abortion. The use of violence by a minority of pro-life advocates clearly undermines the pro-life stance. Morever, such an approach has actually driven people away from the defense of life in the womb because of its hypocrisy and radical actions. But even the more mainstream strategies of the pro-life movement have not had their desired effects. Paul Swope, the head of a pro-life organization, says, "For twenty-five years the pro-life movement has stood up to defend perhaps the most crucial principle in any civilized society, namely the sanctity and value of every human life. However, neither the profundity and scale of the cause, nor the integrity of those who work to support it, necessarily translates into effective action."[41] Why the failure?

Pointing to research on the subject, Swope argues that the movement has failed because it has lacked discernment in making its moral appeal. The pro-life movement has assumed that if women truly knew the moral status and nature of the fetus, they would never choose to abort. But recent research has shown that most women choosing an abortion recognize that they are taking a human life. They generally are weighing three "evils"—motherhood, adoption, and abortion—and "unplanned motherhood . . . represents a threat so great to modern women that it is perceived as equivalent to a 'death of self.'"[42] The research indicates that when women evaluate the abortion decision, they do not formulate the issue as a pro-lifer might. Rather, "their perception of the choice is either 'my life is over' or 'the life of this new child is over.' . . . Abortion is considered the least of three evils because it is perceived as offering the greatest hope for a woman to preserve her own sense of self, her own life."[43] Thus, says Swope, the moral appeal focused exclusively on the life of the unborn does not connect with a woman who feels she has no way out of her dilemma, and it tends to appear unsympathetic.

What is needed? Swope believes the movement cannot abandon its ethical backbone, the dignity and rights of the human life in the womb, but in making its public appeal it must make a connection with a woman's personal sense of well-being. "The pro-life movement must address her side of the equation, and do so in a compassionate manner that affirms her own inner convictions."[44] All of this points to the fact that there are differences among the foundations of our moral commitments, the way we make our moral decisions, the actual moral positions themselves, and the models we employ to implement them in a complex, secular society.

270

Another example of the failure of a given model resulting from a lack of discernment is the slave redemption program focused on Sudan. In 1998, a grade-school class in Colorado captured the attention of people all over North America with their efforts to raise money to buy back slaves in Sudan. For a number of years, the Christian Solidarity International (CSI) organization, based in Switzerland, had been redeeming slaves by purchasing their freedom. CSI's attempt to buy slaves for fifty to one hundred dollars seemed like a great humanitarian effort to end a scourge that had long troubled the Continent. When the fifth graders in Colorado started a campaign to stop slavery by raising money to send through CSI, the media quickly gave the movement impetus, and it caught the imagination of many people. Here was a way to show moral compassion and justice by bringing an end to an old yet modern-day evil. By the end of the 1990s, CSI had freed nearly eight thousand slaves and was being joined by a dozen other groups who were going to Sudan to purchase freedom for slaves.[45]

But some involved in the redemption program, as well as outside observers, began to believe that the good intentions were going awry. By buying the slaves' freedom for fifty or one hundred dollars, which was far higher than what the slave traders themselves were paying for slaves, CSI was fueling a slave economy and only encouraging further raids of villages as well as hoaxes by people who were not actually slave traders. Richard Miniter, who made an investigative visit to Sudan, notes that by 1997, prices in the slave trade had begun to decline drastically, and it appeared that the slave raids might die out. However, suddenly the slave trade began to increase. A typical raiding party grew from four hundred attackers in 1995 to twenty-five hundred attackers in 1999. Miniter writes, "Why in an era of falling prices, did the raiders more than sextuple their overhead? To garner more of the slave redeemers' bounty. It seems certain that without redemption, the raiding parties would have diminished."[46] Essentially, slave redemption was putting more money into the economy, which only allowed more raiders and raids, thus increasing the actual number of slaves. Moreover, some felt the redemption practice showed an implicit acceptance of the notion that it was legitimate for human beings to be bought and sold. Putting more money into an economy in which the average Sudanese earns five hundred dollars per year also fueled hoaxes by people who were not actually involved in the slave trade. When slave redeemers showed up on several occasions, children were suddenly rounded up as if they were slaves, ready to be sent off to freedom, when in fact the supposed traders had simply removed them from their own families and communities.[47]

The moral intention of slave redemption was indeed praiseworthy. It arose out of a commitment to human dignity, freedom, and justice. But the particular strategy failed to take into consideration the economics of the situation and to perceive the way in which good intentions only enhanced the evil the redeemers sought to eradicate. Wisdom, discernment, and a clear comprehension of a situation are essential to choosing strategies and models that can truly carry out Christian moral vision.

Conclusion

This book has attempted to demonstrate that Christian ethics is ultimately rooted in the nature and actions of God and in the worldview derived from the biblical story. All moral principles, commands, virtues, and narratives thus ultimately have a larger and transcendent grounding. But we as Christians apply our worldview and moral directives in a human, fallen, complex world. Thus, the last section of this work examined issues related to connecting a transcultural ethic with the cultures and societies in which we find ourselves. The challenge of moving from transcendent realities to the mundane of this world is no easy task, and clearly the means we use to connect our Christian ethic to society is not of the same status as the ethic itself or the foundations behind the ethic.

The moral task before the Christian church today is immense. We face a world that frequently shares little of the worldview and convictions that inform our way of life. Because of the rise of pluralism, sophisticated technologies, and the postmodern ethos of subjectivity and relativism, the world to which we apply our Christian commitments is complex and challenging. Its ethos is often foreign, sometimes downright hostile, to our biblically informed sentiments.

But God has called us, as he called Esther long ago in Persia, to be a divine presence "for such a time as this." As we seek to think, live, and apply our Christian moral commitments to a complex world, we must do so with both assurance and humility, with both conviction and love, with both transcendent grounding and "worldly" wisdom. In such a world, let us choose the good. Above all, let us choose God, the source of the good and the foundation of all that we are and do.

NOTES

Introduction

1. Taken from David M. Adams and Edward W. Maine, *Business Ethics for the Twenty-First Century* (Mountain View, Calif.: Mayfield, 1998), 409–10.

2. Arthur F. Holmes, *Ethics: Approaching Moral Decisions* (Downers Grove, Ill.: InterVarsity Press, 1984), 10.

3. Steve Wilkens, *Beyond Bumper Sticker Ethics: An Introduction to Theories of Right and Wrong* (Downers Grove, Ill.: InterVarsity Press, 1995), 16.

4. Analytical philosophy, sometimes also called linguistic philosophy, is a twentieth-century philosophical movement devoted primarily to the analysis of concepts and language. It attempts to describe the nature and meaning of certain types of concepts or linguistic expressions. Key thinkers in this diverse movement have included G. E. Moore, Bertrand Russell, Ludwig Wittgenstein, A. J. Ayer, Gilbert Ryle, and John Austin.

5. A. J. Ayer, *Language, Truth, and Logic* (New York: Dover Publications, 1946), 103.

6. This perspective was particularly articulated by Anders Nygren in *Agape and Eros* (Philadelphia: Fortress Press, 1953).

7. Richard Higginson, *Dilemmas: A Christian Approach to Moral Decision Making* (Louisville: Westminster/John Knox Press, 1988), 27.

8. Some thinkers have traditionally referred to these kinds of issues as *adiaphora,* meaning matters of indifference or issues in which there is no clear right or wrong.

9. E. David Cook, "Relativism," in *New Dictionary of Christian Ethics and Pastoral Theology,* ed. David J. Atkinson, David F. Field, Arthur Holmes, and Oliver O'Donovan (Downers Grove, Ill.: InterVarsity Press, 1995), 726–27.

10. James Rachels, *The Right Thing to Do: Basic Readings in Moral Philosophy* (New York: McGraw-Hill College, 1999), 2.

11. Lewis B. Smedes, *Mere Morality: What God Expects of Ordinary People* (Grand Rapids: Eerdmans, 1983), 242.

12. See, for example, Matthew 5:31–32 and 1 Corinthians 7:10–16. Some Christians have contended that a legitimate divorce can go beyond the grounds of these two passages, which seem to allow divorce for unfaithfulness and abandonment by a nonbelieving spouse. But the list for legitimate divorce should always be fairly minimal and contain serious factors.

13. Philip Rieff, *The Triumph of the Therapeutic: Uses of Faith after Freud* (Chicago: University of Chicago Press, 1987).

14. Oliver O'Donovan, *Begotten or Made?* (Oxford: Clarendon Press, 1984), 11.

Chapter 1

1. We should note, however, that teleological ethics is not always a pure consequentialist approach. There is a teleological ethic (i.e., Aristotle and Aquinas) that focuses on the ends toward which humans were made and builds the moral framework around those natural ends.

2. Robert Bellah, Richard Madsen, William Sullivan, Ann Swidler, and Steven Tipton, *Habits of the*

Heart: Individualism and Commitment in American Life (New York: Harper & Row, 1985), 9.

3. Quoted in Louis P. Pojman, *The Moral Life: An Introductory Reader in Ethics and Literature* (New York: Oxford Press, 2000), 552. A similar perspective to Alexander Pope is set forth by Robert G. Olson, who states, "The individual is most likely to contribute to social betterment by rationally pursuing his own best long-range interests" (552).

4. Lucretius, *The Nature of Things* 1.62–71, trans. Frank O. Copley (New York: W. W. Norton, 1977), 3.

5. Stanley Grenz, *The Moral Quest: Foundations of Christian Ethics* (Downers Grove, Ill.: InterVarsity Press, 1997), 78.

6. Adam Smith, *The Wealth of Nations* (New York: Random House), 423.

7. Larry Rasmussen, *Moral Fragments and Moral Community* (Minneapolis: Fortress Press, 1993), 41–42.

8. Ayn Rand, *For the New Intellectual* (New York: Signet, 1961), 80, 82.

9. There is a sense in which Rand at this point is really a utilitarian in disguised form, for she appeals to the larger social consequences (i.e., the world a more orderly place) as the basis for one's personal pursuits of pleasure.

10. Jeremy Bentham, *The Principles of Morals and Legislation* (Darien, Conn.: Hafner, 1949), 1.

11. Ibid., 31.

12. John Stuart Mill, *Utilitarianism* (Indianapolis: Hackett, 1979), 10.

13. Ibid., 21.

14. Joseph Fletcher, *Situation Ethics: The New Morality* (Philadelphia: Westminster Press, 1966), 26.

15. Ibid., 65.

16. Ibid., 120, 129.

17. J. Budziszewski, *Written on the Heart: The Case for Natural Law* (Downers Grove, Ill.: InterVarsity Press, 1997), 145–46.

18. Aristotle, *The Nichomachean Ethics* X-6, trans. David Ross, rev. J. L. Ackrill and J. O. Urmson (New York: Oxford University Press, 1980), 261.

19. Thomas Malthus, *Population: The First Essay* (Ann Arbor, Mich.: University of Michigan Press, 1959), 132.

20. The primary proponent of this theory was biologist Garret Hardin. See his "Carrying Capacity as an Ethical Concept," in *Lifeboat Ethics: The Dilemma of World Hunger,* ed. George R. Lucas (New York: Harper & Row, 1976). In the same volume, Joseph Fletcher, the situationist, argues for much the same on the grounds of a love-based utilitarianism.

21. Steve Wilkens, *Beyond Bumper Sticker Ethics: An Introduction to Theories of Right and Wrong* (Downers Grove, Ill.: InterVarsity Press, 1995), 96.

22. Plato, *Crito,* in *The Works of Plato,* ed. Erwin Edman (New York: Simon & Schuster, 1928), 91–106.

23. Immanuel Kant, *Foundations of the Metaphysics of Morals,* trans. Lewis White Beck (Indianapolis: Bobbs-Merrill, 1959), 16. Further elaboration of his ethics and particularly its rational basis came in his later publication, *The Metaphysics of Ethics.*

24. Kant, *Foundations,* 31.

25. Ibid., 39.

26. Ibid., 47.

27. Newman Smyth, *Christian Ethics* (Edinburgh: T & T Clark, 1893), 102.

28. Paul Ramsey, *Basic Christian Ethics* (New York: Scribners, 1954), 1.

29. Ibid., 115–16.

30. For his emphasis on love as the summation of all moral absolutes, see Norman L. Geisler, *The Christian Ethic of Love* (Grand Rapids: Zondervan, 1973).

31. Norman L. Geisler, *Ethics: Alternatives and Issues* (Grand Rapids: Zondervan, 1971), 114.

32. It should be noted that Geisler is formulating the issue as choosing the greater good, though some Christian theologians and ethicists formulate the issue as choosing the lesser evil. See, for example, Helmet Thielicke's *Theological Ethics,* vol. 1 (Grand Rapids: Eerdmans, 1979), in which he argues that in borderline situations, choosing the lesser evil is still marked by some taint of moral guilt.

33. Allen Verhey, "Is Lying Always Wrong?" *Christianity Today,* 24 May 1999, 68.

Chapter 2

1. The essence of this illustration is taken from Stanley Grenz, *The Moral Quest: Foundations of Christian Ethics* (Downers Grove, Ill.: InterVarsity Press, 1997), 40.

2. Terence R. Anderson, *Walking the Way: Christian Ethics as a Guide* (Toronto: United Church Publishing House, 1993), 111.

3. Iris Murdoch, *The Sovereignty of Good* (New York: Schocken Books, 1971), 37.

4. Aristotle, *The Nichomachean Ethics* I-10, trans. David Ross, rev. J. L. Ackrill and J. O. Urmson (New York: Oxford University Press, 1980), 22.

5. Ibid., I-13, 27.

6. Ibid., II-1, 29.

7. Ibid., II-6, 37.

8. James Rachels, *The Elements of Moral Philosophy*, 3d ed. (Boston: McGraw-Hill, 1999), 179.

9. Aristotle, *The Nichomachean Ethics* V-1, 109, 108.

10. Ibid., II-4, 34.

11. Ibid., II-1, 29.

12. Aristotle, *Politics* I-1, trans. T. A. Sinclair (New York: Penguin Books, 1992), 54.

13. Craig Dykstra, "Moral Development," in *The Westminster Dictionary of Christian Ethics,* ed. James F. Childress and John Macquarrie (Philadelphia: Westminster Press, 1986), 396.

14. The analysis of Gilligan fitting into the virtue tradition is argued cogently by Sharon Meagher, "Histories, Herstories, and Moral Tradition," *Social Theory and Practice* 16 (1990): 61–84. Meagher particularly highlights the narrative dimension of Gilligan in that she is both telling a story (rather than reporting facts) and claiming that narrative is central to moral theory.

15. Lawrence Kohlberg, *The Psychology of Moral Development* (New York: Harper & Row, 1984), 624.

16. Carol Gilligan, *In a Different Voice: Psychological Theory and Women's Development* (Cambridge: Harvard University Press, 1982), 18.

17. Ibid., 19.

18. Carol Gilligan and Jane Attanucci, "Two Moral Orientations," in *Mapping the Moral Domain: A Contribution of Women's Thinking to Psychological Theory and Education,* ed. Carol Gilligan, Jamie Victoria Ward, Jill McLean Taylor, with Betty Bardige (Cambridge: Harvard University Press, 1988), 73.

19. Carol Gilligan, "Adolescent Development Reconsidered," in *Mapping the Moral Domain,* xviii. For a similar ethic of care that is explicitly virtue oriented, see Nel Noddings, *Caring: A Feminine Approach to Ethics and Moral Education* (Berkeley: University of California Press, 1984).

20. Max Stackhouse, "Alasdair MacIntyre: An Overview and Evaluation," *Religious Studies Review* 18, no. 3 (July 1992): 203.

21. Alasdair MacIntyre, *After Virtue: A Study in Moral Theory* (Notre Dame, Ind.: University of Notre Dame Press, 1981), 2.

22. Alasdair MacIntyre, *Whose Justice? Which Rationality?* (Notre Dame, Ind.: University of Notre Dame Press, 1988), 5–6.

23. MacIntyre, *After Virtue,* 11.

24. Ibid., 51.

25. Alasdair MacIntyre, *A Short History of Ethics: A History of Moral Philosophy from the Homeric Age to the Twentieth Century* (New York: Macmillan, 1966), 122–23. For a helpful analysis and critique of MacIntyre's view on Protestantism and the Reformers, see Richard Mouw, *The God Who Commands* (Notre Dame, Ind.: University of Notre Dame Press, 1990), 55–75.

26. MacIntyre, *After Virtue,* 107.

27. Ibid., 139.

28. Ibid., 140.

29. Ibid., 114.

30. Ibid., 201.

31. There are a number of other character/virtue ethicists or works using this perspective. See, for example, Gil Meilaender, *The Theory and Practice of Virtue* (Notre Dame, Ind.: University of Notre Dame Press, 1984); James McClendon Jr., *Systematic Theology: Ethics* (Nashville: Abingdon Press, 1986); Joseph Kotva Jr., *The Christian Case for Virtue Ethics* (Washington, D.C.: Georgetown University Press, 1996); and Jonathan Wilson, *Gospel Virtues: Practicing Faith, Hope, and Love in Uncertain Times* (Downers Grove, Ill.: InterVarsity Press, 1998).

32. Stanley Hauerwas, *Sanctify Them in the Truth: Holiness Exemplified* (Nashville: Abingdon Press, 1998), 29.

33. Ibid., 30.

34. Stanley Hauerwas, *The Peaceable Kingdom: A Primer in Christian Ethics* (Notre Dame, Ind.: University of Notre Dame Press, 1983), 29.

35. Stanley Hauerwas, *Character and the Christian Life: A Study in Theological Ethics* (San Antonio: Trinity University Press, 1975), 8.

36. Edward L. Long, *A Survey of Recent Christian Ethics* (New York: Oxford University Press, 1982), 107.

37. Stanley Hauerwas, *A Community of Character: Toward a Constructive Christian Social Ethic* (Notre Dame, Ind.: University of Notre Dame Press, 1981), 9–12.

38. Hauerwas, *Peaceable Kingdom,* 55. For a more recent treatment, see Stanley Hauerwas, "The Truth about God," in *Sanctify Them in the Truth.*

39. Ibid., 62.

40. Ibid., 76.

41. Stanley Hauerwas, *Naming the Silences: God, Medicine, and the Problem of Suffering* (Grand Rapids: Eerdmans, 1990), 62.

42. Ibid., 11.

43. Ibid., 16.

44. Arthur F. Holmes, *Ethics: Approaching Moral Decisions* (Downers Grove, Ill.: InterVarsity Press, 1984), 115.

45. Hauerwas, *Peaceable Kingdom*, 129.

46. For a helpful critique along these lines, see Paul Nelson, *Narrative and Morality: A Theological Inquiry* (University Park, Pa.: Pennsylvania State University Press, 1987).

47. Hauerwas, *Peaceable Kingdom*, 16, 29.

Chapter 3

1. George F. Will, "Life and Death at Princeton," *Newsweek*, 13 September 1999, 80.

2. Peter Singer, ed., *Ethics* (New York: Oxford University Press, 1994), 5. See also idem, *How Are We to Live* (Amherst, N.Y.: Prometheus Books, 1995); idem, *In Defence of Animals* (Oxford: Blackwell, 1985); and idem and Helga Kuhse, *Should the Baby Live? The Problem of Handicapped Infants* (New York: Oxford University Press, 1985).

3. Terence R. Anderson, *Walking the Way: Christian Ethics as a Guide* (Toronto: United Church Publishing House, 1993), 152.

4. Clifford Geertz, *The Interpretation of Cultures* (New York: Basic Books, 1973), 127.

5. Ibid., 126.

6. Alister McGrath, "Doctrine and Ethics," in *Readings in Christian Ethics*, ed. David K. Clark and Robert V. Rakestraw (Grand Rapids: Baker, 1994), 83.

7. Dorothy L. Sayers, *Creed or Chaos?* (London: Methuen, 1947), 28.

8. Geoffrey Bromiley, "Ethics and Dogmatics," in *International Standard Biblical Encyclopedia*, vol. 2 (Grand Rapids: Eerdmans, 1982), 186–90.

9. Donald Bloesch, *Freedom for Obedience: Evangelical Ethics in Contemporary Times* (San Francisco: Harper & Row, 1987), 65.

10. See, for example, John Kilner, "A Pauline Approach to Ethical Decision-Making," *Interpretation: A Journal of Bible and Theology* 43 (October 1989): 366–78. Kilner writes, "There is an important sense in which the indicative must precede the imperative for Paul, even though the indicative itself

possesses imperative force. Good works always are a fruit of one's new life" (373).

11. Carl F. H. Henry, *Christian Personal Ethics* (Grand Rapids: Eerdmans, 1957), 255.

12. Jonathan R. Cohen, "In God's Garden: Creation and Cloning in Jewish Thought," *Hastings Center Report* 29, no. 4 (1999): 7.

13. Millard J. Erickson, *Christian Theology* (Grand Rapids: Baker, 1986), 310.

14. John Howard Yoder, *The Politics of Jesus* (Grand Rapids: Eerdmans, 1972), 15.

15. Obviously, there is much more that needs to be said about a trinitarian norm than space allows at this point. There has long been a tension between an ethic of creation and an ethic of redemption. If we are truly trinitarian, we will seek to hold creation, redemption, and Spirit discernment and empowerment together. Christ must be given a priority in terms of redemptive history and revelation, but such does not negate a trinitarian ontological grounding for ethics.

16. Edward L. Long, *A Survey of Christian Ethics* (New York: Oxford University Press, 1967), 131–32. See Martin Luther's "Treatise on Christian Liberty," in *Three Treatises* (Philadelphia: Muhlenberg Press, 1943), 249–90; and idem, "Treatise on Good Works," in *Luther's Works*, vol. 44 (Philadelphia: Fortress Press, 1966), 15–114.

17. Jonathan Edwards, *The Nature of True Virtue* (Ann Arbor, Mich.: University of Michigan Press, 1960), 89.

18. Ibid., 25–26.

19. Henry, *Christian Personal Ethics*, 437.

20. Ibid., 438.

21. Vinoth Ramachandra, *Gods That Fail: Modern Idolatry and Christian Mission* (Downers Grove, Ill.: InterVarsity Press, 1996), 64.

22. Roland H. Bainton, *What Christianity Says about Sex, Love, and Marriage* (New York: Association Press, 1957), 30.

23. George Steiner, *Real Presences* (London: Faber and Faber, 1989), 21.

24. Oliver O'Donovan, *Resurrection and the Moral Order: An Outline for Evangelical Ethics* (Grand Rapids: Eerdmans, 1986), 31.

25. This does not imply that socialization of the biological parents is universal but rather that the socialization process most frequently occurs within the family structure, whether that be the extended or the nuclear family. There are some infrequent exceptions.

26. The phrase is taken from Cornelius Plantinga Jr., *Not the Way It's Supposed to Be: A Breviary of Sin* (Grand Rapids: Eerdmans, 1995).

27. Blaise Pascal, *The Pensees* VII-435, trans. W. F. Trotter (New York: Random House, 1941). Pascal deals with this dual dimension of humanity in other places as well; see, for example, his *Thoughts on Religion and Other Subjects* (London: Routledge, n.d.), chaps. 23–26.

28. Albert M. Wolters, *Creation Regained: Biblical Basics for a Reformational Worldview* (Grand Rapids: Eerdmans, 1985), 48.

29. J. E. Cowell, "Sin," in *New Dictionary of Theology*, ed. Sinclair Ferguson, David Wright, and J. I. Packer (Downers Grove, Ill.: InterVarsity Press, 1988), 642.

30. Quoted in Plantinga, *Not the Way It's Supposed to Be*, 62.

31. Ibid., 99.

32. Geoffrey Bromiley, "Sin," in *International Standard Biblical Encyclopedia*, vol. 3, 521.

33. George Steiner, *Extra-Territorial: Papers on Literature and the Language of Revolution* (New York: Atheneum, 1971), 36.

34. Greg Foster, *Sin, Structure, and Responsibility* (Bramcote Notts, Great Britain: Grove Books, 1978), 4.

35. Ibid., 5.

36. C. H. Dodd, *The Johannine Epistles* (New York: Harper, 1946), 42.

37. See, for example, Hendrikus Berkof, *Christ and the Powers* (Scottdale, Pa.: Mennonite Publishing House, 1962); Walter Wink, *The Powers That Be* (New York: Doubleday, 1998); idem, *Unmasking the Powers* (Philadelphia: Fortress Press, 1986); and Peter O'Brien, "Principalities and Powers and Their Relationship to Structures," *Evangelical Review of Theology* (April 1982): 50–61.

38. Wolters, *Creation Regained*, 60.

39. For a helpful overview of the history and varying interpretations of sanctification, see Donald Alexander, ed., *Christian Spirituality: Five Views of Sanctification* (Downers Grove, Ill.: InterVarsity Press, 1988); and Stanley M. Burgess, ed., *Reaching Beyond: Chapters in the History of Perfectionism* (Peabody, Mass.: Hendrickson, 1986).

40. Quoted in Leon O. Hynson, *To Reform the Nation: Theological Foundations of Wesley's Ethics* (Grand Rapids: Zondervan, 1984), 9.

41. Wolters, *Creation Regained*, 58.

42. Henry, *Christian Personal Ethics*, 219.

43. George P. Eckman, *When Christ Comes Again* (New York: Abingdon Press, 1917), 154. It should be pointed out that not all dispensationalists rejected social reform efforts. For a helpful overview of the entire premillennial movement, see Timothy P. Weber, *Living in the Shadow of the Second Coming: American Premillennialism, 1875–1982* (Grand Rapids: Zondervan, 1983). Weber shows that there was not a monolithic response to social reform even among the dispensational variety of premillennialism.

44. Rousas J. Rushdoony, "Government and the Christian," *The Rutherford Institute* 1 (July–August 1984): 7.

45. F. F. Bruce, "Eschatology," in *Evangelical Dictionary of Theology*, ed. Walter Elwell (Grand Rapids: Baker, 1984), 365.

46. Miroslav Volf, "On Loving with Hope: Eschatology and Social Responsibility," *Transformation* (July/September 1990): 29.

47. Ibid.

48. Richard Bauckham and Trevor Hart, *Hope against Hope: Christian Eschatology at the Turn of the Millennium* (Grand Rapids: Eerdmans, 1999), 181.

49. David W. Gill, "Hope," in *New Dictionary of Christian Ethics and Pastoral Theology*, ed. David Atkinson, David Field, Arthur Holmes, and Oliver O'Donovan (Downers Grove, Ill.: InterVarsity Press, 1995), 456.

50. Ibid., 457.

Chapter 4

1. Anthony Giddens, *The Consequences of Modernity* (Stanford, Calif.: Stanford University Press, 1990), 1.

2. Larry Rasmussen, *Moral Fragments and Moral Community: A Proposal for Church and Society* (Minneapolis: Fortress Press, 1993), 29.

3. Lesslie Newbigin, *Truth and Authority in Modernity* (Valley Forge, Pa.: Trinity Press International, 1996), 65.

4. Ibid.

5. Elizabeth Bounds, *Coming Together, Coming Apart: Religion, Community, and Modernity* (New York: Routledge, 1997), 29.

6. Newbigin, *Truth and Authority*, 11, 3.

7. L. T. Hobhouse, *Morals in Evolution* (1906; reprint, London: Chapman & Hall, 1951), 636.

8. Colin Gunton, *The One, the Three, and the Many: God, Creation, and the Culture of Modernity*

(Cambridge: Cambridge University Press, 1993), 28.

9. Jennifer A. Herdt, "Religious Ethics, History, and the Rise of Modern Moral Philosophy," *Journal of Religious Ethics* 28, no. 2 (summer 2000): 169.

10. Ibid., 172.

11. Ibid., 175.

12. Franklin Gamwell, *The Divine Good: Modern Moral Theory and the Necessity of God* (Dallas: Southern Methodist University Press, 1996), 4.

13. Gabriel Marcel, "The Sacred in the Technological Age," *Theology Today* 19 (1962): 28.

14. H. H. Gerth and C. Wright Mills, eds., *From Max Weber: Essays in Sociology* (London: Kegan Paul, 1948), 293.

15. Peter Berger, Brigitte Berger, and Hansfriel Kellner, *The Homeless Mind: Modernization and Consciousness* (New York: Random, 1973), 181.

16. Bryan Wilson, *Religion in Sociological Perspective* (Oxford: Oxford University Press, 1982), 156.

17. Jacques Ellul, *The Technological Society* (New York: Vintage Books, 1964). His more recent work on technology is *The Technological Bluff* (Grand Rapids: Eerdmans, 1990).

18. Marcel, "Sacred in the Technological Age," 29.

19. Bryan Wilson, *Contemporary Transformations of Religion* (Oxford: Clarendon Press, 1976), 1.

20. Oliver O'Donovan, *Begotten or Made?* (Oxford: Clarendon Press, 1984), 3.

21. Anthony Giddens, "The Global Revolution in Family and Personal Life," in *Family in Transition,* 11th ed., ed. Arlene Skolnick and Jerome Skolnick (Boston: Allyn & Bacon, 2001), 19.

22. David Lyon, *The Steeple's Shadow: On the Myths and Realities of Secularization* (Grand Rapids: Eerdmans, 1987), 53.

23. Ellul, *Technological Society,* 74.

24. Bryan Wilson, "Morality in the Evolution of the Modern Social System," *The British Journal of Sociology* 36, no. 3 (September 1985): 326.

25. Ibid.

26. Ibid., 328–29.

27. Emile Durkheim, *The Division of Labor in Society* (London: Macmillan, 1984), 2.

28. Robert Bellah, Richard Madsen, William Sullivan, Ann Swidler, and Steven Tipton, *Habits of the Heart: Individualism and Commitment in American Life* (New York: Harper & Row, 1985), 277.

29. Agnes Heller, *A Theory of Modernity* (Oxford: Blackwell, 1999), 202, 203.

30. Berger, *Homeless Mind,* 37.

31. Peter Berger, *The Sacred Canopy: Elements of a Sociological Theory of Religion* (Garden City, N.J.: Anchor Books, 1967), 48.

32. Lyon, *Steeple's Shadow,* 31.

33. Jeffrey Hadden, "Toward Desacralizing Secularization Theory," *Social Forces* 65, no. 3 (March 1989): 588.

34. Berger, *Sacred Canopy,* 107.

35. Karel Dobbelaere, "Secularization Theories and Sociological Paradigms: Convergences and Divergences," *Sociological Analysis* (1985): 378.

36. See Peter Berger, ed., *The Desecularization of the World: Resurgent Religion and World Politics* (Grand Rapids: Eerdmans, 1999); and Paul J. Fitzgerald, "Faithful Sociology: Peter Berger's Religious Project," *Religious Studies Review* 27, no. 1 (January 2001): 10–17.

37. Wilson, *Contemporary Transformations of Religion,* 10.

38. Bellah, *Habits of the Heart,* 45.

39. Karl Mannheim, *Essays on the Sociology of Knowledge* (London: Routledge and Kegan Paul, 1952), 269.

40. Heller, *Theory of Modernity,* 8.

41. Jose Ortega y Gasset, *The Revolt of the Masses* (New York: Mentor, 1932), 31–32.

42. Newbigin, *Truth and Authority,* 73.

Chapter 5

1. Anthony Giddens, *The Consequences of Modernity* (Stanford, Calif.: Stanford University Press, 1990), 51.

2. Larry Rasmussen, *Moral Fragments and Moral Community: A Proposal for Church and Society* (Minneapolis: Fortress Press, 1993), 31.

3. Gene Veith, "Postmodern Times: Facing a World of New Challenges and Opportunities," *Modern Reformation* (September/October 1995): 17.

4. Stanley Grenz, *A Primer on Postmodernism* (Grand Rapids: Eerdmans, 1996), 43.

5. Jean-François Lyotard, *The Postmodern Condition: A Report on Knowledge* (Minneapolis: University of Minnesota Press, 1984), xxiv.

6. Grenz, *Primer on Postmodernism,* 49.

7. Andrew Sullivan, "Disappointed," *New Republic* 28 (September 1992): 45.

8. Veith, "Postmodern Times," 17.

9. Jacques Derrida, "White Mythology," *New Literary History* 5 (1974): 9.

Notes

10. Jacques Derrida, *Margins of Philosophy* (Chicago: University of Chicago Press, 1982), 329.

11. Jacques Derrida, *Of Grammatology* (Baltimore: Johns Hopkins Press, 1976), 158. For a modified version of Derrida, see John D. Caputo, *The Prayers and Tears of Jacques Derrida: Religion without Religion* (Bloomington, Ind.: Indiana University Press, 1997).

12. Richard Rorty, *Objectivity, Relativism, and Truth, Philosophical Papers,* vol. 1 (Cambridge: Cambridge University Press, 1991), 1.

13. Kevin Vanhoozer, *Is There a Meaning in This Text?* (Grand Rapids: Zondervan, 1998), 100.

14. Stanley Fish, *Is There a Text in This Class? The Authority of Interpretive Communities* (Cambridge: Harvard University Press, 1980), 13.

15. Paul Rabinow, ed., *The Foucault Reader* (New York: Pantheon Books, 1984), 74–75.

16. Michel Foucault, *Language, Counter Memory, Practice* (Ithaca, N.Y.: Cornell University Press, 1977), 151.

17. Elisabeth Schüssler Fiorenza, *In Memory of Her: A Feminist Theological Reconstruction of Christian Origins* (New York: Crossroad, 1983), 32.

18. Vanhoozer, *Is There a Meaning?* 181.

19. Walter Truett Anderson, *Reality Isn't What It Used to Be* (San Francisco: Harper & Row, 1990), 75.

20. Vanhoozer, *Is There a Meaning?* 58–59.

21. David Wells, *God in the Wasteland* (Grand Rapids: Eerdmans, 1994), 48.

22. Mark Taylor and Esa Saarinen, *Imagologies: Media Philosophy* (New York: Routledge, 1994), 9.

23. Simon Frith, *Performing Rites: On the Value of Popular Music* (Cambridge: Harvard University Press, 1996), 243.

24. Quoted in Tom Beaudoin, *Virtual Faith: The Irreverent Spiritual Quest of Generation X* (San Francisco: Jossey-Bass, 1998), 25.

25. Robert Wuthnow, *After Heaven: Spirituality in America since the 1950s* (Berkeley: University of California Press, 1998), 2.

26. George Lindbeck, *The Nature of Doctrine: Religion and Theology in a Postliberal Age* (Philadelphia: Westminster Press, 1984), 126.

27. Alasdair MacIntyre, *After Virtue: A Study in Moral Theory* (Notre Dame, Ind.: University of Notre Dame Press, 1981), 11.

28. Martin Marty, *By Way of Response* (Nashville: Abingdon Press, 1981), 81.

29. *Webster's Encyclopedic Unabridged Dictionary of the English Language* (New York: Gramercy Books, 1989), 1491.

30. Robert Benne, *The Paradoxical Vision: A Public Theology for the Twenty-First Century* (Minneapolis: Fortress Press, 1995), 12. Benne gives this portrayal based on a personal conversation with Tinder.

31. Stan Gaede, *When Tolerance Is No Virtue: Political Correctness, Multiculturalism, and the Future of Truth and Justice* (Downers Grove, Ill.: InterVarsity Press, 1993), 27.

32. Ibid., 82.

33. Andrew Neil, "Laid Bare," *Sunday Times Magazine,* 18 October 1992, 20.

34. Quoted in Nancy Gibbs, "Baby, It's You! And You, and You . . . , " *Time,* 19 February 2001, 50.

35. Gaede, *When Tolerance Is No Virtue,* 89.

36. Richard Mouw, *Uncommon Decency: Christian Civility in an Uncivil World* (Downers Grove, Ill.: InterVarsity Press, 1992), 136.

37. Philip Rieff, *The Triumph of the Therapeutic: Uses of Faith after Freud* (Chicago: University of Chicago Press, 1987), 62, 13.

38. Ibid., 22.

39. Ibid., 253.

40. James Davison Hunter, *The Death of Character: Moral Education in an Age without Good or Evil* (New York: Basic Books, 2000), xiii.

41. Ibid., 70.

42. Ibid., 84, 100.

43. Ibid., 122.

44. Ibid., 152.

45. David Wells, *Losing Our Virtue: Why the Church Must Recover Its Moral Vision* (Grand Rapids: Eerdmans, 1998), 42.

46. Ibid., 70.

47. Philip Turner, "Sex and the Single Life," *First Things* 33 (May 1993): 15.

48. See Charles Taylor, *The Sources of the Self: The Making of Modern Identity* (Cambridge: Harvard University Press, 1989).

49. Turner, "Sex and the Single Life," 18, 17.

50. Ibid., 19.

51. Vanhoozer, *Is There a Meaning?* 186.

52. Rasmussen, *Moral Fragments,* 32.

Chapter 6

1. Bernard Adeney, *Strange Virtues: Ethics in a Multicultural World* (Downers Grove, Ill.: InterVarsity Press, 1995), 13–14.

2. Edward L. Long, *A Survey of Christian Ethics* (New York: Oxford University Press, 1967). Long

has more recently written *A Survey of Recent Christian Ethics* (New York: Oxford University Press, 1982).

3. Long, *Survey of Christian Ethics,* 45.

4. Thomas Aquinas, *Summa Theologica* (New York: Benziger Brothers, 1947), vol. 1, pt I-II, Q. 49, art. 4.

5. Ibid., vol. 1, pt I-II, Q. 91, art. 1.

6. Ibid., art. 2.

7. Ibid., Q. 96, art. 1.

8. Ibid., Q. 95, art. 2.

9. Ibid., Q. 99, art. 2.

10. Ibid., vol. 2, pt II-II, Q. 40, art. 1.

11. Ibid.

12. Pope Pius XII, "On the Function of the State in the Modern World" *(Summi Pontificatus),* in Anne Fremantle, *The Papal Encyclicals in Their Historical Context* (New York: New American Library, 1956), 264.

13. Richard McCormick, *How Brave a New World? Dilemmas in Bioethics* (Garden City, N.Y.: Doubleday, 1981), 9.

14. Richard McCormick, "Theology and Biomedical Ethics," *Eglise et Theologie* 13 (1982): 313. For another contemporary version of natural law ethics in the Thomistic tradition, see Jean Porter, "Contested Categories: Reason, Nature, and Natural Order in Medieval Accounts of the Natural Law," *Journal of Religious Ethics* 24, no. 2 (fall 1996): 207–32; and idem, "Recent Studies in Aquinas' Virtue Ethic: A Review Essay," *Journal of Religious Ethics* 26, no. 1 (spring 1998): 191–215.

15. Quoted in Long, *Survey of Christian Ethics,* 60.

16. Ibid., 65. For Paul Ramsey's basic theoretical framework, see his *Basic Christian Ethics* (New York: Scribners, 1950).

17. Reinhold Niebuhr, *An Interpretation of Christian Ethics* (New York: Harper, 1935). See also his *Moral Man and Immoral Society* (New York: Scribners, 1932).

18. Long, *Survey of Recent Christian Ethics,* 15.

19. James Gustafson, *Theology and Christian Ethics* (Philadelphia: Pilgrim Press, 1974), 109. See also his *Ethics from a Theocentric Perspective,* vols. 1, 2 (Chicago: University of Chicago Press, 1981, 1984).

20. C. S. Lewis, *Mere Christianity* (New York: Macmillan, 1952), 7.

21. C. S. Lewis, *The Latin Letters of C. S. Lewis/Don Giovanni Calabra* (Ann Arbor, Mich.: Servant Books, 1988), 89.

22. Kenneth Myers, "Natural Law without Shame," *Crisis* (February 1994): 15.

23. Long, *Survey of Christian Ethics,* 73.

24. *The Shorter Catechism Explained from Scripture* (Edinburgh: Banner of Trust, 1980), 13.

25. Richard Baxter, *A Christian Directory: Or, A Summ of Practical Theologie, and Cases of Conscience,* 2d ed. (London: R. White for N. Simmons, 1967), vol. I, chap. xix, 6, Q. 1.

26. C. H. Dodd, *Gospel and Law: The Relation of Faith and Ethics in Early Christianity* (New York: Columbia University Press, 1951), 52.

27. John Calvin, *Institutes of the Christian Religion,* trans. Henry Beveridge (Grand Rapids: Eerdmans, 1957), book IV, X-7.

28. Ibid., book II, VII-12.

29. Carl F. H. Henry, *Christian Personal Ethics* (Grand Rapids: Eerdmans, 1957), 192.

30. Ibid., 255.

31. Ibid., 219.

32. Carl F. H. Henry, *Aspects of Christian Social Ethics* (Grand Rapids: Eerdmans, 1964), 17.

33. Richard Mouw, *The God Who Commands: A Study in Divine Command Ethics* (Notre Dame, Ind.: University of Notre Dame, 1990), 2.

34. Ibid., 10.

35. Richard Mouw, *Politics and the Biblical Drama* (Grand Rapids: Eerdmans, 1976), 12.

36. John Howard Yoder, *The Politics of Jesus* (Grand Rapids: Eerdmans, 1972), 15.

37. Ibid., 23.

38. Ibid., 63.

39. For an overview of contemporary evangelical thinking that includes Henry, Mouw, and Yoder, see Dennis Hollinger and David Gushee, "Evangelical Ethics: Profile of a Movement Coming of Age," *Annual of the Society of Christian Ethics* 20 (2000): 183–203.

40. Long, *Survey of Christian Ethics,* 117.

41. Ibid., 119.

42. Bruce C. Birch and Larry L. Rasmussen, *Bible and Ethics in the Christian Life* (Minneapolis: Augsburg Press, 1989), 1.

43. Ibid., 32.

44. Ibid., 181.

45. See Long, *Survey of Christian Ethics,* 129–38.

46. Jonathan Edwards, *The Nature of True Virtue* (Ann Arbor, Mich.: University of Michigan Press, 1960), 24.

47. Nigel Biggar, *The Hastening That Waits: Karl Barth's Ethics* (Oxford: Oxford University Press, 1995), 7.

48. Karl Barth, *Ethics,* ed. Dietrich Braun (New York: Seabury Press, 1981), 18.

49. Karl Barth, *The Christian Life: Church Dogmatics Vol. IV, Part 4, Lecture Fragments* (Grand Rapids: Eerdmans, 1981), 33.

50. Ibid., 34.

51. Karl Barth, *Church Dogmatics,* 4 vols., II-2 (Edinburgh: T & T Clark, 1936–77), 700.

52. Ibid., III-4, 462. For a more detailed account of Barth's views on war, see John Howard Yoder, *Karl Barth and the Problem of War* (Nashville: Abingdon Press, 1970).

53. Barth, *Church Dogmatics,* III-4, 427.

54. Emil Brunner, *The Divine Imperative: A Study in Christian Ethics* (Philadelphia: Westminster, 1947), 111.

55. Stanley Hauerwas, *Visions and Virtue: Essays in Christian Ethical Reflection* (Notre Dame, Ind.: University of Notre Dame, 1981), 2.

56. Stanley Hauerwas, *Sanctify Them in the Truth: Holiness Exemplified* (Nashville: Abingdon Press, 1998), 43.

57. Ibid., 57.

58. Rosemary Radford Ruether, *Gaia and God: An Ecofeminist Theology of Earth Healing* (San Francisco: Harper & Row, 1992), 258.

59. Ibid., 253.

60. Rosemary Radford Ruether, *The Church against Itself* (New York: Herder & Heider, 1967), 61, 226–27.

61. Rosemary Radford Ruether, *To Change the World: Christology and Cultural Criticism* (New York: Crossroad, 1981), 4–5.

62. Birch and Rasmussen, *Bible and Ethics,* 81. Such a statement, taken at face value, appears to reduce transcendence to the faith community itself.

Chapter 7

1. Boaz Johnson, a native of India who has ministered in that part of the country, indicates that the people of that area believe their practice stems from the Old Testament, for they see themselves as a remnant of one of the tribes of Israel.

2. Robin Scroggs, "The Bible as Foundational Document," *Interpretation* 49, no. 1 (January 1995): 19.

3. Wayne Meeks, *The Origins of Christian Morality: The First Two Centuries* (New Haven: Yale University Press, 1993), 216.

4. Jack T. Sanders, *Ethics in the New Testament: Change and Development* (Philadelphia: Fortress Press, 1975), 130.

5. Paul Jersild, *Spirit Ethics: Scripture and the Moral Life* (Minneapolis: Fortress Press, 2000), 78–79.

6. Ibid., 82, 80.

7. Sallie McFague, *Models of God: Theology for an Ecological, Nuclear Age* (Philadelphia: Fortress Press, 1987), 43.

8. D. A. Carson, *The Gagging of God: Christianity Confronts Pluralism* (Grand Rapids: Zondervan, 1996), 151.

9. Richard Hays, "The Church as a Scripture-Shaped Community: The Problem of Methos in New Testament Ethics," *Interpretation* 44 (1990): 51.

10. Richard Hays, "New Testament Ethics. The Theological Task," *The Annual: Society of Christian Ethics* 15 (1995): 104.

11. Stephen Mott, *Jesus and Social Ethics* (Bramcote Notts, Great Britain: Grove Books, 1984), 19.

12. See, for example, Luke 2:12, where Jesus in the manger is called *brephos.* See also Luke 18:15; Acts 7:19; and 2 Timothy 3:15—all texts in which the same term used for the baby in Mary's womb is utilized for a child.

13. Ronald J. Sider, *Rich Christians in an Age of Hunger* (Downers Grove, Ill.: InterVarsity Press, 1977), 94–95. See also S. R. Driver, *Commentary on Deuteronomy* (Edinburgh: T & T Clark, 1895), 266–67.

14. We should note that in the Old Testament there does seem to be some differentiation between capital punishment for murder and for the various other offences. Walter Kaiser notes that "while there apparently was a 'ransom' or 'substitute' payment available for all the other crimes that demanded a capital punishment in the Old Testament, Numbers 35:31 explicitly denied this option in the case of first degree murder" (Walter Kaiser, *Toward Old Testament Ethics* [Grand Rapids: Zondervan, 1983], 165).

15. Ibid., 282, 270–71.

16. Peter Craigie, "Yahweh Is a Man of Wars," *Scottish Journal of Theology* 22 (1969): 186. See also Peter Craigie, *The Problem of War in the Old Testament* (Grand Rapids: Eerdmans, 1978).

17. While the permanence of marriage is the moral norm, there appear to be two exceptions in which divorce was allowed: adultery (Matt. 5:32;

19:9) and an unbelieving spouse who leaves (1 Cor. 7:15).

18. Oliver M. T. O'Donovan, "Towards an Interpretation of Biblical Ethics," *Tyndale Bulletin* 27 (1976): 60.

19. See, for example, C. G. Montefiore, *Rabbinic Literature and Gospel Teaching* (New York: Ktav, 1970), 316–17; also Kaiser, *Toward Old Testament Ethics,* 44–48.

20. Bernard Adeney, *Strange Virtues: Ethics in a Multicultural World* (Downers Grove, Ill.: InterVarsity Press, 1995), 101.

21. Ibid. For a similar treatment of these issues, see Christopher J. H. Wright, *An Eye for an Eye: The Place of Old Testament Ethics Today* (Downers Grove, Ill.: InterVarsity Press, 1983), 174–96.

22. O'Donovan, "Towards an Interpretation," 66.

23. For the role of culture in this issue, see William J. Webb, *Slaves, Women, and Homosexuals: Exploring the Hermeneutics of Cultural Analysis* (Downers Grove, Ill.: InterVarsity Press, 2001). Webb sets forth what he calls a redemptive-movement hermeneutic in which he establishes criteria for determining the ethical normativity of certain biblical teachings.

24. See, for example, Norman Geisler, *The Christian Ethics of Love* (Grand Rapids: Zondervan, 1973), 76–97; and idem, *Ethics: Alternatives and Issues* (Grand Rapids: Zondervan, 1971), 114–36.

25. See, for example, James Gustafson, *Theology and Christian Ethics* (Philadelphia: Pilgrim Press, 1974), 309–16; and Edward LeRoy Long, "The Use of the Bible in Christian Ethics," *Interpretation* 19 (1965): 149–62.

26. Albrecht Alt, *Essays in Old Testament History and Religion* (Oxford: Blackwell, 1966), 81–132.

27. Kaiser, *Toward Old Testament Ethics,* 65.

28. Gordon Dahl, *Work, Play, and Worship in a Leisure-Oriented Society* (Minneapolis: Augsburg Press, 1972), 12.

29. For an insightful and helpful application of the Decalogue to contemporary issues, see Lewis Smedes, *Mere Morality: What God Expects of Ordinary People* (Grand Rapids: Eerdmans, 1983).

30. Stanley Hauerwas, *A Community of Character: Toward a Constructive Christian Social Ethic* (Notre Dame, Ind.: University of Notre Dame Press, 1981), 58.

31. Richard Longenecker, *New Testament Social Ethics for Today* (Grand Rapids: Eerdmans, 1984), 27.

For a similar perspective, see Webb, *Slaves, Women, and Homosexuals.*

32. Ibid., 29.

33. Christine Pohl, *Making Room: Recovering Hospitality as a Christian Tradition* (Grand Rapids: Eerdmans, 1999), 4.

34. Ibid., 16.

35. Reinhold Niebuhr, *The Children of Light and the Children of Darkness* (New York: Scribners, 1944), xiii.

36. For a full unfolding of these concepts, see Dennis Hollinger, "A Theology of Death and Dying," *Journal of Medical Ethics* 12, no. 3 (1996): 60–65.

37. Ibid., 64–65.

38. Christopher J. H. Wright, *Walking in the Ways of the Lord: The Ethical Authority of the Old Testament* (Downers Grove, Ill.: InterVarsity Press, 1995), 36.

39. Ibid., 63.

40. Richard Hays, *The Moral Vision of the New Testament: A Contemporary Introduction to New Testament Ethics* (San Francisco: Harper, 1996), 196–98.

41. Ibid., 449.

42. Stanley Hauerwas and David Burrell, "From Story to Story: An Alternative Pattern for Rationality in Ethics," in *Why Narrative? Readings in Narrative Theology,* ed. Stanley Hauerwas and Gregory Jones (Grand Rapids: Eerdmans, 1989), 190.

43. Richard Bauckham, "Scripture and Authority," *Transformation* (April/June 1998): 8.

Chapter 8

1. Alan Geyer, "Toward an Ecumenical Political Ethics: A Marginal View," in *Perspectives on Political Ethics,* ed. K. Srisang (Geneva: WCC, 1983), 135.

2. For helpful overviews of these positions, see Roland Bainton, *Christian Attitudes toward War and Peace: A Historical Survey and Critical Evaluation* (Nashville: Abingdon Press, 1960); and Robert Clouse, ed., *War: Four Christian Views* (Downers Grove, Ill.: InterVarsity Press, 1981).

3. John Howard Yoder, *When War Is Unjust: Being Honest in Just-War Thinking* (Minneapolis: Augsburg Press, 1984), 79.

4. For recent overviews of these issues, see James Turner Johnson, *Morality and Contemporary Warfare* (New Haven: Yale University Press, 1999); and

Richard B. Miller, *Interpretations of Conflict: Ethics, Pacifism, and the Just-War Tradition* (Chicago: University of Chicago Press, 1991).

5. Lester B. Lave and Hadi Dowlatabadi, "Climate Change: The Effects of Personal Beliefs and Scientific Uncertainty," *Environmental Science Technology* 27, no. 10 (1993): 1963.

6. S. George Philander, *Is the Temperature Rising? The Uncertain Science of Global Warming* (Princeton, N.J.: Princeton University Press, 1998), 3.

7. Joby Warrick, "Panel Seeks Cease-Fire on Air Quality but Gets a War," *Washington Post*, 6 February 1997, p. A21.

8. Quoted in "10 Billion for Dinner, Please," *U.S. News & World Report*, 12 September 1994, 57.

9. Quoted in Jeffrey Marsh, "From Malthus to Al Gore," *Book World*, 28 August 1994, 4. For the debate, see Norman Myers and Julian Simon, *Scarcity or Abundance? A Debate on the Environment* (New York: Norton, 1994).

10. Marsh, "From Malthus to Al Gore," 4.

11. Enrique Dussel, "The Market from the Ethical Viewpoint of Liberation Theology," in *Outside the Market No Salvation*, ed. Dietmar Mieth and Marciano Vidal (London: SCM Press, 1997), 97. See also Robert Andelson and James Dawsey, *From Wasteland to Promised Land: Liberation Theology for a Post-Marxist World* (Maryknoll, N.Y.: Orbis, 1992).

12. This scenario is to some degree reflected in Michael Novak, who notes that Latin America, earlier in its history, was richer than North America in natural resources and developed industries but in recent history has been far surpassed by its northern neighbors. Why? "The answer appears to lie in the quite different nature of the Latin American political system, economic system, and moral-cultural system. The last is probably decisive" (Michael Novak, *The Spirit of Democratic Capitalism* [New York: Simon & Schuster, 1982], 275).

13. David S. Landes, *The Wealth and Poverty of Nations* (New York: Norton, 1999), 317. See also Stephen Monsma, "Poverty, Civil Society, and the Public Policy Impass," in *Toward a Just and Caring Society: Christian Responses to Poverty in America*, ed. David P. Gushee (Grand Rapids: Baker, 1999), 71.

14. William Graham Sumner, *Folkways: A Study of the Sociological Importance of Usages, Manners, Customs, Mores, and Morals* (Boston: Ginn and Co., 1940). See particularly 30–31 and 75–82.

15. Yasuko Kawashima, "Policy-making Processes for Global Environmental Problems: A Comparative Analysis beween Japan and the United States," *Keikaku Gyosei* 17, no. 3 (1994): 13.

16. Talcott Parsons, *The Social System* (Glencoe, Ill.: The Free Press, 1951), 354, 349.

17. Donald Bloesch, *Freedom for Obedience: Evangelical Ethics in Contemporary Times* (San Francisco: Harper & Row, 1987), 250.

18. Talcott Parsons, "An Approach to the Sociology of Knowledge," in *Transactions of the Fourth World Congress of Sociology*, ed. Milan and Stressa (London: International Sociological Association, 1959), 38.

19. Elisabeth Schüssler Fiorenza, "Feminist Theology as a Critical Theology of Liberation," in *Woman: New Dimensions*, ed. Walter J. Burghardt (New York: Paulist Press, 1977), 40.

20. See Justin Watson, *The Christian Coalition: Dreams of Restoration, Demands for Recognition* (New York: St. Martin's Press, 1997).

21. Quoted in "FDA Chief Says Nicotine Is Bolstered," *The Boston Globe*, 22 June 1994, 12.

22. See, for example, Tom Tyler and Heather Smith, "Social Justice and Social Movements," in *The Handbook of Social Psychology*, 4th ed., vol. 2, ed. Daniel Gilbert, Susan Fiske, and Gardner Lindzey (New York: Oxford University Press, 1998), 595–622.

23. Michael J. Apter, "Reversal Theory: What Is It?" *The Psychologist* 10, no. 5 (May 1997). Cited 29 May 2001. Online: www.swin.edu.au/sbs/pub/rt/bpsapter.htm. See also Michael J. Apter, *Reversal Theory: Motivation, Emotion, and Personality* (London: Routledge, 1989).

24. Lave and Dowlatabadi, "Climate Change," 1965.

25. See, for example, Cynthia Crossen, *Tainted Truth: The Manipulation of Fact in America* (New York: Simon & Schuster, 1994).

26. Robert J. Samuelson, "The Triumph of the Psycho-Fact," *Washington Post*, 4 May 1994, p. A23.

27. T. S. Eliot, "The Hollow Men," in *The Complete Poems and Plays 1909–1950* (New York: Harcourt, Brace and Co., 1952), 58.

Chapter 9

1. H. Richard Niebuhr, *Christ and Culture* (New York: Harper & Row, 1951).

2. See, for example, Robert Webber, *The Church in the World: Opposition, Tension, or Transformation* (Grand Rapids: Zondervan, 1986), 81–144, in

which he sets forth three models: antithesis, paradox, and transformation. See also John Howard Yoder, *The Original Revolution* (Scottdale, Pa.: Herald Press, 1971), 18–26, in which he develops a kind of typology in examining the various options of relating faith to the world in Jesus' day: realism (Herodians and Saducees), revolution (Zealots), withdrawal (Essenes), and separation of secular/sacred (Pharisees).

3. For an analysis of these and other critiques, see Glen Stassen, Diane Yeager, and John Howard Yoder, *Authentic Transformation: A New Vision of Christ and Culture* (Nashville: Abingdon Press, 1996).

4. H. Richard Niebuhr, "Types of Christian Ethics," in *Authentic Transformation,* 16.

5. Niebuhr, *Christ and Culture,* 45.

6. Quoted in ibid., 54.

7. Tertullian, *De Spectaculis,* in *Tertullian-Minucius Felix,* trans. T. Glover and G. Rendall, Loeb Classical Library (New York: Putnam, 1931).

8. Tertullian, "On the Proscription of Heretics 7," in *The Ante-Nicene Fathers: Translations of the Writings of the Fathers Down to A.D. 325,* vol. 3, ed. Alexander Roberts (Grand Rapids: Eerdmans, 1963), 246.

9. Tertullian, "On Idolatry 10," in ibid., 66–67.

10. George Forell, *History of Christian Ethics: From the New Testament to Augustine,* vol. 1 (Minneapolis: Augsburg Press, 1979), 60.

11. Edward L. Long, *A Survey of Christian Ethics* (New York: Oxford University Press, 1967), 257–58.

12. J. Philip Wogaman, *Christian Ethics: A Historical Introduction* (Louisville: Westminster/John Knox, 1993), 63.

13. *The Little Flowers of St. Francis of Assisi,* trans. Dom Roger Hudleston (London: Burns Oates, 1953), xiii.

14. Suzanne Noffke, ed. and trans., *The Prayers of Catherine of Siena* (New York: Paulist Press, 1983), 90.

15. R. B. Blakney, trans., *Meister Eckhart, A Modern Translation* (New York: Harper, 1941), 79.

16. Niebuhr, *Christ and Culture,* 56.

17. See John Howard Yoder, "How H. Richard Niebuhr Reasoned: A Critique of *Christ and Culture,*" in *Authentic Transformation,* 31–89.

18. "The Schleitheim Confession of Faith," in John C. Wenger, *Glimpses of Mennonite History and Doctrine* (Scottdale, Pa.: Herald Press, 1957), 209, 211.

19. Niebuhr, *Christ and Culture,* 57.

20. Quoted in ibid., 64.

21. Leo Tolstoy, "The Kingdom of God Is within You," *The Tolstoy Centenary Edition,* vol. 22 (London: H. Milford, 1928–37), 275.

22. Niebuhr, *Christ and Culture,* 68, 69.

23. Ibid., 83.

24. Ibid., 90.

25. Quoted in ibid.

26. Quoted in R. E. O. White, *Christian Ethics: The Historical Development* (Atlanta: John Knox Press, 1981), 115.

27. Niebuhr, *Christ and Culture,* 90.

28. For a description of Fosdick's thought, see William R. Hutchison, *The Modernist Impulse in American Protestantism* (New York: Oxford University Press, 1976), 280–87.

29. Niebuhr, *Christ and Culture,* 93.

30. Ernst Troeltsch, *Christian Thought: Its History and Application* (New York: Meridian Books, 1957), 59.

31. Quoted in Donald Bloesch, *Freedom for Obedience: Evangelical Ethics in Contemporary Times* (San Francisco: Harper & Row, 1987), 265.

32. See, for example, Kathy Rudy, *Sex and the Church: Gender, Homosexuality, and the Transformation of Christian Ethics* (Boston: Beacon, 1997); and Anne Bathurst Gilson, *Eros Breaking Free: Interpreting Sexual Theo-Ethics* (Cleveland: Pilgrim Press, 1995).

33. See, for example, Robert H. Schuller, *Self Esteem: The New Reformation* (Waco: Word, 1982).

34. Niebuhr, *Christ and Culture,* 110.

35. H. Richard Niebuhr, *The Kingdom of God in America* (New York: Harper & Row, 1959), 193.

36. Forell, *History of Christian Ethics,* 74.

37. Clement of Alexandria, "The Rich Man's Salvation," in *Ante-Nicene Fathers,* vol. 2, 595, par. 13.

38. Niebuhr, *Christ and Culture,* 124.

39. Ibid., 129.

40. Aquinas, *Summa Theologica* (New York: Benziger Brothers, 1947), vol. I, pt I-II, Q. 62, art. 1.

41. Richard McBrien, *Catholicism* (Minneapolis: Winston Press, 1981), 84, 151.

42. Niebuhr, *Christ and Culture,* 143.

43. Ibid., 145.

44. Luther makes a distinction between the invisible church, composed of all true believers, and the visible church, composed of all baptized members of society.

45. Martin Luther, "Temporal Authority: To What Extent It Should Be Obeyed," in *Luther's Works*, vol. 45 (Philadelphia: Fortress Press, 1962), 89, 91.

46. Martin Luther, "An Open Letter Concerning the Hard Book against the Peasants," in *Luther's Works*, vol. 47, 70.

47. H. Richard Niebuhr does briefly mention Reinhold as an example of this type in an earlier essay. See his "Types of Christian Ethics," in *Authentic Transformation*, 27.

48. Reinhold Niebuhr, *Moral Man and Immoral Society* (New York: Scribners, 1932), xi.

49. Ibid., xx, xxii.

50. Reinhold Niebuhr, *An Interpretation of Christian Ethics* (London: SCM Press, 1936), 61.

51. Niebuhr, *Christ and Culture*, 185.

52. For a discussion of thinkers who see a link between Nazism and Luther's thought, as well as a critique of such analysis, see George W. Forell, *Faith Active in Love: An Investigation of the Principles Underlying Luther's Social Ethics* (Minneapolis: Augsburg Press, 1954), 16–43.

53. Niebuhr, *Christ and Culture*, 194.

54. Quoted in White, *Christian Ethics*, 184. White draws these quotes from various places within the *Institutes*.

55. John Calvin, *Institutes of the Christian Religion*, trans. Henry Beveridge ((Grand Rapids: Eerdmans, 1957), book 4, XX-2.

56. Ibid., book 4, XX-3.

57. Ibid., book 4, XX-32.

58. W. Fred Graham, *The Constructive Revolutionary: John Calvin and His Socio-Economic Impact* (Atlanta: John Knox, 1978), 19.

59. Good examples of this can be seen in Albert M. Wolters, *Creation Regained: Biblical Basics for a Reformational Worldview* (Grand Rapids: Eerdmans, 1985); Richard Mouw, *Politics and the Biblical Drama* (Grand Rapids: Eerdmans, 1976); and idem, *The God Who Commands* (Notre Dame, Ind.: University of Notre Dame Press, 1990).

60. Walter Rauschenbusch, *Christianizing the Social Order* (New York: Macmillan, 1912), 93.

61. Ibid., 125.

62. Gustavo Gutierrez, *A Theology of Liberation* (Maryknoll, N.Y.: Orbis, 1973), 26–27.

63. Ibid., 88. For more recent examples of liberation thought in other contexts, see Dwight Hopkins, *Introducing Black Theology of Liberation* (Maryknoll, N.Y.: Orbis, 1999); Ivone Gebara, *Longing for Running Water: Ecofeminism and Liberation* (Minneapolis: Fortress Press, 1999); and Joseph Comblin, *Called for Freedom: The Changing Context of Liberation Theology* (Maryknoll, N.Y.: Orbis, 1998).

64. Jerry Falwell, Ed Dobson, and Ed Hindson, *The Fundamentalist Phenomenon* (Garden City, N.Y.: Doubleday, 1981), 187–88.

65. Ralph Reed, *Active Faith: How Christians Are Changing the Soul of American Politics* (New York: Free Press, 1996), 9.

66. Ibid., 157.

67. Ernst Troeltsch, *The Social Teachings of the Christian Churches*, vol. 1 (New York: Harper & Row, 1960), 345.

68. Cal Thomas and Ed Dobson, *Blinded by Might: Can the Religious Right Save America?* (Grand Rapids: Zondervan, 1999), 47.

Chapter 10

1. Bart Barnes, "Mick Mantle, Legend of Baseball, Dies at 63," *Washington Post*, 14 August 1995. Online: www.washingtonpost.com/wp-srv/sports/longterm/memories.

2. "Mantle Illness Impacts Organ Donor Program," Associated Press, 14 August 1995. Online: http://archive.sportserver.com/newsroom.

3. "Critical Data: U.S. Facts about Transplantation," from the United Network of Organ Sharing, www.unog.org. The 77,000 is for July 2001, and the number of organ transplants (22,854) is for the year 2000.

4. Peter Richardson, "Justice," in *Baker's Dictionary of Christian Ethics*, ed. Carl F. H. Henry (Grand Rapids: Baker, 1973), 361.

5. Stephen Mott, *Biblical Ethics and Social Change* (New York: Oxford University Press, 1982), 59.

6. Nicholas Wolterstorff, "Justice and Peace," in *New Dictionary of Christian Ethics and Pastoral Theology*, ed. David J. Atkinson, David F. Field, Arthur Holmes, and Oliver O'Donovan (Downers Grove, Ill.: InterVarsity Press, 1995), 18.

7. Emil Brunner, *Justice and the Social Order* (London: Lutterworth Press, 1945), 115.

8. Ibid., 117.

9. In some of the earlier writings of Carl Henry, we find this view. See, for example, Carl Henry, *Aspects of Christian Social Ethics* (Grand Rapids: Eerdmans, 1964), 146–71.

285

10. Reinhold Niebuhr, *The Nature and Destiny of Man,* vol. 2, *Human Destiny* (New York: Scribners, 1964), 87–88.

11. Reinhold Niebuhr, *Moral Man and Immoral Society* (New York: Scribners, 1932), 257.

12. Richard Higginson, *Dilemmas: A Christian Approach to Moral Decision Making* (Louisville: Westminster/John Knox Press, 1988), 110.

13. Ibid., 183.

14. Ibid., 178.

15. Ibid., 180–81.

16. John Stuart Mill, *On Liberty* (New York: F. S. Crofts, 1947), 95.

17. See, for example, Robert Nozick, *Anarchy, State, and Utopia* (New York: Basic Books, 1974).

18. Earle Cairns, *Saints and Society: The Social Impact of Eighteenth-Century English Revivals and Its Contemporary Relevance* (Chicago: Moody Press, 1960).

19. Dennis Hollinger, "The Purpose of the State: A Theological Perspective," in *Politics and Public Policy: A Christian Response,* ed. Tim Demy and Gary Stewart (Grand Rapids: Kregel, 2000).

20. There have been other definitions offered and other typologies proposed. For a range of definitions and proponents, see Karen Lebacqz, *Six Theories of Justice: Perspectives from Philosophical and Theological Ethics* (Minneapolis: Augsburg Press, 1986).

21. Ronald Nash, *Social Justice and the Christian Church* (Milford, Mich.: Mott Media, 1983), 57.

22. Ibid., 37.

23. E. Calvin Beisner, *Prosperity and Poverty: The Compassionate Use of Resources in a World of Scarcity* (Westchester, Ill.: Crossway, 1988), 54.

24. Nozick, *Anarchy, State, and Utopia,* 155.

25. Ibid., 334.

26. Higginson, *Dilemmas,* 173.

27. For a helpful overview of Rawls's framework and principles of justice, see Lebacqz, *Six Theories,* 33–50.

28. John Rawls, *A Theory of Justice* (Cambridge: Harvard University Press, 1971), 302.

29. Ibid., 15.

30. Lebacqz, *Six Theories,* 40.

31. "Legislator Isn't Kidding about 'Potty Parity,'" *Elkhart Truth,* 9 May 1988, p. A1.

32. For a Christian defense of this perspective and the need for redress, see Mott, *Biblical Ethics and Social Change,* 65–72.

33. Karl Marx, *Critique of the Gotha Programme* (Peking: Foreign Language Press, 1972), 18.

34. Mott, *Biblical Ethics and Social Change,* 66.

35. Ibid., 68.

36. Stephen Mott and Ronald Sider, "Economic Justice: A Biblical Paradigm," in *Toward a Just and Caring Society: Christian Responses to Poverty in America,* ed. David P. Gushee (Grand Rapids: Baker, 1999), 27.

37. William Werpehowski, "Justice," in *The Westminster Dictionary of Christian Ethics,* ed. John MacQuaire (Philadelphia: Westminster Press, 1986), 331.

38. There has been considerable debate about this issue, whether God ordained the state from creation or whether it was a providential concession resulting from sin's entrance into the world with the fall.

39. For an excellent treatment of the role marriage and family play in poverty, see David P. Gushee, "Rebuilding Marriage and the Family," in *Toward a Just and Caring Society,* 499–530. Gushee combs through the literature showing the relationship between poverty and both marital dissolution and childbirth outside of marriage.

Chapter 11

1. Max Stackhouse, *Public Theology and Political Economy: Christian Stewardship in Modern Society* (Grand Rapids: Eerdmans, 1987), 157.

2. Richard Rorty, *Objectivity, Relativism, and Truth: Philosophical Papers,* vol. 1 (New York: Cambridge University Press, 1991), 24.

3. My intent in using the language of truth is not to argue for a particular philosophical theory of truth but to contend that biblical faith compels us to speak of truth and affirm that there are realities that are final and ultimate, of which we can speak adequately and to which we can make commitments.

4. See, for example, Emile Durkheim, *The Elementary Forms of the Religious Life* (New York: Free Press, 1965), 466–70.

5. Ian Markham, *Plurality and Christian Ethics* (Cambridge: Cambridge University Press, 1994), 2.

6. Tom Driver, "Towards a Theocentric Christology," *Christianity and Crisis* (11 November 1985): 450.

7. For a detailed analysis of this history, see Dennis Hollinger, *Individualism and Social Ethics: An Evangelical Syncretism* (Lanham, Md.: University Press of America, 1983); and Robert Booth Fowler,

A New Engagement: Evangelical Political Thought, 1966–1976 (Grand Rapids: Eerdmans, 1982).

8. Charles Krauthammer, "Will It Be Coffee, Tea or He?" *Time,* 15 June 1998, 92.

9. John Rawls, *Political Liberalism* (New York: Columbia University Press, 1993), 135, 134.

10. Ibid., 218. For a similar rendition of privatization in political philosophy, see Robert Audi, especially his dialogue with Nicholas Wolterstorff in *Religion in the Public Square: The Place of Religious Convictions in Political Debate* (London: Rowman and Littlefield, 1997).

11. Tristram Engelhardt Jr., *The Foundations of Bioethics* (New York: Oxford University Press, 1986), 12.

12. Ibid., 54.

13. Tristram Engelhardt Jr., *The Foundations of Christian Bioethics* (Lisse, Netherlands: Swets & Zeitlinger, 2000), 3. It should be pointed out that Engelhardt previously noted the distinction between a faith-grounded content-full morality and a thin secular morality, but now it is clear where his hope lies.

14. Quoted in John Murray Cuddihy, *No Offense: Civil Religion and Protestant Taste* (New York: Seabury Press, 1978), 108.

15. See, for example, Michael Creuzet, *Toleration and Liberalism* (Chumleigh, Great Britain: Augustine, 1979). Creuzet argues that tolerance is possible only when we rule out absolute truth claims.

16. Jeffrey Stout, *Ethics after Babel: The Language of Morals and Their Discontents* (Boston: Beacon Press, 1988), 163.

17. The term *theocratic* refers to a rule by God, while the term *Constantinian* refers to a historic situation that began with Constantine in the fourth century. Constantine tolerated Christianity, and subsequent emperors made it the privileged religion of the Empire. Some use the term *Christendom* for this position.

18. Quoted in a book review of *The American Pope,* a book on the life and thought of Spellman, in *New York Times Book Review,* 28 October 1984, 11.

19. T. S. Eliot, *The Idea of a Christian Society* (New York: Harcourt, Brace and World, 1968), 27.

20. Markham, *Plurality and Christian Ethics,* 55.

21. Rousas John Rushdoony, *Christianity and the State* (Vallecito, Calif.: Ross House Books, 1986), 7.

22. Greg Bahnsen, "Christ and the Role of Civic Government: The Theonomic Perspective," *Transformation* 5, no. 2 (April/July 1988): 24.

23. Ibid., 26. For a detailed analysis of reconstructionism, see William Barker and W. Robert Godfrey, eds., *Theonomy: A Reformed Critique* (Grand Rapids: Zondervan, 1990); and H. Wayne House and Thomas Ice, *Dominion Theology: Blessing or Curse* (Portland, Ore.: Multnomah Press, 1988).

24. Carl Henry, "The New Coalitions," *Christianity Today,* 17 November 1989, 27.

25. St. Augustine, *The City of God,* trans. Demetrius Zema and Gerald Walsh (Washington, D.C.: The Catholic University of America Press, 1950), VI:5, 6. Augustine's reference to civil religion comes in the context of a discussion of Marcus Varro, who had noted various kinds of religion including the civic. He notes that the religions Varro discussed are non-Christian and of no value to believers.

26. Jean Jacques Rousseau, *The Social Contract,* trans. Christopher Betts (Oxford: Oxford University Press, 1994), IV-8.

27. Will Herberg, *Protestant, Catholic, Jew* (Garden City, N.Y.: Anchor Books, 1960), 263.

28. Robert Bellah, "Civil Religion in America" *Daedalus* 96, no. 1 (winter 1967): 1.

29. Robert Bellah, *The Broken Covenant. American Civil Religion in Time of Trial* (New York: Seabury Press, 1975), 3.

30. Harold Berman, *The Interaction of Law and Religion* (Nashville: Abingdon Press, 1974), 73.

31. Ibid., 125.

32. This is the thrust of Bellah's *Broken Covenant.*

33. Dale Evans Rogers, *Let Freedom Ring!* (Old Tappan, N.J.: Revell, 1975), 21–22.

34. Herberg, *Protestant, Catholic, Jew,* 268.

35. Quoted in Stan D. Gaede, *When Tolerance Is No Virtue* (Downers Grove, Ill.: InterVarsity Press, 1993), 27.

36. See ibid., and Markham, *Plurality and Christian Ethics.*

37. Gaede, *When Tolerance Is No Virtue,* 28.

38. Stephen C. Carter, *The Culture of Disbelief* (New York: Anchor Books, 1993) was a welcome analysis, as he called into question the secularizing trivialization of religion in pluralistic America.

39. Audi and Wolterstorff, *Religion in the Public Square,* 114.

40. For a helpful suggestion on the bilingual approach, see Walter Brueggemann, *Interpretation and Obedience: From Faithful Reading to Faithful Living* (Minneapolis: Augsburg/Fortress, 1991), 41–65.

Drawing from 2 Kings 18, he speaks of "a conversation at the wall of the city" and "a conversation behind the wall."

41. Richard Mouw and Sander Griffioen, *Pluralisms and Horizons: An Essay in Christian Public Philosophy* (Grand Rapids: Eerdmans, 1993), 175.

Chapter 12

1. Ronald J. Sider, *Rich Christians in an Age of Hunger: A Biblical Study* (Downers Grove, Ill.: InterVarsity Press, 1984), 191–92.

2. Guenter B. Risse, *Mending Bodies, Saving Souls: A History of Hospitals* (New York: Oxford University Press, 1999), 7.

3. Rosemary Stevens, *In Sickness and in Wealth: American Hospitals in the Twentieth Century* (New York: Basic Books, 1989), 23.

4. See, for example, Claude E. Schindler Jr. with Pacheco Pyle, *Still Educating for Eternity: The Case for Christian Schools* (Colorado Springs: Association of Christian Schools International, 1997). This work notes, for example, that according to the U.S. population census, even public school teachers enroll their kids in private schools at twice the national rate (6). For a history of Christian schools, see Paul A. Kienel, *A History of Christian School Education* (Colorado Springs: Association of Christian Schools International, 1998).

5. See, for example, Christian Smith and David Sikkink, "Is Private School Privatizing?" *First Things* 92 (April 1999): 16–20.

6. For a helpful analysis of how the crisis pregnancy center developed as a mechanism for dealing with abortion, see Frederica Mathews-Green, *Real Choices: Offering Practical Life-Affirming Alternatives to Abortion* (Sisters, Ore.: Multnomah, 1994).

7. Richard Mouw, "Evangelism and Social Ethics," *Perkins Journal* 35, no. 1 (autumn 1981): 14.

8. For a helpful overview of the intersection of evangelism and social justice, see Ronald Sider, *Evangelism, Salvation, and Social Justice* (Bramcote Notts, Great Britain: Grove Books, 1977).

9. A Joint Publication of the Lausanne Committee for World Evangelization and the World Evangelical Fellowship, *Evangelism and Social Responsibility: An Evangelical Commitment* (Wheaton: Lausanne Committee for World Evangelization, 1982), 21.

10. Ibid, 22.

11. Ibid., 23.

12. See Stephen Mott, *Biblical Ethics and Social Change* (New York: Oxford University Press, 1982), 110–12.

13. William Booth, *In Darkest England and the Way Out* (London: International Headquarters of the Salvation Army, 1890), 53.

14. Frederick Buechner, *Telling the Truth* (New York: HarperCollins, 1977), 18.

15. David Gushee and Robert Long, *The Bolder Pulpit: Reclaiming the Moral Dimension of Preaching* (Valley Forge, Pa.: Judson Press, 1998), 4.

16. National Conference of Catholic Bishops, *Economic Justice for All: Pastoral Letter on Catholic Social Teaching and the U.S. Economy* (Washington, D.C.: U.S. Catholic Conference, 1986); and National Conference of Catholic Bishops, *The Challenge of Peace: God's Promise and Our Response: A Pastoral Letter on War and Peace* (Washington, D.C.: U.S. Catholic Conference, 1983).

17. Quoted from "Vatican Council for Justice and Peace Calls for Complete Debt Cancellation," at www.J2000.org/updates/vatican1 (1 February 2001). Pope John Paul II personally supported the Jubilee 2000 debt cancellation in "Incarnationis Mysterium: Bull of Indiction of the Great Jubilee of the Year 2000."

18. W. A. Visser 't Hooft and J. H. Oldham, *The Church and Its Function in Society* (Chicago: Willet, Clark, 1937), 193.

19. William Temple, *Christianity and Social Order* (London: SCM Press, 1950), 47.

20. Regarding this criticism relative to Jubilee 2000, see Stephen Smith, "Christian Ethics and Forgiving Third World Debt," *Stillpoint* (fall 2000): 22–23. Smith favors the Heavily Indebted Poor Country initiative of the World Bank, which stipulates reform measures on the part of indebted countries. He believes, however, that the outright canceling of debts does not address the root issues of dysfunctional governments, misplaced priorities, and mismanaged tax policy.

21. Ken Kollman, *Outside Lobbying: Public Opinion and Interest Group Strategies* (Princeton, N.J.: Princeton University Press, 1998), 3.

22. Kevin Hula, *Lobbying Together: Interest Group Coalitions in Legislative Politics* (Washington, D.C.: Georgetown University Press, 1999), 3.

23. See Luke Ebersole, *Church Lobbying in the Nation's Capital* (New York: Macmillan, 1951).

24. Keith Graber Miller, *Wise as Serpents, Innocent as Doves: American Mennonites Engage Wash-*

ington (Knoxville: University of Tennessee Press, 1996), 42.

25. Jeffrey K. Hadden, *The Gathering Storm in the Churches: A Sociologist Looks at the Widening Gap between Clergy and Laymen* (Garden City, N.Y.: Anchor Books, 1969).

26. "About the MCD," www.mcdpolitics.org/about/welcome.htm, 31 May 2001.

27. My thanks to Jerry Herbert, who has done research on the movement and has given lectures but has not yet published his materials, which he graciously shared with me.

28. Stephen L. Carter, *God's Name in Vain: The Wrongs and Rights of Religion in Politics* (New York: Basic Books, 2000), 1.

29. Mott, *Biblical Ethics and Social Change,* 142.

30. William D. Watley, *Roots of Resistance: The Nonviolent Ethic of Martin Luther King, Jr.* (Valley Forge, Pa.: Judson Press, 1985), 14. For more on King's ethics, see Ervin Smith, *The Ethics of Martin Luther King, Jr.* (New York: Edwin Mellen Press, 1981).

31. Martin Luther King, *Stride toward Freedom: The Montgomery Story* (New York: Harper, 1958), 215.

32. For a thoughtful essay on this issue, see Tim Stafford, "In Reluctant Praise of Extremism," *Christianity Today,* 26 October 1992, 18–22.

33. Mott, *Biblical Ethics and Social Change,* 133.

34. John Howard Yoder, *The Politics of Jesus* (Grand Rapids: Eerdmans, 1972), 111.

35. Ibid., 153.

36. Stanley Hauerwas, *Vision and Virtue* (Notre Dame, Ind.: Fides, 1974), 221.

37. Larry Christenson, *A Charismatic Approach to Social Action* (Minneapolis: Bethany Fellowship, 1974), 75, 93.

38. Mott, *Biblical Ethics and Social Change,* 139.

39. Carl F. H. Henry, *Aspects of Christian Social Ethics* (Grand Rapids: Eerdmans, 1964), 99–100.

40. N. T. Wright, *For All God's Worth: True Worship and the Calling of the Church* (Grand Rapids: Eerdmans, 1997), 101.

41. Paul Swope, "Abortion: A Failure to Communicate," *First Things* 82 (April 1998): 31.

42. Ibid., 32.

43. Ibid.

44. Ibid., 33.

45. For a helpful overview of this story and the controversy surrounding it, see "Special News Report: Sudan, Slave Redemption," *Christianity Today,* 9 August 1999, 28–33.

46. Richard Miniter, "The False Promise of Slave Redemption," *Atlantic Monthly,* July 1999, part 2, 2. Online: www.theatlantic.com/issues.

47. Ibid., 5.

Index

293